Ultra Maniac

Story and Art by
Wataru Yoshizumi

Vol. 5

Characters

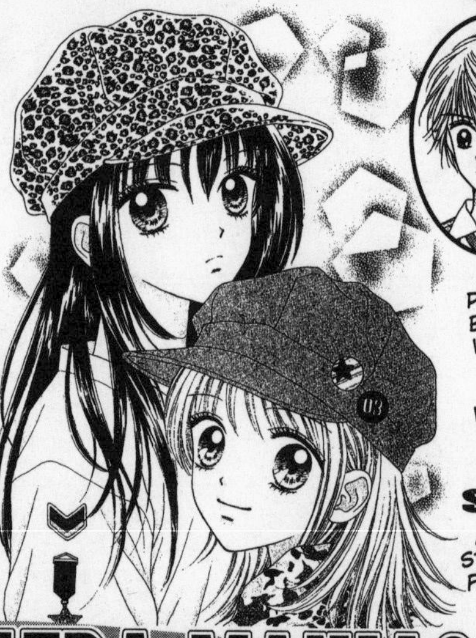

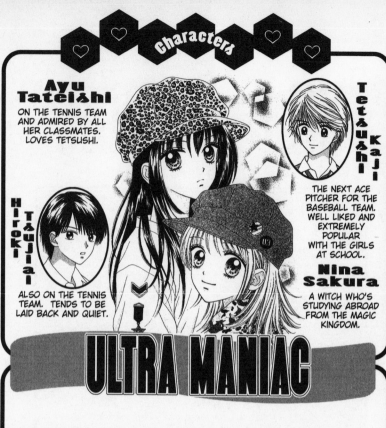

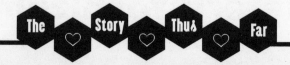

Ayu Tateishi

ON THE TENNIS TEAM AND ADMIRED BY ALL HER CLASSMATES. LOVES TETSUSHI.

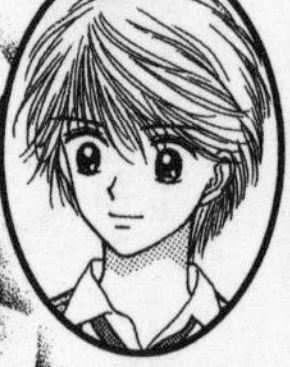

Tetsushi Kaji

THE NEXT ACE PITCHER FOR THE BASEBALL TEAM. WELL LIKED AND EXTREMELY POPULAR WITH THE GIRLS AT SCHOOL.

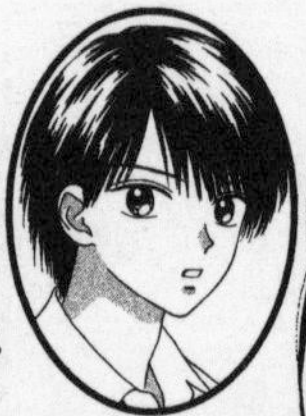

Hiroki Tsujiai

ALSO ON THE TENNIS TEAM. TENDS TO BE LAID BACK AND QUIET.

Nina Sakura

A WITCH WHO'S STUDYING ABROAD FROM THE MAGIC KINGDOM.

ULTRA MANIAC

AYU IS A NORMAL SEVENTH GRADE STUDENT WHO HAS A CRUSH ON TETSUSHI, THE MOST POPULAR BOY IN HER CLASS. AFTER A CHANCE ENCOUNTER WITH A GIRL NAMED NINA, HER LIFE SUDDENLY TURNS UPSIDE DOWN. NINA, AS IT TURNS OUT, IS A WITCH, AND AYU HAS LEARNED THAT SHE'S A TRANSFER STUDENT FROM A PLACE CALLED THE MAGIC KINGDOM!

DURING SUMMER VACATION AN ANONYMOUS PRANK LETTER IS SENT TO NINA. THE NOTE SAYS, "GO BACK TO THE MAGIC KINGDOM!" BACK AT SCHOOL, THE AUTHOR OF THE LETTER IS REVEALED TO BE A GIRL NAMED SAYAKA. SHE'S A HALF-WITCH AND SHE'S JEALOUS OF ALL THE ATTENTION NINA GETS ON CAMPUS. AFTER A DRAMATIC CONFRONTATION IN THE SCHOOL'S GYMNASIUM, NINA IS ABLE TO MAKE FRIENDS WITH HER RIVAL.

THINGS GET COMPLICATED, HOWEVER, WHEN A BOY NAMED HIROKI CONFESSES HIS LOVE FOR NINA. AS IT TURNS OUT, SAYAKA HAS A CRUSH ON HIROKI AND WANTS NINA TO BACK OFF. TWO WITCHES, ONE CUTE BOY: CAN MAGIC HELP UNTANGLE THIS MESSY KNOT OF LOVE?

The Story Thus Far

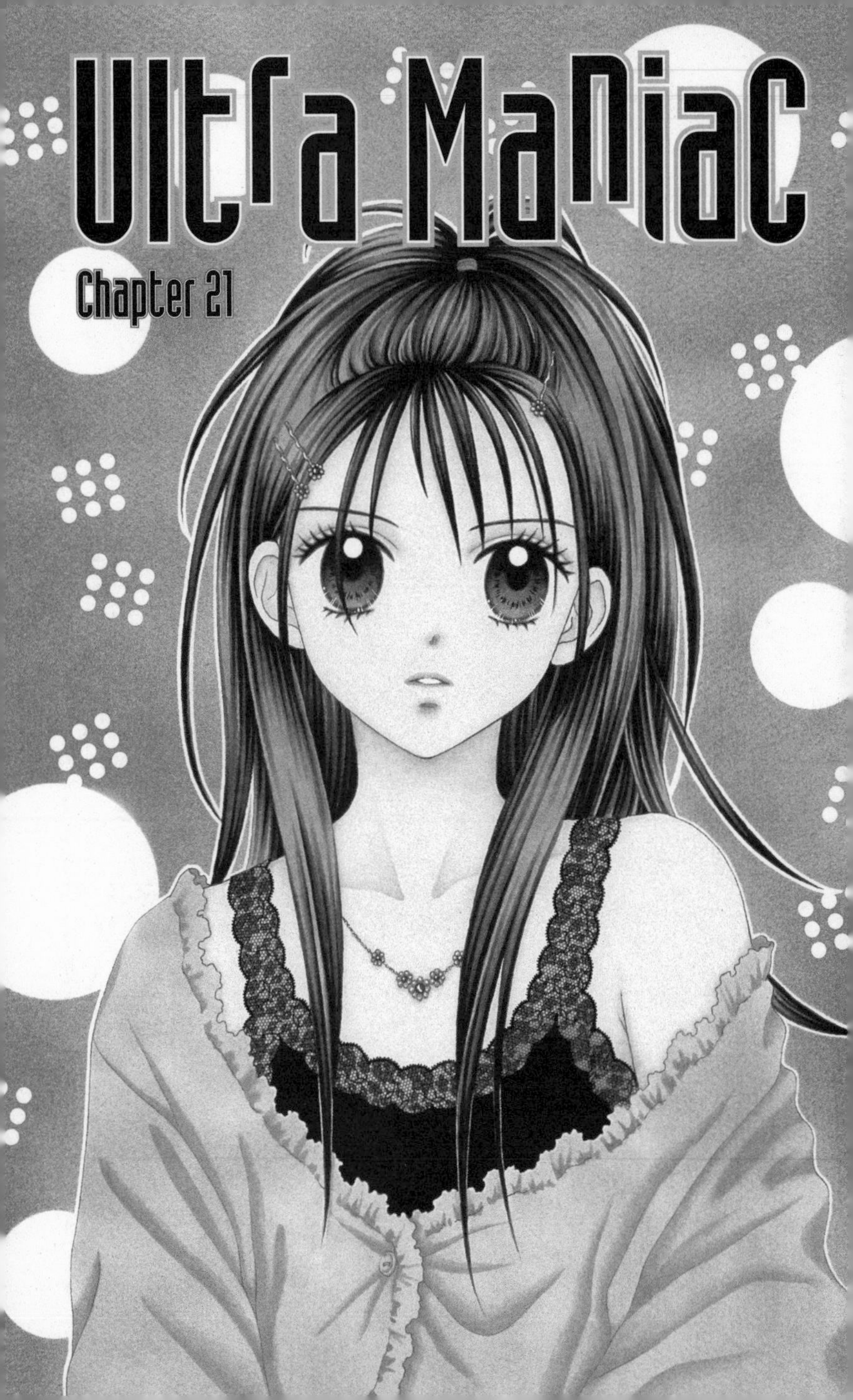
Ultra Maniac
Chapter 21

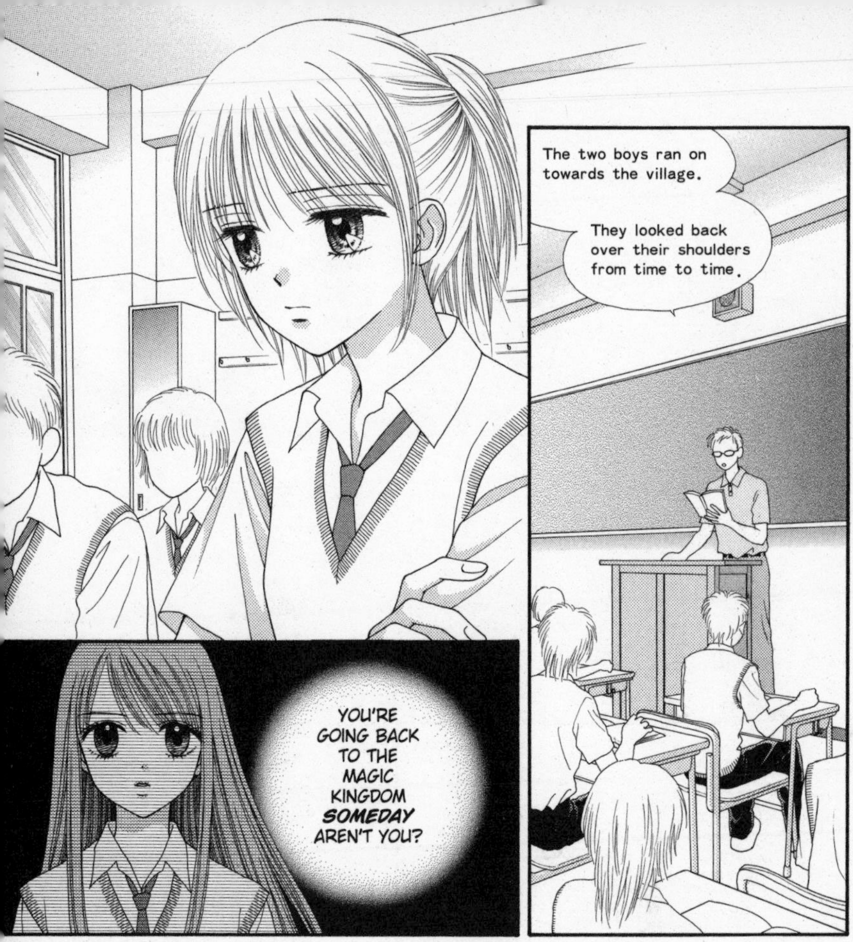
The two boys ran on towards the village.
They looked back over their shoulders from time to time.
YOU'RE GOING BACK TO THE MAGIC KINGDOM *SOMEDAY* AREN'T YOU?

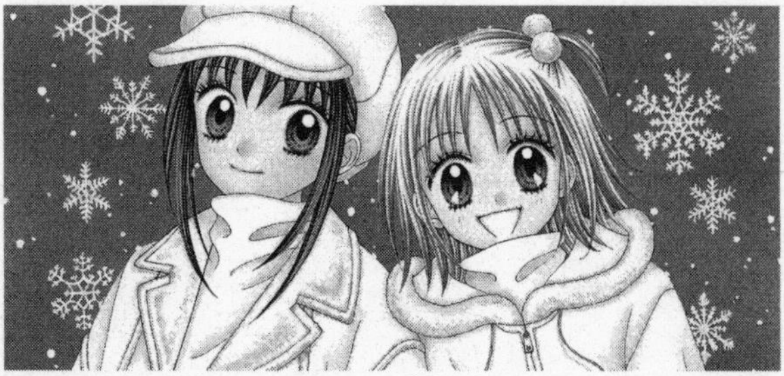

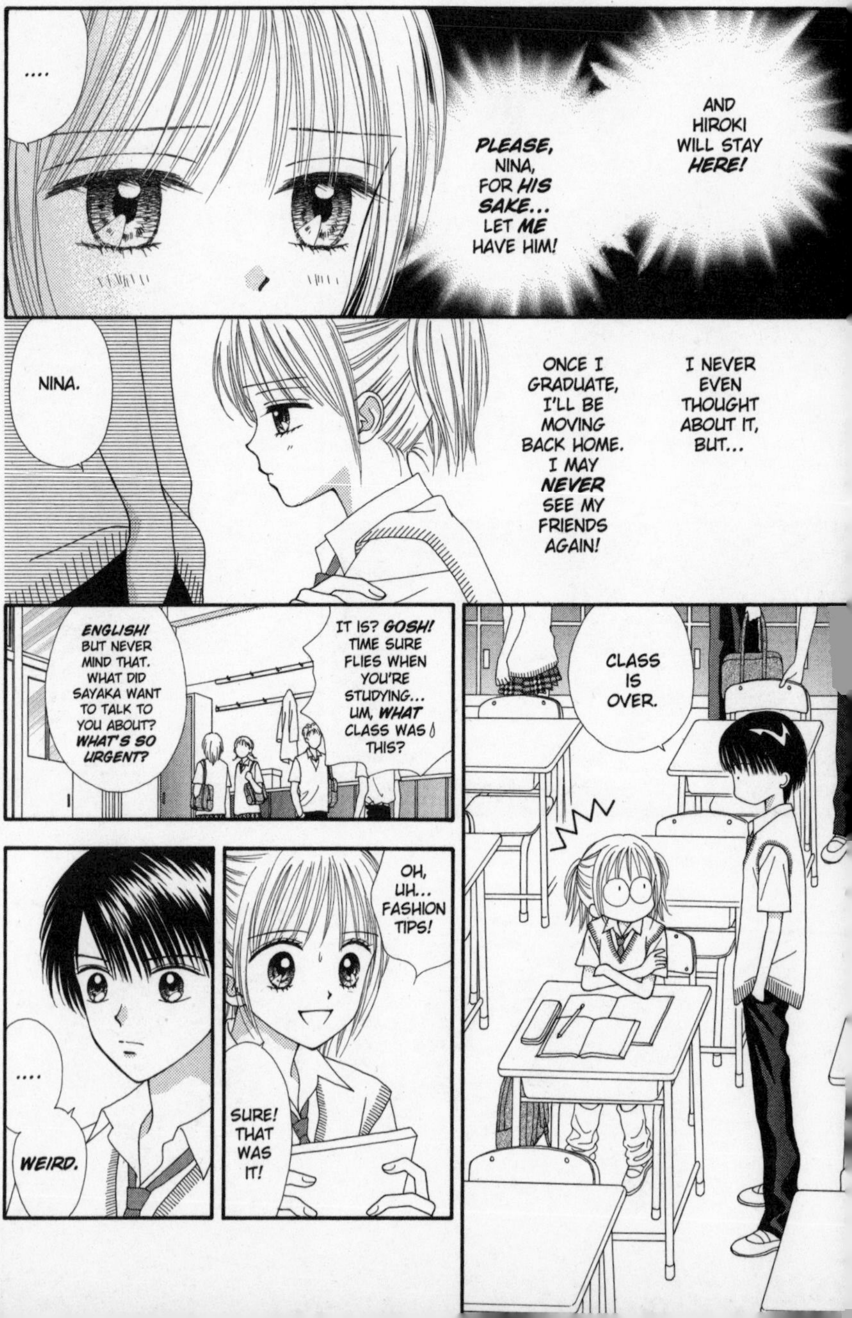
PLEASE, NINA, FOR HIS SAKE... LET ME HAVE HIM!
AND HIROKI WILL STAY HERE!
....
I NEVER EVEN THOUGHT ABOUT IT, BUT...
ONCE I GRADUATE, I'LL BE MOVING BACK HOME. I MAY NEVER SEE MY FRIENDS AGAIN!
NINA.
CLASS IS OVER.
IT IS? GOSH! TIME SURE FLIES WHEN YOU'RE STUDYING... UM, WHAT CLASS WAS THIS?
ENGLISH! BUT NEVER MIND THAT. WHAT DID SAYAKA WANT TO TALK TO YOU ABOUT? WHAT'S SO URGENT?
OH, UH... FASHION TIPS!
SURE! THAT WAS IT!
....
WEIRD.

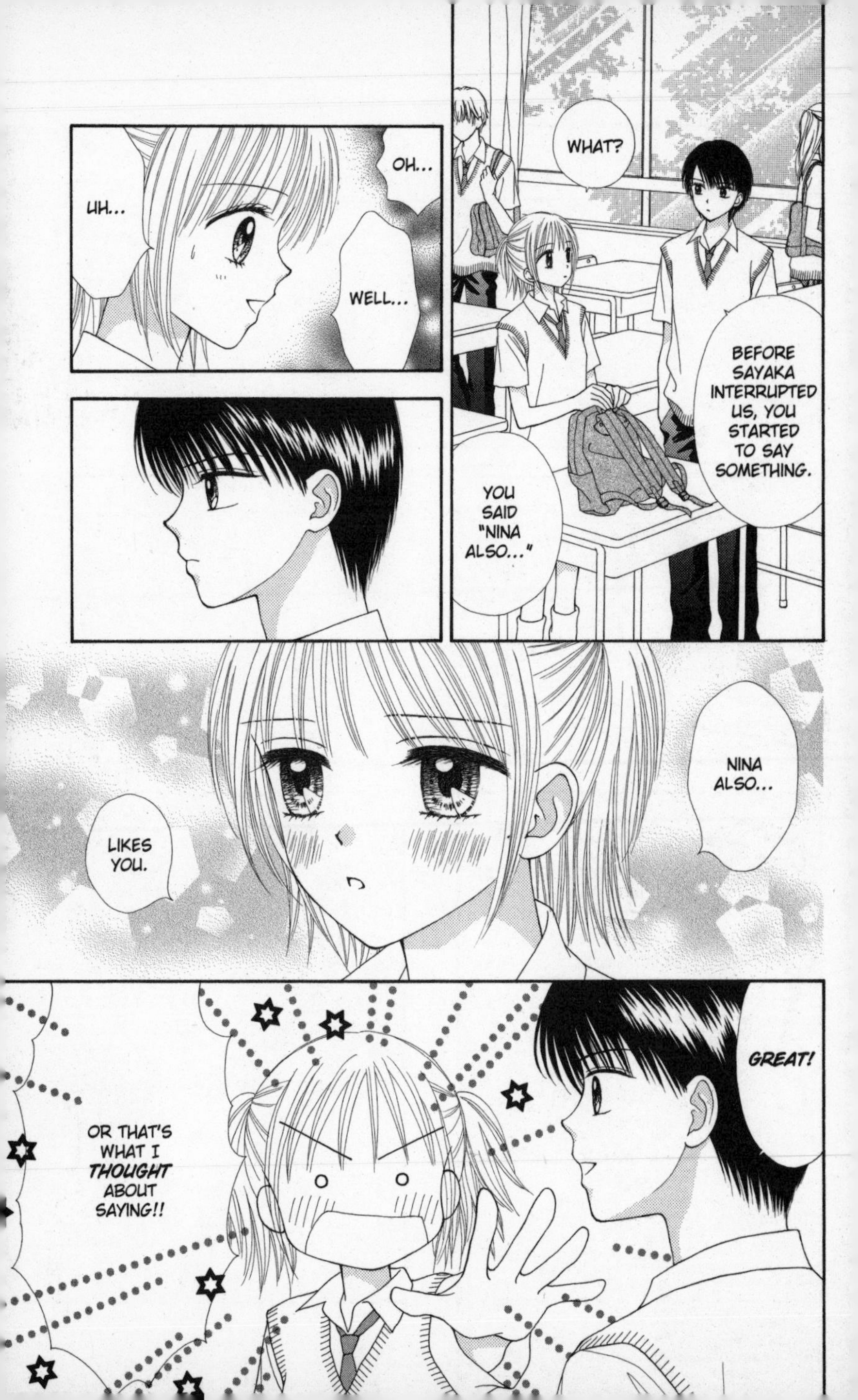

WHAT?
BEFORE SAYAKA INTERRUPTED US, YOU STARTED TO SAY SOMETHING.
YOU SAID "NINA ALSO..."
OH...
WELL...
UH...
NINA ALSO...
LIKES YOU.
GREAT!
OR THAT'S WHAT I *THOUGHT* ABOUT SAYING!!

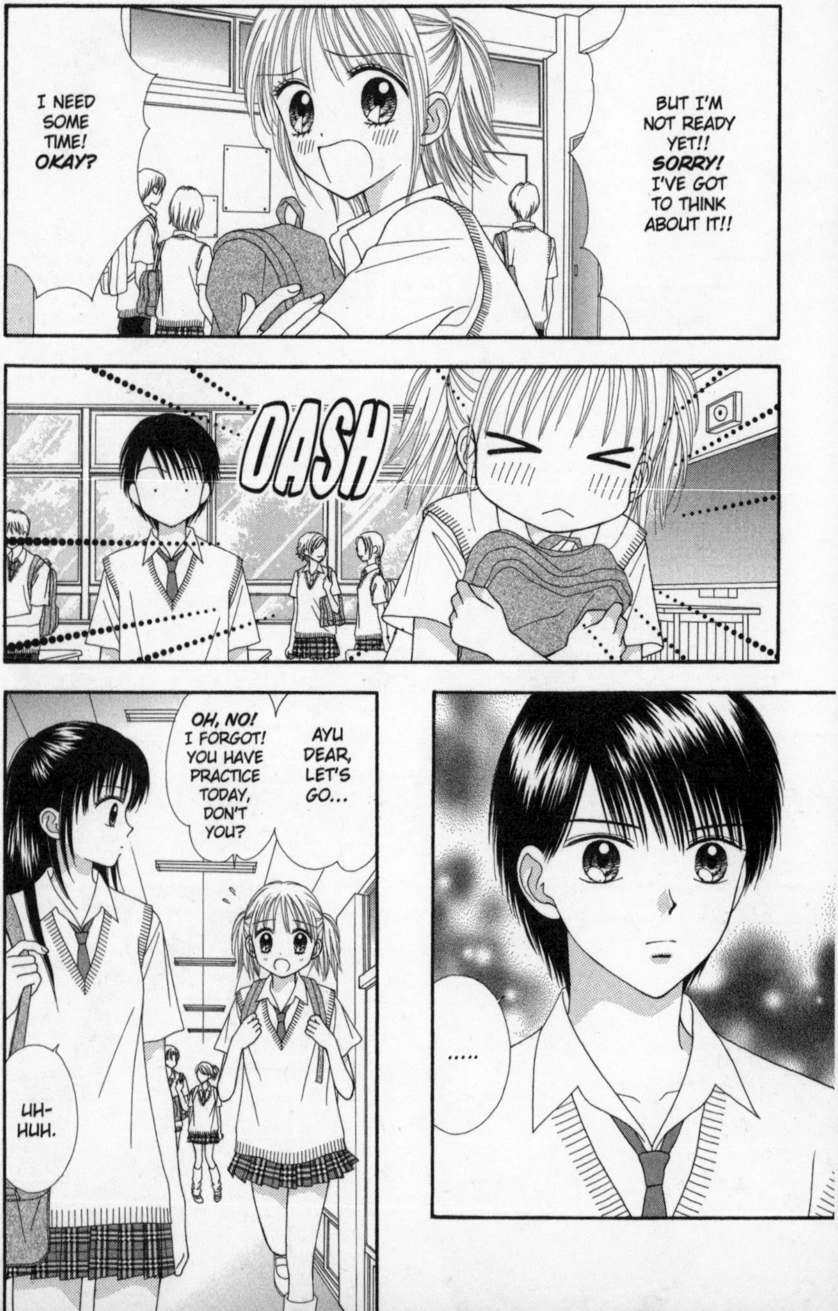
BUT I'M NOT READY YET!! SORRY! I'VE GOT TO THINK ABOUT IT!!
I NEED SOME TIME! OKAY?
DASH
.....
AYU DEAR, LET'S GO...
OH, NO! I FORGOT! YOU HAVE PRACTICE TODAY, DON'T YOU?
UH-HUH.

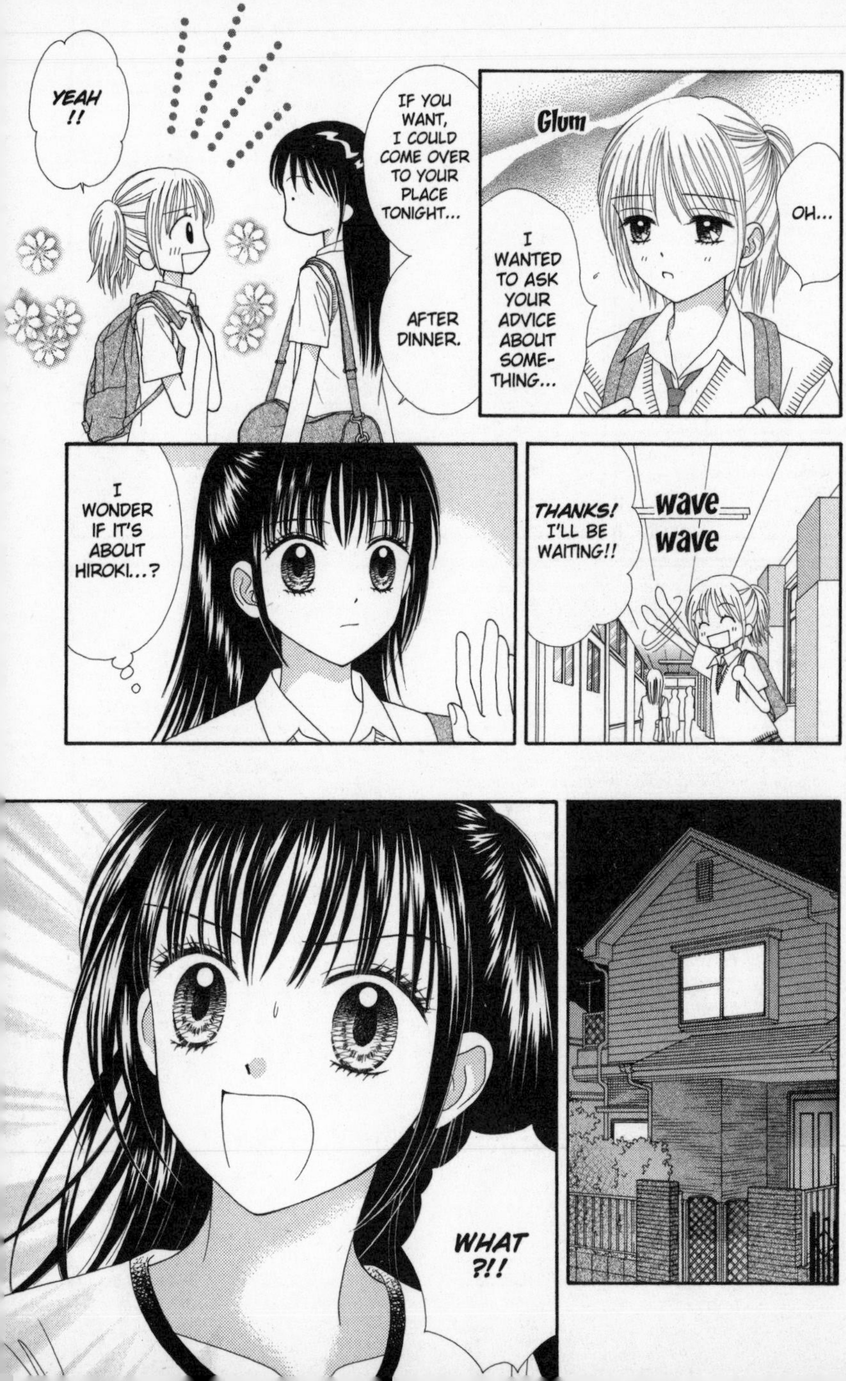
Glum
OH...
I WANTED TO ASK YOUR ADVICE ABOUT SOME-THING...
IF YOU WANT, I COULD COME OVER TO YOUR PLACE TONIGHT...
AFTER DINNER.
YEAH !!
THANKS! I'LL BE WAITING!!
wave wave
I WONDER IF IT'S ABOUT HIROKI...?
WHAT ?!!

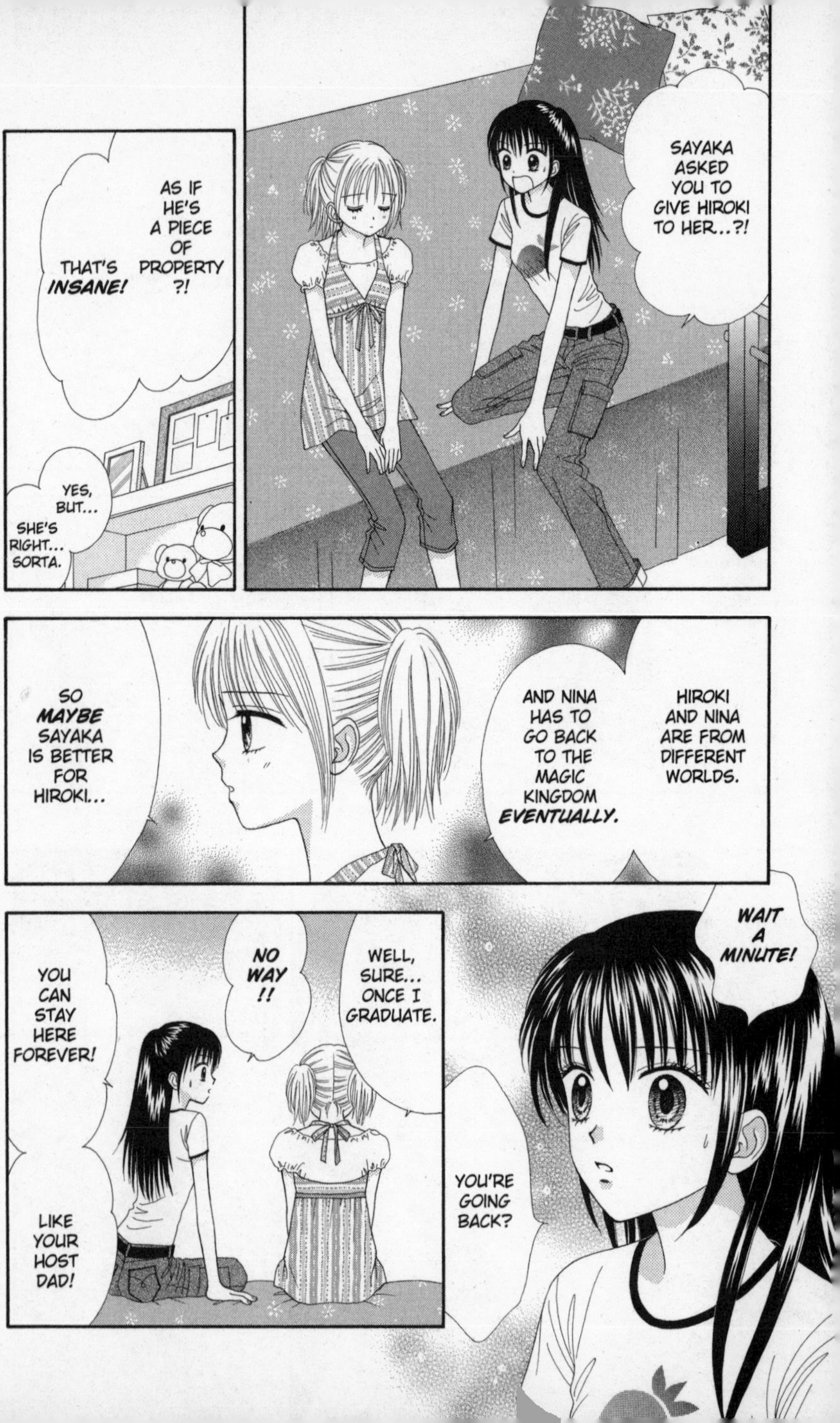
SAYAKA ASKED YOU TO GIVE HIROKI TO HER...?!
THAT'S INSANE! AS IF HE'S A PIECE OF PROPERTY?!
YES, BUT... SHE'S RIGHT... SORTA.
HIROKI AND NINA ARE FROM DIFFERENT WORLDS.
AND NINA HAS TO GO BACK TO THE MAGIC KINGDOM EVENTUALLY.
SO MAYBE SAYAKA IS BETTER FOR HIROKI...
WAIT A MINUTE!
YOU'RE GOING BACK?
WELL, SURE... ONCE I GRADUATE.
NO WAY!!
YOU CAN STAY HERE FOREVER!
LIKE YOUR HOST DAD!

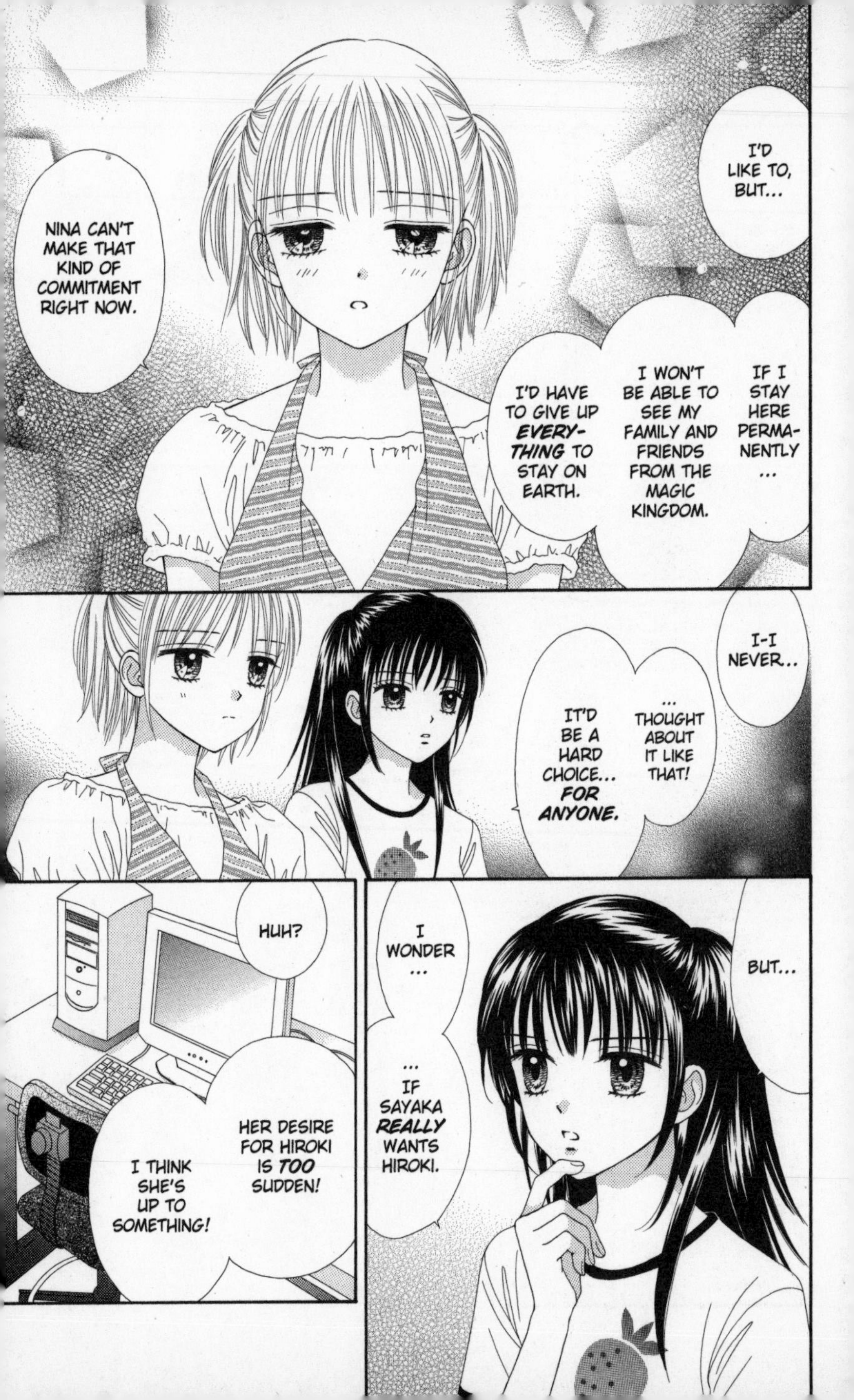
I'D LIKE TO, BUT...
IF I STAY HERE PERMANENTLY...
I WON'T BE ABLE TO SEE MY FAMILY AND FRIENDS FROM THE MAGIC KINGDOM.
I'D HAVE TO GIVE UP EVERYTHING TO STAY ON EARTH.
NINA CAN'T MAKE THAT KIND OF COMMITMENT RIGHT NOW.
I-I NEVER...
...THOUGHT ABOUT IT LIKE THAT!
IT'D BE A HARD CHOICE... FOR ANYONE.
BUT...
I WONDER...
...IF SAYAKA REALLY WANTS HIROKI.
HUH?
HER DESIRE FOR HIROKI IS TOO SUDDEN!
I THINK SHE'S UP TO SOMETHING!

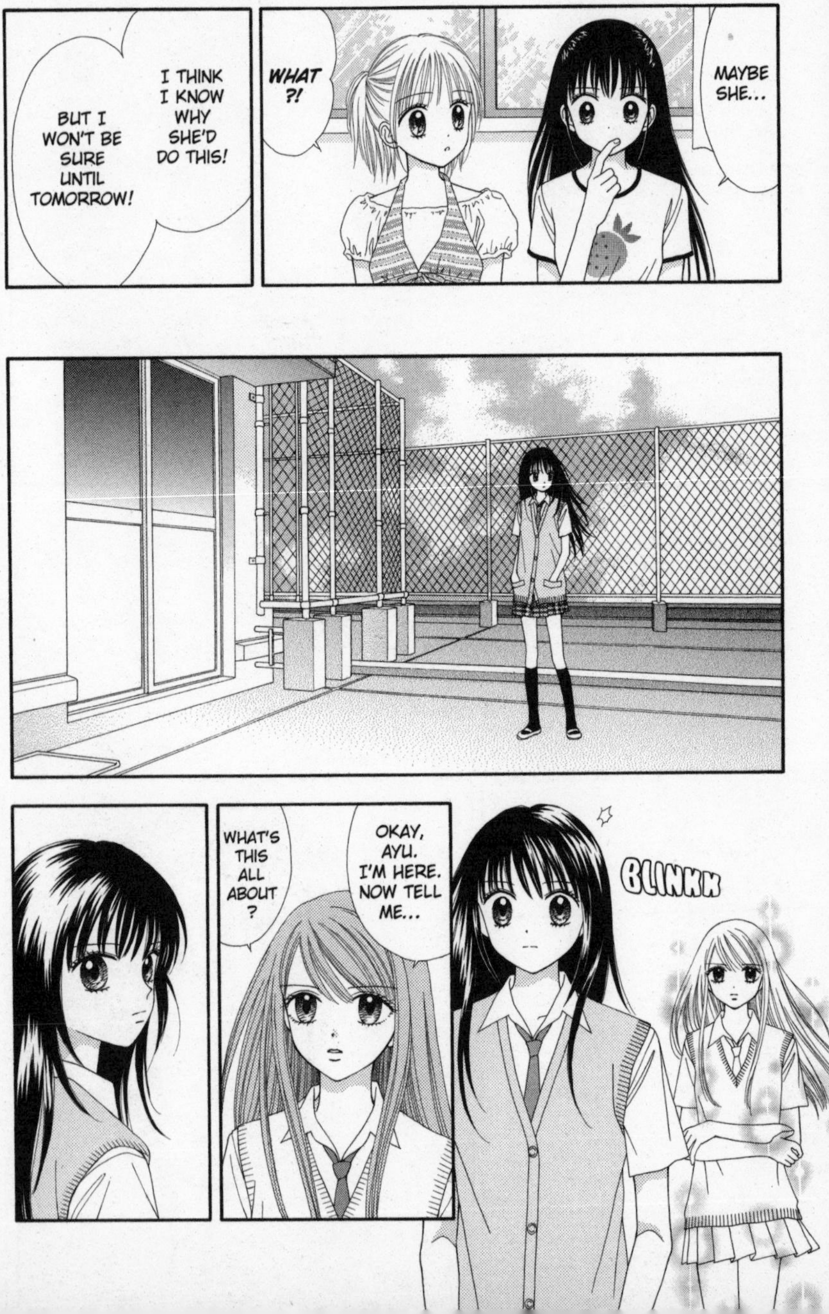
MAYBE SHE...
WHAT ?!
I THINK I KNOW WHY SHE'D DO THIS!
BUT I WON'T BE SURE UNTIL TOMORROW!
BLINKK
OKAY, AYU. I'M HERE. NOW TELL ME...
WHAT'S THIS ALL ABOUT ?

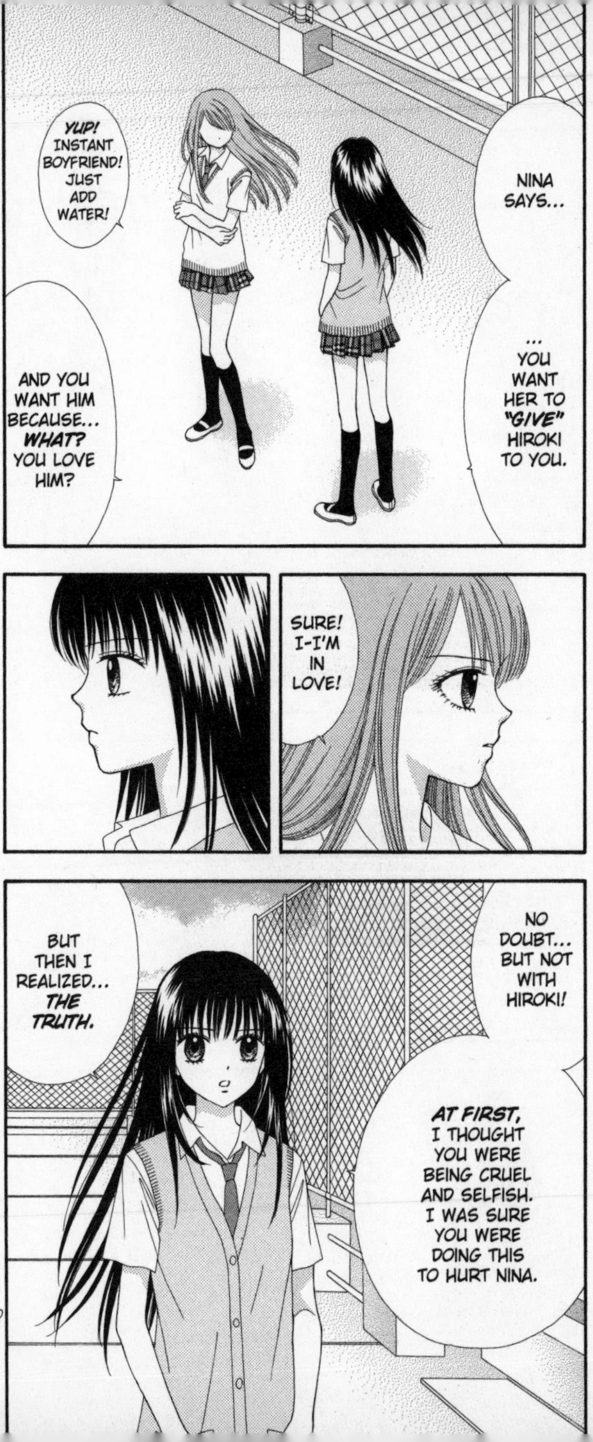
NINA SAYS...
... YOU WANT HER TO "GIVE" HIROKI TO YOU.
YUP! INSTANT BOYFRIEND! JUST ADD WATER!
AND YOU WANT HIM BECAUSE... WHAT? YOU LOVE HIM?
SURE! I-I'M IN LOVE!
NO DOUBT... BUT NOT WITH HIROKI!
AT FIRST, I THOUGHT YOU WERE BEING CRUEL AND SELFISH. I WAS SURE YOU WERE DOING THIS TO HURT NINA.
BUT THEN I REALIZED... THE TRUTH.

FREE TALK 1

It's been about three months since *Ultra Maniac* ended and I'm supposed to be on vacation--recharging my batteries before I begin my next series. But things haven't gone as planned. Instead of resting, I'm working on *The Complete Works of Marmalade Boy*!

If it was a standard RMC (Ribon Mascot Comic), the paper size and style would all be pre-determined. So all I'd have to do is make some corrections and updates. But a "complete works" is different. Every aspect of it can be tweaked. So it's a lot of work, but also a lot of fun!!

I changed the cover design to be a bit more adult and chic. Plus I added more color to the illustrations. For the cover stock, I chose a paper called Helios, which is slightly cream colored.

The first volume has Miki and Yuu on the cover. The second volume is Miki alone. And Vol. 3 has Yuu and Ginta. (I won't tell you who's on the covers of Vol. 4-6. I want it to be a surprise! ♡

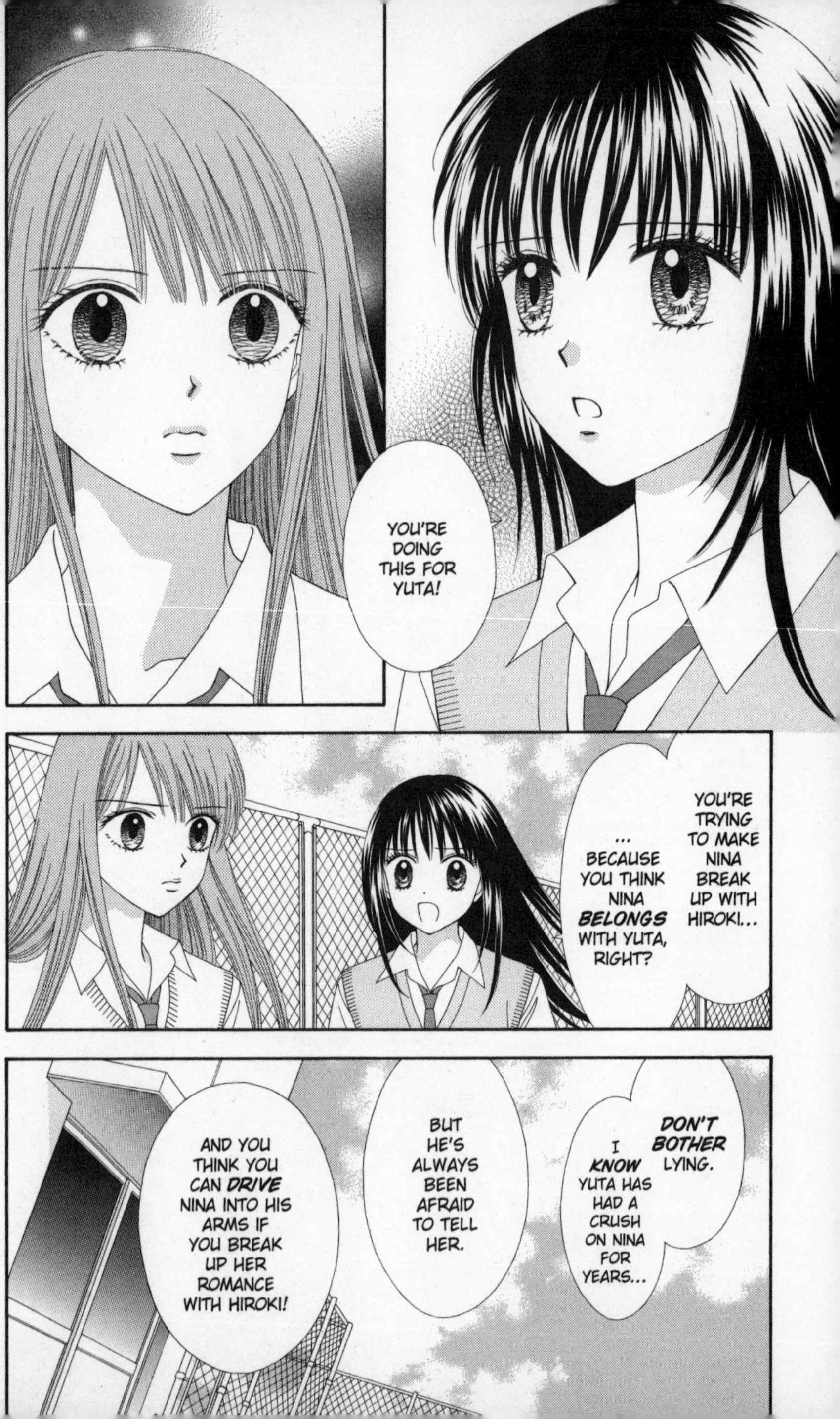
YOU'RE DOING THIS FOR YUTA!
YOU'RE TRYING TO MAKE NINA BREAK UP WITH HIROKI...
...BECAUSE YOU THINK NINA BELONGS WITH YUTA, RIGHT?
DON'T BOTHER LYING.
I KNOW YUTA HAS HAD A CRUSH ON NINA FOR YEARS...
BUT HE'S ALWAYS BEEN AFRAID TO TELL HER.
AND YOU THINK YOU CAN DRIVE NINA INTO HIS ARMS IF YOU BREAK UP HER ROMANCE WITH HIROKI!

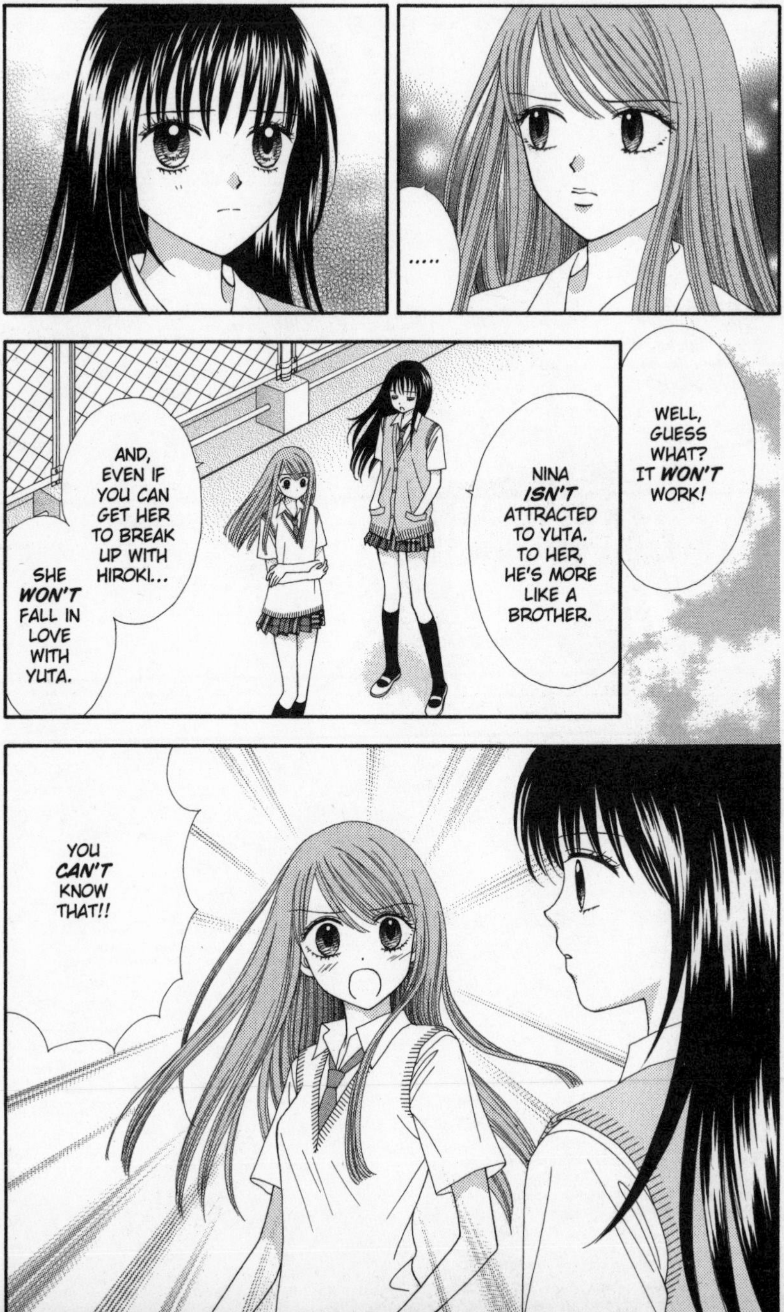
.....
WELL, GUESS WHAT? IT *WON'T* WORK!
NINA *ISN'T* ATTRACTED TO YUTA. TO HER, HE'S MORE LIKE A BROTHER.
AND, EVEN IF YOU CAN GET HER TO BREAK UP WITH HIROKI...
SHE *WON'T* FALL IN LOVE WITH YUTA.
YOU *CAN'T* KNOW THAT!!

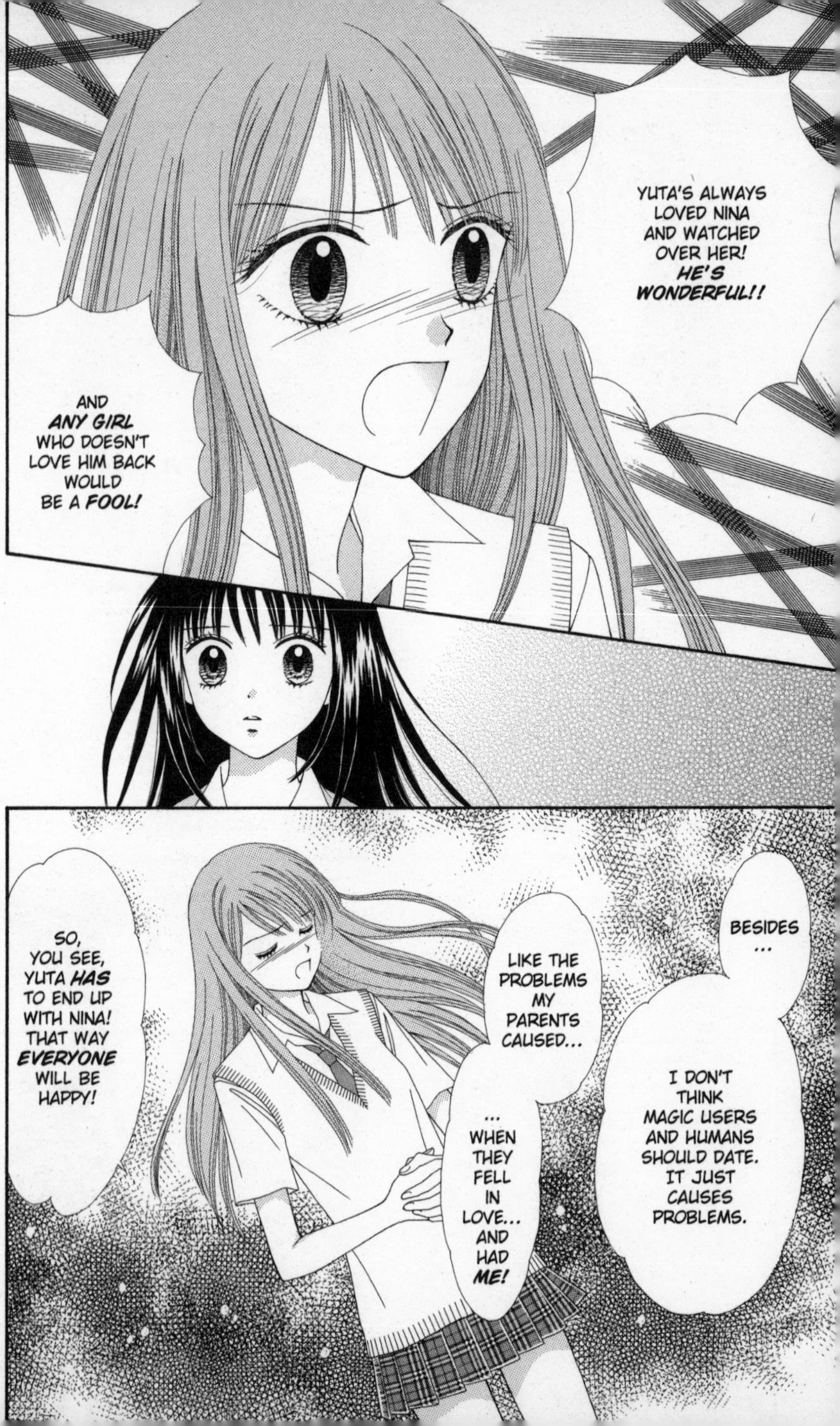
YUTA'S ALWAYS LOVED NINA AND WATCHED OVER HER! HE'S WONDERFUL!!
AND ANY GIRL WHO DOESN'T LOVE HIM BACK WOULD BE A FOOL!
BESIDES...
I DON'T THINK MAGIC USERS AND HUMANS SHOULD DATE. IT JUST CAUSES PROBLEMS.
LIKE THE PROBLEMS MY PARENTS CAUSED...
... WHEN THEY FELL IN LOVE... AND HAD ME!
SO, YOU SEE, YUTA HAS TO END UP WITH NINA! THAT WAY EVERYONE WILL BE HAPPY!

FREE TALK 2

The dustcover for **The Complete Works of Marmalade Boy** looks like tracing paper, but is actually a sturdy, semi-transparent vellum. Selecting types of paper and materials is one of the fun parts of designing the book. Originally, I was going to have the interior of the book be printed on beige paper to match the color of the cover. But I decided to make the interior pages match the main color of the "next episode" page.

I also had to decide which black and white illustrations to include as well as their placement and size. I also had to fix any inconsistencies and adjust the size of the dialog text.

I actually only had to redo the covers, but I wanted to revise the content and add screen tones. But if I started doing that, there would be no end to all the changes I'd make. And, I have to admit, there's something to be said for leaving things alone—so that I don't accidentally lose any of the qualities that made readers love the series. So I'm restraining myself. (Laughs!)

Unlike the comics, **The Complete Works** are much larger and easier to read. The color pages from the original publications are printed in their original colors. The filler illustrations are also placed exactly where they were in the original magazines--unlike how they're bunched together in the books. Doing this increases the cost of **The Complete Works**, but to offset it, I did a simple no-frills cover, and other cost-cutting measures. The end result, though, is beautiful!

EVERY-ONE?
WHAT ABOUT YOU, SAYAKA?
YOU LIKE YUTA DON'T YOU?
......
I DON'T MATTER.
I JUST WANT YUTA TO BE HAPPY.
HE'S BEEN SO KIND TO ME.
I'D DO ANYTHING FOR HIM!

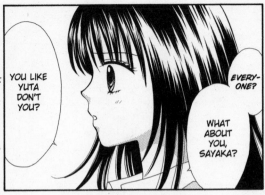

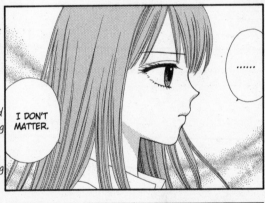

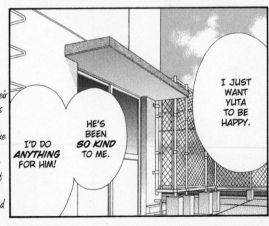

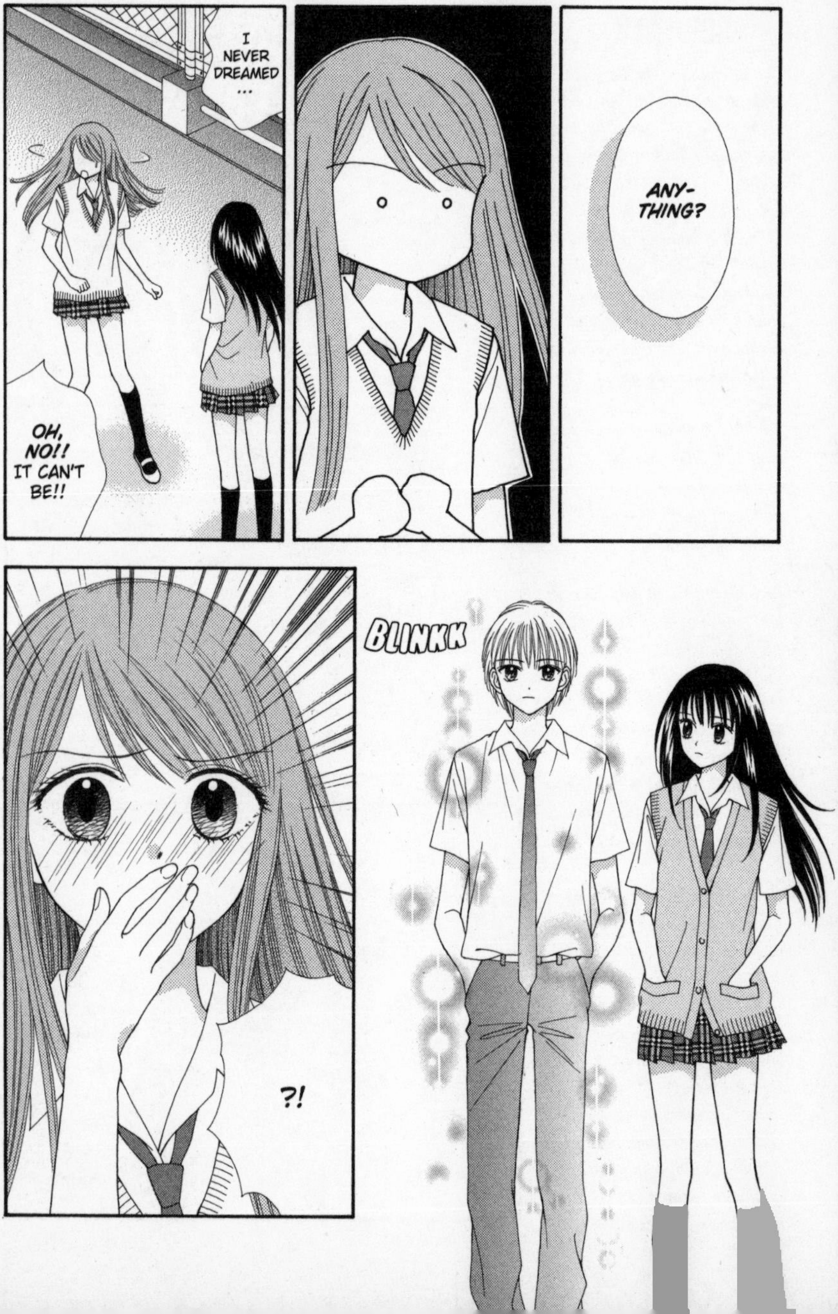
ANY-THING?
I NEVER DREAMED...
OH, NO!! IT CAN'T BE!!
BLINKK
?!

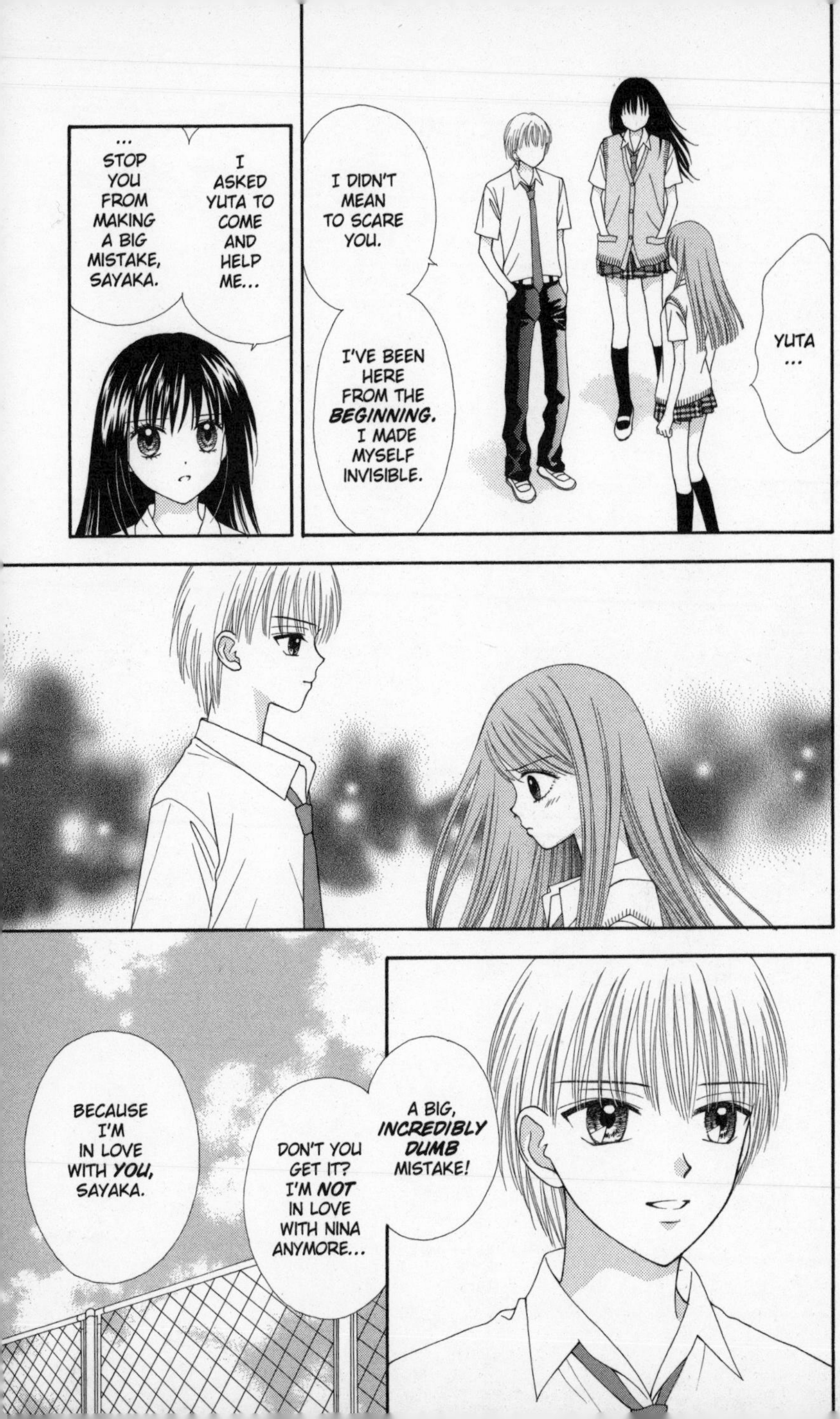
YUTA...
I DIDN'T MEAN TO SCARE YOU.
I'VE BEEN HERE FROM THE *BEGINNING.* I MADE MYSELF INVISIBLE.
I ASKED YUTA TO COME AND HELP ME...
... STOP YOU FROM MAKING A BIG MISTAKE, SAYAKA.
A BIG, *INCREDIBLY DUMB* MISTAKE!
DON'T YOU GET IT? I'M *NOT* IN LOVE WITH NINA ANYMORE...
BECAUSE I'M IN LOVE WITH *YOU,* SAYAKA.

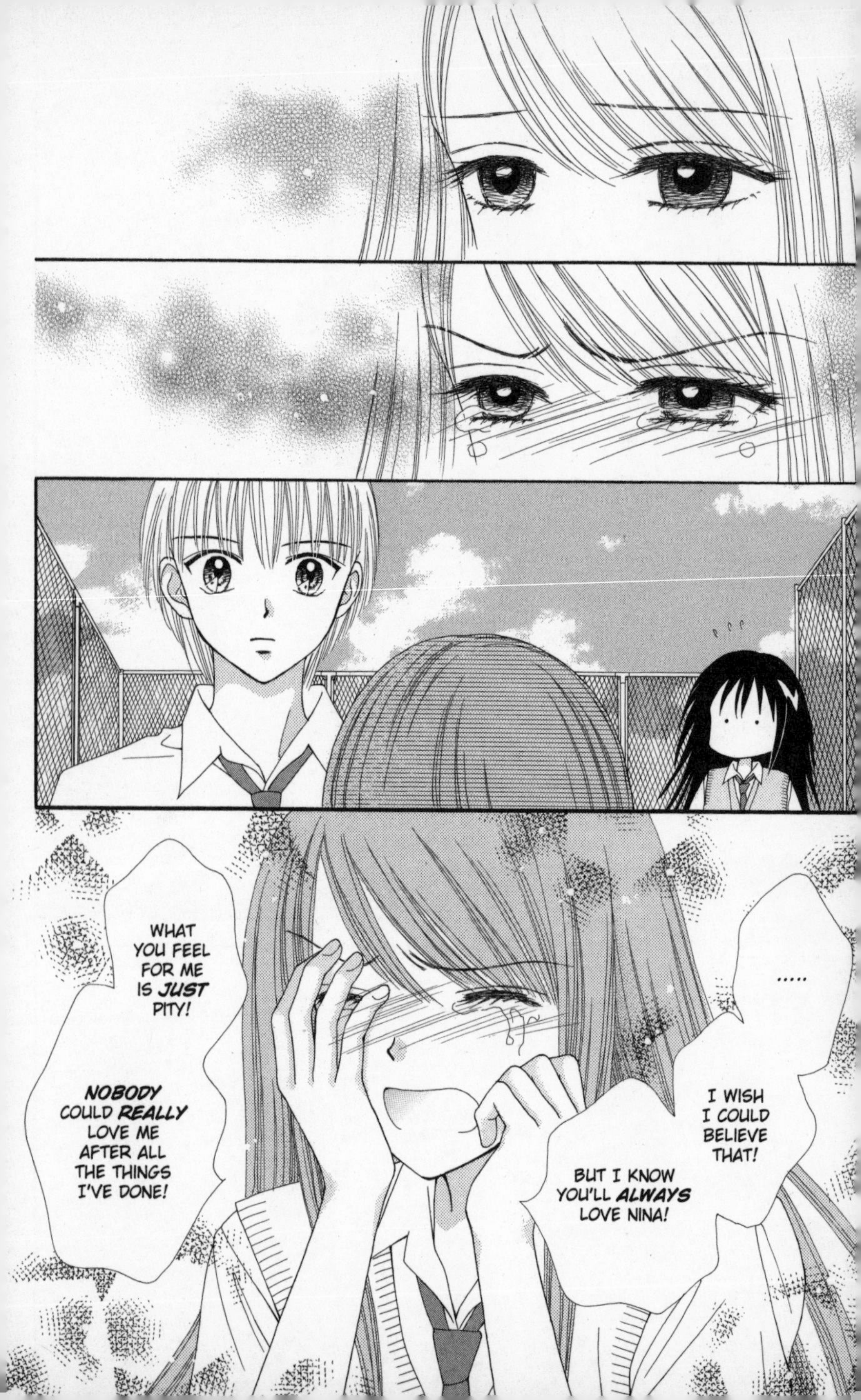

.....
I WISH I COULD BELIEVE THAT!
BUT I KNOW YOU'LL ALWAYS LOVE NINA!
WHAT YOU FEEL FOR ME IS JUST PITY!
NOBODY COULD REALLY LOVE ME AFTER ALL THE THINGS I'VE DONE!

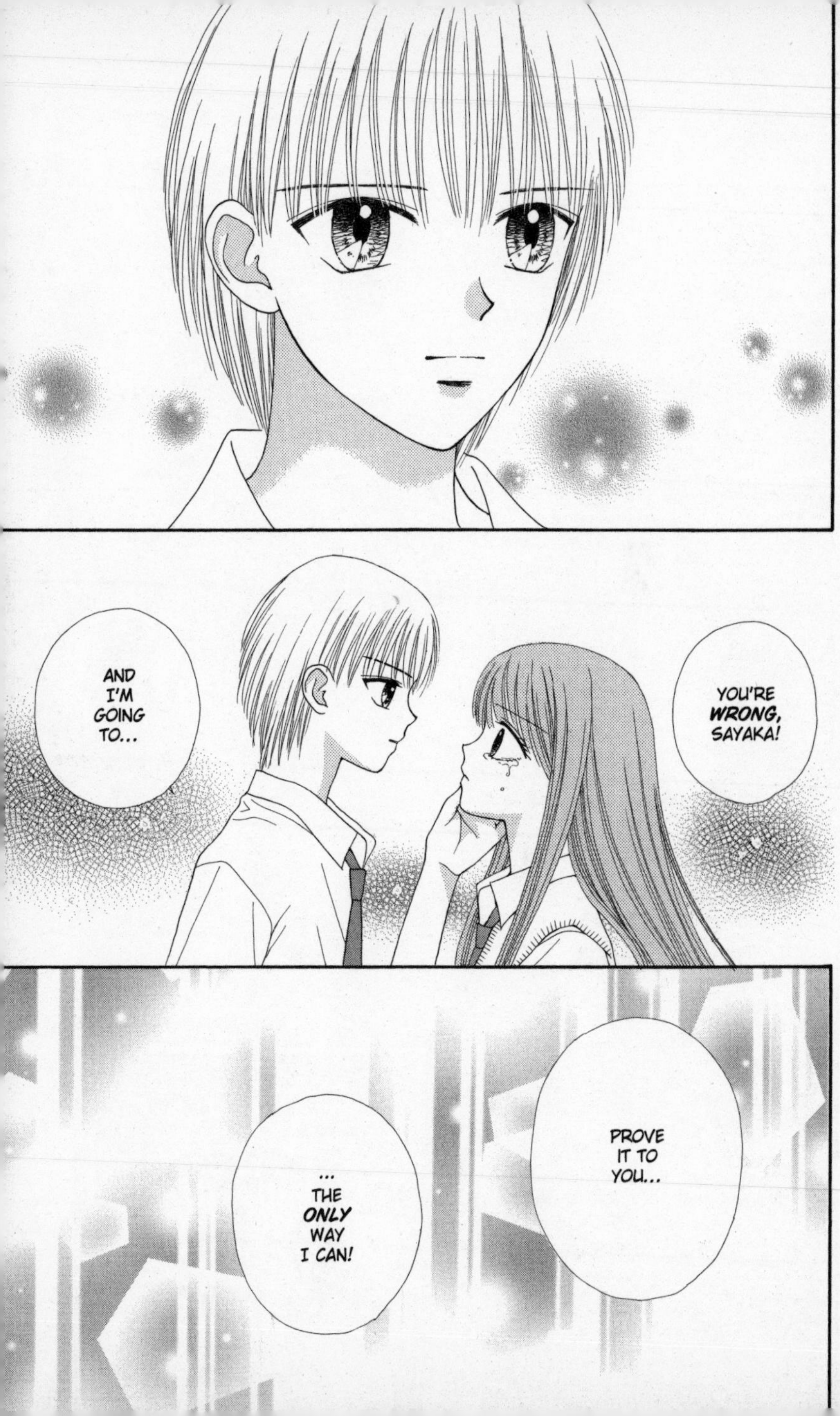
YOU'RE WRONG, SAYAKA!
AND I'M GOING TO...
PROVE IT TO YOU...
...THE ONLY WAY I CAN!

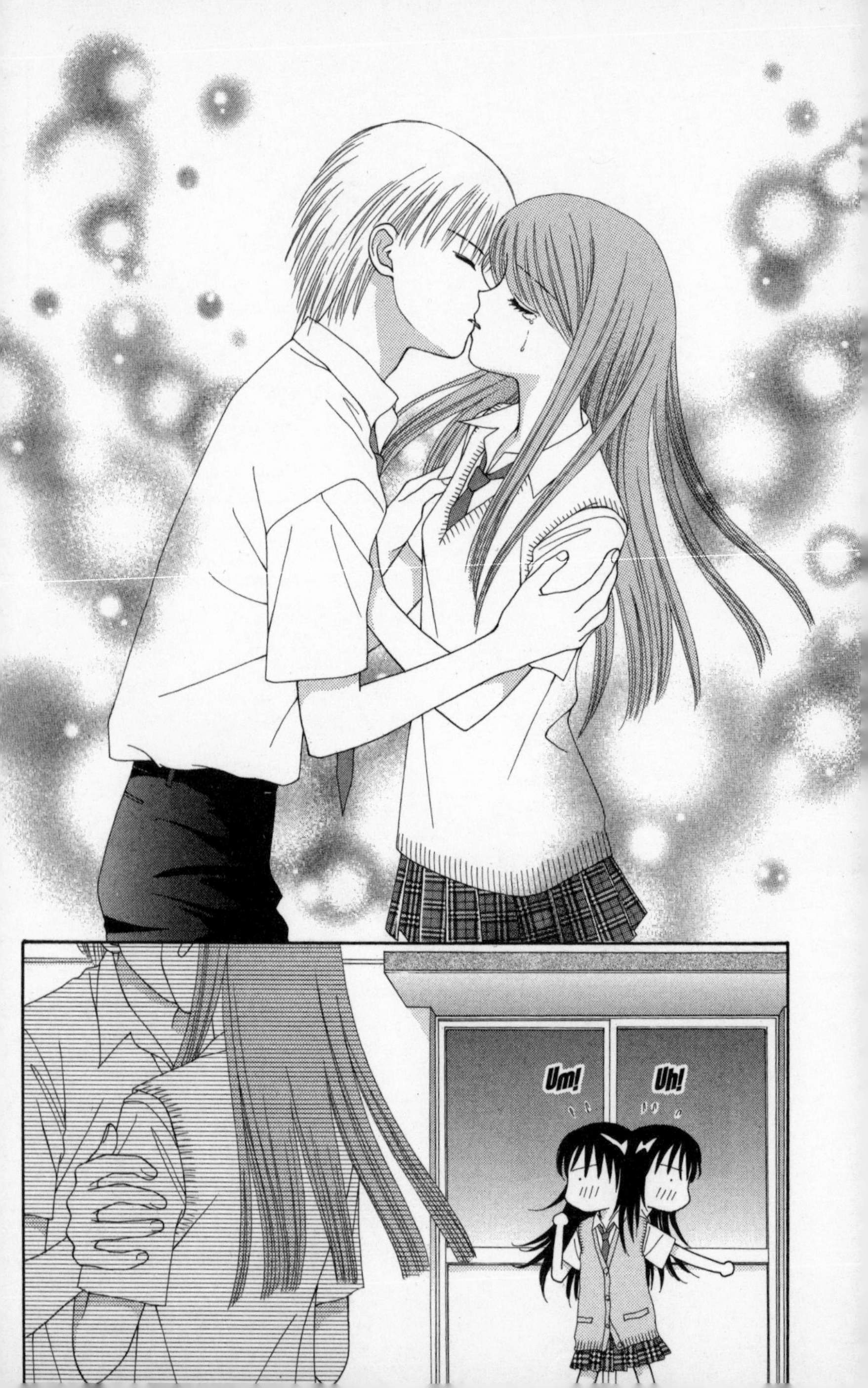
Uh!
Um!

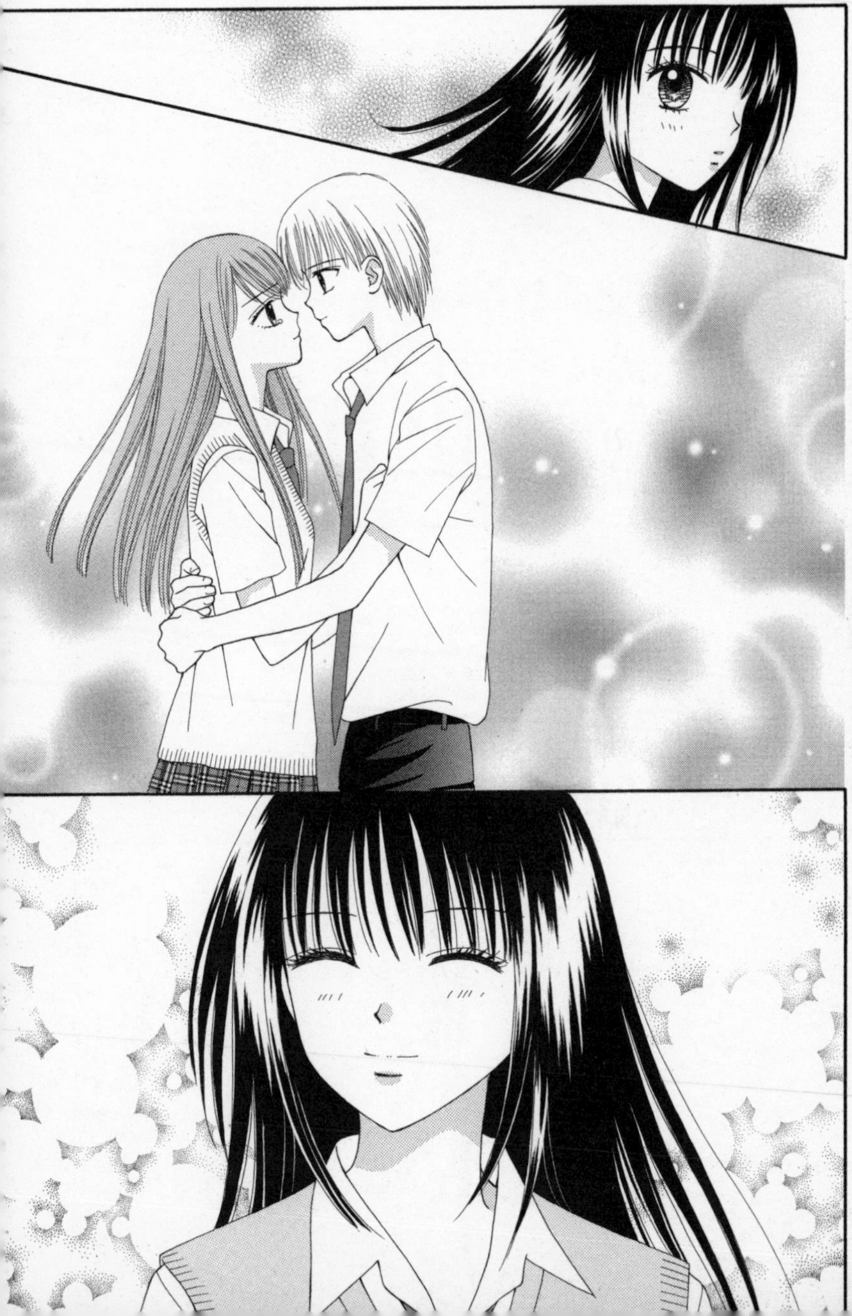

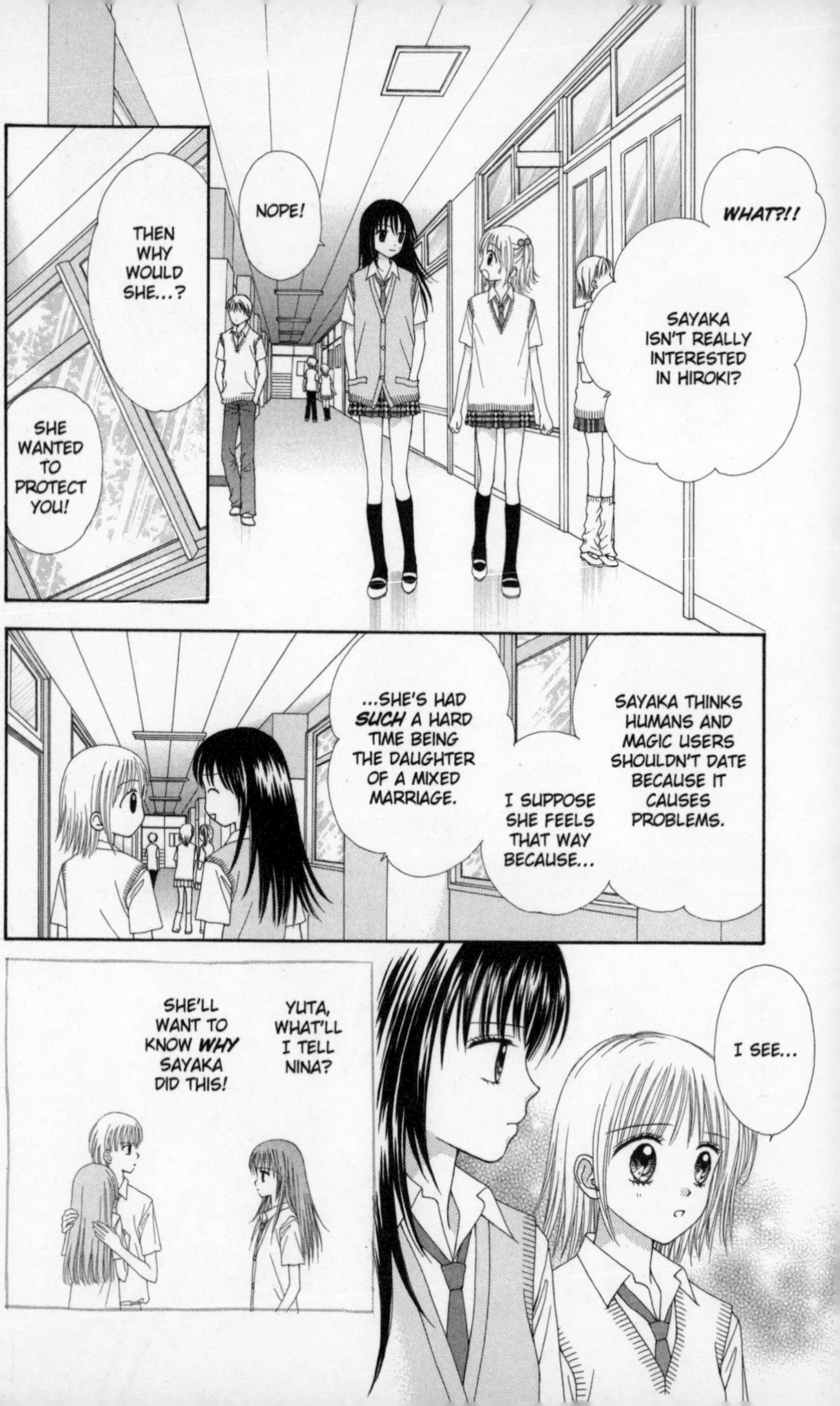
WHAT?!!
SAYAKA ISN'T REALLY INTERESTED IN HIROKI?
NOPE!
THEN WHY WOULD SHE...?
SHE WANTED TO PROTECT YOU!
SAYAKA THINKS HUMANS AND MAGIC USERS SHOULDN'T DATE BECAUSE IT CAUSES PROBLEMS.
I SUPPOSE SHE FEELS THAT WAY BECAUSE...
...SHE'S HAD SUCH A HARD TIME BEING THE DAUGHTER OF A MIXED MARRIAGE.
I SEE...
YUTA, WHAT'LL I TELL NINA?
SHE'LL WANT TO KNOW WHY SAYAKA DID THIS!

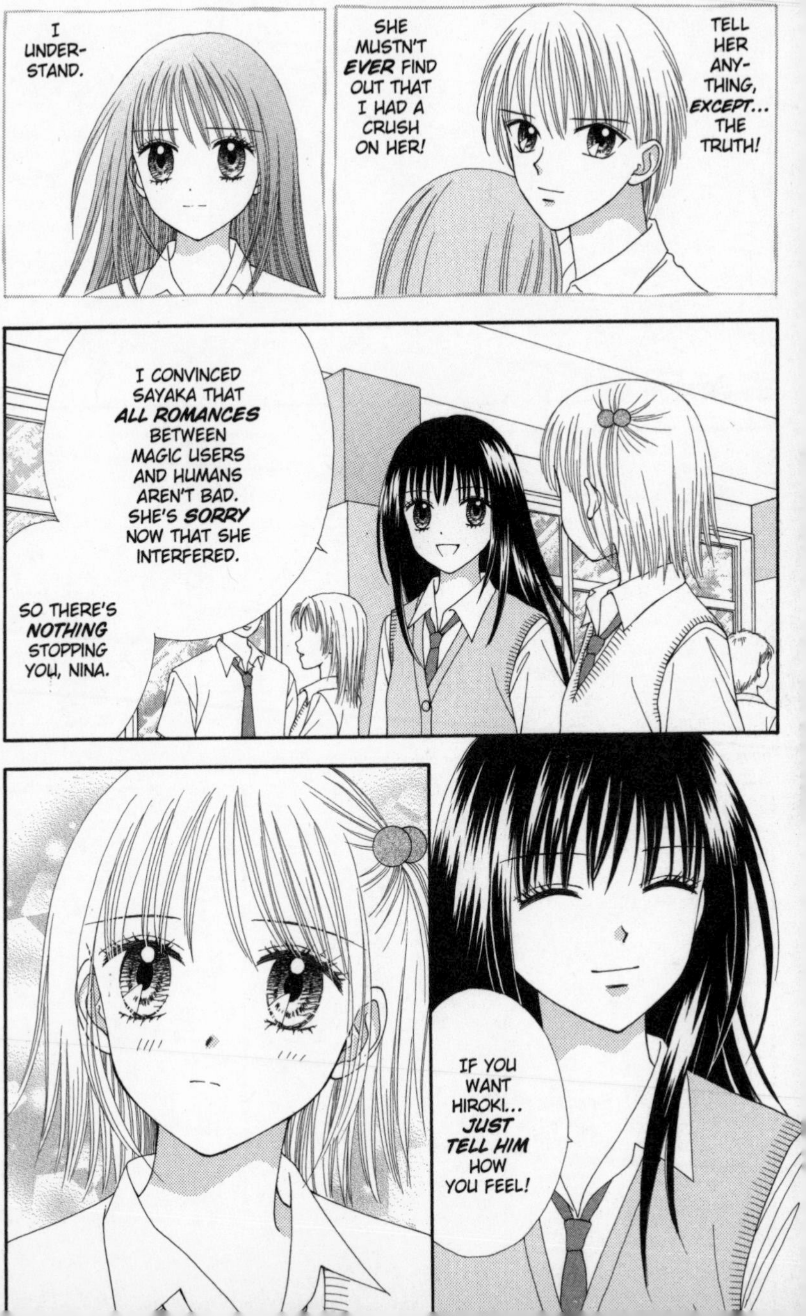
TELL HER ANY-THING, EXCEPT... THE TRUTH!
SHE MUSTN'T EVER FIND OUT THAT I HAD A CRUSH ON HER!
I UNDER-STAND.
I CONVINCED SAYAKA THAT ALL ROMANCES BETWEEN MAGIC USERS AND HUMANS AREN'T BAD. SHE'S SORRY NOW THAT SHE INTERFERED.
SO THERE'S NOTHING STOPPING YOU, NINA.
IF YOU WANT HIROKI... JUST TELL HIM HOW YOU FEEL!

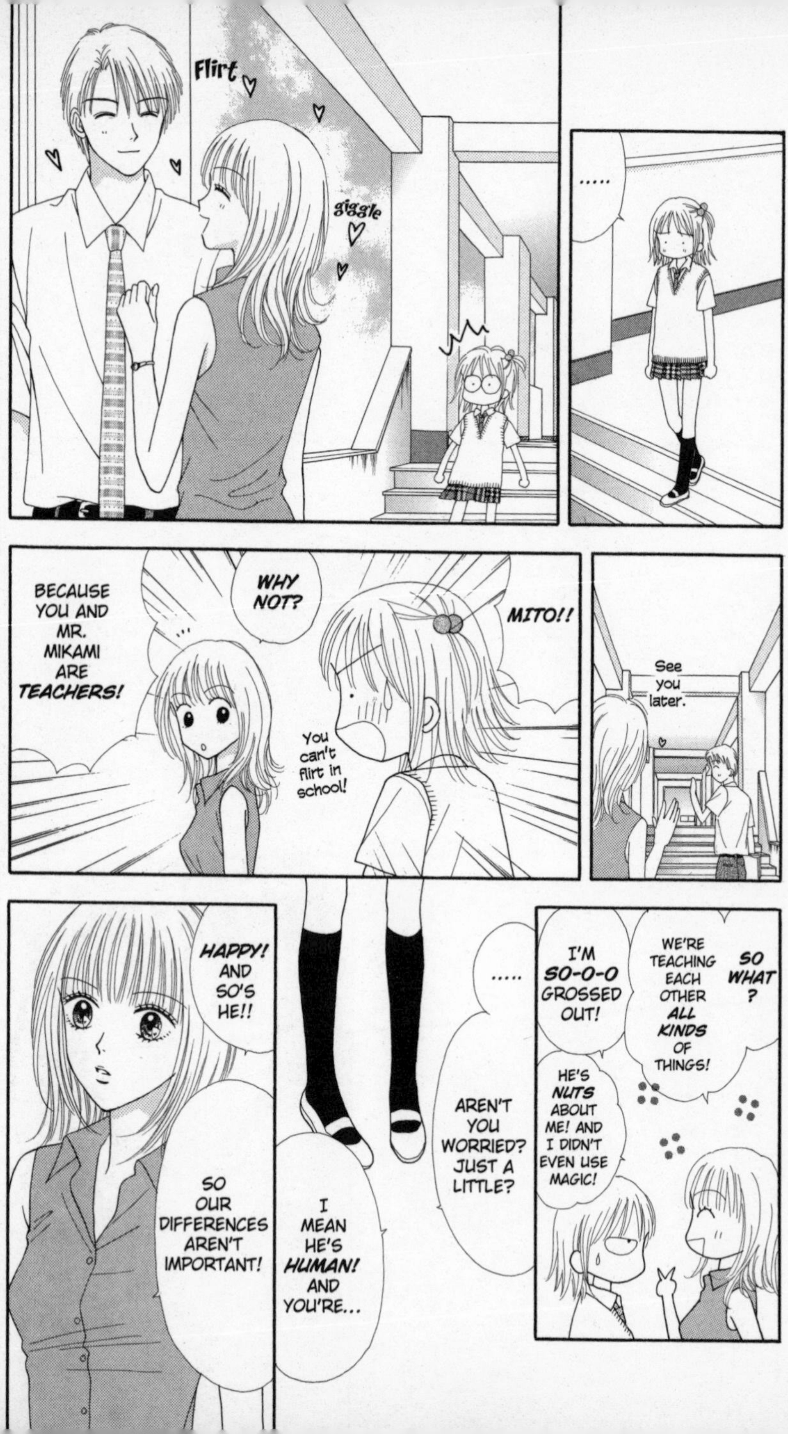
.....
Flirt
giggle
See you later.
MITO!!
You can't flirt in school!
WHY NOT?
...
BECAUSE YOU AND MR. MIKAMI ARE TEACHERS!
SO WHAT?
WE'RE TEACHING EACH OTHER ALL KINDS OF THINGS!
I'M SO-O-O GROSSED OUT!
HE'S NUTS ABOUT ME! AND I DIDN'T EVEN USE MAGIC!
.....
AREN'T YOU WORRIED? JUST A LITTLE?
I MEAN HE'S HUMAN! AND YOU'RE...
SO OUR DIFFERENCES AREN'T IMPORTANT!
HAPPY! AND SO'S HE!!

FREE TALK 3

Ultra Maniac, Vol. 5 and **The Complete Works of Marmalade Boy** Vol. 3 are coming out at the same time. This is the first time I've ever had two books published simultaneously! I really feel fortunate! **The Complete Works** has a lot of extras—initial sketches and character design sheets that I did in preparing to do *Marmalade Boy*.

For Vol. 4, I'm going to include lots of extra sketches and a color opening. Plus I plan on doing plenty of new, eye-popping illustrations in addition to the cover!

Normally, the inside story pages are the most important part of a book. But a lot of attention was put into this collection, and the staff did its best to make the book really special. So I hope you'll buy it and put it on your bookshelf!

A special illustrated collection of *Marmalade Boy* was printed before this. But, because it was released while the series was still being published, the color illustrations from the last eight chapters are missing. Those missing illustrations and a bunch of other color pages are included in **The Complete Works**, so those of you who own **The Illustrated Collection**, please buy this collection too!

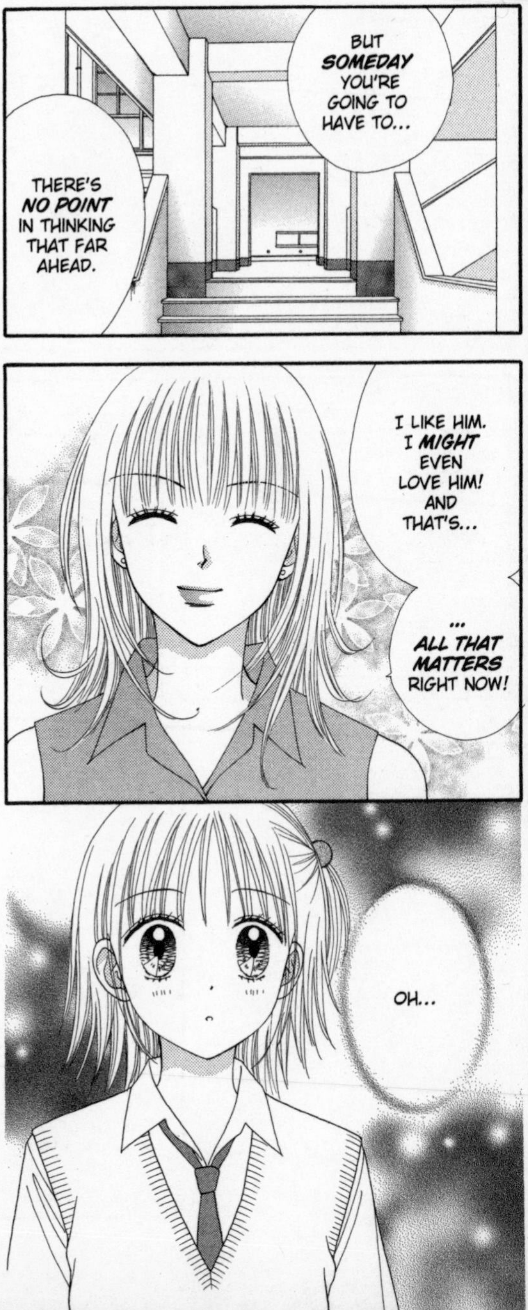
BUT SOMEDAY YOU'RE GOING TO HAVE TO...
THERE'S NO POINT IN THINKING THAT FAR AHEAD.
I LIKE HIM. I MIGHT EVEN LOVE HIM! AND THAT'S...
...ALL THAT MATTERS RIGHT NOW!
OH...

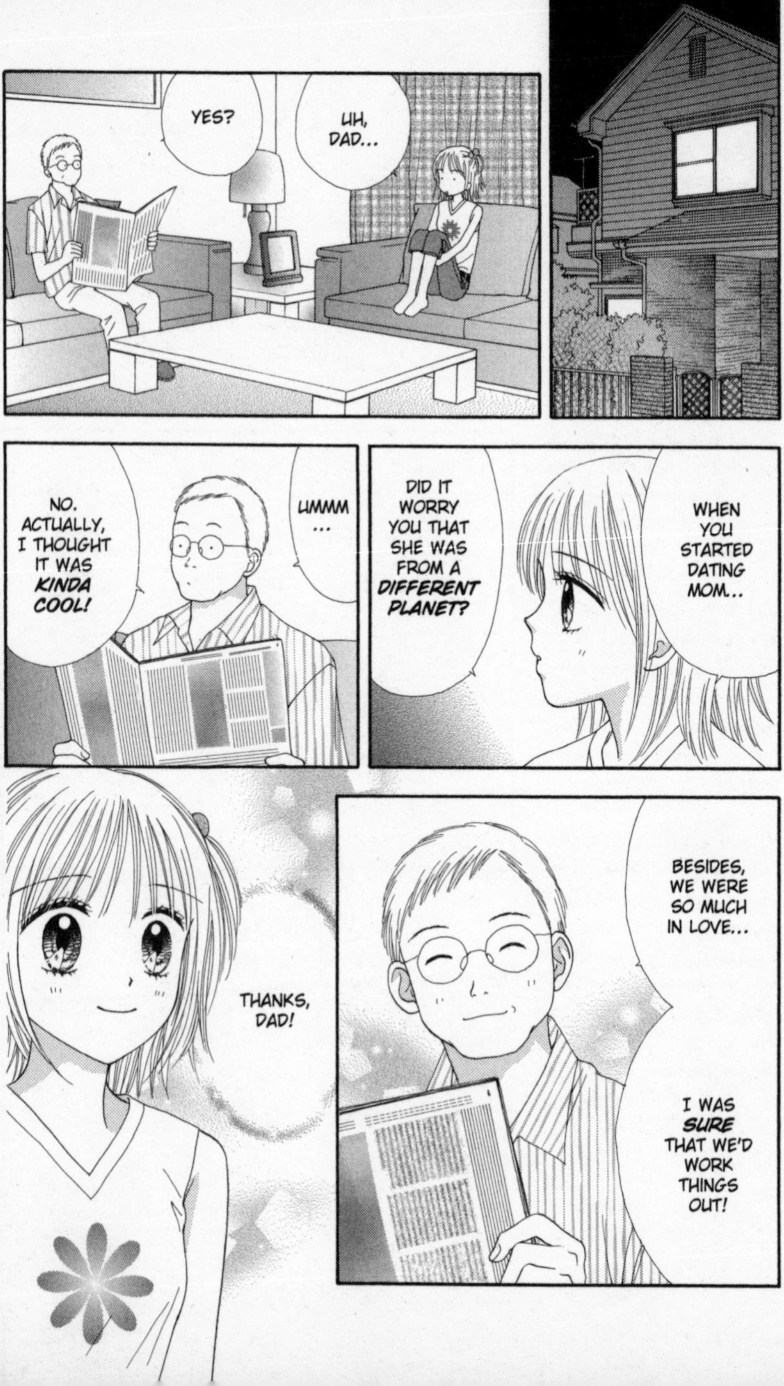
UH, DAD...
YES?
WHEN YOU STARTED DATING MOM...
DID IT WORRY YOU THAT SHE WAS FROM A *DIFFERENT PLANET?*
UMMM ...
NO. ACTUALLY, I THOUGHT IT WAS *KINDA COOL!*
BESIDES, WE WERE SO MUCH IN LOVE...
I WAS *SURE* THAT WE'D WORK THINGS OUT!
THANKS, DAD!

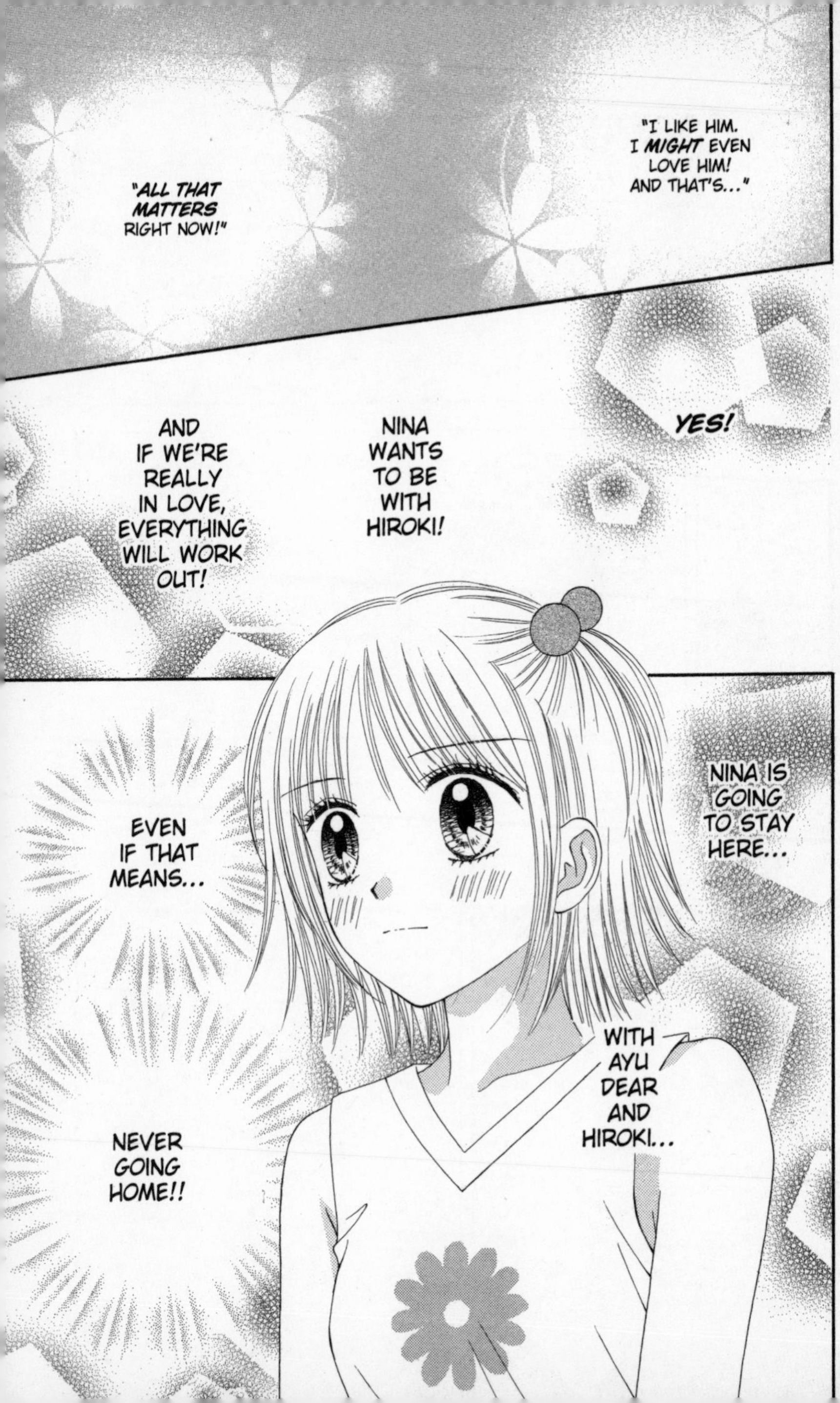
"I LIKE HIM. I MIGHT EVEN LOVE HIM! AND THAT'S..."
"ALL THAT MATTERS RIGHT NOW!"
YES!
NINA WANTS TO BE WITH HIROKI!
AND IF WE'RE REALLY IN LOVE, EVERYTHING WILL WORK OUT!
NINA IS GOING TO STAY HERE...
WITH AYU DEAR AND HIROKI...
EVEN IF THAT MEANS...
NEVER GOING HOME!!

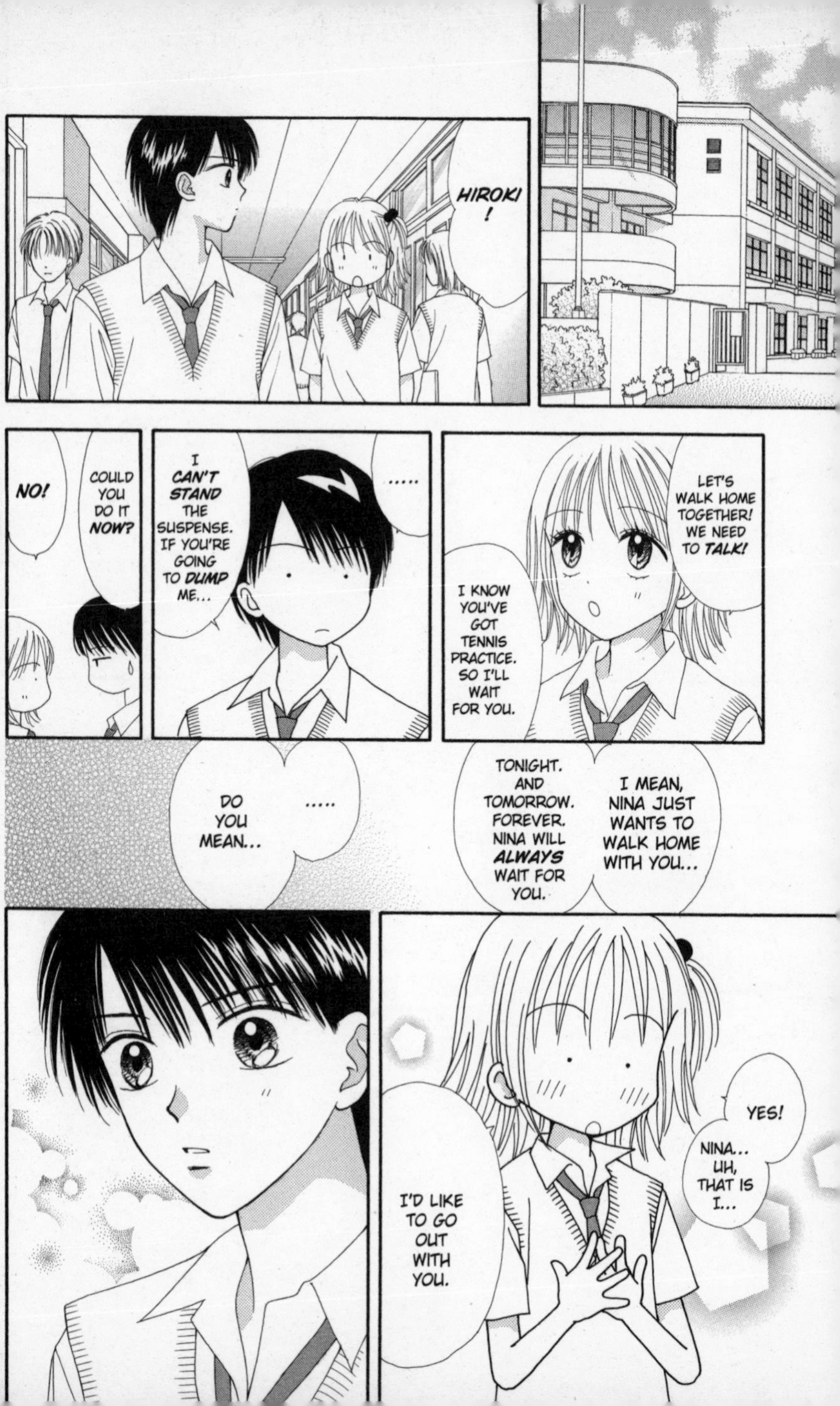
HIROKI!
LET'S WALK HOME TOGETHER! WE NEED TO TALK!
I KNOW YOU'VE GOT TENNIS PRACTICE. SO I'LL WAIT FOR YOU.
.....
I CAN'T STAND THE SUSPENSE. IF YOU'RE GOING TO DUMP ME...
COULD YOU DO IT NOW?
NO!
I MEAN, NINA JUST WANTS TO WALK HOME WITH YOU...
TONIGHT. AND TOMORROW. FOREVER. NINA WILL ALWAYS WAIT FOR YOU.
.....
DO YOU MEAN...
YES!
NINA... UH, THAT IS I...
I'D LIKE TO GO OUT WITH YOU.

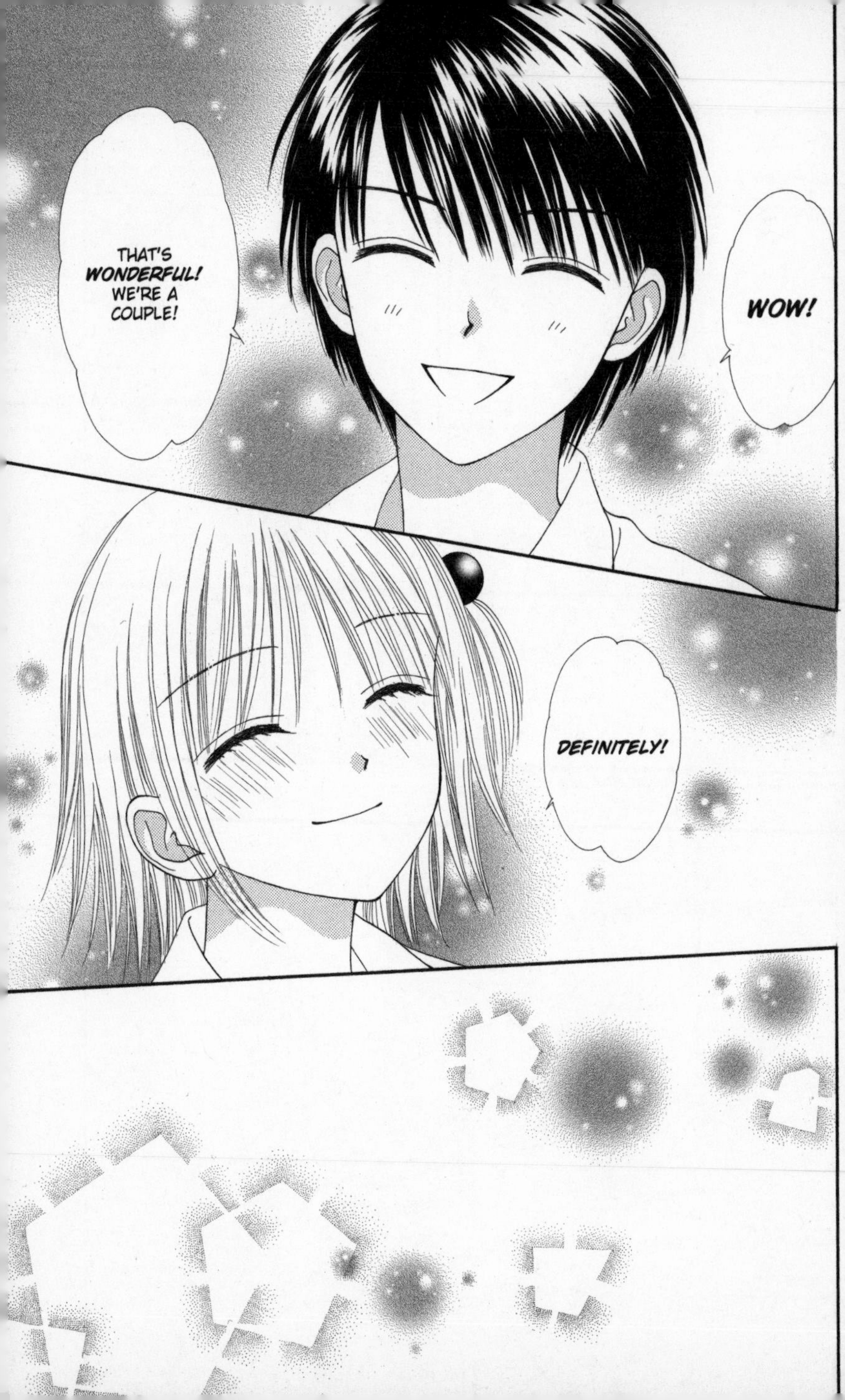
WOW!
THAT'S WONDERFUL! WE'RE A COUPLE!
DEFINITELY!

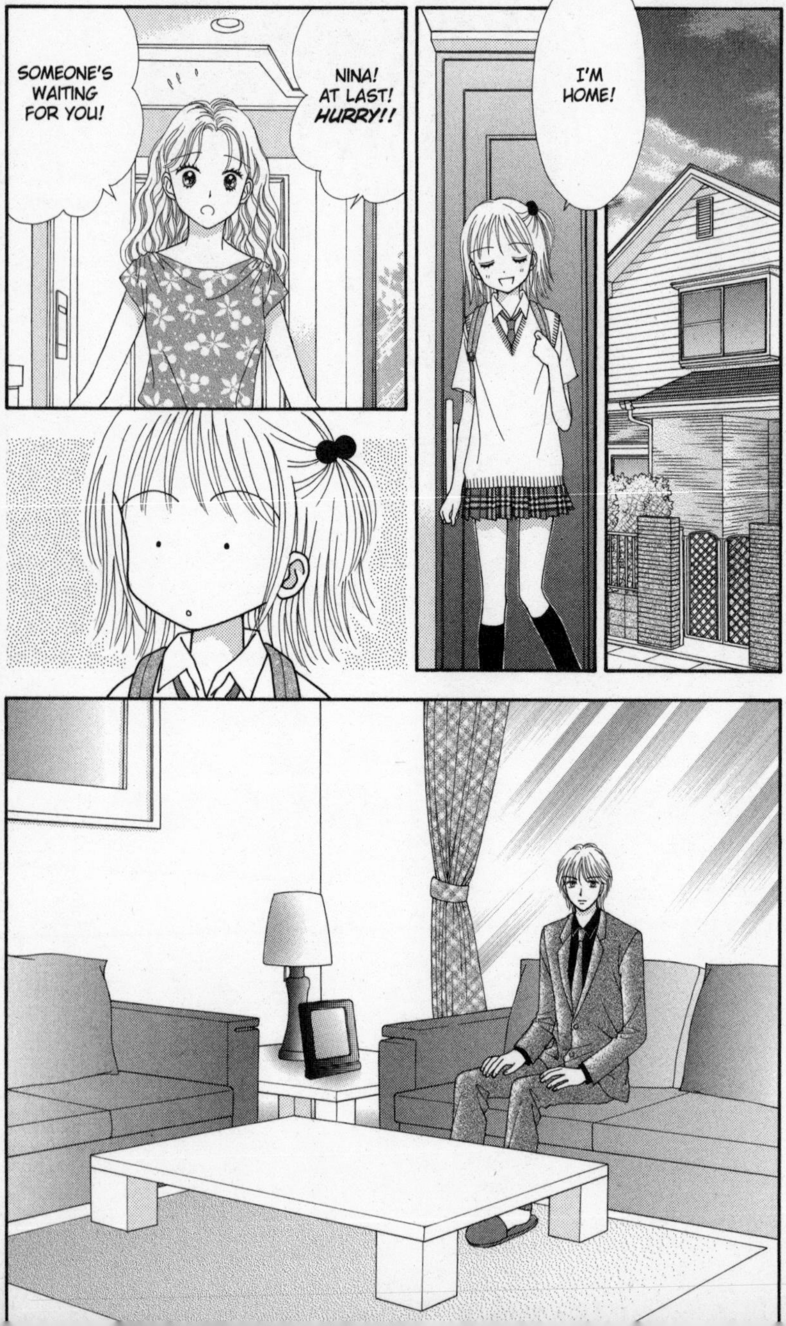
I'M HOME!
NINA! AT LAST! HURRY!!
SOMEONE'S WAITING FOR YOU!

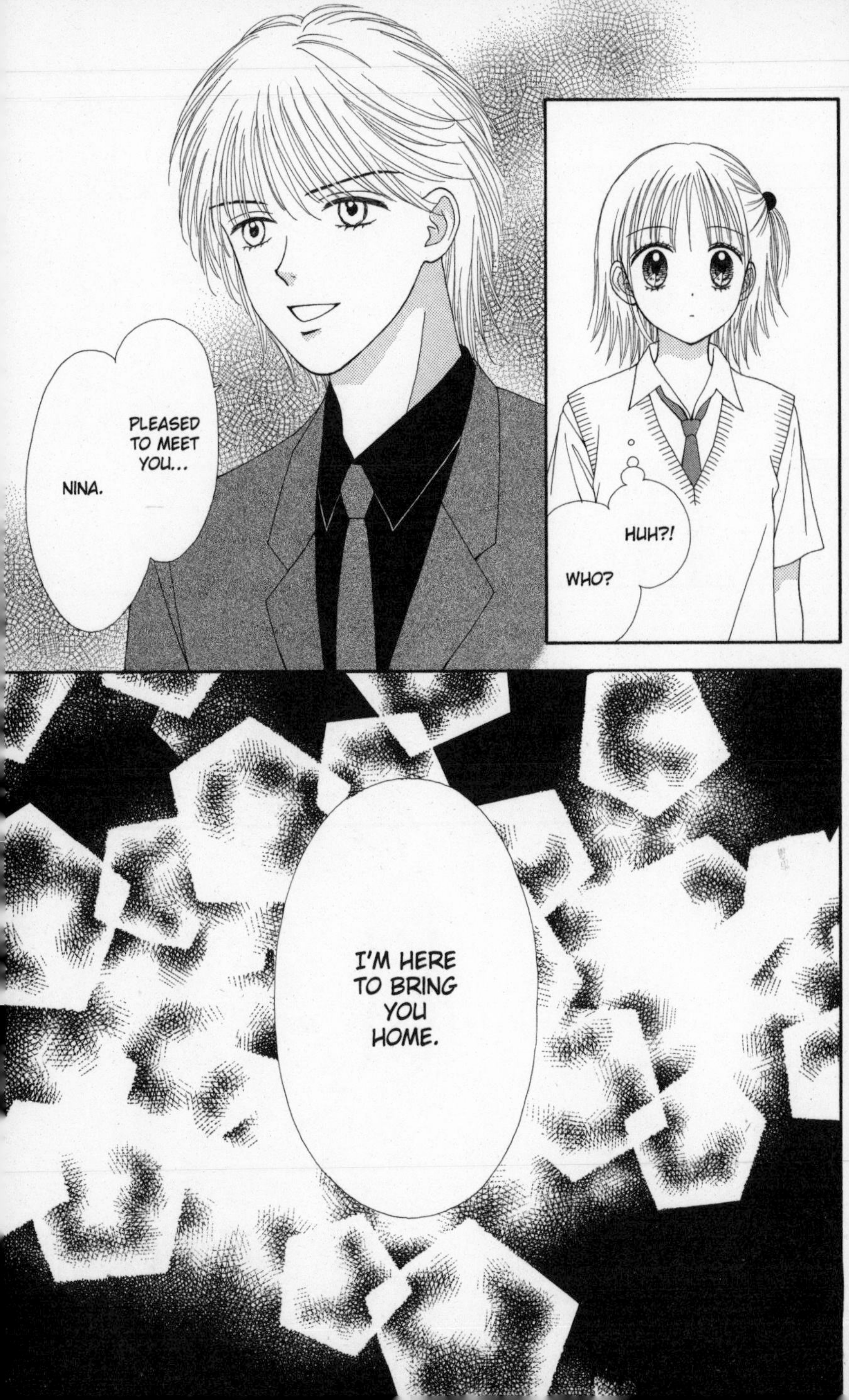
PLEASED TO MEET YOU... NINA.
HUH?! WHO?
I'M HERE TO BRING YOU HOME.

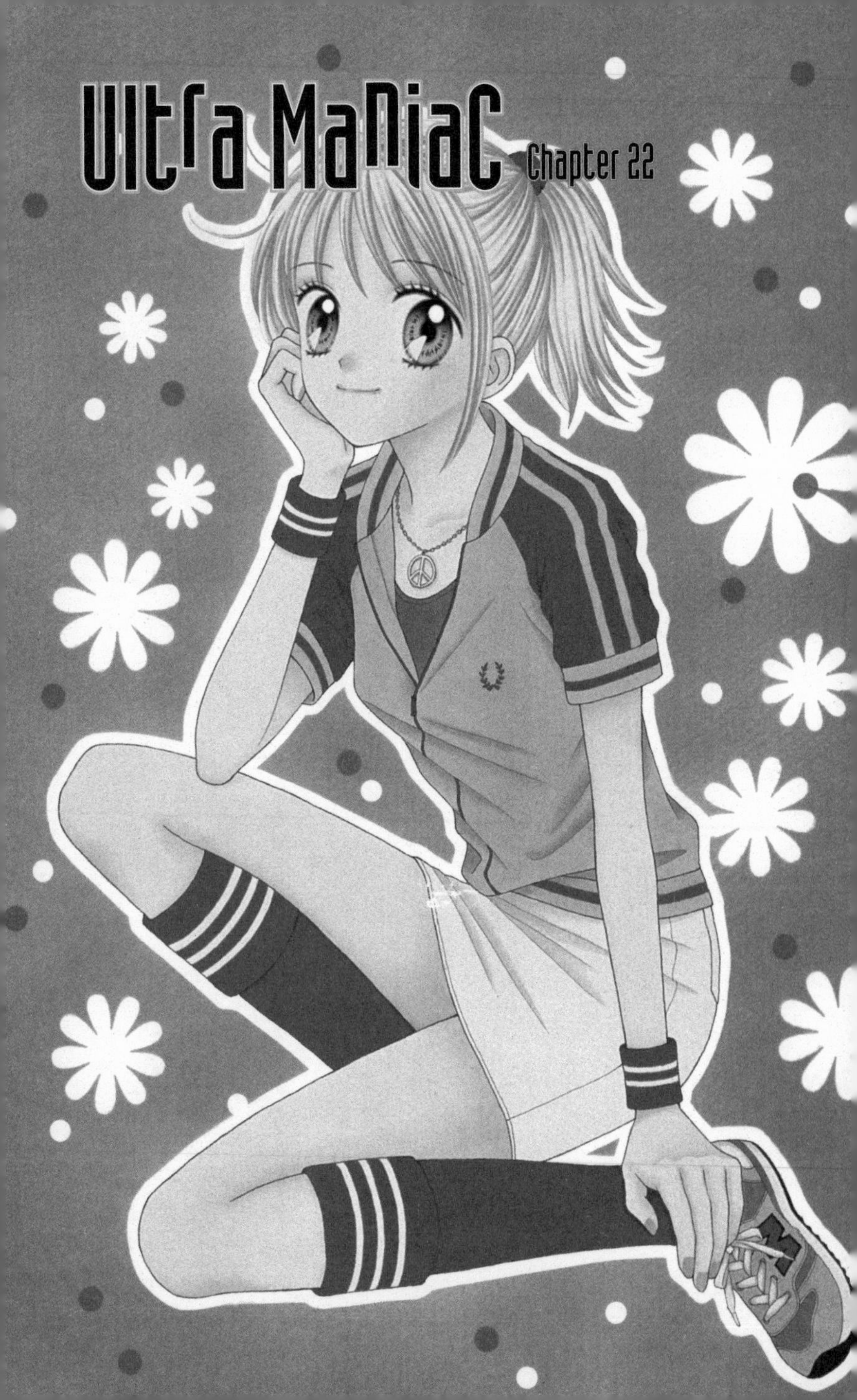
Ultra Maniac
Chapter 22

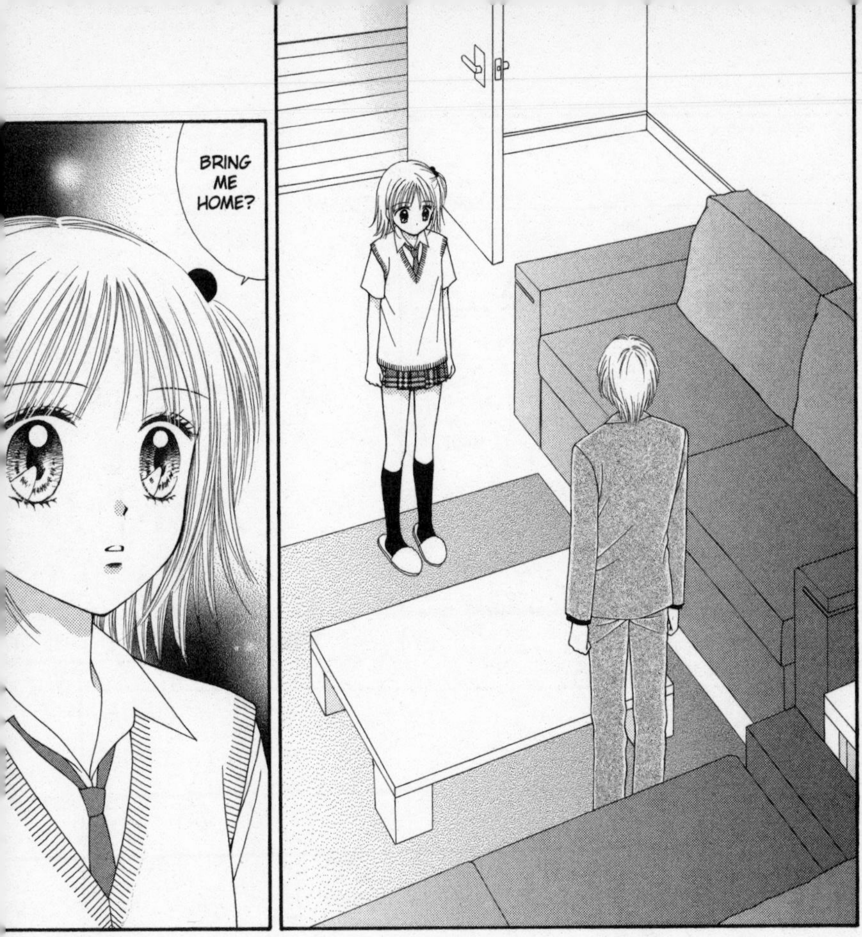
BRING ME HOME?

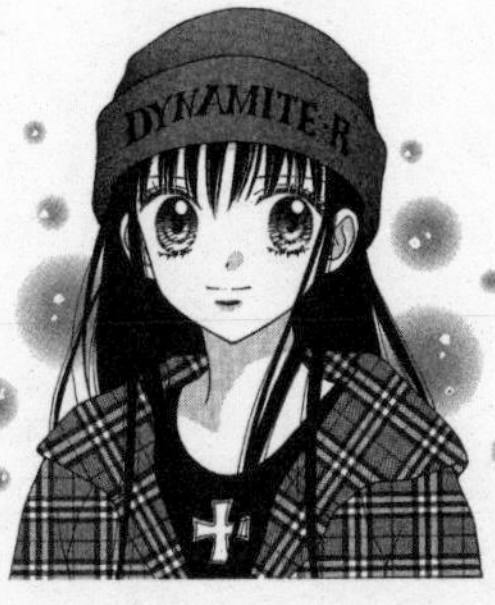
DYNAMITE-R

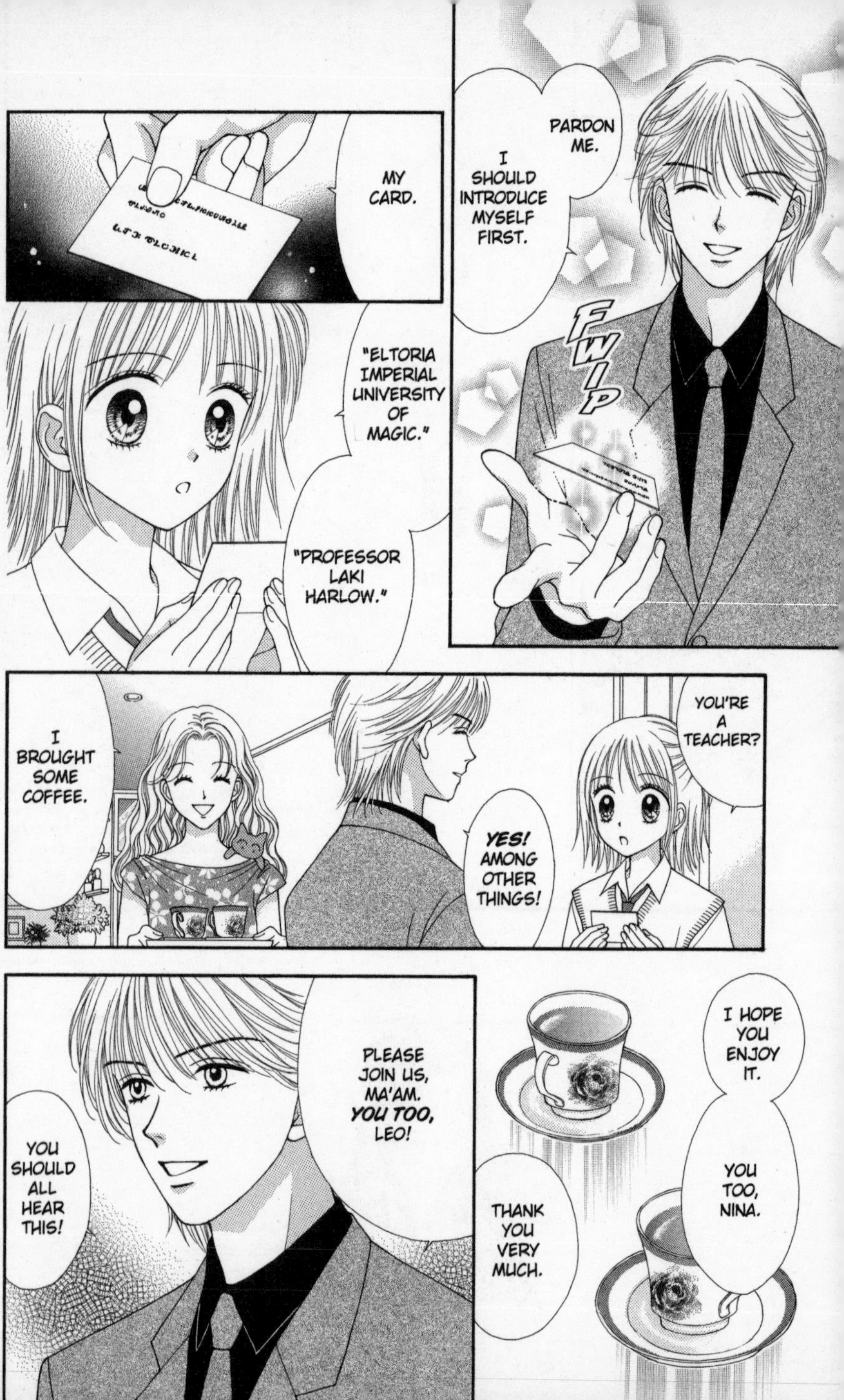
PARDON ME.
I SHOULD INTRODUCE MYSELF FIRST.
FWIP
MY CARD.
"ELTORIA IMPERIAL UNIVERSITY OF MAGIC."
"PROFESSOR LAKI HARLOW."
YOU'RE A TEACHER?
YES! AMONG OTHER THINGS!
I BROUGHT SOME COFFEE.
I HOPE YOU ENJOY IT.
YOU TOO, NINA.
THANK YOU VERY MUCH.
PLEASE JOIN US, MA'AM. **YOU TOO,** LEO!
YOU SHOULD ALL HEAR THIS!

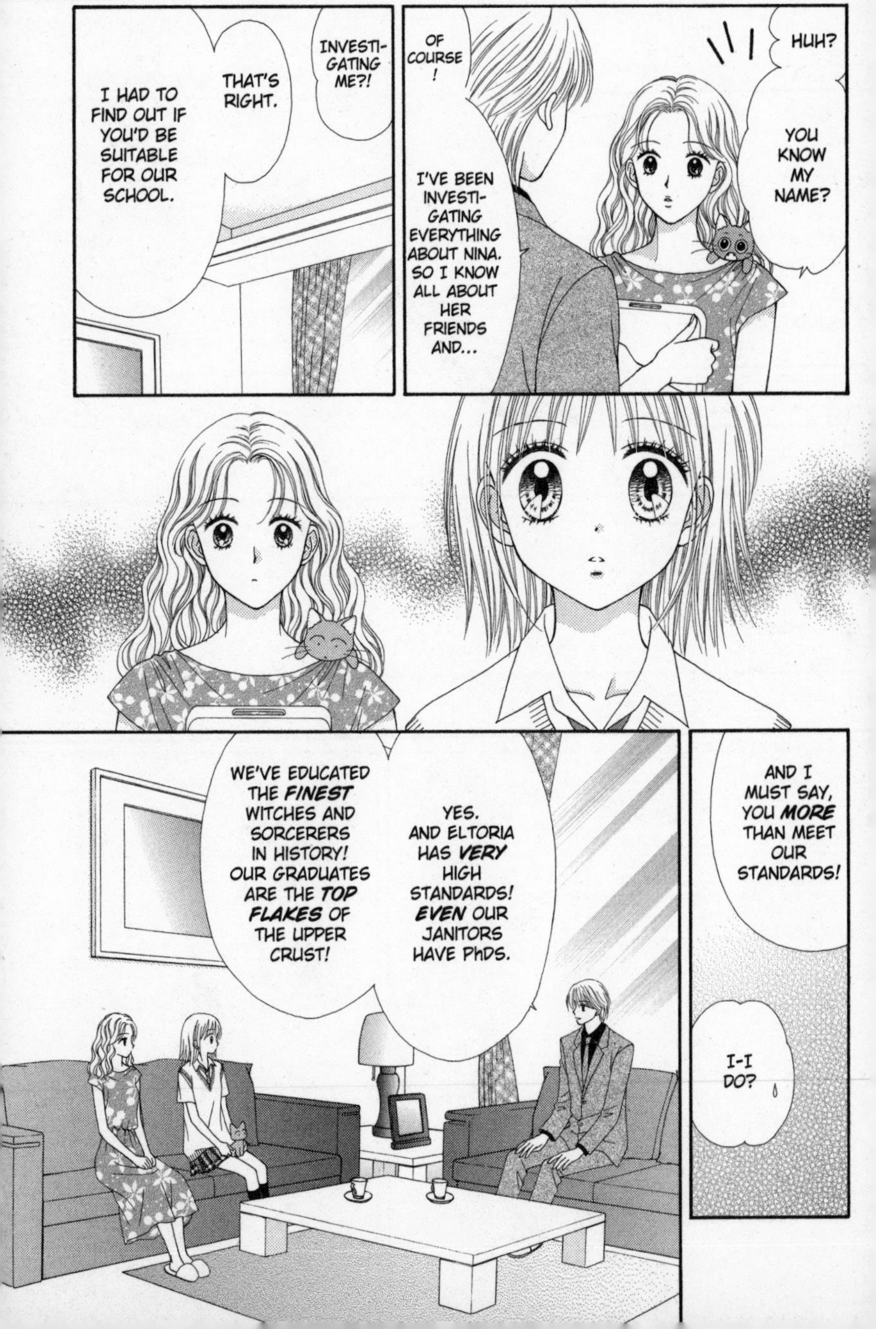
HUH?
YOU KNOW MY NAME?
OF COURSE!
I'VE BEEN INVESTIGATING EVERYTHING ABOUT NINA. SO I KNOW ALL ABOUT HER FRIENDS AND...
INVESTIGATING ME?!
THAT'S RIGHT.
I HAD TO FIND OUT IF YOU'D BE SUITABLE FOR OUR SCHOOL.
AND I MUST SAY, YOU ***MORE*** THAN MEET OUR STANDARDS!
I-I DO?
YES. AND ELTORIA HAS ***VERY*** HIGH STANDARDS! ***EVEN*** OUR JANITORS HAVE PhDS.
WE'VE EDUCATED THE ***FINEST*** WITCHES AND SORCERERS IN HISTORY! OUR GRADUATES ARE THE ***TOP FLAKES*** OF THE UPPER CRUST!

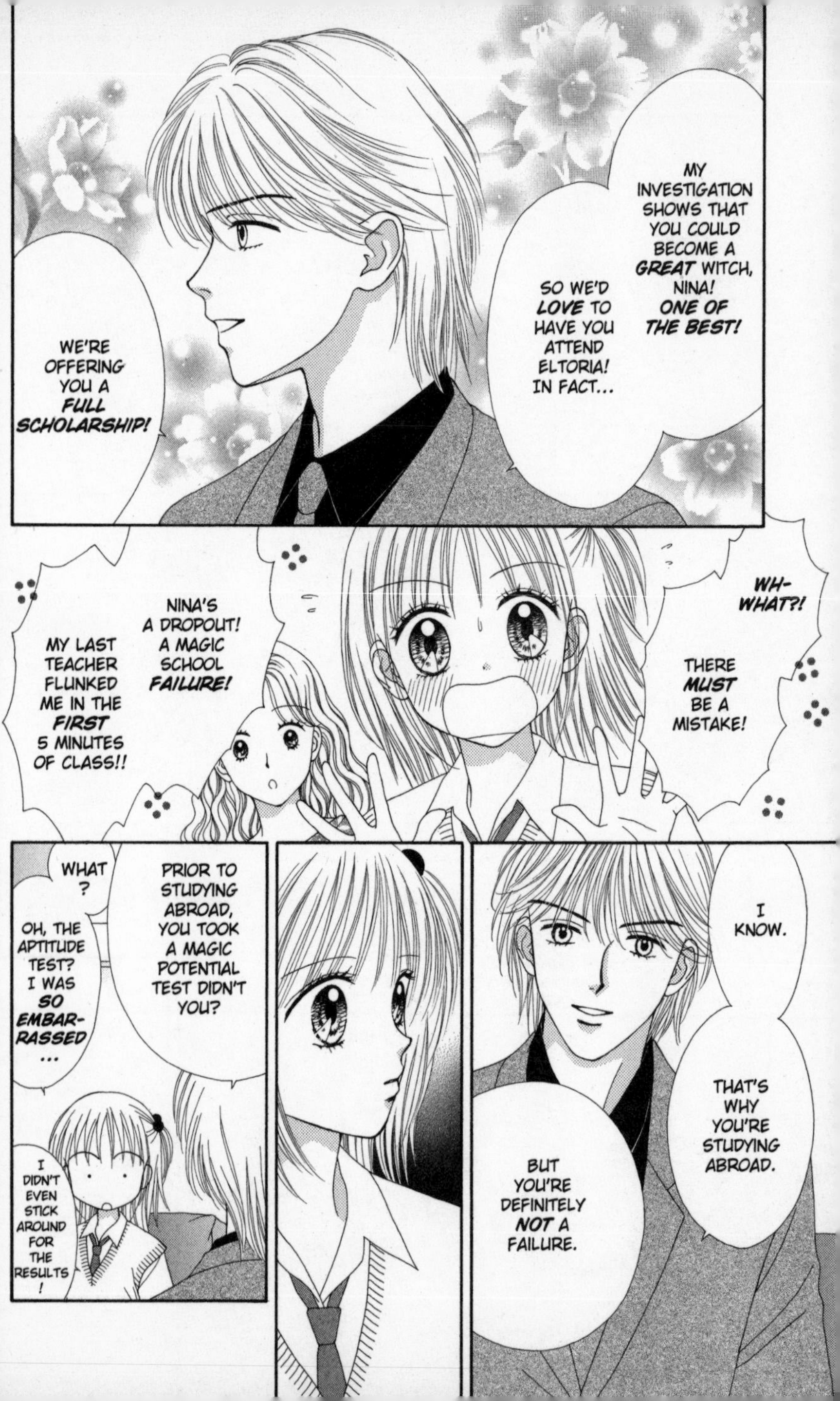

MY INVESTIGATION SHOWS THAT YOU COULD BECOME A GREAT WITCH, NINA! ONE OF THE BEST!
SO WE'D LOVE TO HAVE YOU ATTEND ELTORIA! IN FACT...
WE'RE OFFERING YOU A FULL SCHOLARSHIP!
WH-WHAT?!
THERE MUST BE A MISTAKE!
NINA'S A DROPOUT! A MAGIC SCHOOL FAILURE!
MY LAST TEACHER FLUNKED ME IN THE FIRST 5 MINUTES OF CLASS!!
I KNOW.
THAT'S WHY YOU'RE STUDYING ABROAD.
BUT YOU'RE DEFINITELY NOT A FAILURE.
PRIOR TO STUDYING ABROAD, YOU TOOK A MAGIC POTENTIAL TEST DIDN'T YOU?
WHAT?
OH, THE APTITUDE TEST? I WAS SO EMBAR-RASSED...
I DIDN'T EVEN STICK AROUND FOR THE RESULTS!

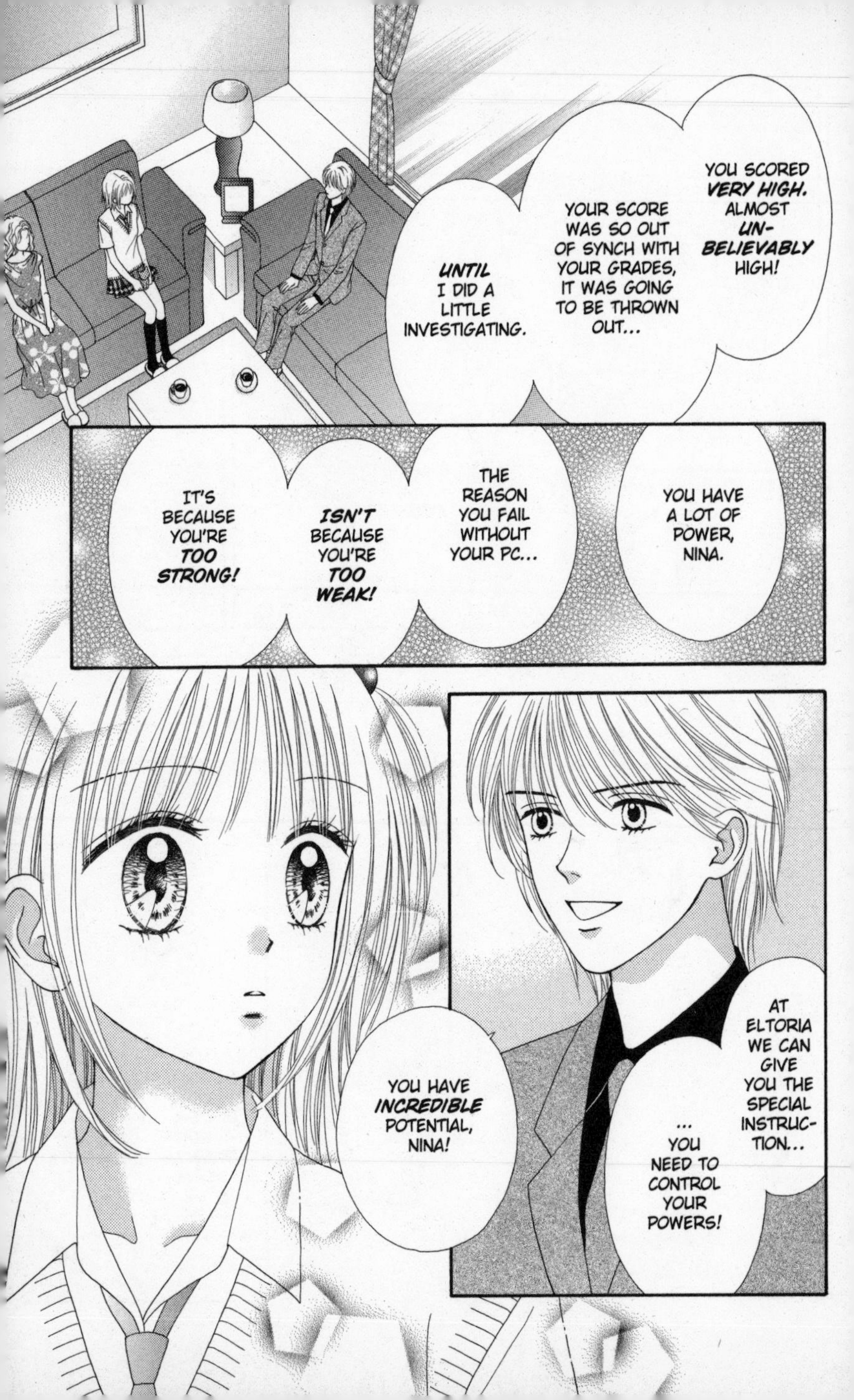
YOU SCORED VERY HIGH. ALMOST UN-BELIEVABLY HIGH!
YOUR SCORE WAS SO OUT OF SYNCH WITH YOUR GRADES, IT WAS GOING TO BE THROWN OUT...
UNTIL I DID A LITTLE INVESTIGATING.
YOU HAVE A LOT OF POWER, NINA.
THE REASON YOU FAIL WITHOUT YOUR PC...
ISN'T BECAUSE YOU'RE TOO WEAK!
IT'S BECAUSE YOU'RE TOO STRONG!
AT ELTORIA WE CAN GIVE YOU THE SPECIAL INSTRUC-TION...
...YOU NEED TO CONTROL YOUR POWERS!
YOU HAVE INCREDIBLE POTENTIAL, NINA!

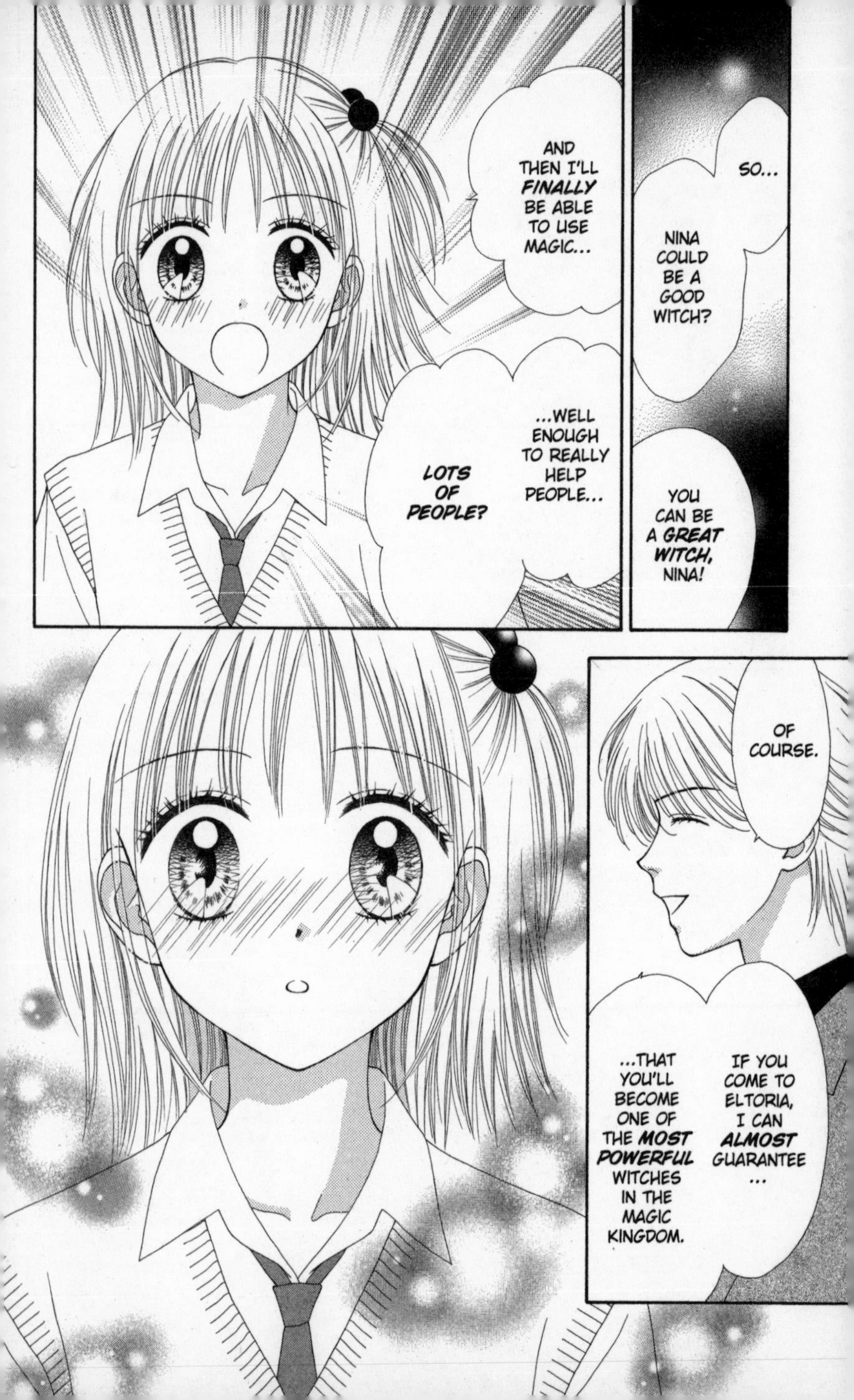
SO...
NINA COULD BE A GOOD WITCH?
YOU CAN BE A GREAT WITCH, NINA!
AND THEN I'LL FINALLY BE ABLE TO USE MAGIC...
...WELL ENOUGH TO REALLY HELP PEOPLE...
LOTS OF PEOPLE?
OF COURSE.
IF YOU COME TO ELTORIA, I CAN ALMOST GUARANTEE...
...THAT YOU'LL BECOME ONE OF THE MOST POWERFUL WITCHES IN THE MAGIC KINGDOM.

FREE TALK 4

In February, there was a wrap party for the *Ultra Maniac* anime series. It was great to get together with the staff and cast again. It was so much fun that I ended up going to all three rounds of the party. (Ha ha!) The third round ended up at anime producer Mr. Otsuki's favorite karaoke bar. Some of the people singing there weren't amateurs, though.

Tapiko, the vocalist of the band can/goo (which recorded the *Ultra Maniac* opening theme song) sang can/goo's song "Maboroshi." Plus, Yui Horie (the voice of Ayu) sang "Peach Colored Unrequited Love"! Yui's super-cute, frilled figure stole the heart of the male customers and they were screaming, "Encore! Encore!" She was so good that Mr. Otsuki said, "Shouldn't you be singing the main theme yourself?!"

Apparently Mr. Otsuki has also taken Mariko Kunifuda to that karaoke bar to sing the *Marmalade Boy* theme. I'm so jealous. (Ha ha.)

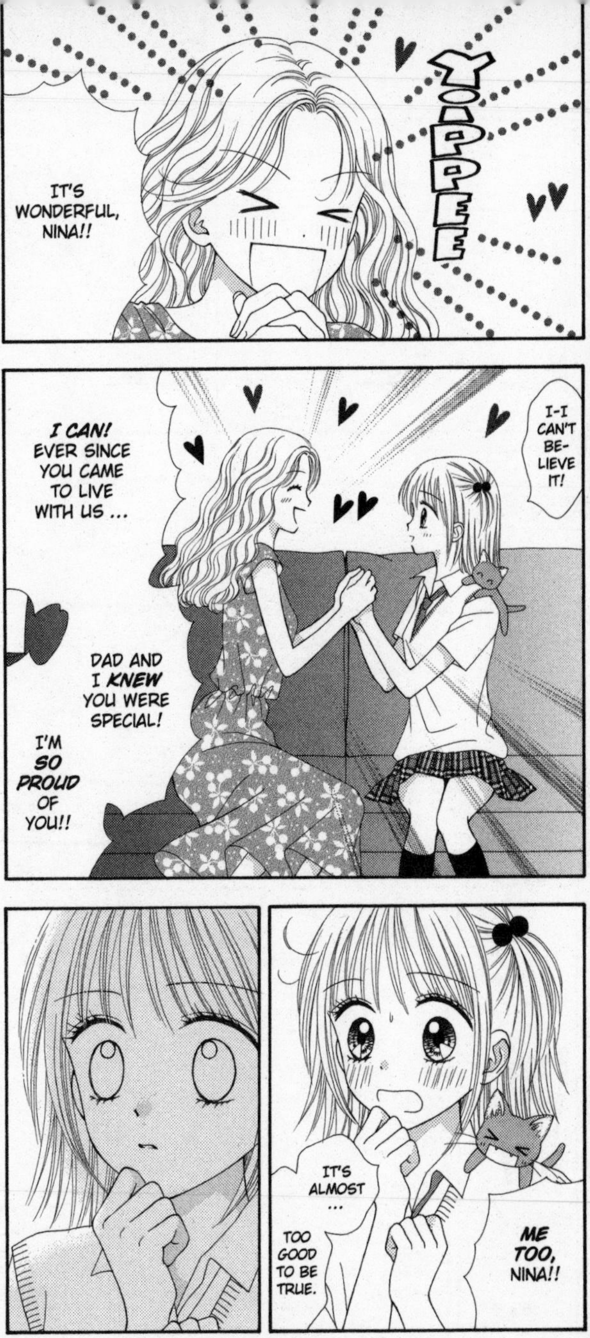
YOIPPEE
IT'S WONDERFUL, NINA!!
I-I CAN'T BE-LIEVE IT!
I CAN! EVER SINCE YOU CAME TO LIVE WITH US ...
DAD AND I KNEW YOU WERE SPECIAL!
I'M SO PROUD OF YOU!!
IT'S ALMOST ...
TOO GOOD TO BE TRUE.
ME TOO, NINA!!

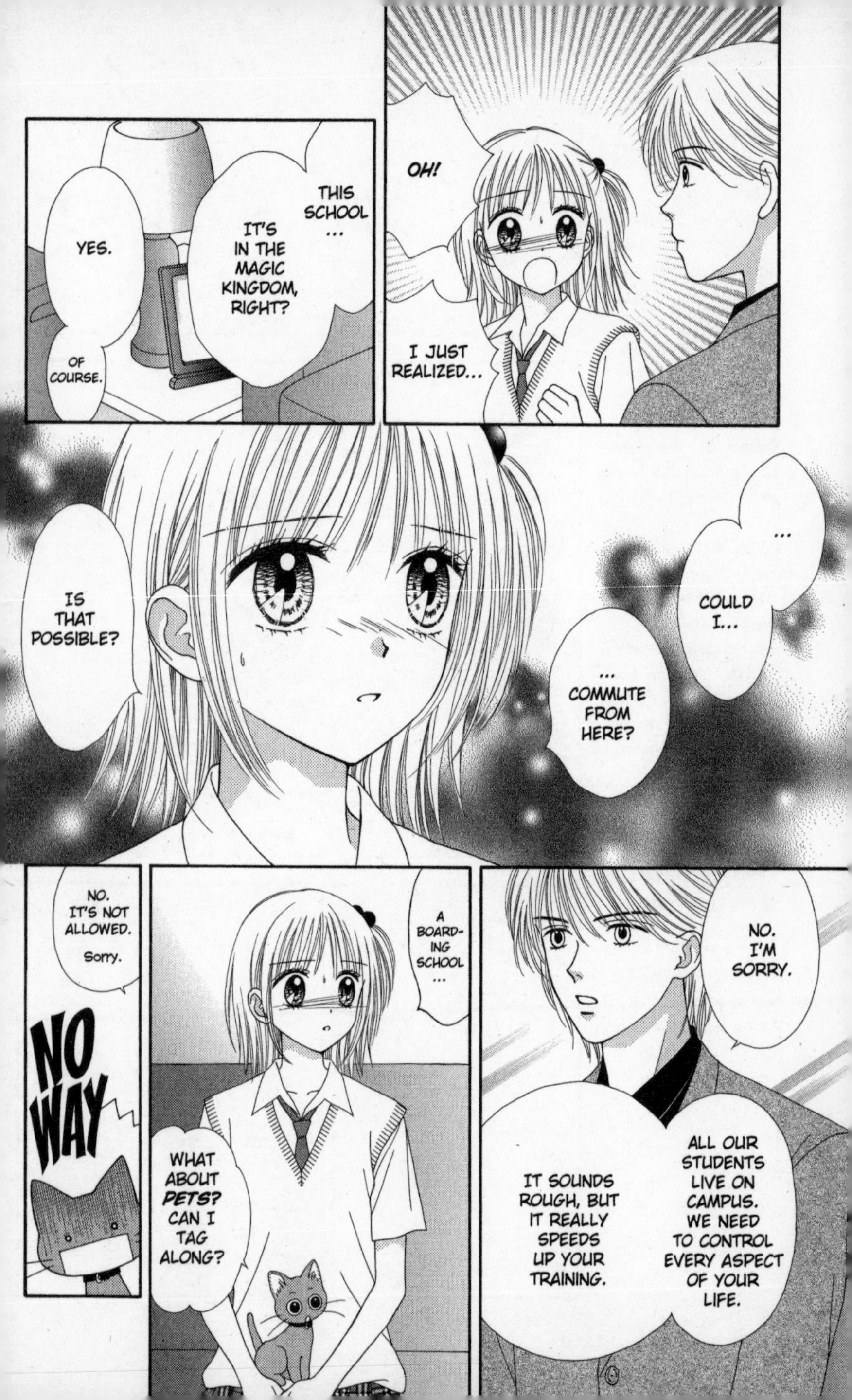
OH!
I JUST REALIZED...
THIS SCHOOL ...
IT'S IN THE MAGIC KINGDOM, RIGHT?
YES.
OF COURSE.
...
COULD I...
... COMMUTE FROM HERE?
IS THAT POSSIBLE?
NO. I'M SORRY.
ALL OUR STUDENTS LIVE ON CAMPUS. WE NEED TO CONTROL EVERY ASPECT OF YOUR LIFE.
IT SOUNDS ROUGH, BUT IT REALLY SPEEDS UP YOUR TRAINING.
A BOARDING SCHOOL ...
WHAT ABOUT *PETS?* CAN I TAG ALONG?
NO. IT'S NOT ALLOWED.
Sorry.
NO WAY

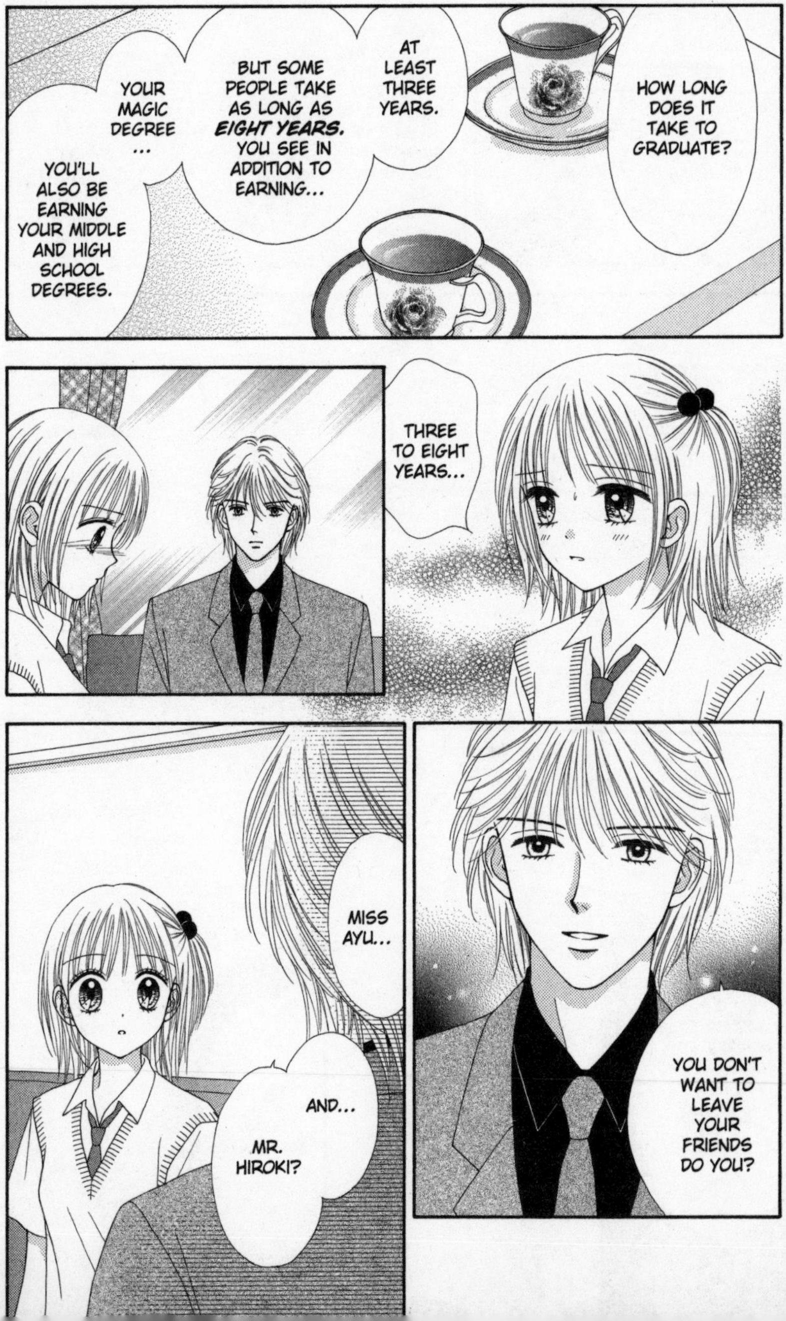
HOW LONG DOES IT TAKE TO GRADUATE?
AT LEAST THREE YEARS.
BUT SOME PEOPLE TAKE AS LONG AS *EIGHT YEARS.* YOU SEE IN ADDITION TO EARNING...
YOUR MAGIC DEGREE ...
YOU'LL ALSO BE EARNING YOUR MIDDLE AND HIGH SCHOOL DEGREES.
THREE TO EIGHT YEARS...
YOU DON'T WANT TO LEAVE YOUR FRIENDS DO YOU?
MISS AYU...
AND...
MR. HIROKI?

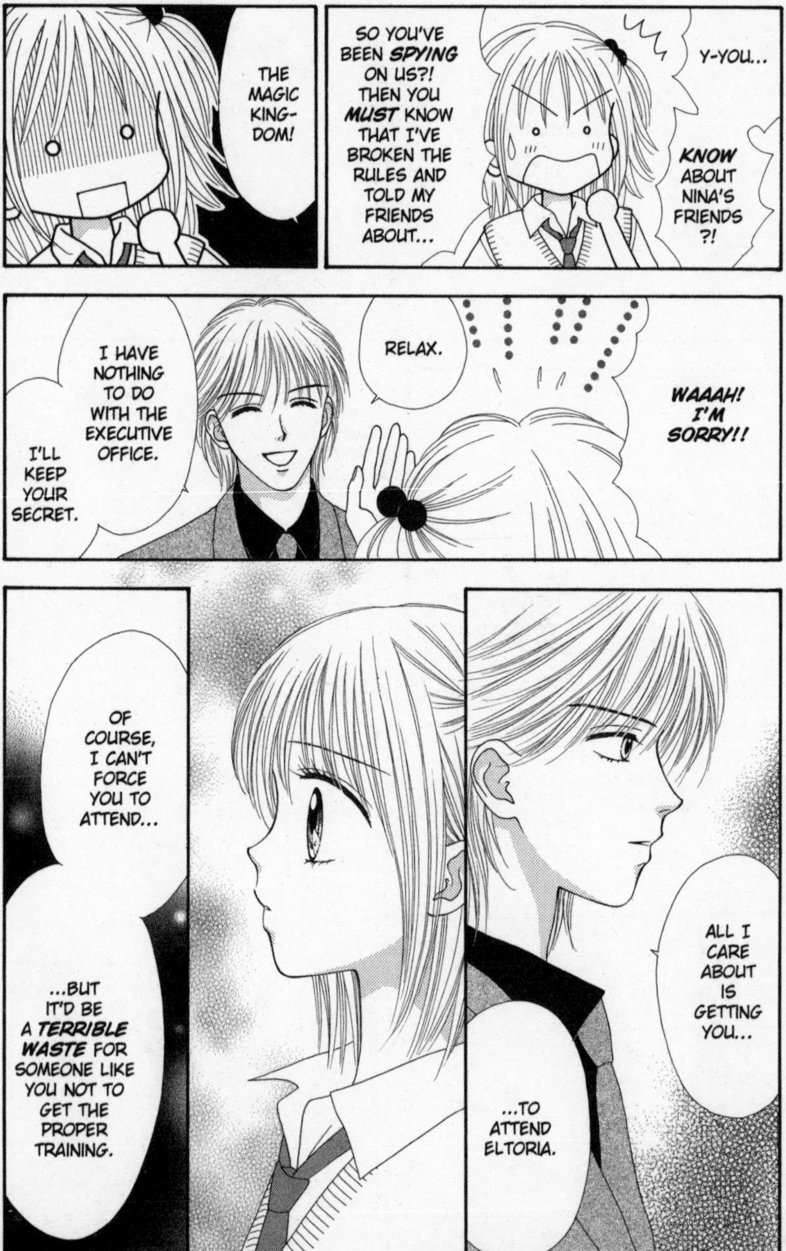
Y-YOU...
KNOW ABOUT NINA'S FRIENDS?!
SO YOU'VE BEEN SPYING ON US?! THEN YOU MUST KNOW THAT I'VE BROKEN THE RULES AND TOLD MY FRIENDS ABOUT...
THE MAGIC KING-DOM!
WAAAH! I'M SORRY!!
RELAX.
I HAVE NOTHING TO DO WITH THE EXECUTIVE OFFICE.
I'LL KEEP YOUR SECRET.
ALL I CARE ABOUT IS GETTING YOU...
...TO ATTEND ELTORIA.
OF COURSE, I CAN'T FORCE YOU TO ATTEND...
...BUT IT'D BE A TERRIBLE WASTE FOR SOMEONE LIKE YOU NOT TO GET THE PROPER TRAINING.

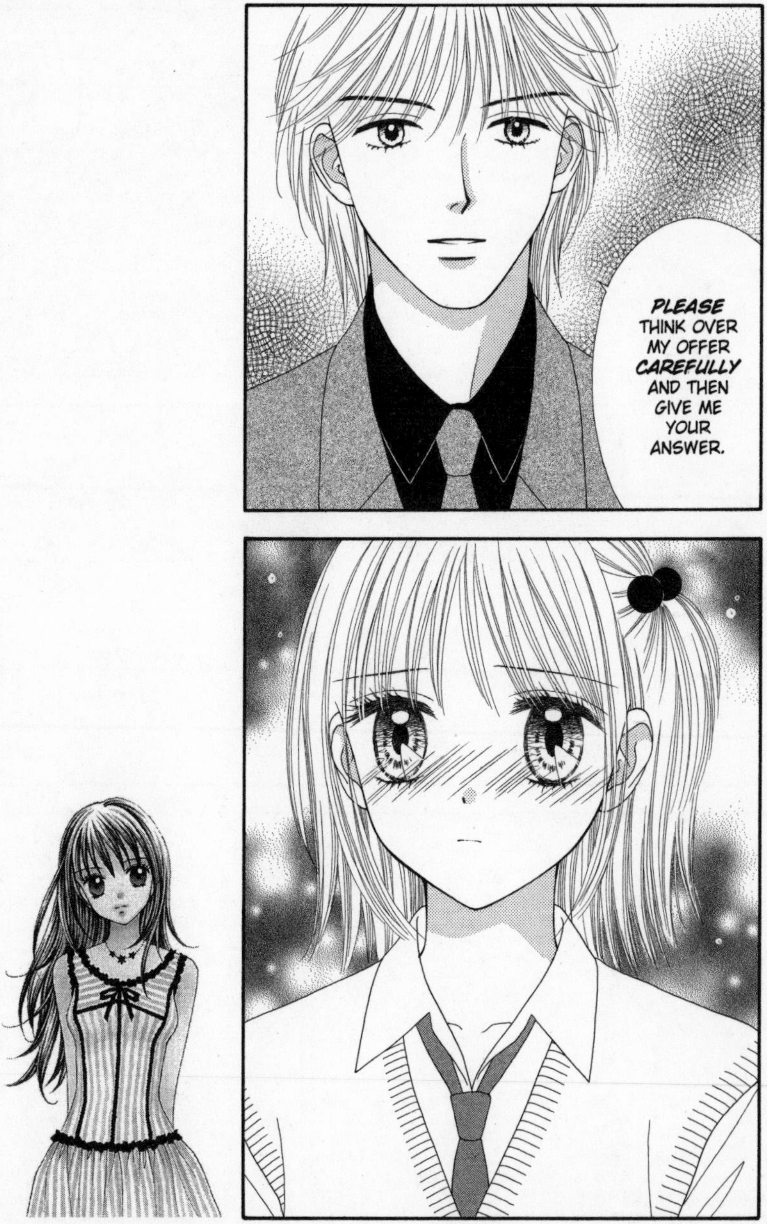
PLEASE THINK OVER MY OFFER CAREFULLY AND THEN GIVE ME YOUR ANSWER.

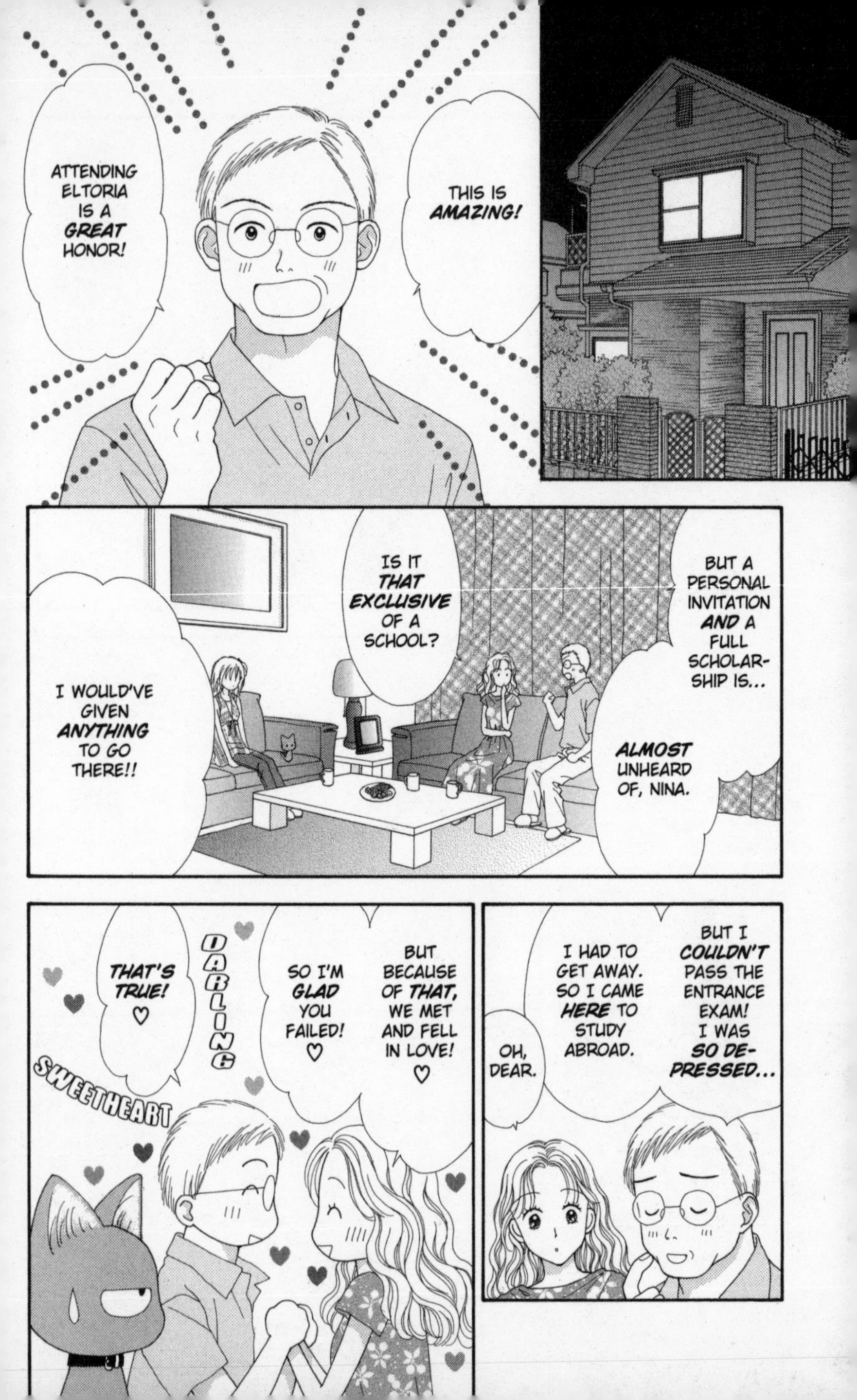
THIS IS AMAZING!
ATTENDING ELTORIA IS A GREAT HONOR!
BUT A PERSONAL INVITATION AND A FULL SCHOLARSHIP IS...
ALMOST UNHEARD OF, NINA.
IS IT THAT EXCLUSIVE OF A SCHOOL?
I WOULD'VE GIVEN ANYTHING TO GO THERE!!
BUT I COULDN'T PASS THE ENTRANCE EXAM! I WAS SO DEPRESSED...
I HAD TO GET AWAY. SO I CAME HERE TO STUDY ABROAD.
OH, DEAR.
BUT BECAUSE OF THAT, WE MET AND FELL IN LOVE! ♡
SO I'M GLAD YOU FAILED! ♡
DARLING
THAT'S TRUE! ♡
SWEETHEART

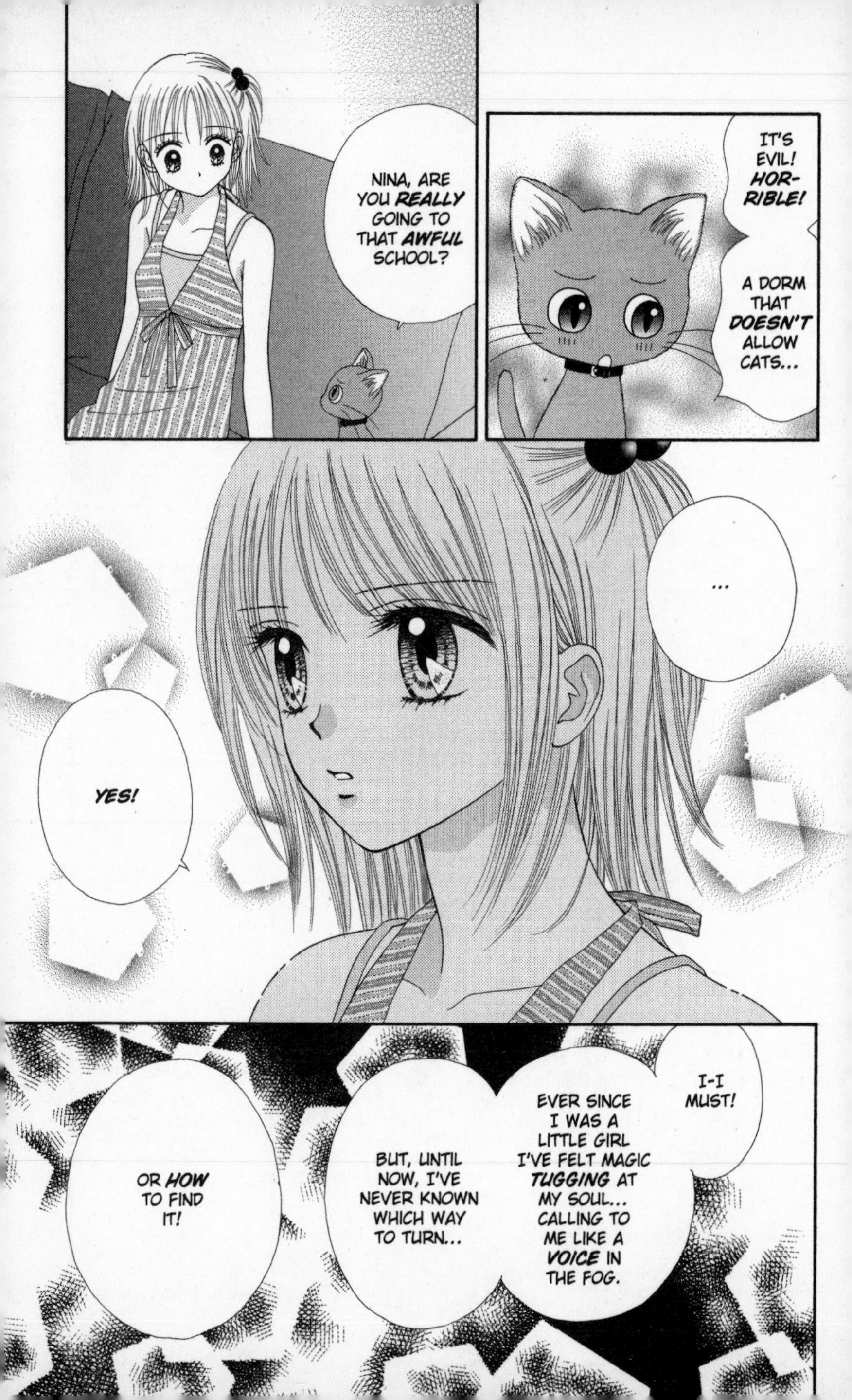
IT'S EVIL! HOR-RIBLE!
A DORM THAT DOESN'T ALLOW CATS...
NINA, ARE YOU REALLY GOING TO THAT AWFUL SCHOOL?
...
YES!
I-I MUST!
EVER SINCE I WAS A LITTLE GIRL I'VE FELT MAGIC TUGGING AT MY SOUL... CALLING TO ME LIKE A VOICE IN THE FOG.
BUT, UNTIL NOW, I'VE NEVER KNOWN WHICH WAY TO TURN...
OR HOW TO FIND IT!

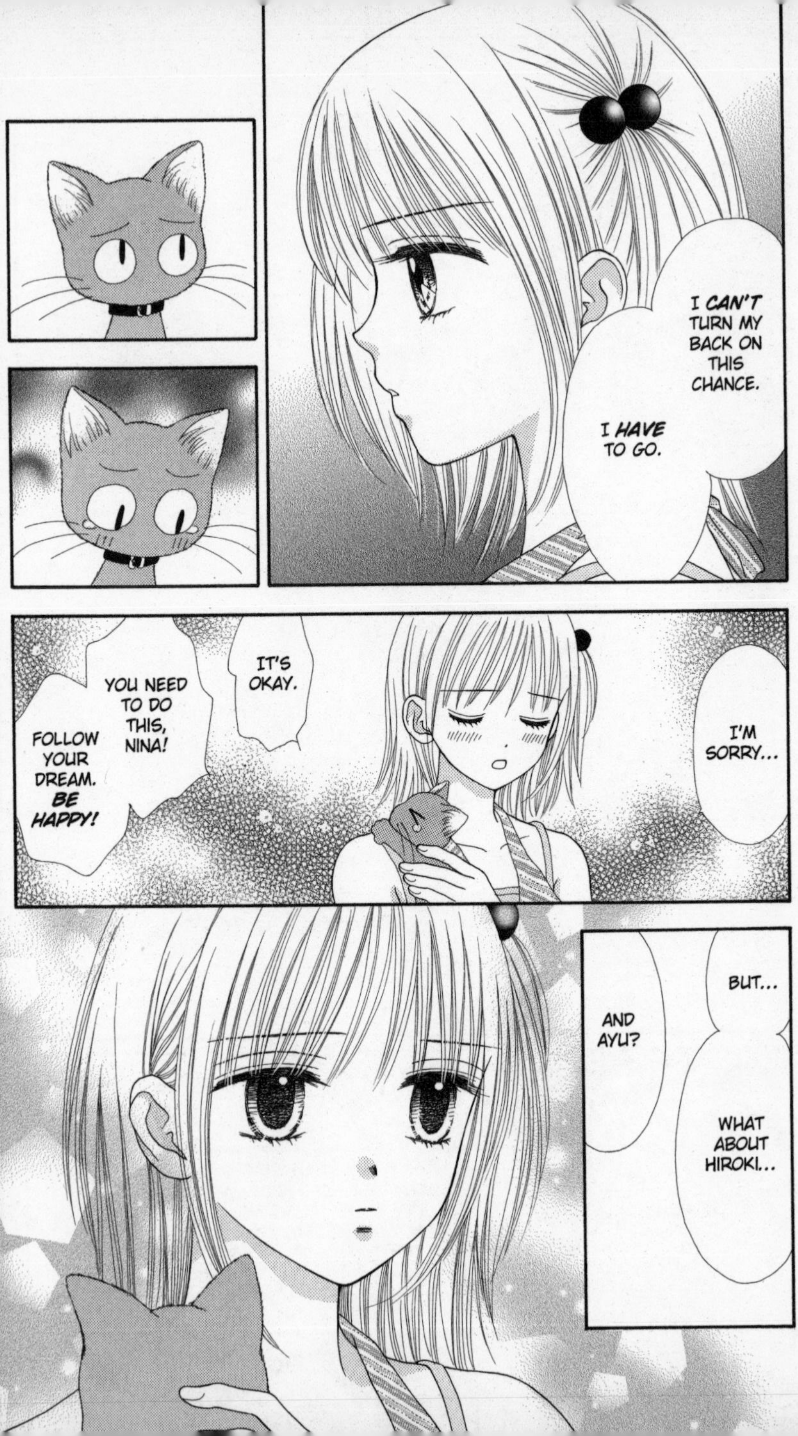
I CAN'T TURN MY BACK ON THIS CHANCE.
I HAVE TO GO.
I'M SORRY...
IT'S OKAY.
YOU NEED TO DO THIS, NINA!
FOLLOW YOUR DREAM. BE HAPPY!
BUT...
WHAT ABOUT HIROKI...
AND AYU?

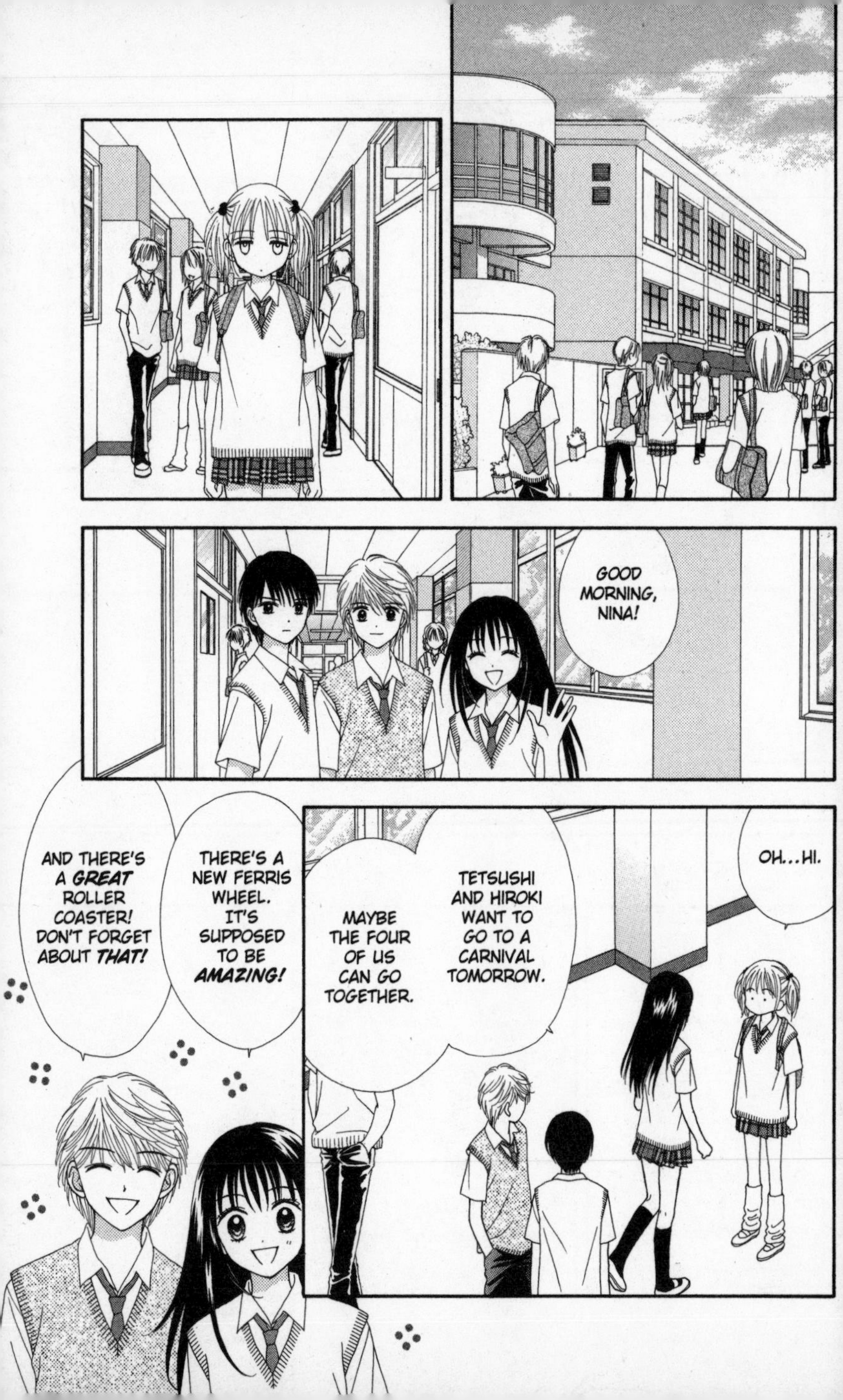
GOOD MORNING, NINA!
OH...HI.
TETSUSHI AND HIROKI WANT TO GO TO A CARNIVAL TOMORROW.
MAYBE THE FOUR OF US CAN GO TOGETHER.
THERE'S A NEW FERRIS WHEEL. IT'S SUPPOSED TO BE *AMAZING!*
AND THERE'S A *GREAT* ROLLER COASTER! DON'T FORGET ABOUT *THAT!*

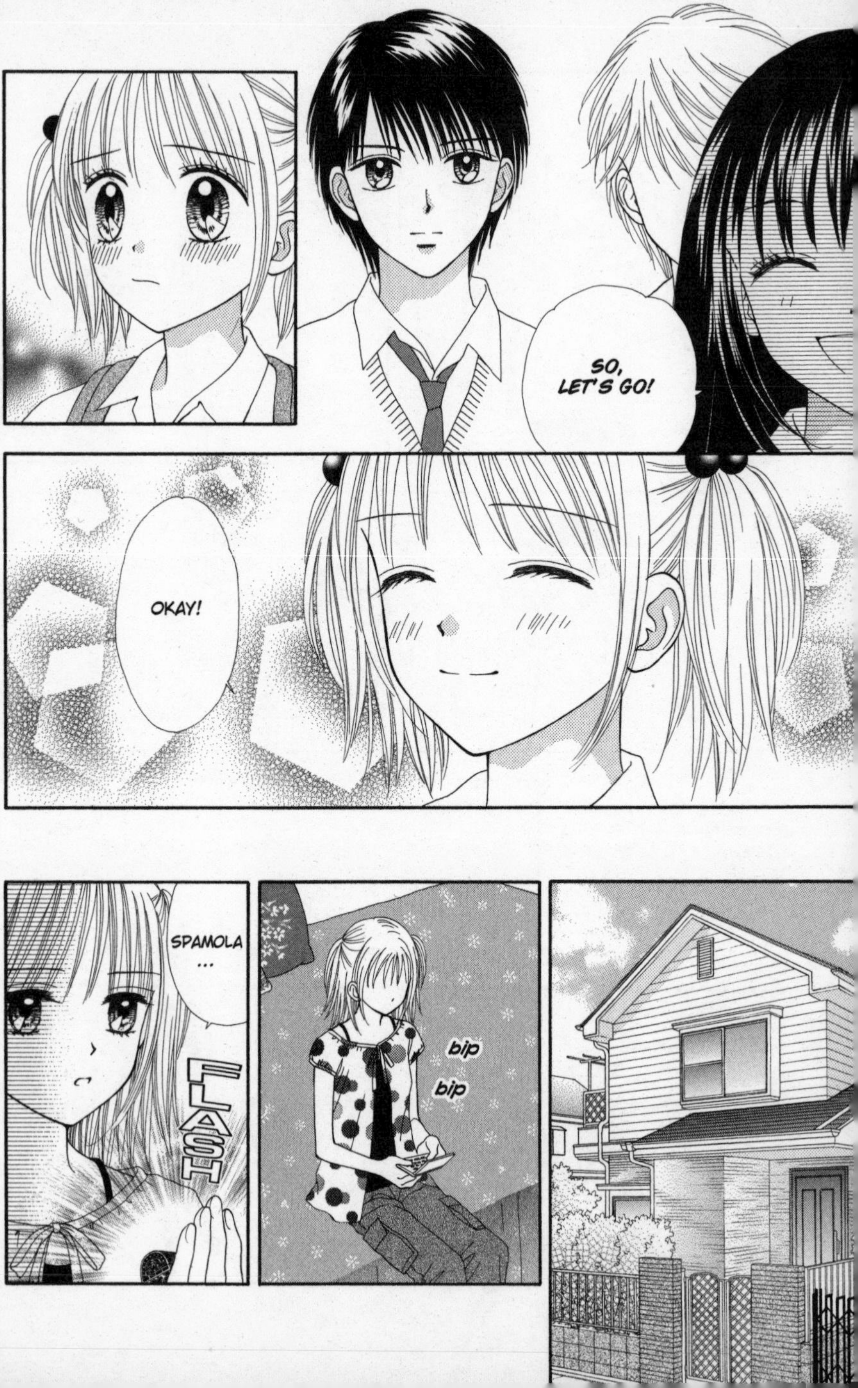
SO, LET'S GO!
OKAY!
bip
bip
SPAMOLA ...
FLASH

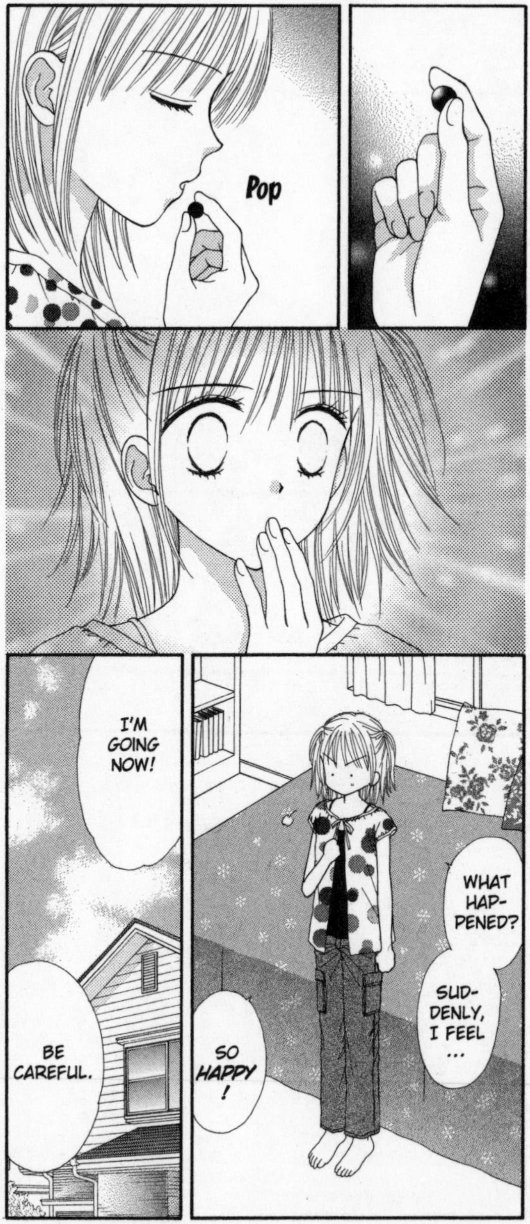
Pop
WHAT HAP-PENED?
SUD-DENLY, I FEEL ...
SO *HAPPY*!
I'M GOING NOW!
BE CAREFUL.

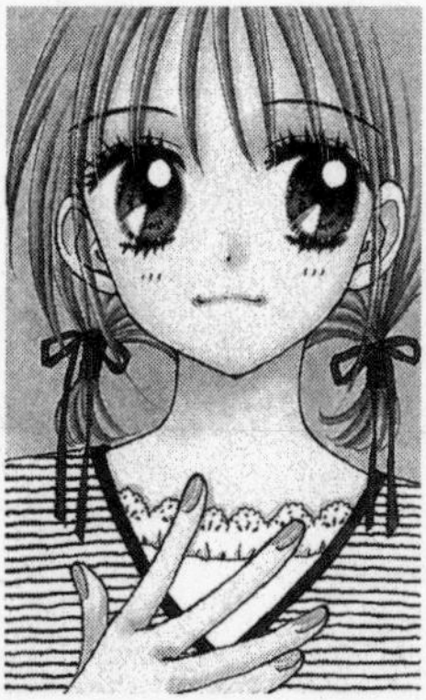

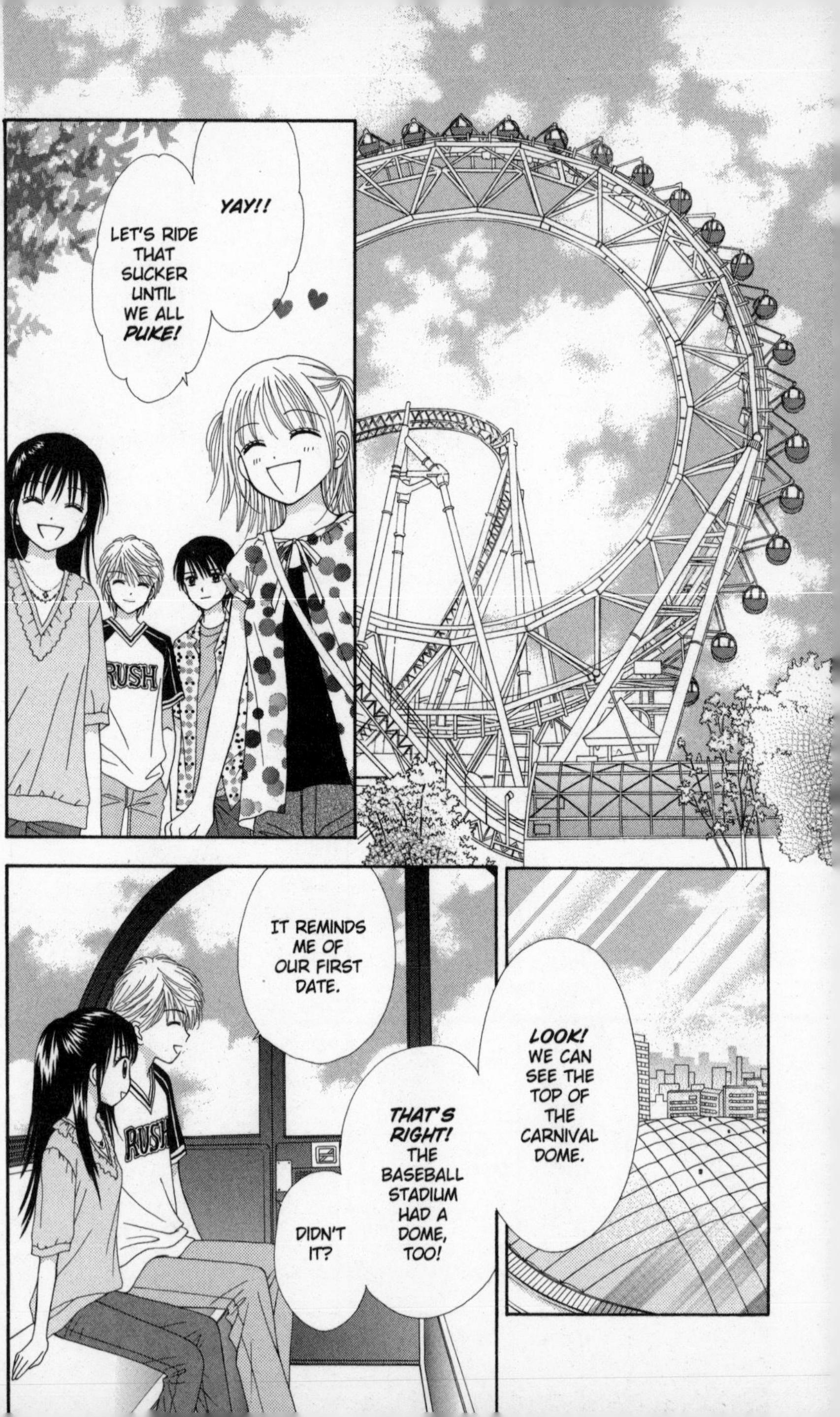
YAY!!
LET'S RIDE THAT SUCKER UNTIL WE ALL PUKE!
LOOK! WE CAN SEE THE TOP OF THE CARNIVAL DOME.
IT REMINDS ME OF OUR FIRST DATE.
THAT'S RIGHT! THE BASEBALL STADIUM HAD A DOME, TOO!
DIDN'T IT?

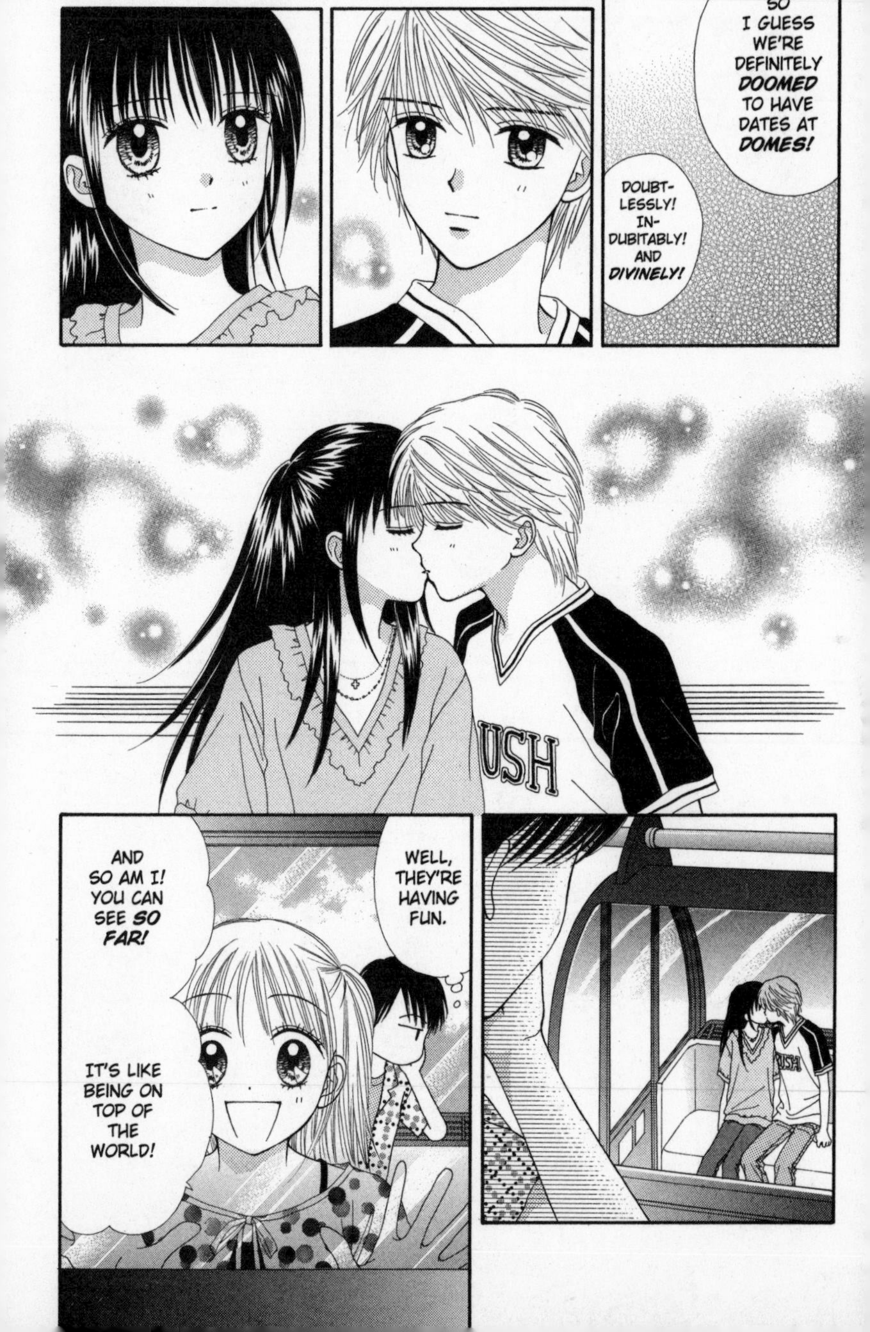
SO I GUESS WE'RE DEFINITELY DOOMED TO HAVE DATES AT DOMES!
DOUBT-LESSLY! IN-DUBITABLY! AND DIVINELY!
USH
WELL, THEY'RE HAVING FUN.
AND SO AM I! YOU CAN SEE SO FAR!
IT'S LIKE BEING ON TOP OF THE WORLD!

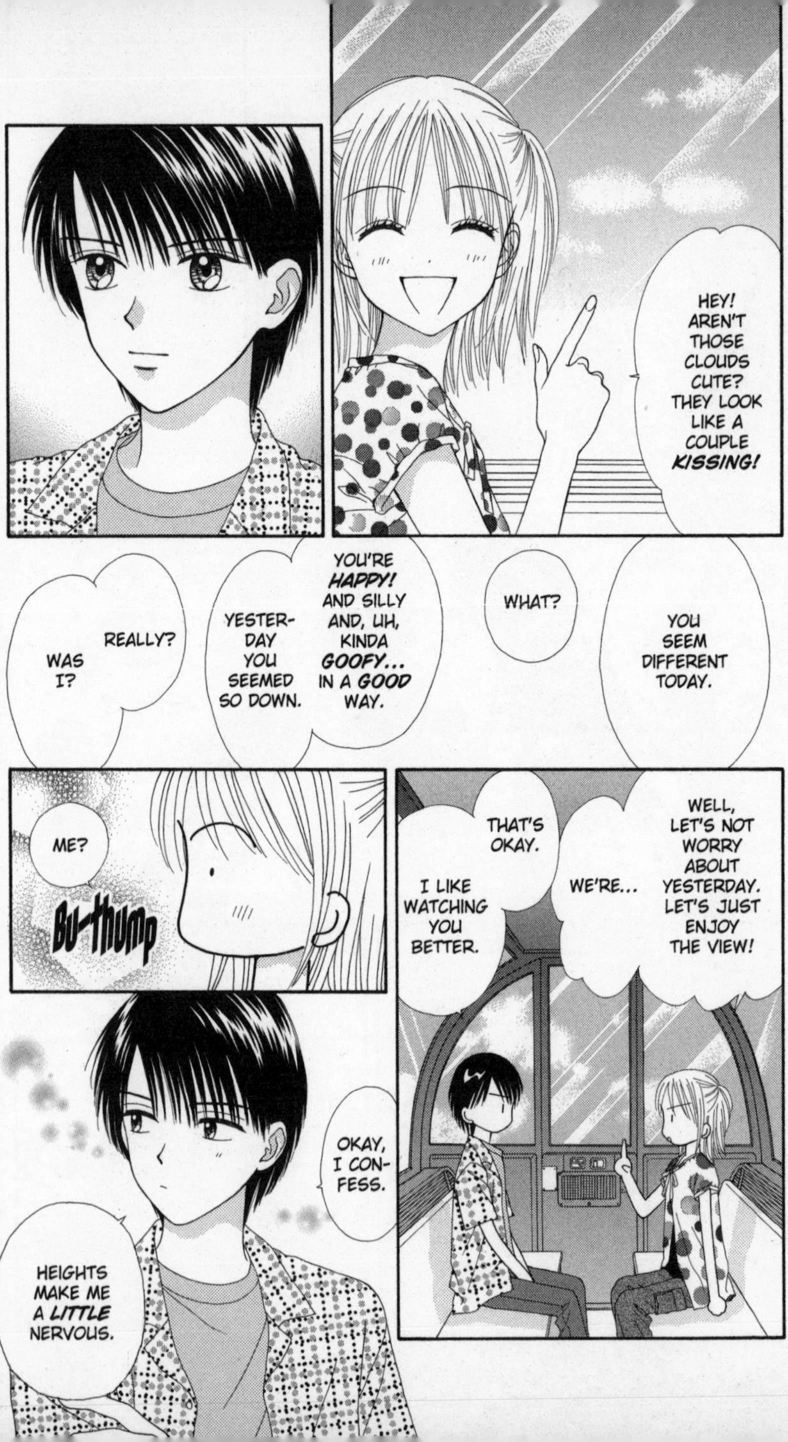
HEY! AREN'T THOSE CLOUDS CUTE? THEY LOOK LIKE A COUPLE *KISSING!*
YOU SEEM DIFFERENT TODAY.
WHAT?
YOU'RE *HAPPY!* AND SILLY AND, UH, KINDA *GOOFY...* IN A *GOOD* WAY.
YESTERDAY YOU SEEMED SO DOWN.
REALLY?
WAS I?
WELL, LET'S NOT WORRY ABOUT YESTERDAY. LET'S JUST ENJOY THE VIEW!
WE'RE...
THAT'S OKAY.
I LIKE WATCHING YOU BETTER.
ME?
Bu-thump
OKAY, I CONFESS.
HEIGHTS MAKE ME A *LITTLE* NERVOUS.

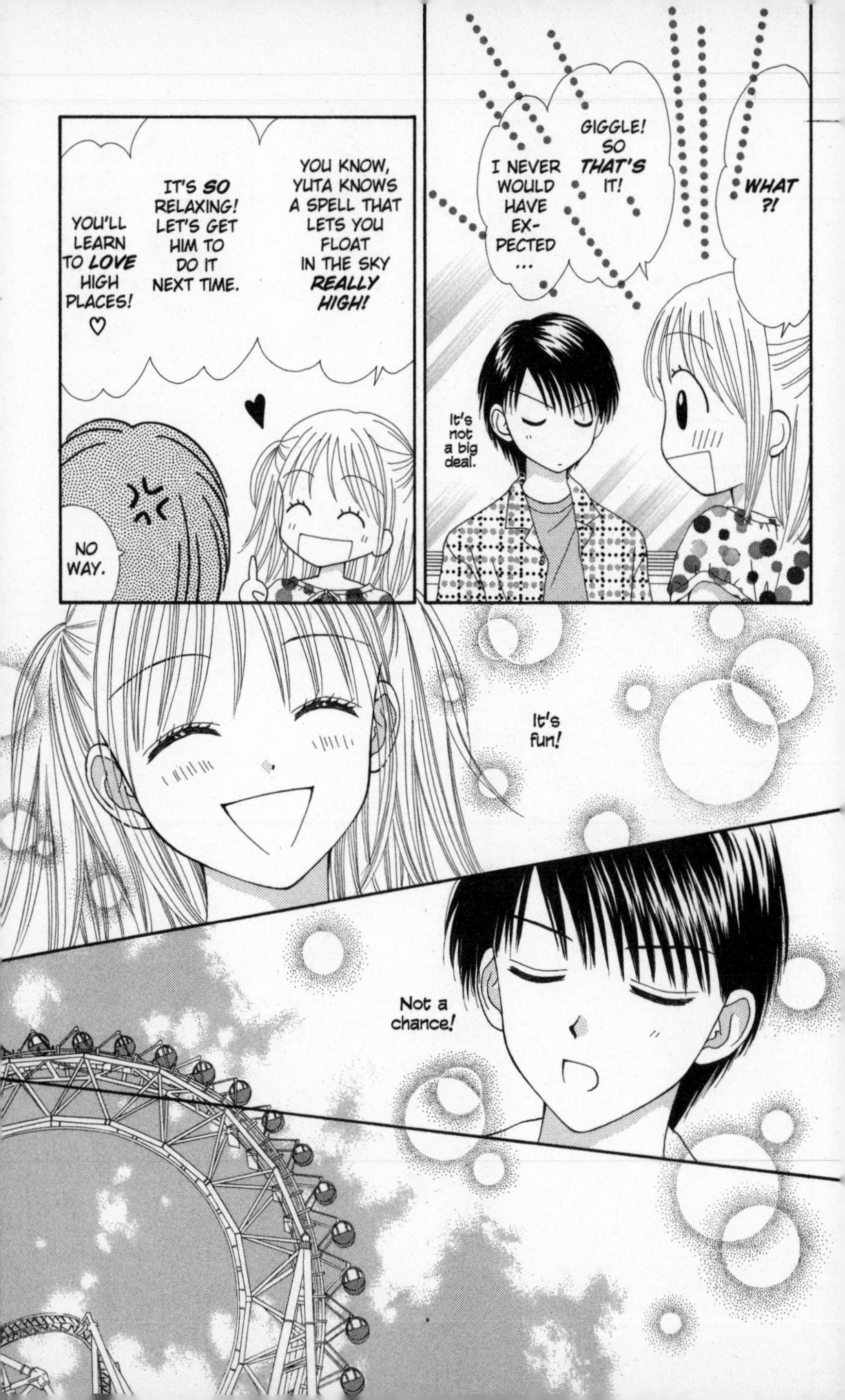
WHAT?!
GIGGLE! SO THAT'S IT!
I NEVER WOULD HAVE EX-PECTED...
It's not a big deal.
YOU KNOW, YUTA KNOWS A SPELL THAT LETS YOU FLOAT IN THE SKY REALLY HIGH!
IT'S SO RELAXING! LET'S GET HIM TO DO IT NEXT TIME.
YOU'LL LEARN TO LOVE HIGH PLACES! ♡
NO WAY.
It's fun!
Not a chance!

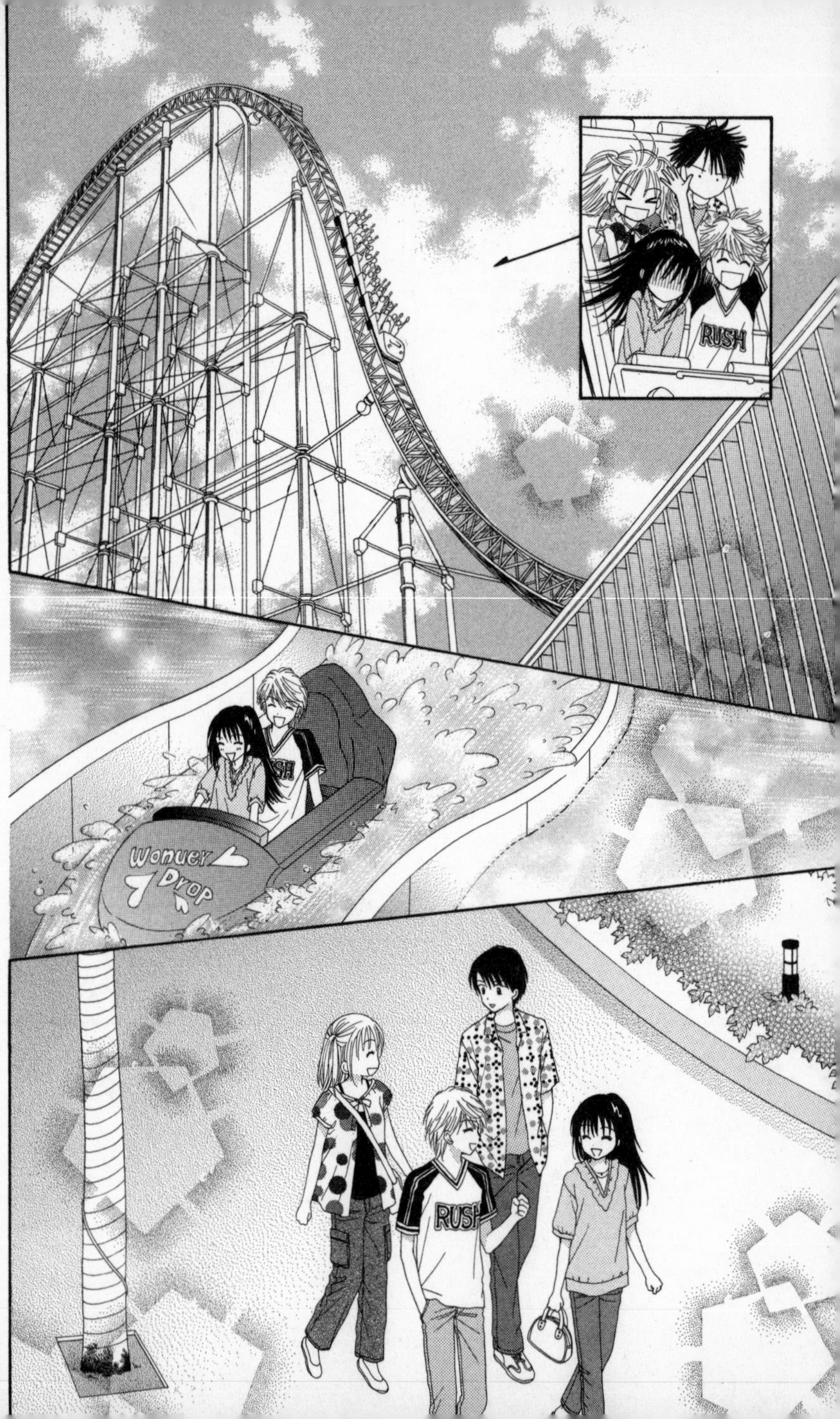
RUSH
RUSH

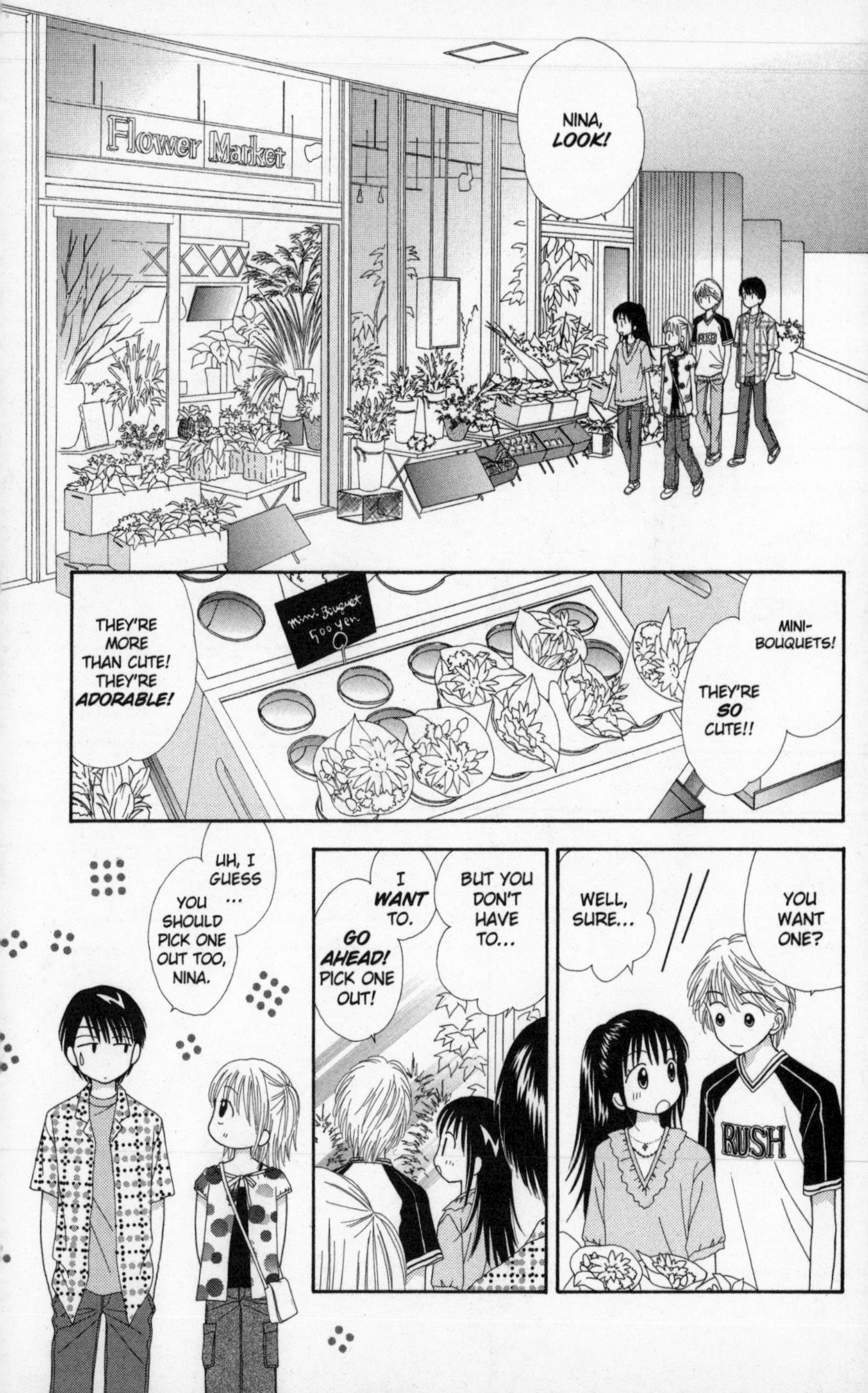
Flower Market
NINA, **LOOK!**
MINI-BOUQUETS!
THEY'RE **SO** CUTE!!
mini Bouquet 500 yen
THEY'RE MORE THAN CUTE! THEY'RE **ADORABLE!**
YOU WANT ONE?
WELL, SURE...
BUT YOU DON'T HAVE TO...
I **WANT** TO. **GO AHEAD!** PICK ONE OUT!
UH, I GUESS ... YOU SHOULD PICK ONE OUT TOO, NINA.

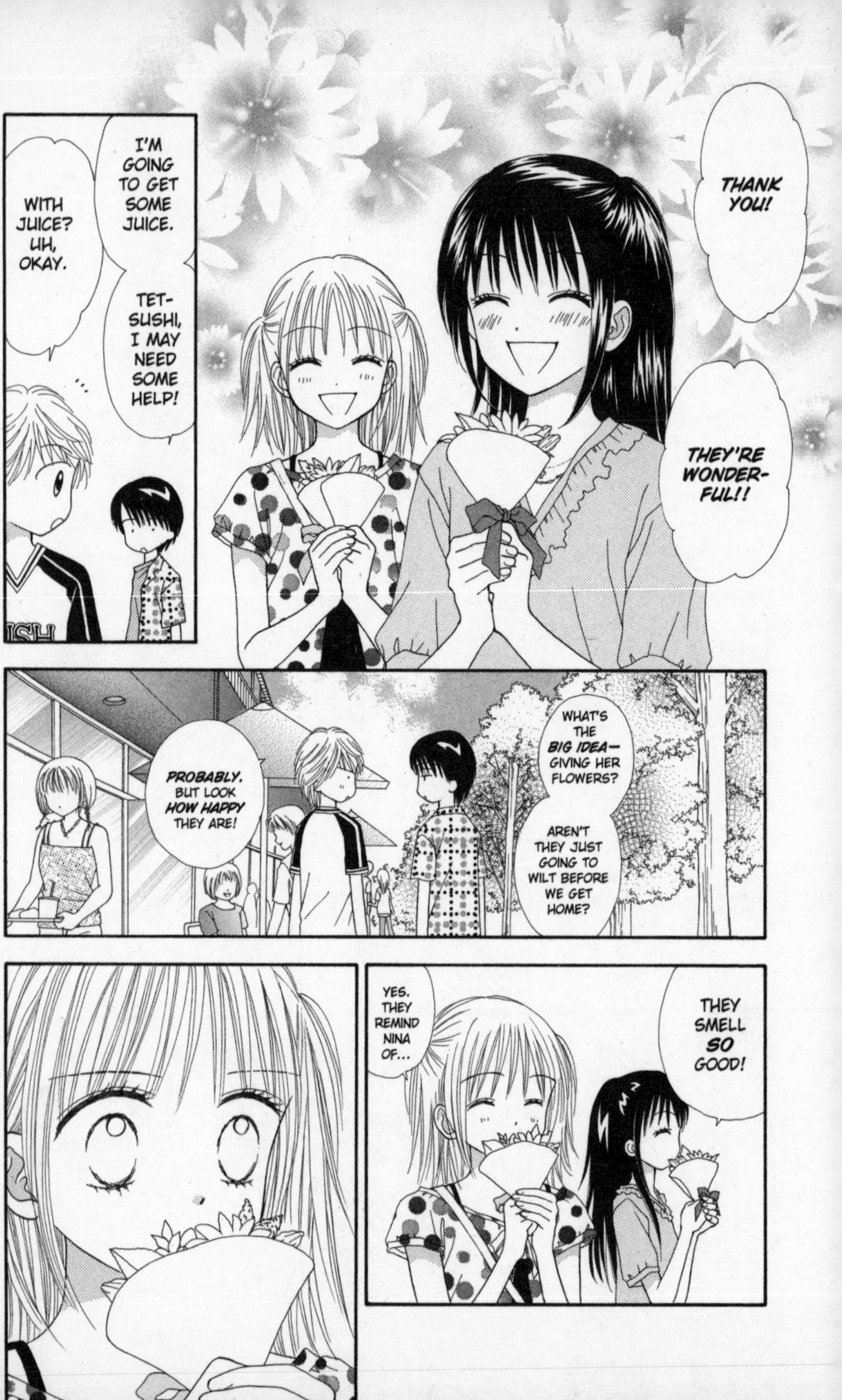
THANK YOU!
THEY'RE WONDER-FUL!!
I'M GOING TO GET SOME JUICE.
TET-SUSHI, I MAY NEED SOME HELP!
WITH JUICE? UH, OKAY.
...
WHAT'S THE BIG IDEA—GIVING HER FLOWERS?
AREN'T THEY JUST GOING TO WILT BEFORE WE GET HOME?
PROBABLY. BUT LOOK HOW HAPPY THEY ARE!
THEY SMELL SO GOOD!
YES. THEY REMIND NINA OF...

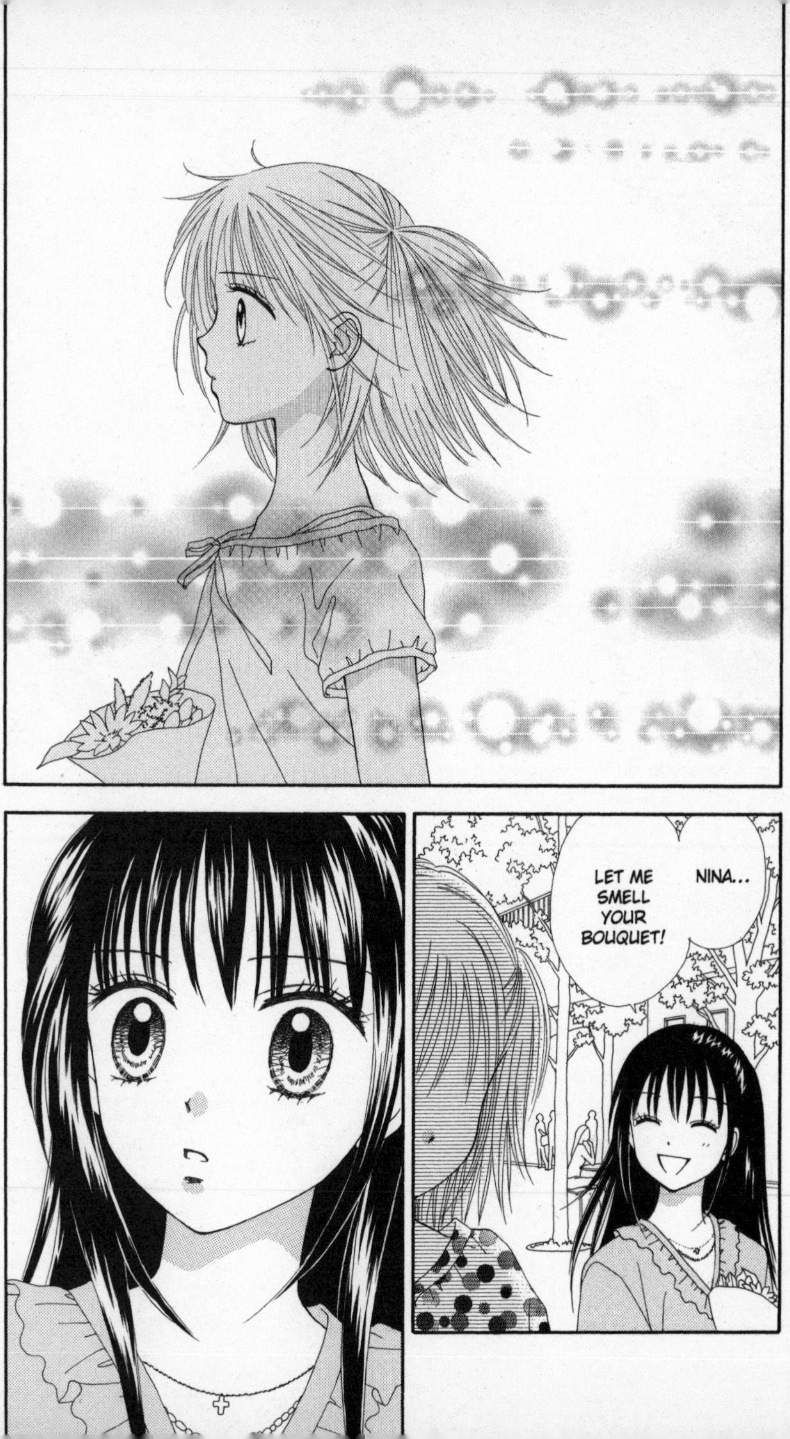
NINA...
LET ME SMELL YOUR BOUQUET!

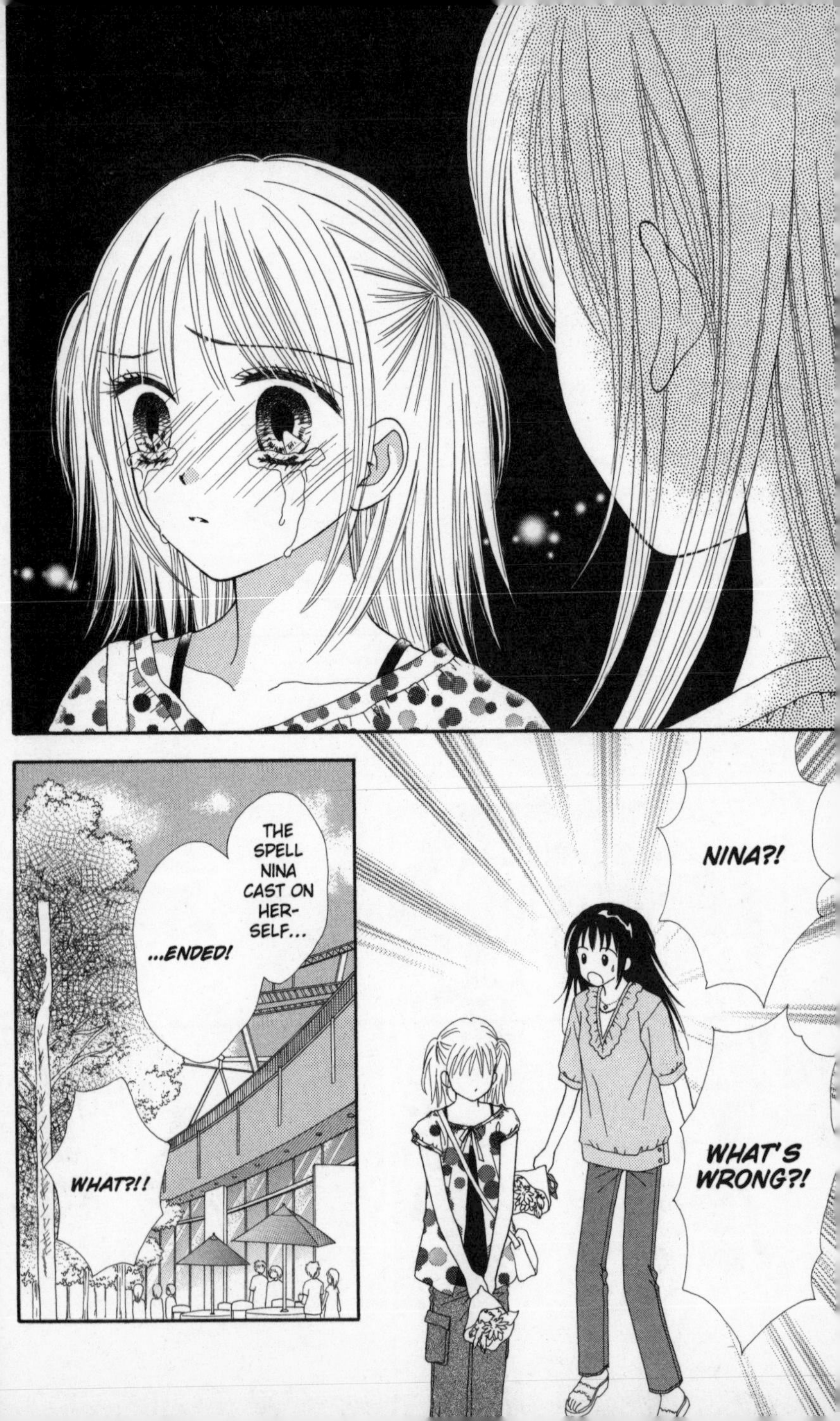
NINA?!
WHAT'S WRONG?!
THE SPELL NINA CAST ON HER-SELF...
...ENDED!
WHAT?!!

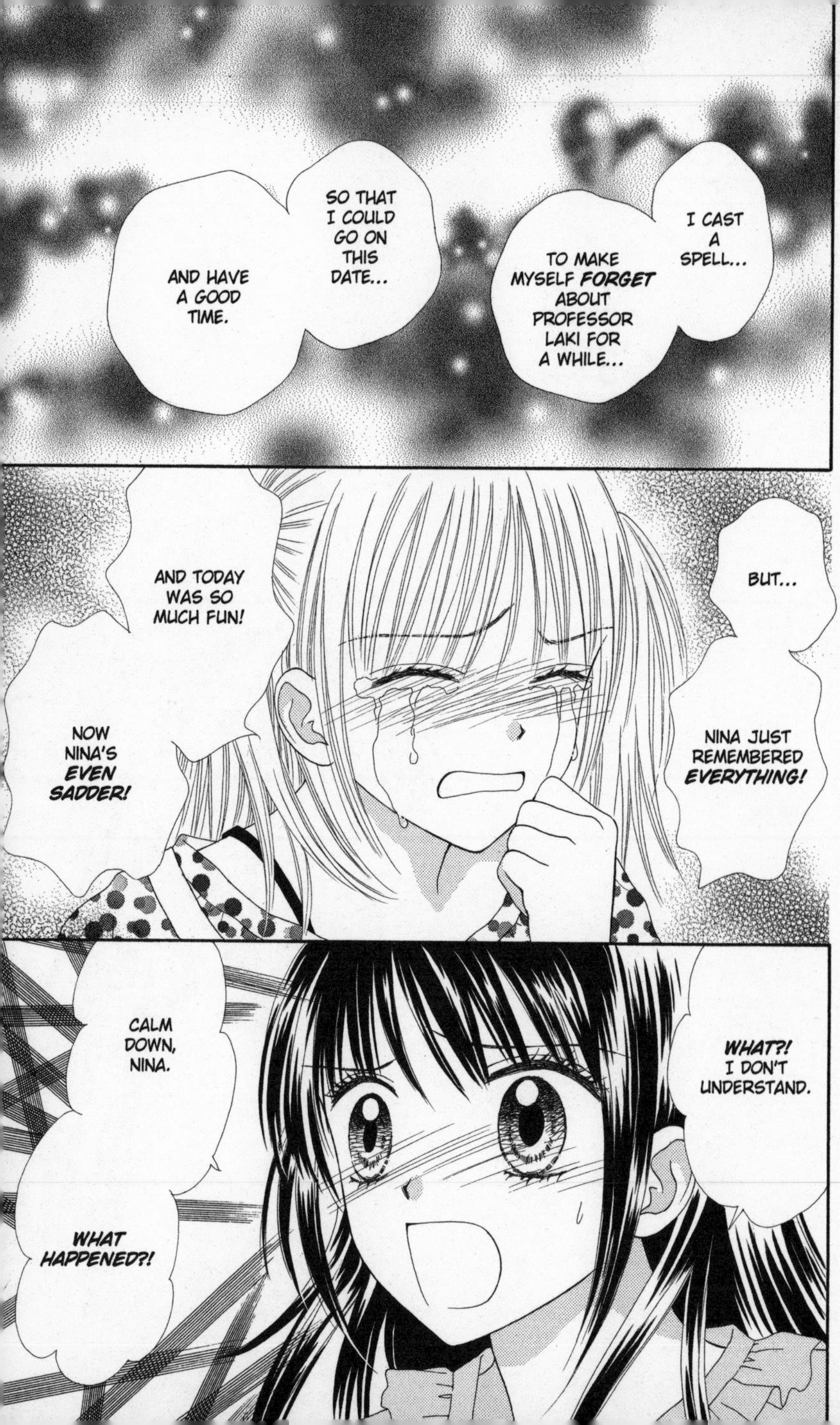
I CAST A SPELL...
TO MAKE MYSELF *FORGET* ABOUT PROFESSOR LAKI FOR A WHILE...
SO THAT I COULD GO ON THIS DATE...
AND HAVE A GOOD TIME.
BUT...
NINA JUST REMEMBERED *EVERYTHING!*
AND TODAY WAS SO MUCH FUN!
NOW NINA'S *EVEN SADDER!*
WHAT?! I DON'T UNDERSTAND.
CALM DOWN, NINA.
WHAT HAPPENED?!

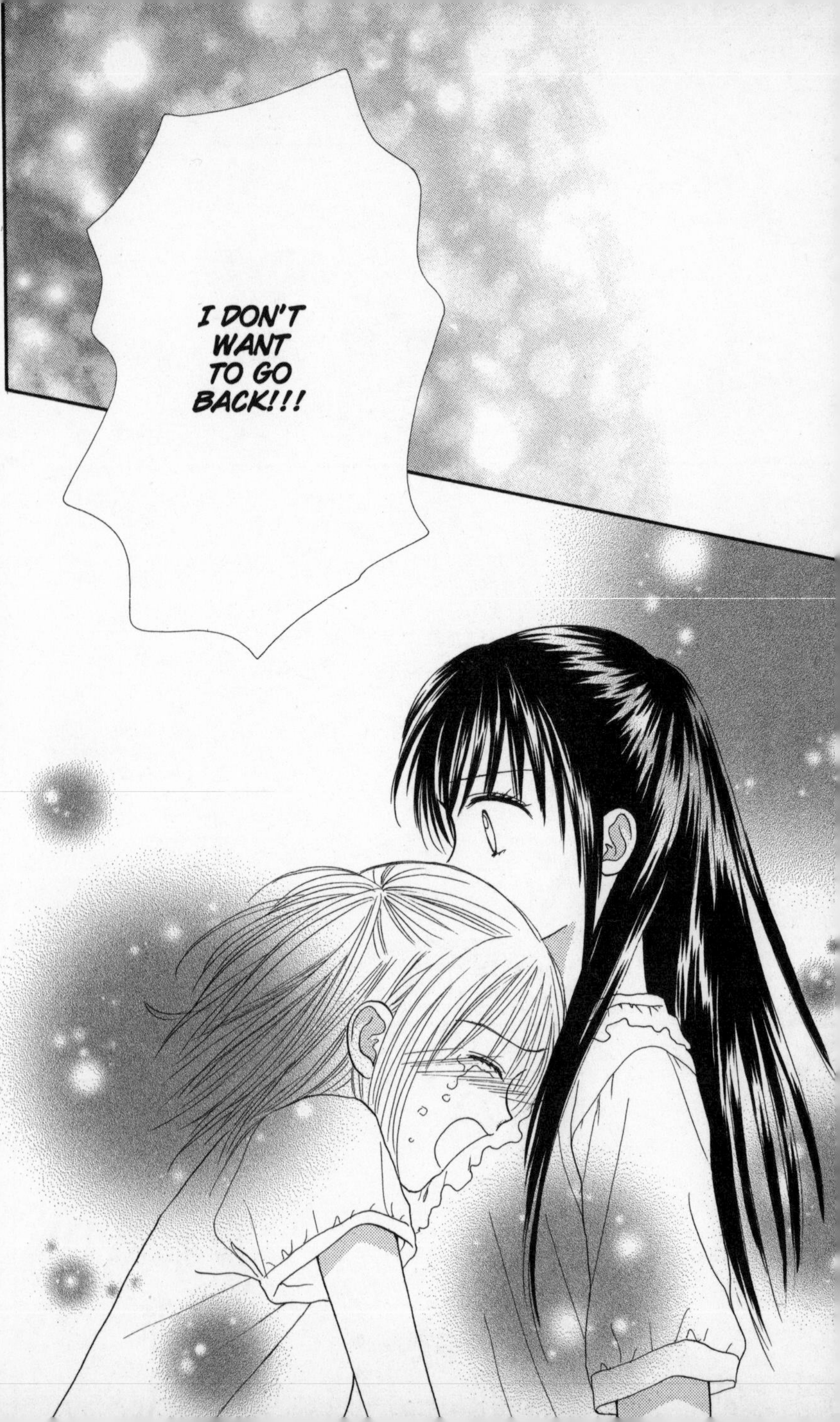
I DON'T WANT TO GO BACK!!!

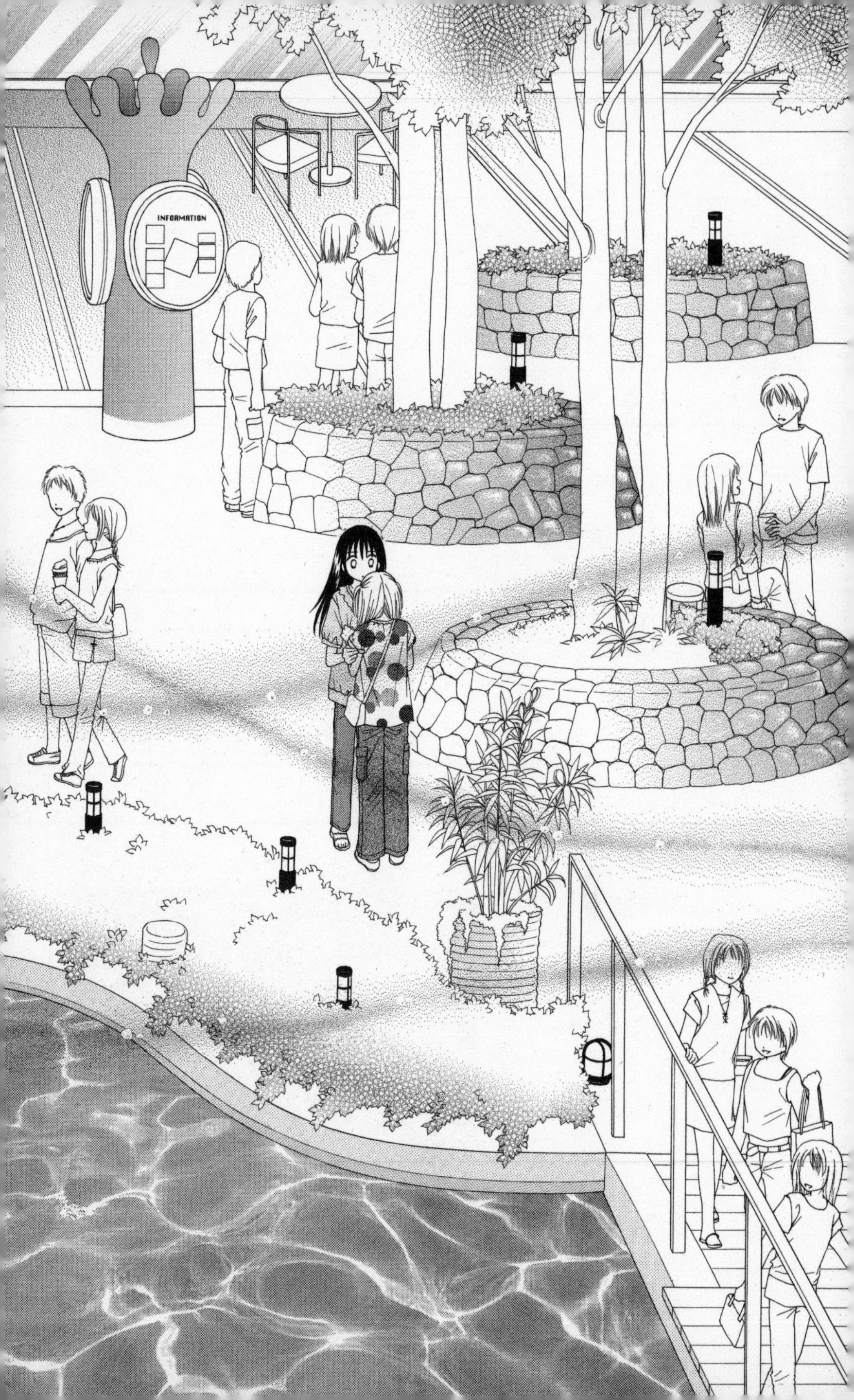
INFORMATION

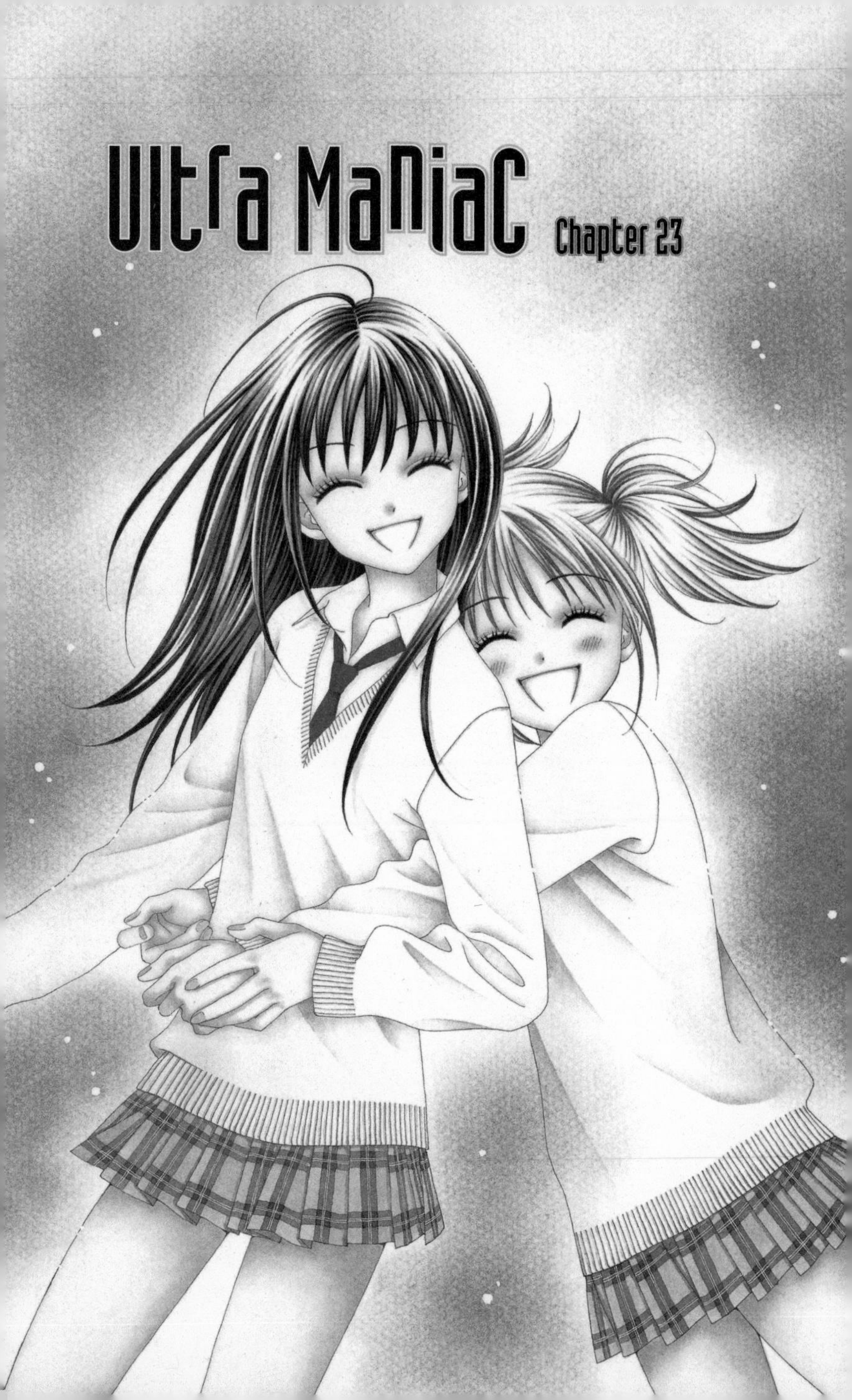

Ultra Maniac
Chapter 23

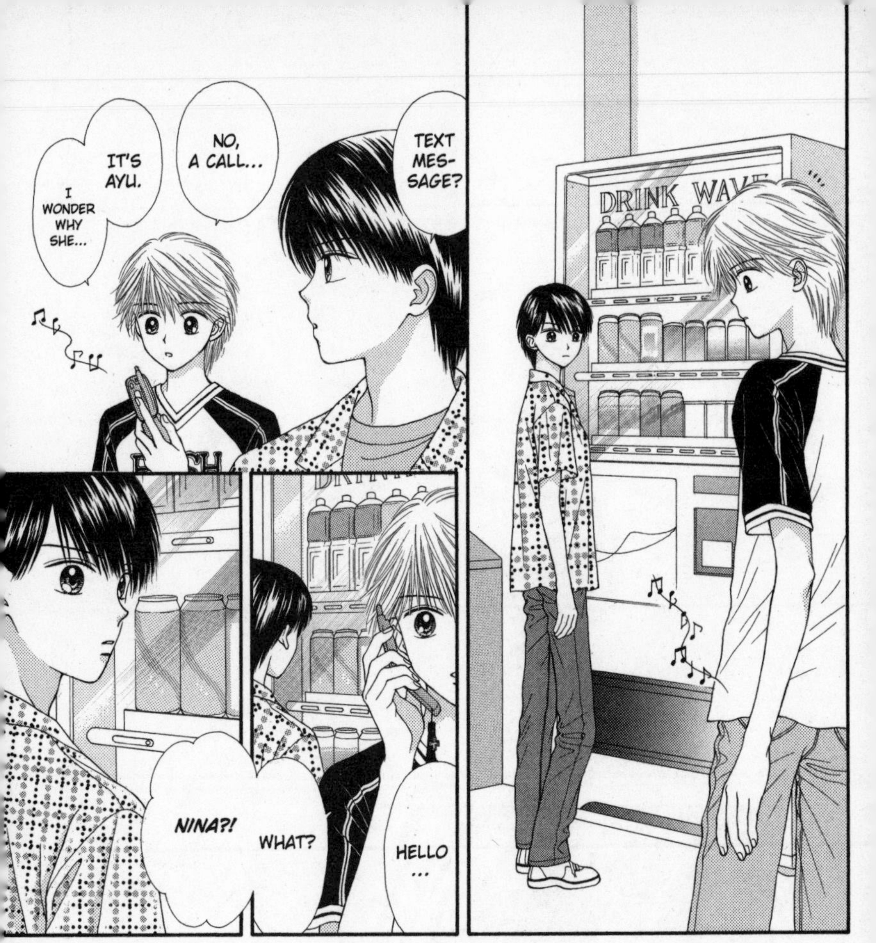
TEXT MES-SAGE?
NO, A CALL...
IT'S AYU.
I WONDER WHY SHE...
HELLO ...
WHAT?
NINA?!

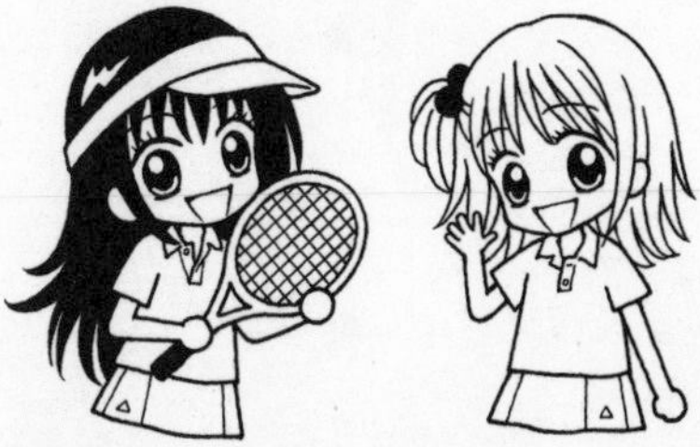

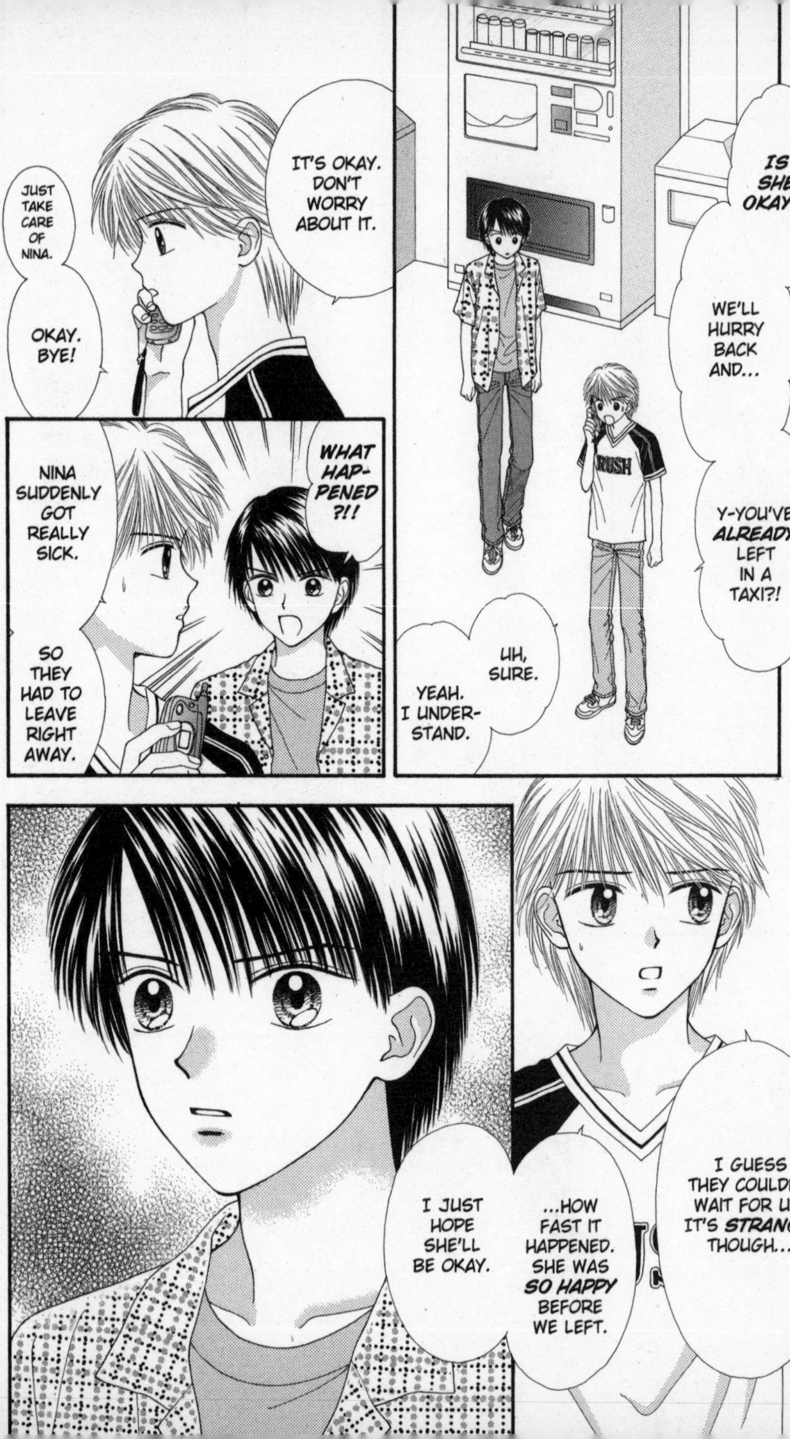
IS SHE OKAY?!
WE'LL HURRY BACK AND...
Y-YOU'VE ALREADY LEFT IN A TAXI?!
UH, SURE.
YEAH. I UNDER-STAND.
IT'S OKAY. DON'T WORRY ABOUT IT.
JUST TAKE CARE OF NINA.
OKAY. BYE!
WHAT HAP-PENED?!!
NINA SUDDENLY GOT REALLY SICK.
SO THEY HAD TO LEAVE RIGHT AWAY.
I GUESS THEY COULDN'T WAIT FOR US. IT'S STRANGE, THOUGH...
...HOW FAST IT HAPPENED. SHE WAS SO HAPPY BEFORE WE LEFT.
I JUST HOPE SHE'LL BE OKAY.

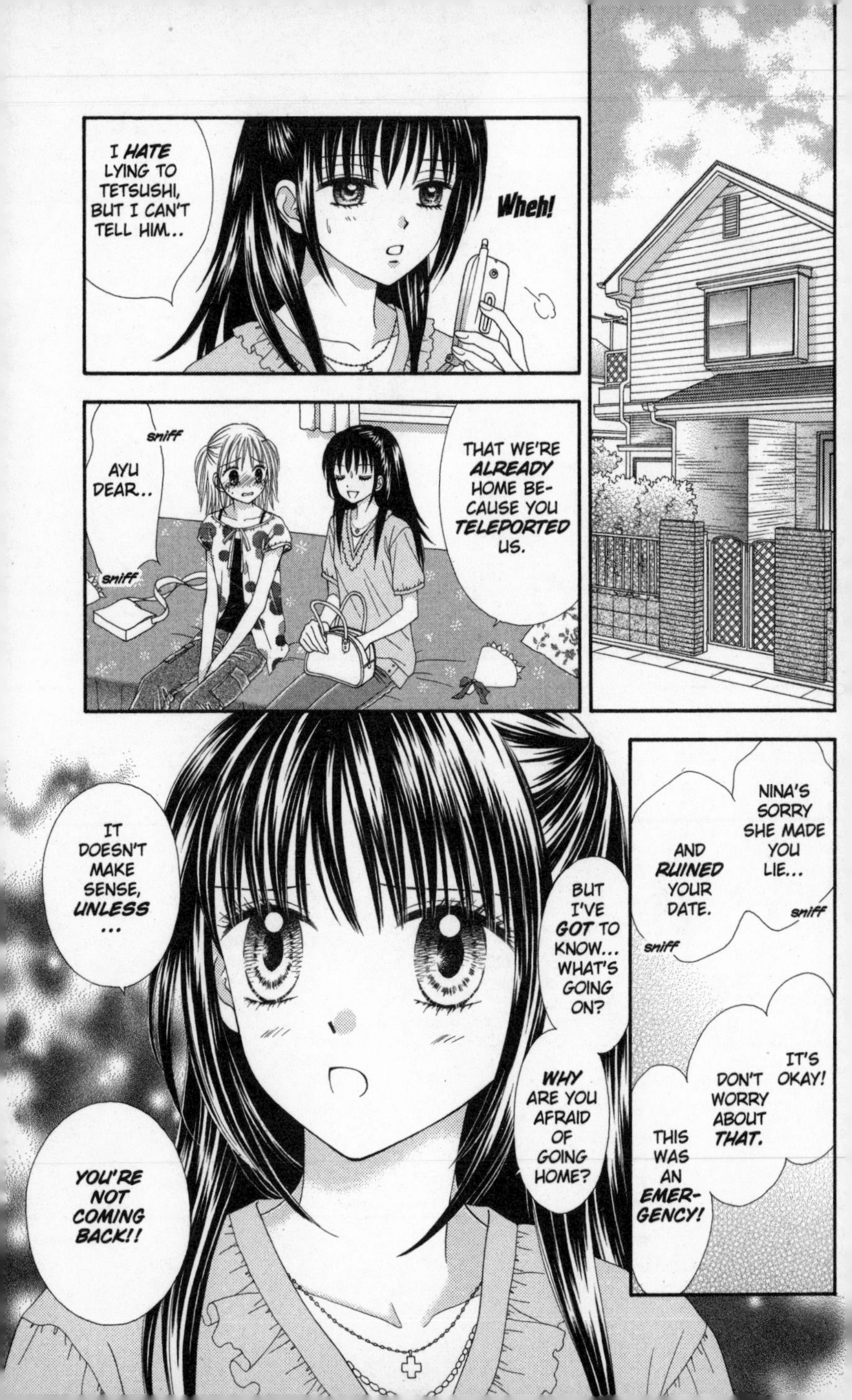
I HATE LYING TO TETSUSHI, BUT I CAN'T TELL HIM...
Wheh!
THAT WE'RE ALREADY HOME BECAUSE YOU TELEPORTED US.
sniff
AYU DEAR...
sniff
NINA'S SORRY SHE MADE YOU LIE...
sniff
AND RUINED YOUR DATE.
sniff
IT'S OKAY!
DON'T WORRY ABOUT THAT.
THIS WAS AN EMERGENCY!
BUT I'VE GOT TO KNOW... WHAT'S GOING ON?
WHY ARE YOU AFRAID OF GOING HOME?
IT DOESN'T MAKE SENSE, UNLESS...
YOU'RE NOT COMING BACK!!

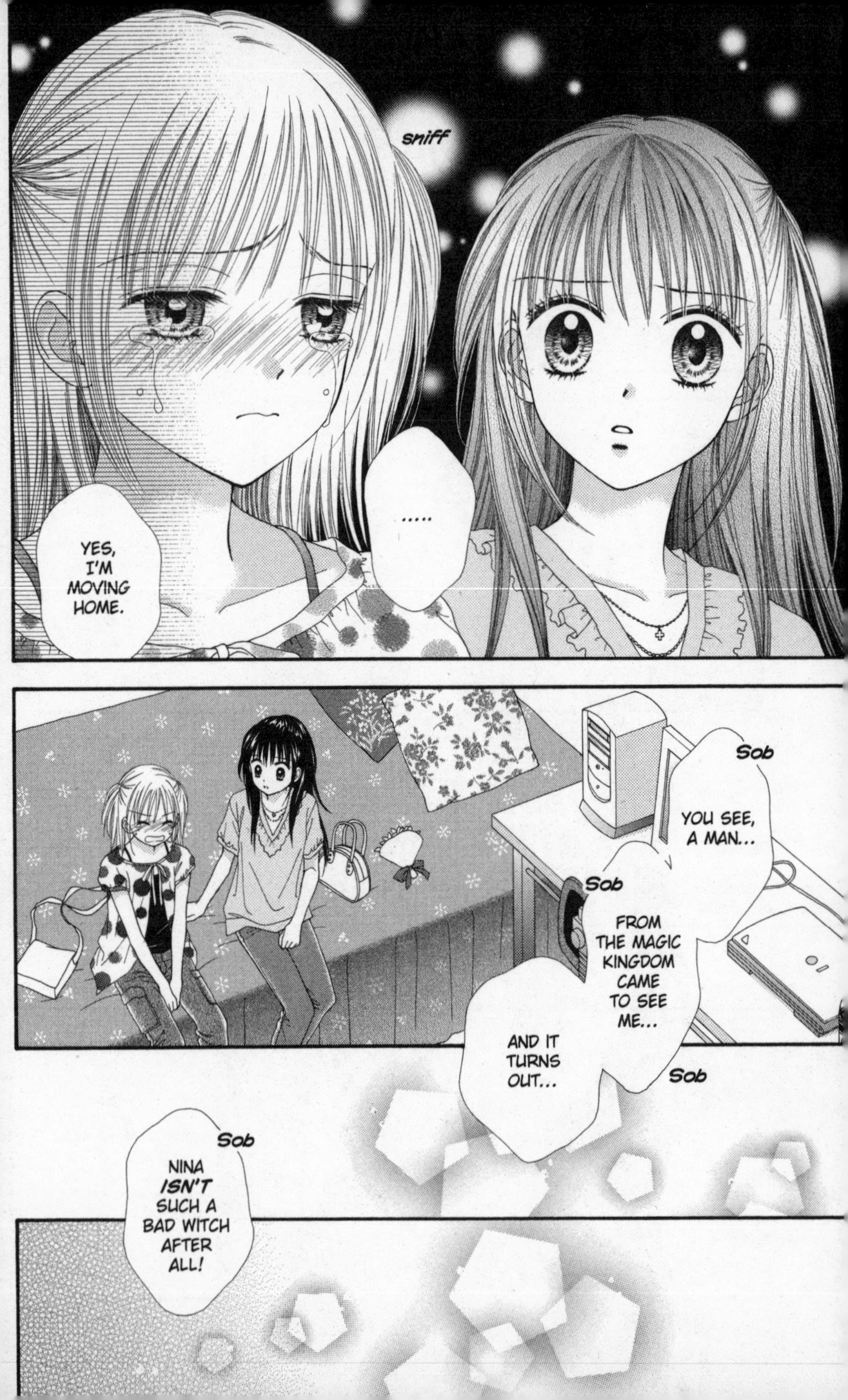
sniff
......
YES, I'M MOVING HOME.
Sob
YOU SEE, A MAN...
Sob
FROM THE MAGIC KINGDOM CAME TO SEE ME...
AND IT TURNS OUT...
Sob
Sob
NINA *ISN'T* SUCH A BAD WITCH AFTER ALL!

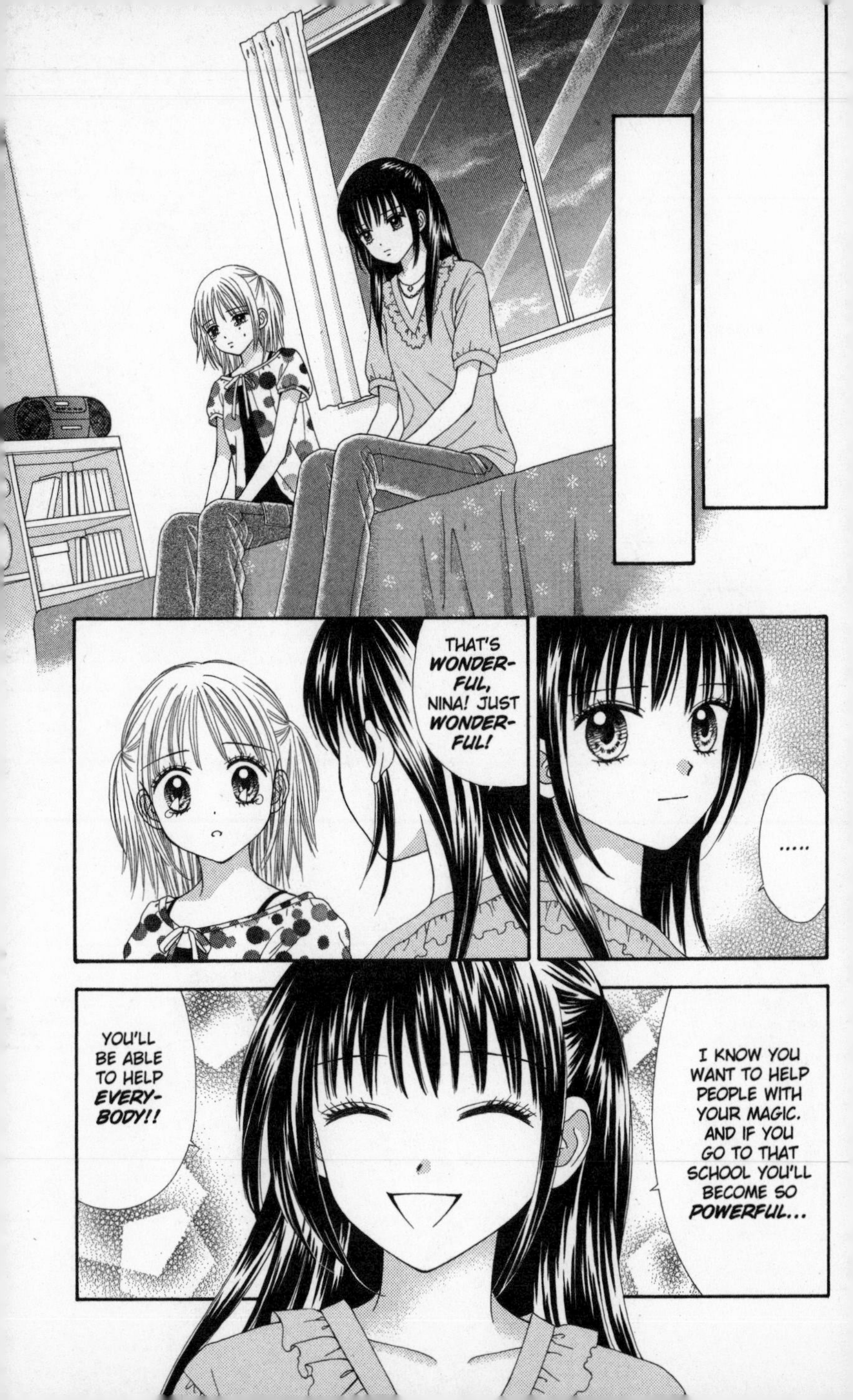
.....
THAT'S WONDERFUL, NINA! JUST WONDERFUL!
I KNOW YOU WANT TO HELP PEOPLE WITH YOUR MAGIC. AND IF YOU GO TO THAT SCHOOL YOU'LL BECOME SO POWERFUL...
YOU'LL BE ABLE TO HELP EVERYBODY!!

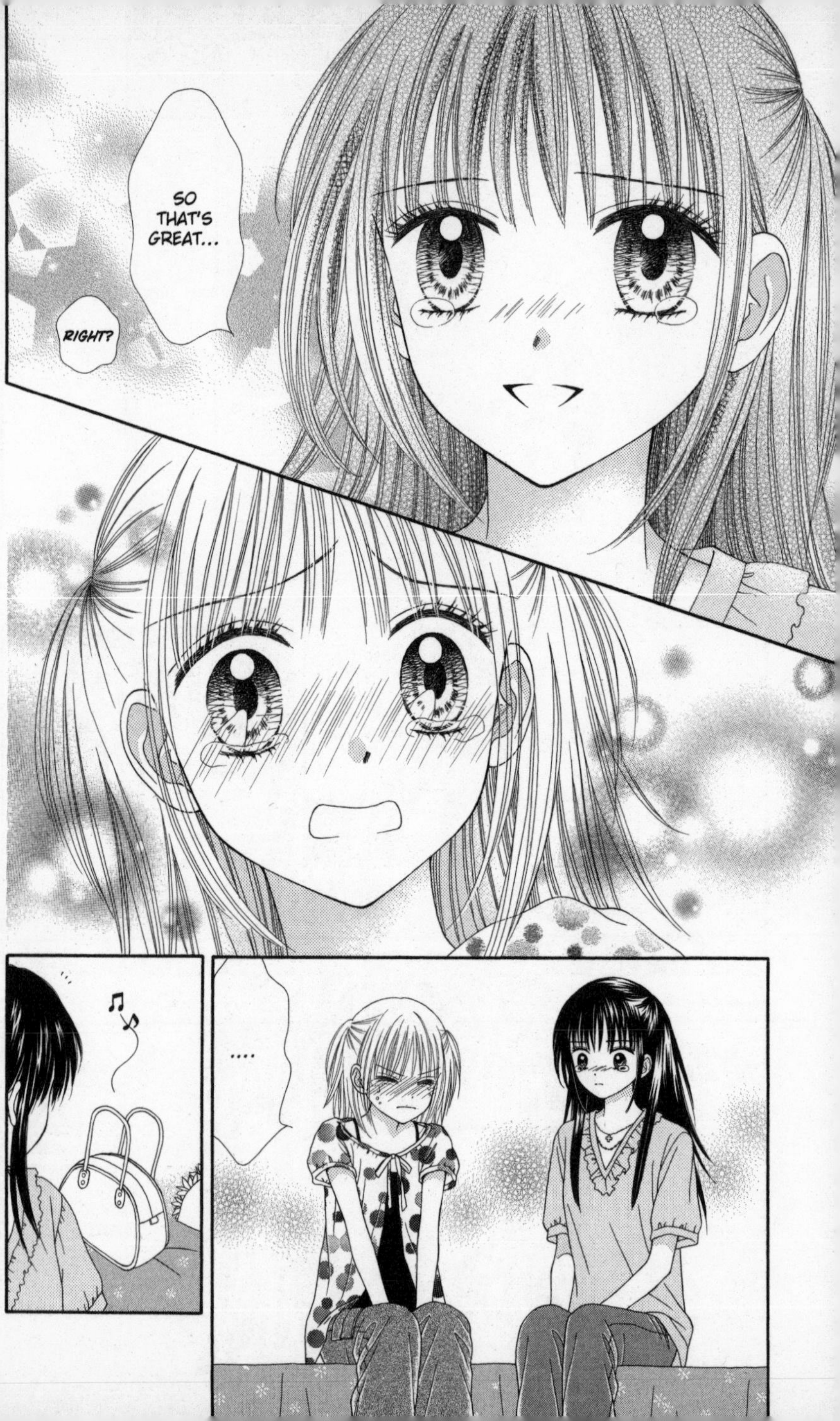
SO THAT'S GREAT...
RIGHT?
....

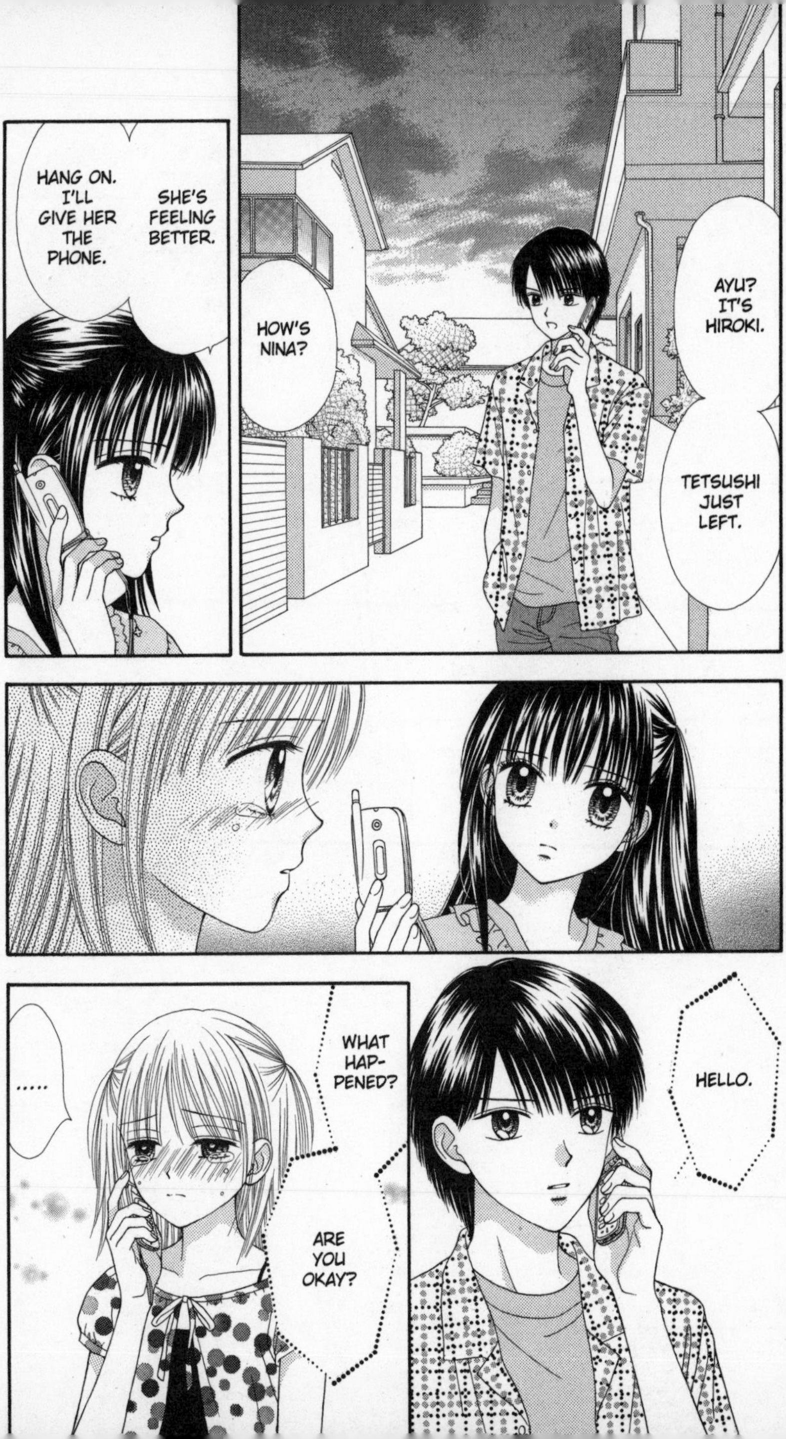
AYU? IT'S HIROKI.
TETSUSHI JUST LEFT.
HOW'S NINA?
SHE'S FEELING BETTER.
HANG ON. I'LL GIVE HER THE PHONE.
HELLO.
WHAT HAP-PENED?
ARE YOU OKAY?
.....

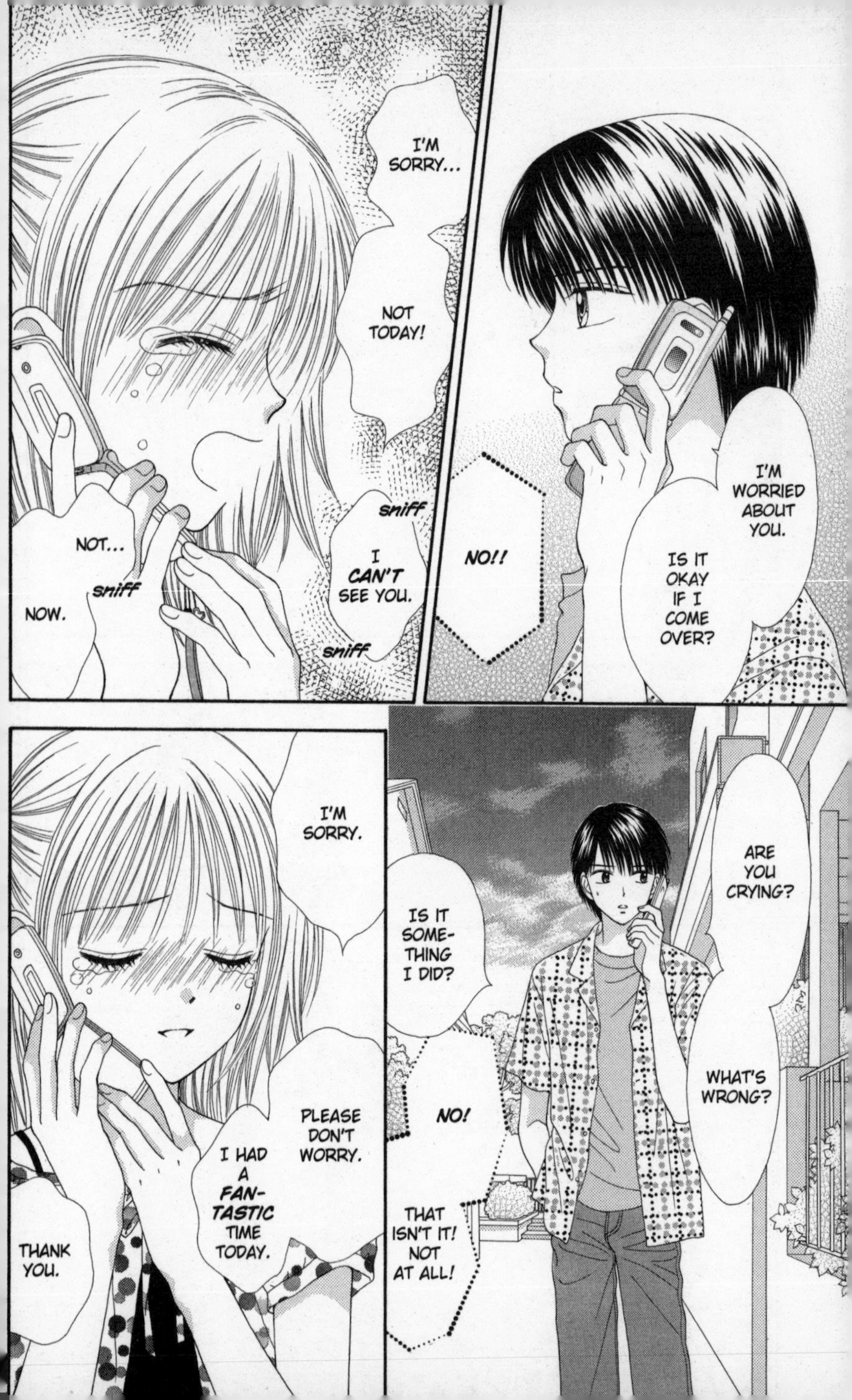
I'M WORRIED ABOUT YOU.
IS IT OKAY IF I COME OVER?
NO!!
I'M SORRY...
NOT TODAY!
sniff
I CAN'T SEE YOU.
sniff
NOT...
sniff
NOW.
ARE YOU CRYING?
WHAT'S WRONG?
IS IT SOMETHING I DID?
NO!
THAT ISN'T IT! NOT AT ALL!
I'M SORRY.
PLEASE DON'T WORRY.
I HAD A FANTASTIC TIME TODAY.
THANK YOU.

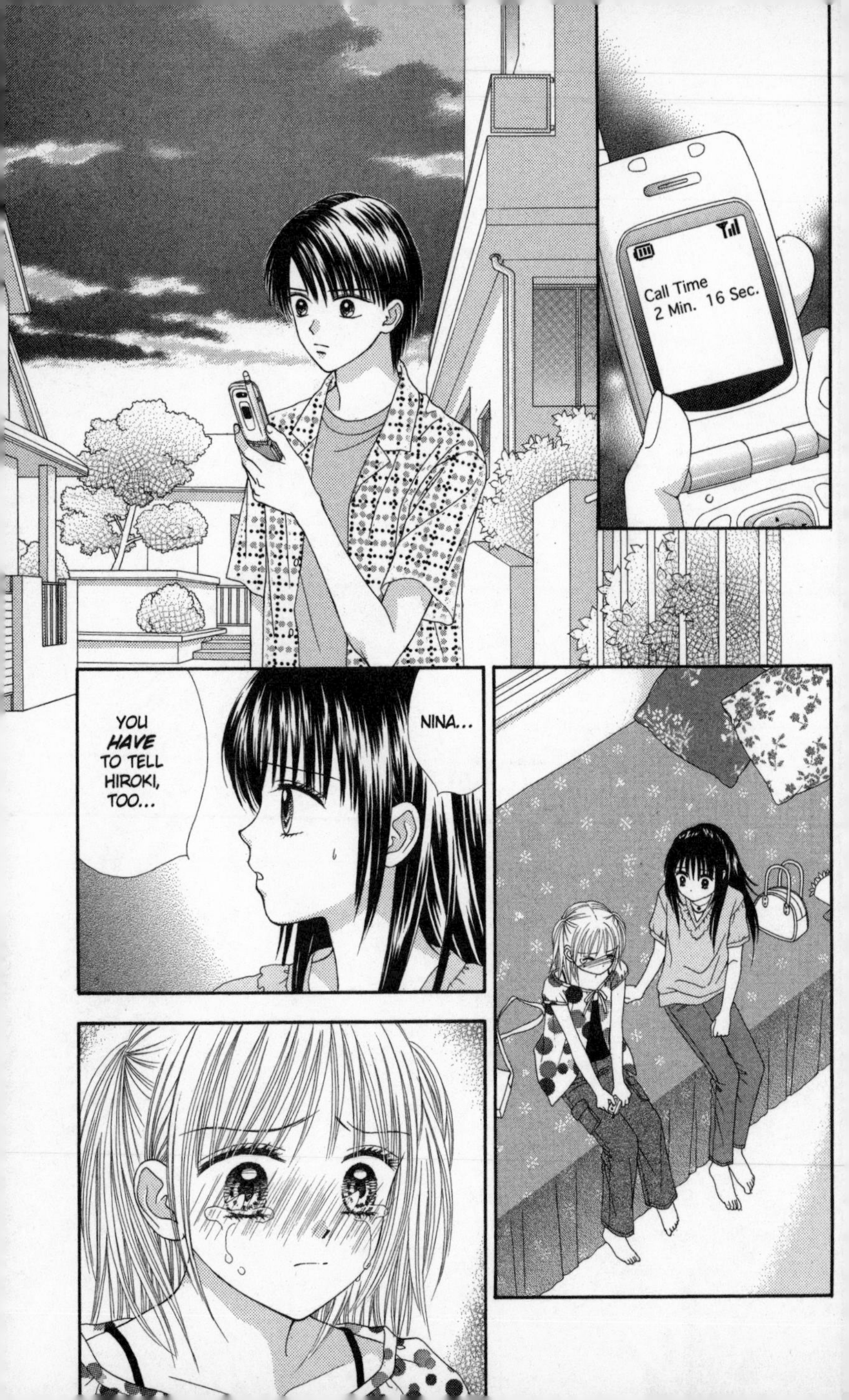
Call Time
2 Min. 16 Sec.
NINA...
YOU *HAVE* TO TELL HIROKI, TOO...

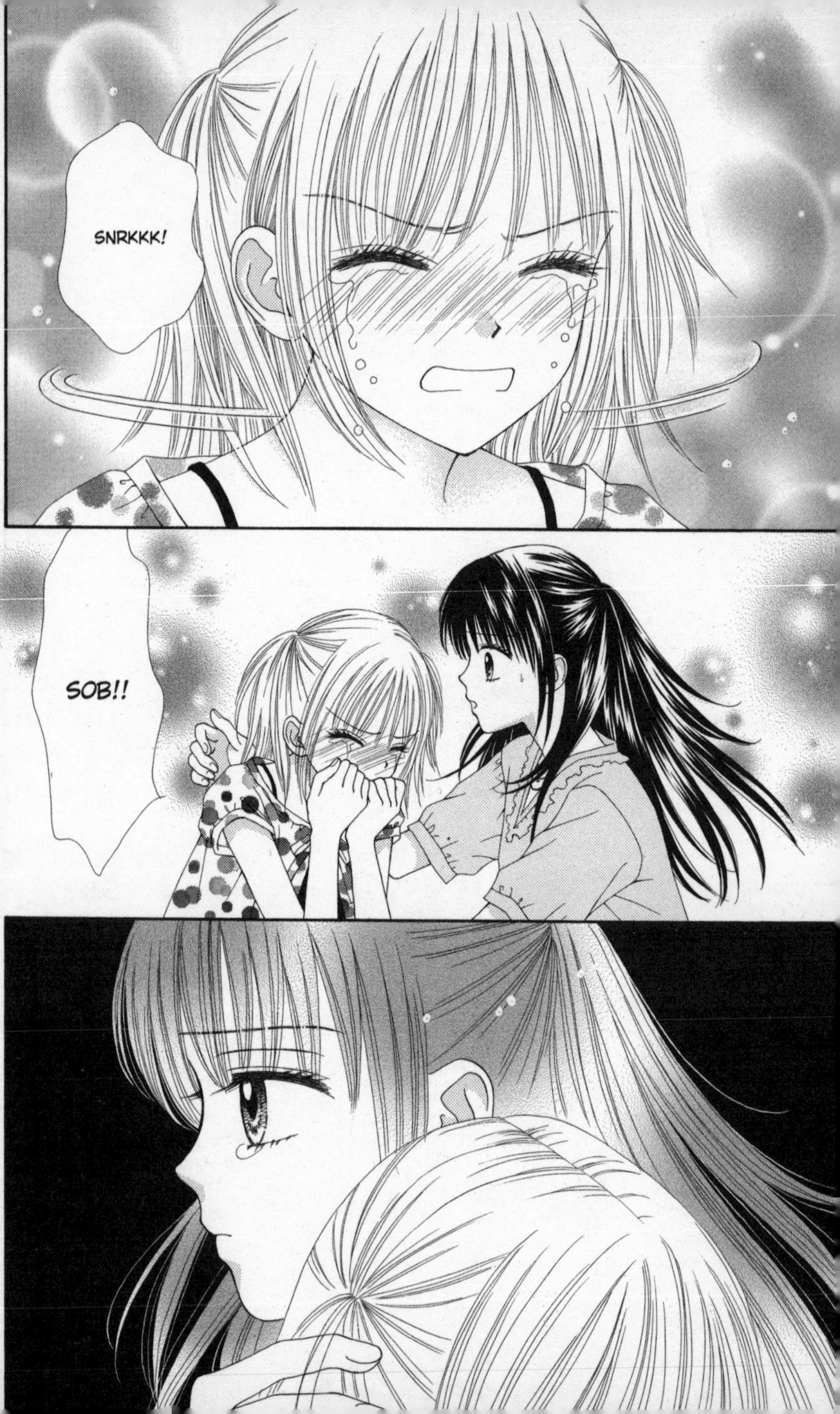
SNRKKK!
SOB!!

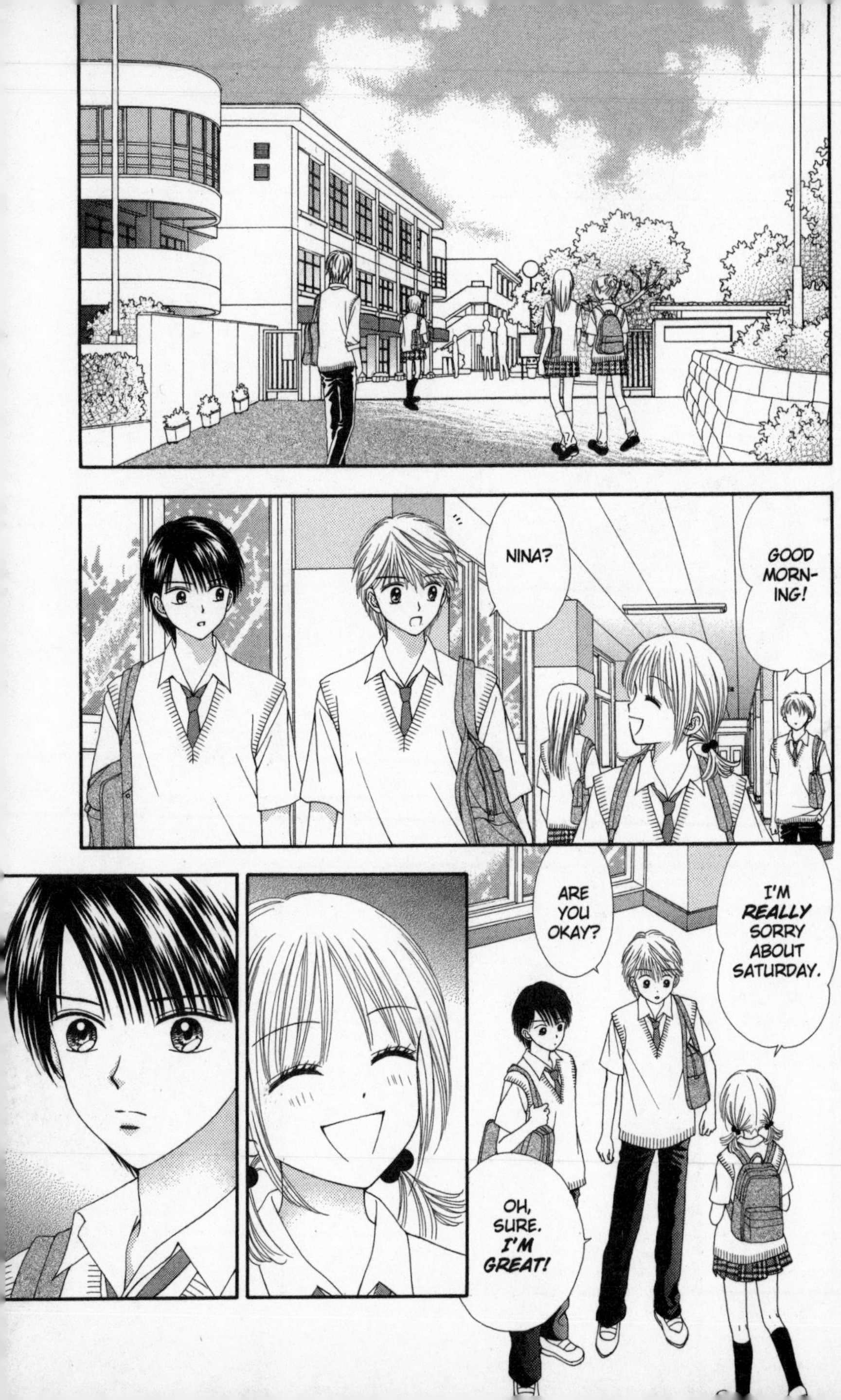
GOOD MORNING!
NINA?
I'M *REALLY* SORRY ABOUT SATURDAY.
ARE YOU OKAY?
OH, SURE. *I'M GREAT!*

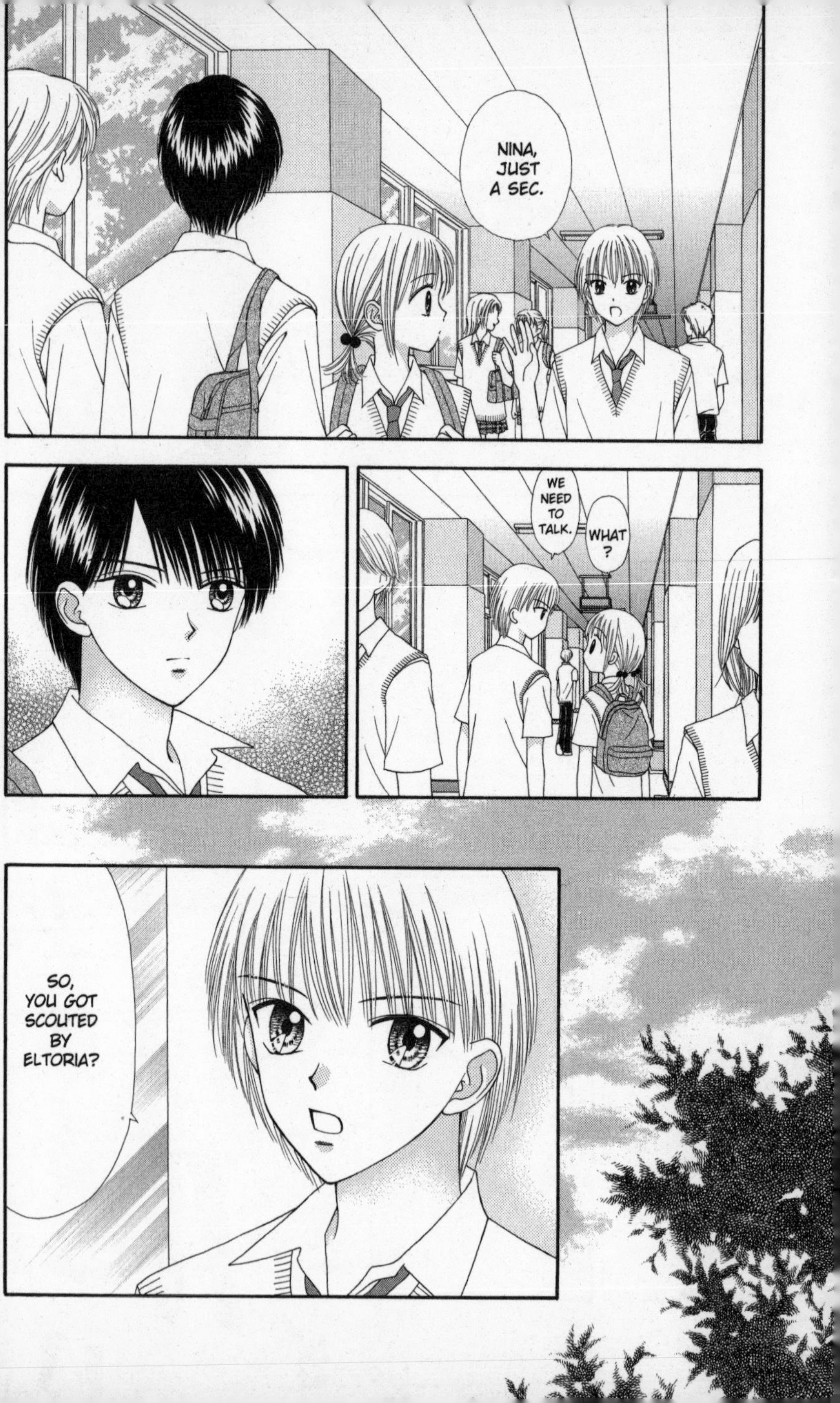
NINA, JUST A SEC.
WHAT?
WE NEED TO TALK.
SO, YOU GOT SCOUTED BY ELTORIA?

FREE TALK 5

Two days ago I went to a fan-club event for voice actress/singer Yui Horie. Or at least. . .that's where I thought I was going.

It was a beautiful day and I felt great, but I was a total bonehead and got the dates mixed up! So when I got there, Sakura Nogawa was doing a live concert instead. The Yuie Horie event had been the week before!

Miss Nogawa was also in Ultra Maniac, so I wanted to go. But I didn't have a ticket, so I slunk home. (Sob!)

By the way, the voice of Nina (Akemi Kanda) recently got a cat and named it Leo. It's a black cat, so I thought it would be named Shinosuke. But she liked Leo's name better. It's definitely neat to have people name their pets after my characters.

The main run of the anime is over, but it's on DVDs now, so please check it out. ♡

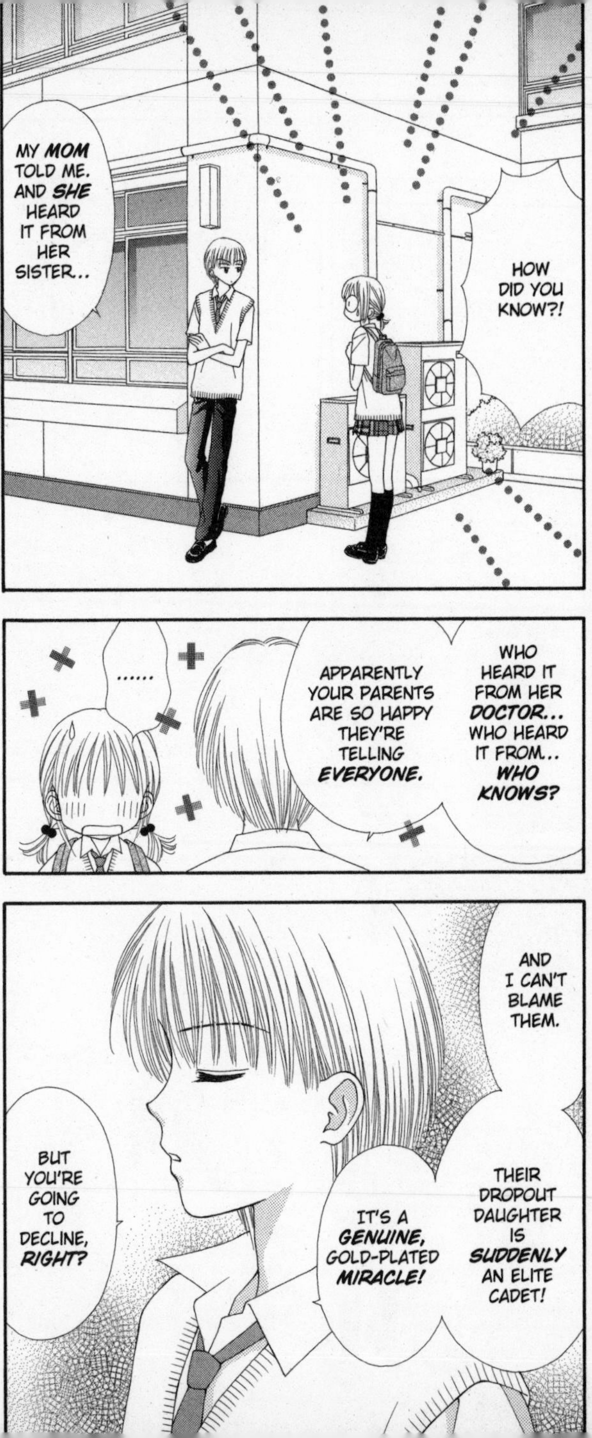
HOW DID YOU KNOW?!
MY MOM TOLD ME. AND SHE HEARD IT FROM HER SISTER...
WHO HEARD IT FROM HER DOCTOR... WHO HEARD IT FROM... WHO KNOWS?
APPARENTLY YOUR PARENTS ARE SO HAPPY THEY'RE TELLING EVERYONE.
......
AND I CAN'T BLAME THEM.
THEIR DROPOUT DAUGHTER IS SUDDENLY AN ELITE CADET!
IT'S A GENUINE, GOLD-PLATED MIRACLE!
BUT YOU'RE GOING TO DECLINE, RIGHT?

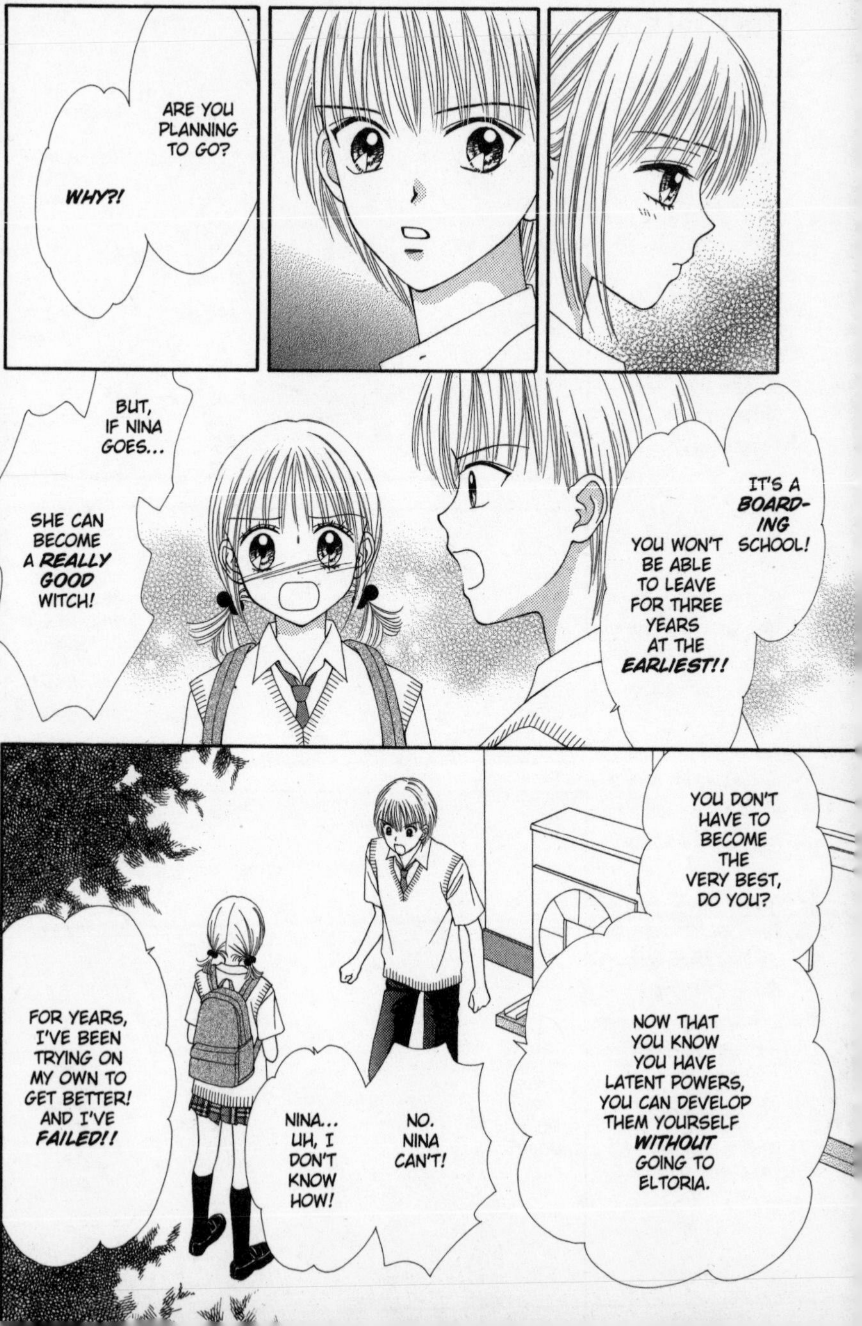
ARE YOU PLANNING TO GO?
WHY?!
IT'S A BOARDING-ING SCHOOL!
YOU WON'T BE ABLE TO LEAVE FOR THREE YEARS AT THE EARLIEST!!
BUT, IF NINA GOES...
SHE CAN BECOME A REALLY GOOD WITCH!
YOU DON'T HAVE TO BECOME THE VERY BEST, DO YOU?
NOW THAT YOU KNOW YOU HAVE LATENT POWERS, YOU CAN DEVELOP THEM YOURSELF WITHOUT GOING TO ELTORIA.
NO. NINA CAN'T!
NINA... UH, I DON'T KNOW HOW!
FOR YEARS, I'VE BEEN TRYING ON MY OWN TO GET BETTER! AND I'VE FAILED!!

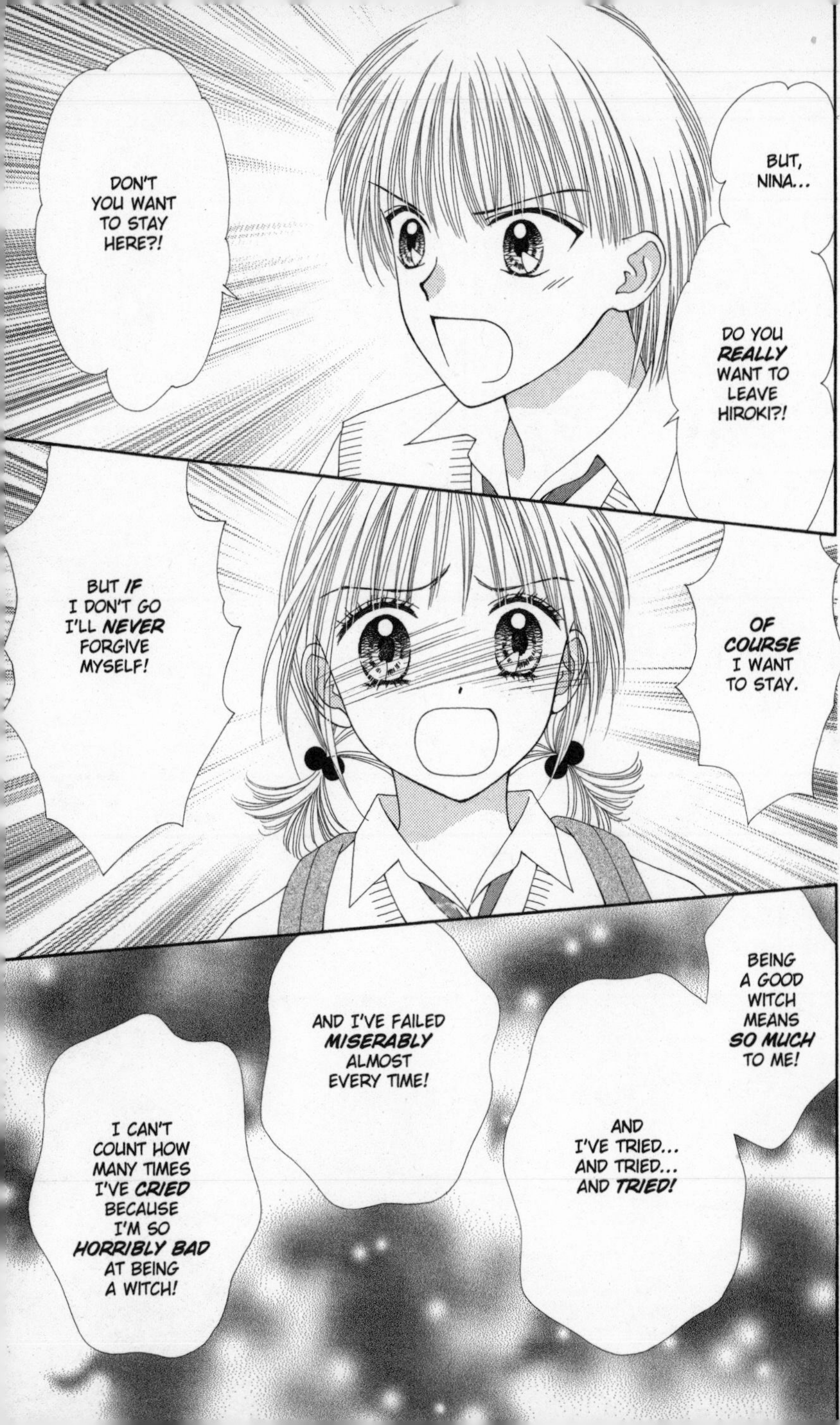
BUT, NINA...
DO YOU *REALLY* WANT TO LEAVE HIROKI?!
DON'T YOU WANT TO STAY HERE?!
OF COURSE I WANT TO STAY.
BUT *IF* I DON'T GO I'LL *NEVER* FORGIVE MYSELF!
BEING A GOOD WITCH MEANS *SO MUCH* TO ME!
AND I'VE TRIED... AND TRIED... AND *TRIED!*
AND I'VE FAILED *MISERABLY* ALMOST EVERY TIME!
I CAN'T COUNT HOW MANY TIMES I'VE *CRIED* BECAUSE I'M SO *HORRIBLY BAD* AT BEING A WITCH!

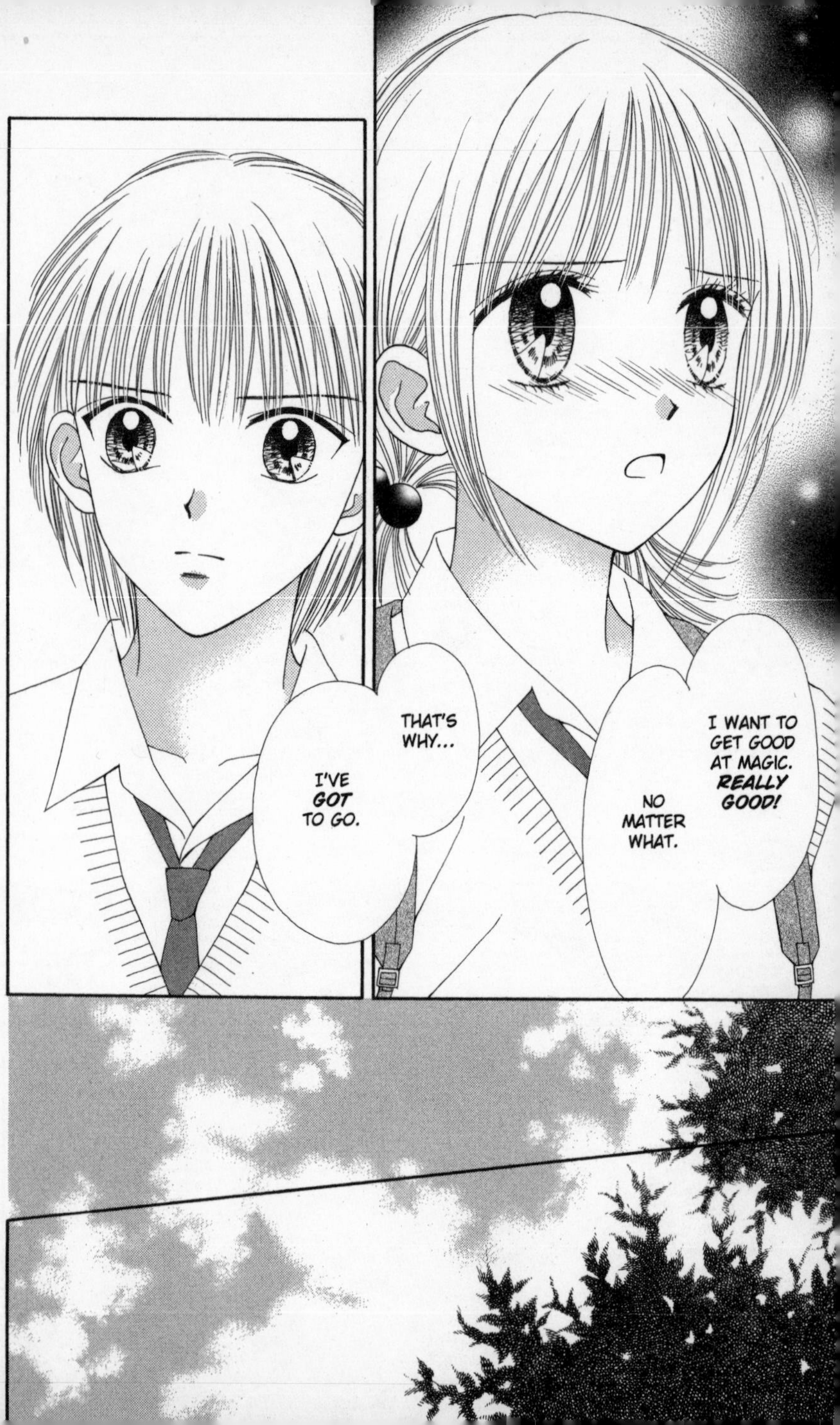
I WANT TO GET GOOD AT MAGIC. **REALLY GOOD!**
NO MATTER WHAT.
THAT'S WHY...
I'VE **GOT** TO GO.

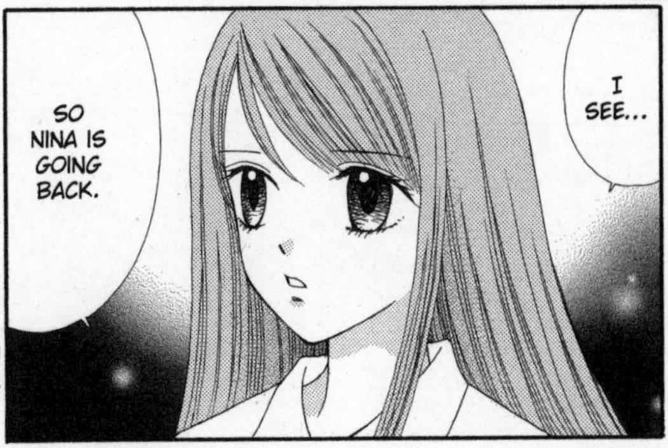
I SEE...
SO NINA IS GOING BACK.

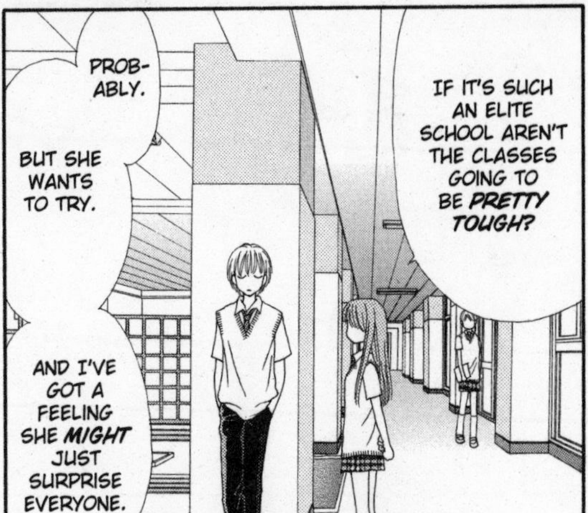
IF IT'S SUCH AN ELITE SCHOOL AREN'T THE CLASSES GOING TO BE PRETTY TOUGH?
PROB-ABLY.
BUT SHE WANTS TO TRY.
AND I'VE GOT A FEELING SHE MIGHT JUST SURPRISE EVERYONE.

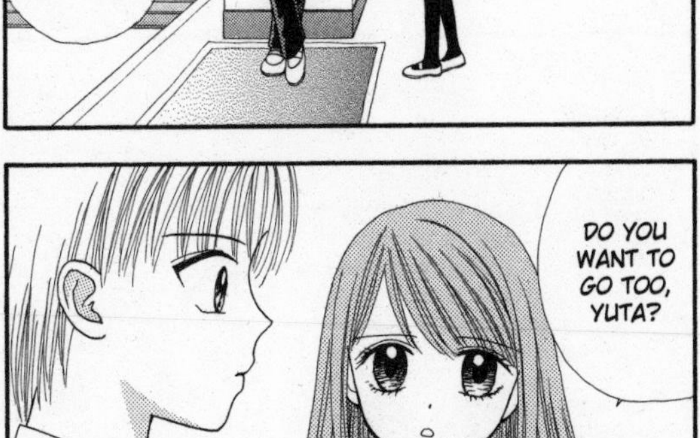
DO YOU WANT TO GO TOO, YUTA?

FREE TALK 6

Near the end of January, I went on my dream vacation (Another one!) to see the Aurora Borealis. My fellow travelers were Ryou Atsuki and Mio Katagiri. They'd previously gone to Canada to see the Aurora Borealis. This time they were going to Scandinavia to see it. When they found out that I wanted to tag along, they were agreeable.

Actually, the two of them are more likes friends of a friend. I never really knew them that well before. (At New Year's parties and events, I basically just said hello to them.) We're all **Ribon** creators and we had a lot to talk about. So it was a really enjoyable trip. But the all-important Aurora B.!

I was able to see it, but it was **very** subtle. (Laughs.)

I had imagined that the Aurora Borealis could be seen overhead in three-dimensions as a blaze of colors. But what I saw was far off near the horizon and appeared flat.

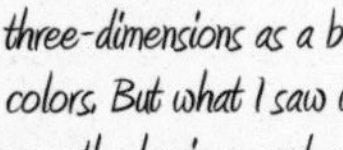

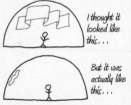

I thought it looked like this...

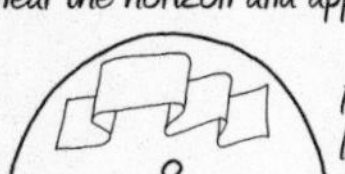

But it was actually like this...

It was almost ethereal, like a fast moving yellow-green cloud.

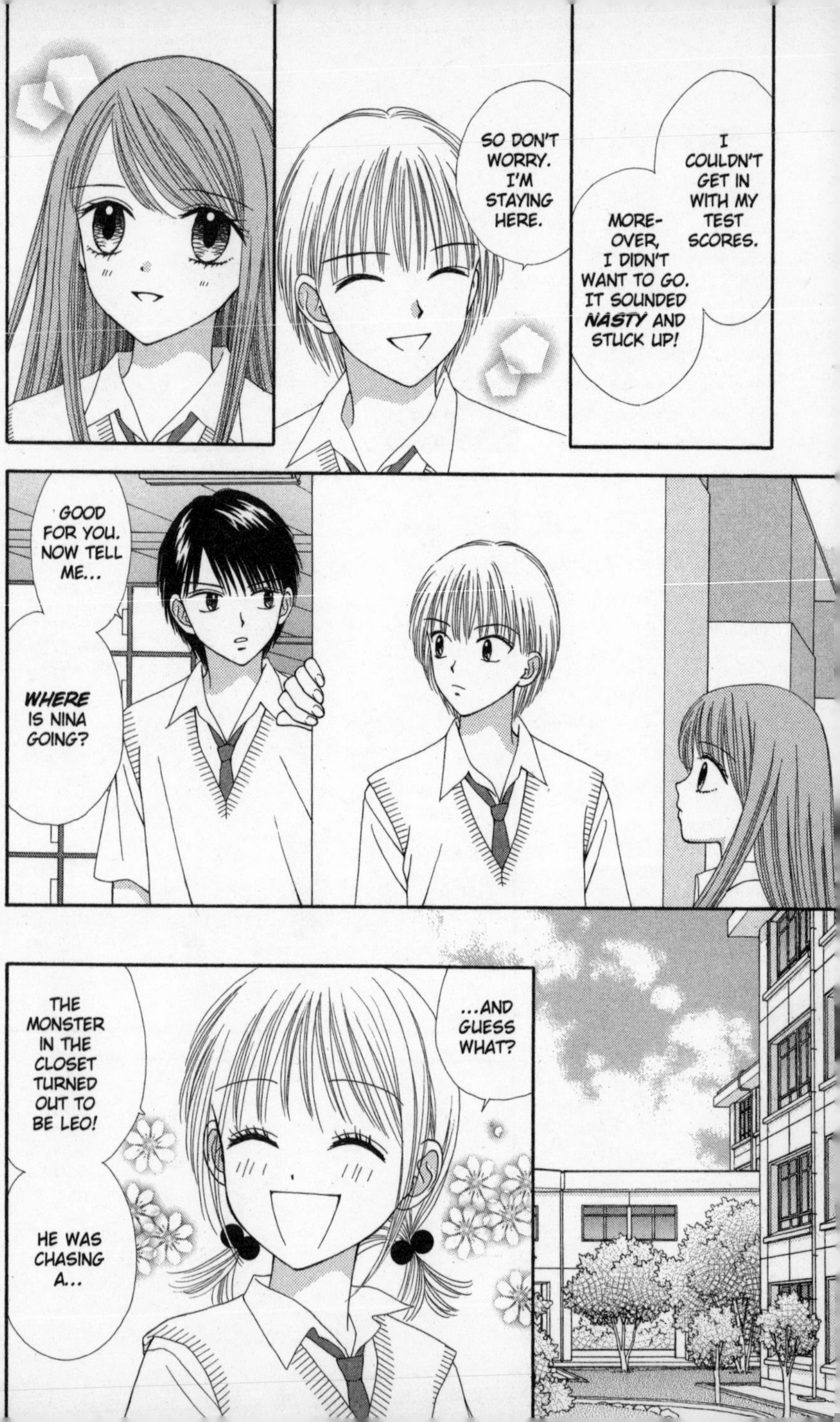
I COULDN'T GET IN WITH MY TEST SCORES.
MORE-OVER, I DIDN'T WANT TO GO. IT SOUNDED NASTY AND STUCK UP!
SO DON'T WORRY. I'M STAYING HERE.
GOOD FOR YOU. NOW TELL ME...
WHERE IS NINA GOING?
...AND GUESS WHAT?
THE MONSTER IN THE CLOSET TURNED OUT TO BE LEO!
HE WAS CHASING A...

FREE TALK 7

Unlike tours I've heard about in Canada and Alaska, the Scandinavian tour didn't take you to a specific point at night to view the Aurora Borealis. Instead, the tour people said, "This is an area where the Aurora appears. So please feel free and roam about outside the hotel to catch it." It was really too bright in town, so it seemed like a poor place to see the Aurora B. So, next time, we decided we'd go to Alaska.

But Scandinavia is really neat! Everyone is so nice, and you feel really good. Plus, the area is famous for its furniture. So there were really nice chairs and tables wherever you went. I want to go there again in summer and see the midnight sun.

The most memorable part of the trip was that I was able to see snowflakes with my naked eye. The flakes must have been around five mm in size. The snow seemed unusually glittery. And lo and behold, it was crystallized! Even the falling snow that clung to our hats and clothes were crystallized! We all shrieked in happiness and took pictures, but they didn't turn out. Too bad.

We also toured a hotel made completely out of ice. (Even the chandelier and the bar glasses!) We also rode dog sleds and snowmobiles; explored a cave; and saw the fjords. So I did a lot and came home feeling very refreshed.

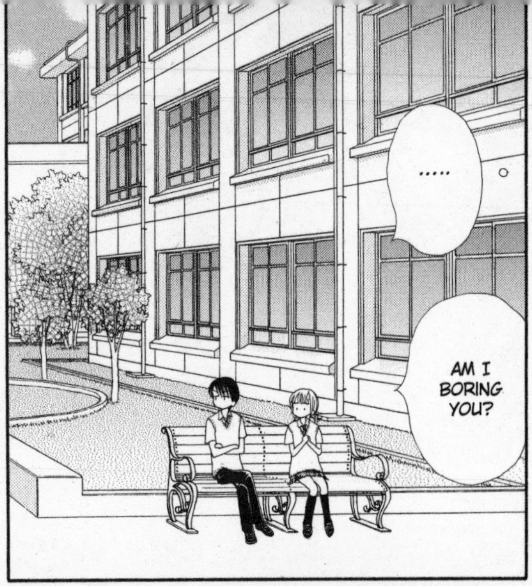
.....
AM I BORING YOU?

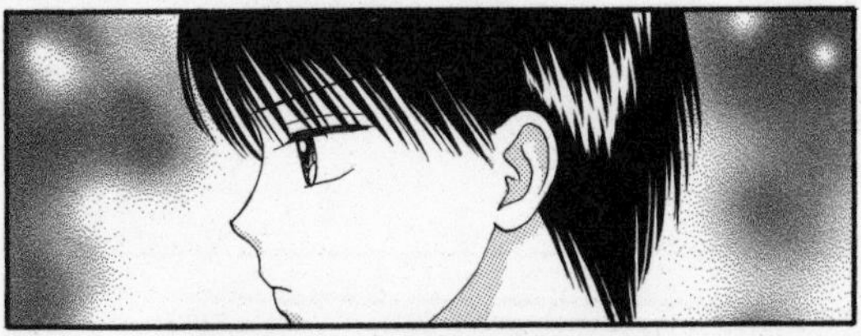

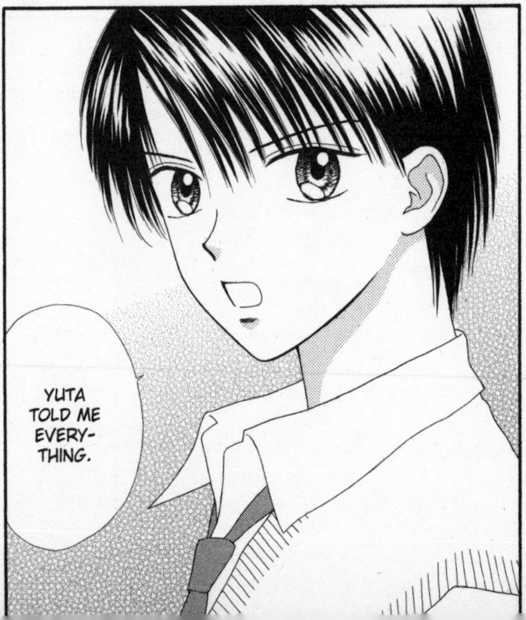
YUTA TOLD ME EVERY-THING.

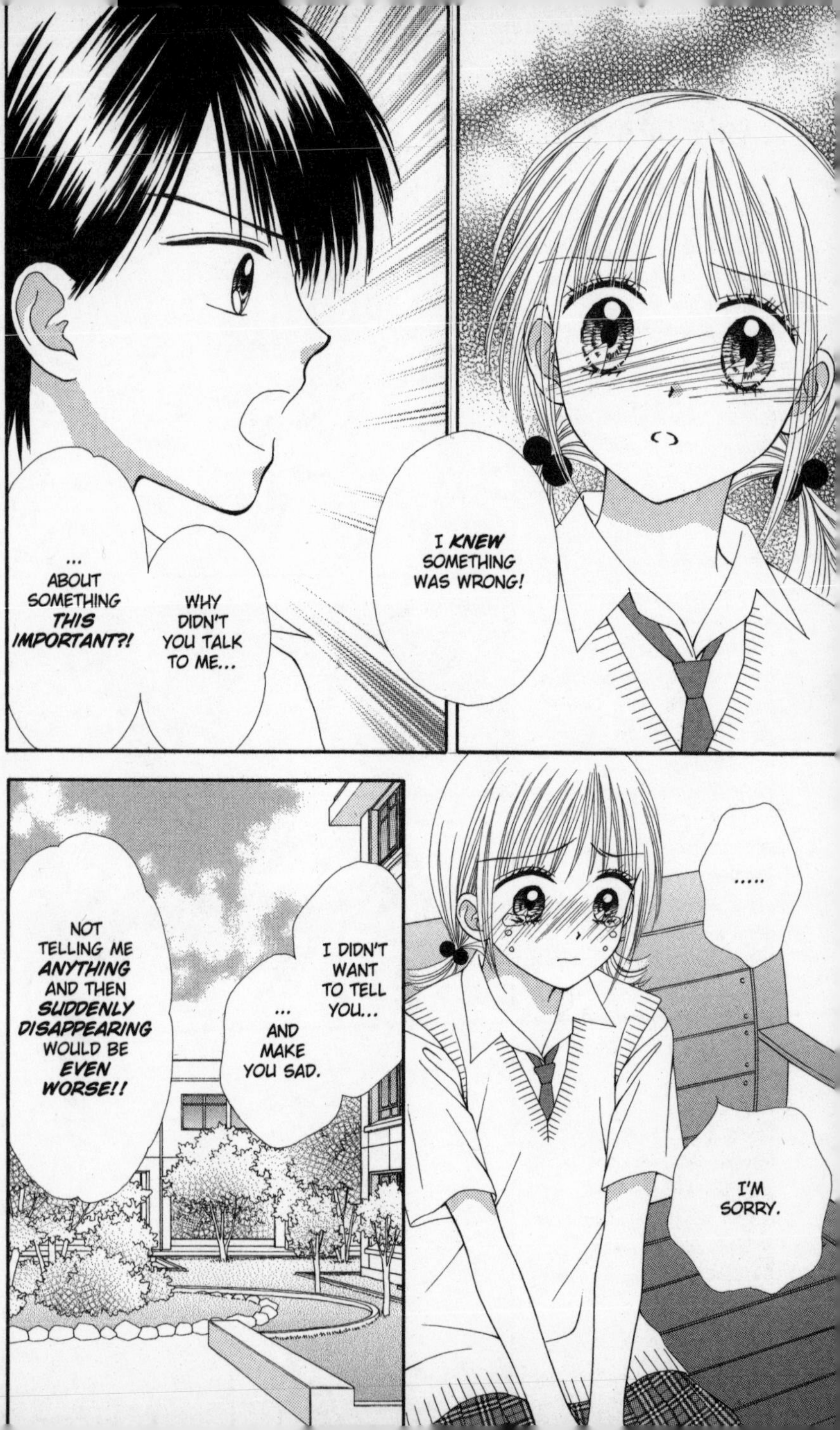
I KNEW SOMETHING WAS WRONG!
WHY DIDN'T YOU TALK TO ME...
... ABOUT SOMETHING THIS IMPORTANT?!
.....
I'M SORRY.
I DIDN'T WANT TO TELL YOU...
... AND MAKE YOU SAD.
NOT TELLING ME ANYTHING AND THEN SUDDENLY DISAPPEARING WOULD BE EVEN WORSE!!

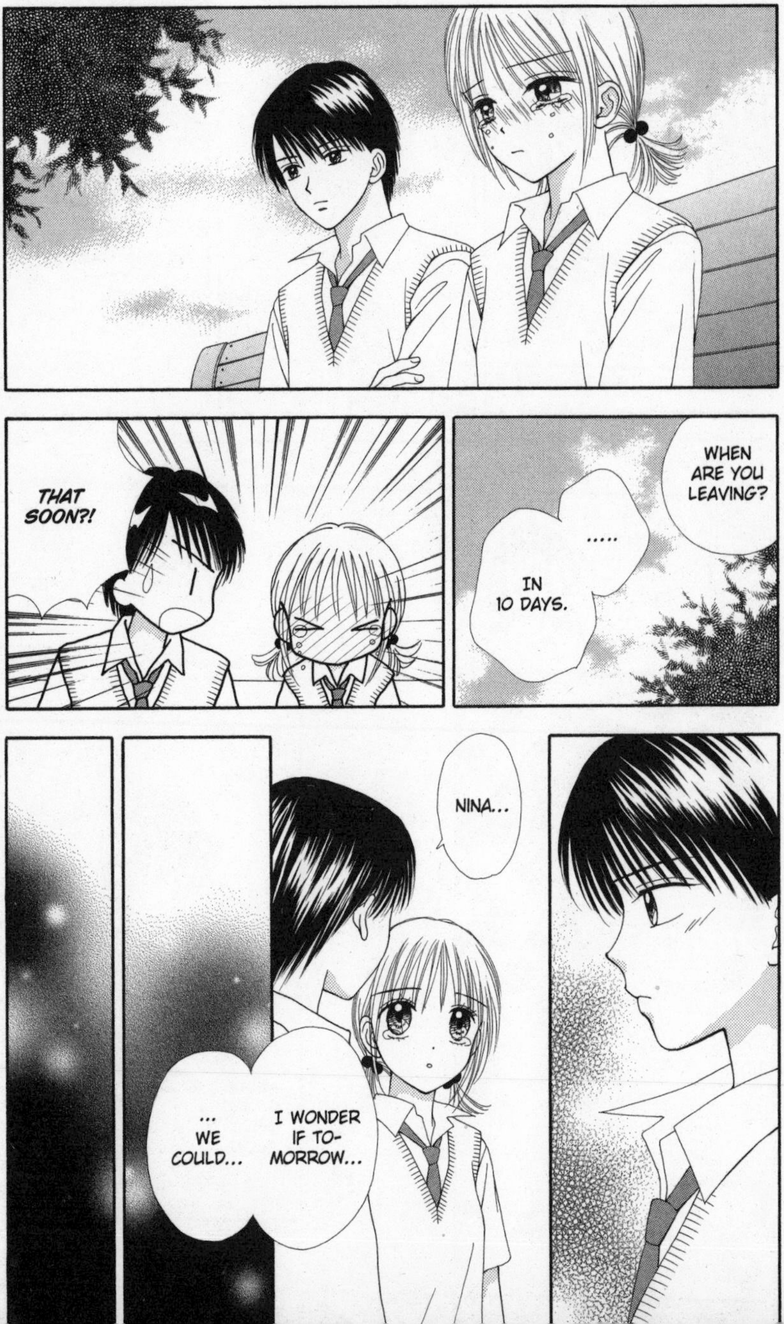
WHEN ARE YOU LEAVING?
.....
IN 10 DAYS.
THAT SOON?!
NINA...
I WONDER IF TO-MORROW...
... WE COULD...

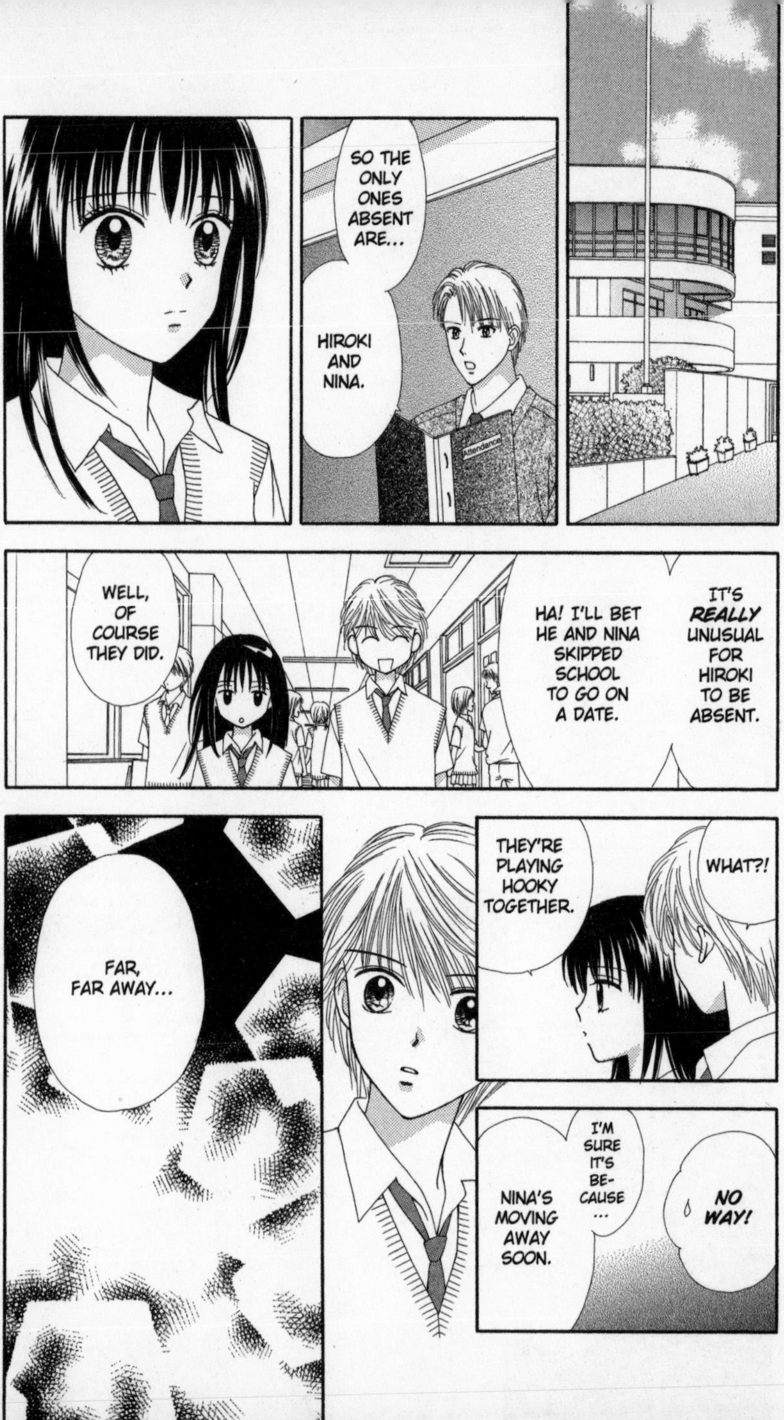
SO THE ONLY ONES ABSENT ARE...
HIROKI AND NINA.
IT'S *REALLY* UNUSUAL FOR HIROKI TO BE ABSENT.
HA! I'LL BET HE AND NINA SKIPPED SCHOOL TO GO ON A DATE.
WELL, OF COURSE THEY DID.
WHAT?!
THEY'RE PLAYING HOOKY TOGETHER.
NO WAY!
I'M SURE IT'S BE-CAUSE...
NINA'S MOVING AWAY SOON.
FAR, FAR AWAY...

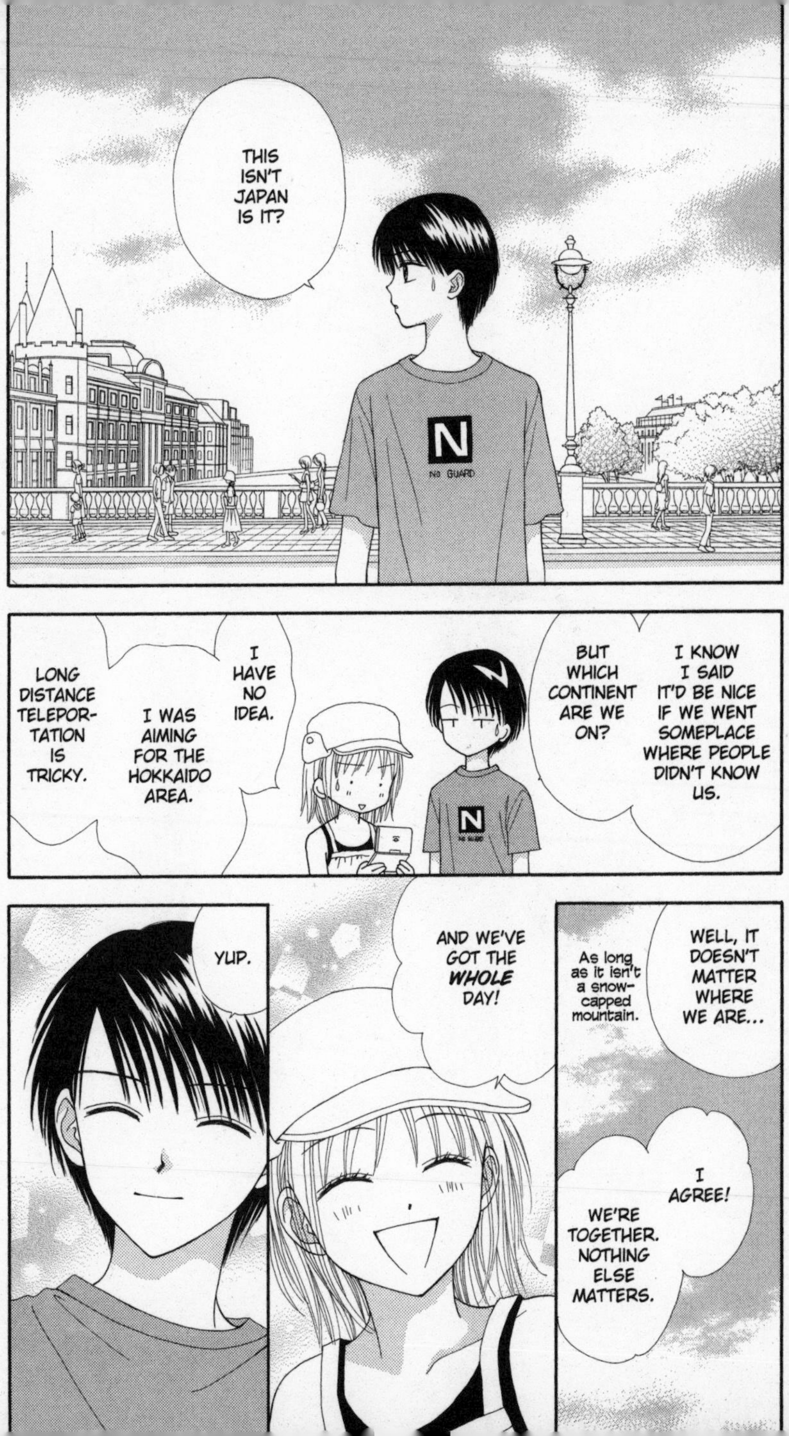
THIS ISN'T JAPAN IS IT?
I KNOW I SAID IT'D BE NICE IF WE WENT SOMEPLACE WHERE PEOPLE DIDN'T KNOW US.
BUT WHICH CONTINENT ARE WE ON?
I HAVE NO IDEA.
I WAS AIMING FOR THE HOKKAIDO AREA.
LONG DISTANCE TELEPOR-TATION IS TRICKY.
WELL, IT DOESN'T MATTER WHERE WE ARE...
As long as it isn't a snow-capped mountain.
I AGREE!
WE'RE TOGETHER. NOTHING ELSE MATTERS.
AND WE'VE GOT THE *WHOLE* DAY!
YUP.

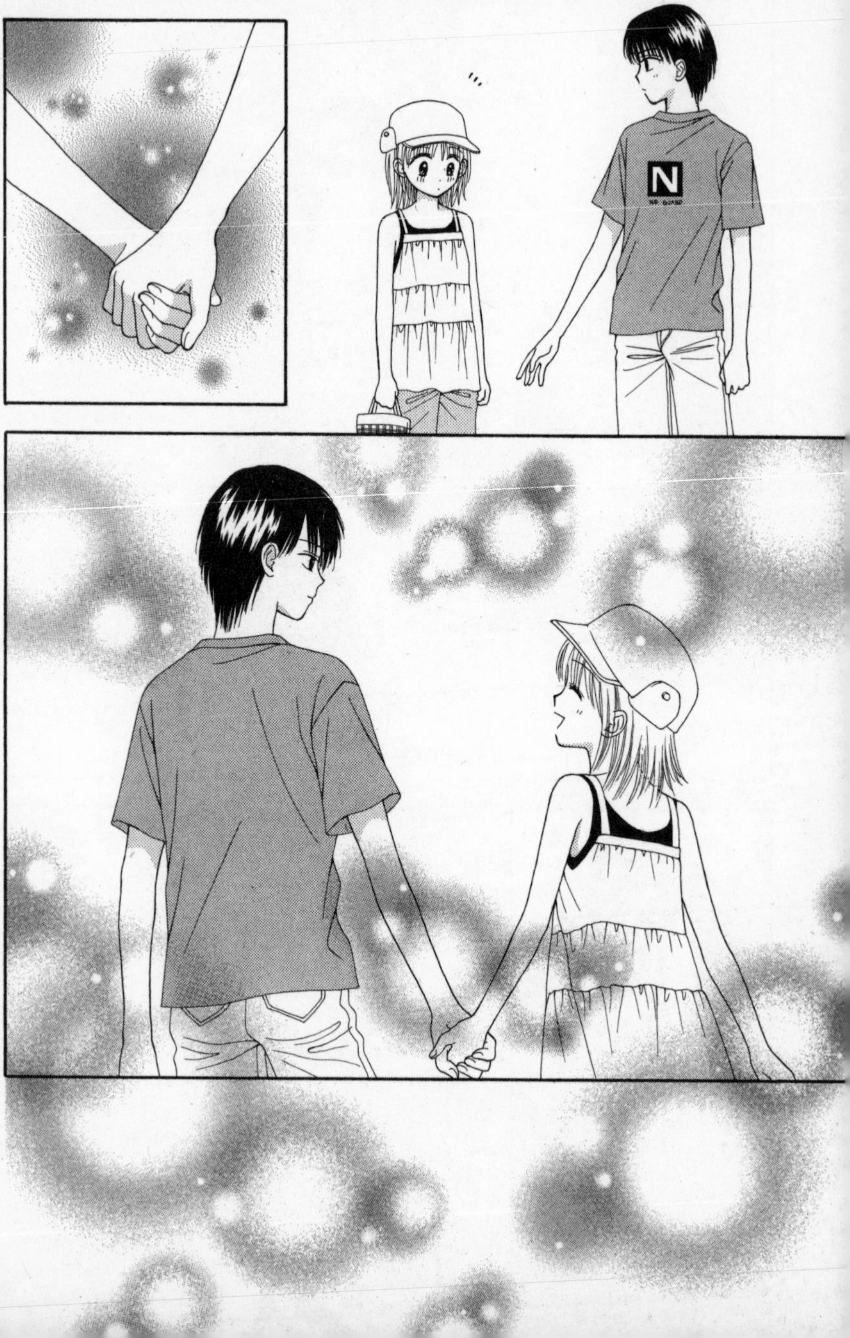
N

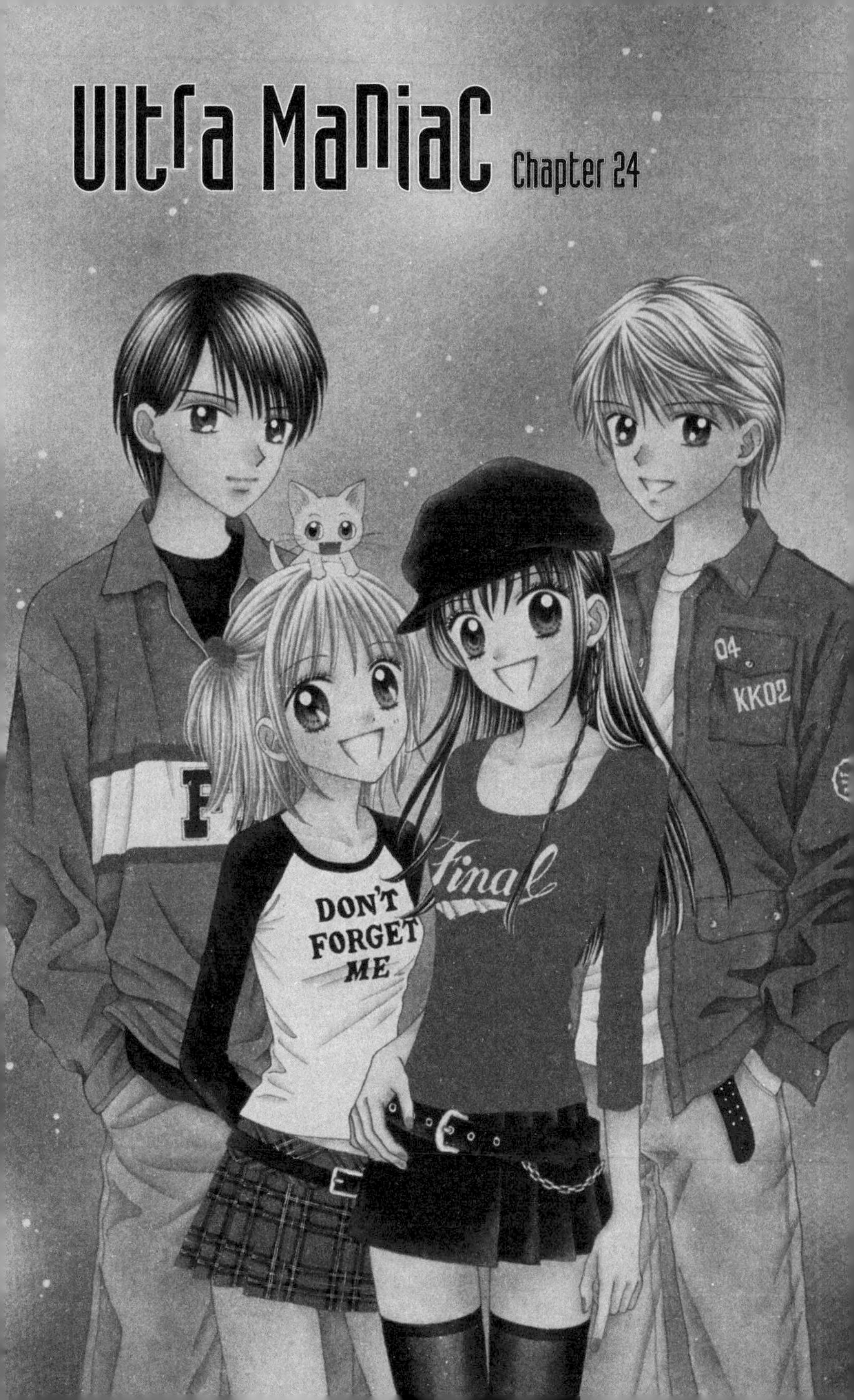
Ultra Maniac
Chapter 24
DON'T FORGET ME
final
Q4
KK02
F

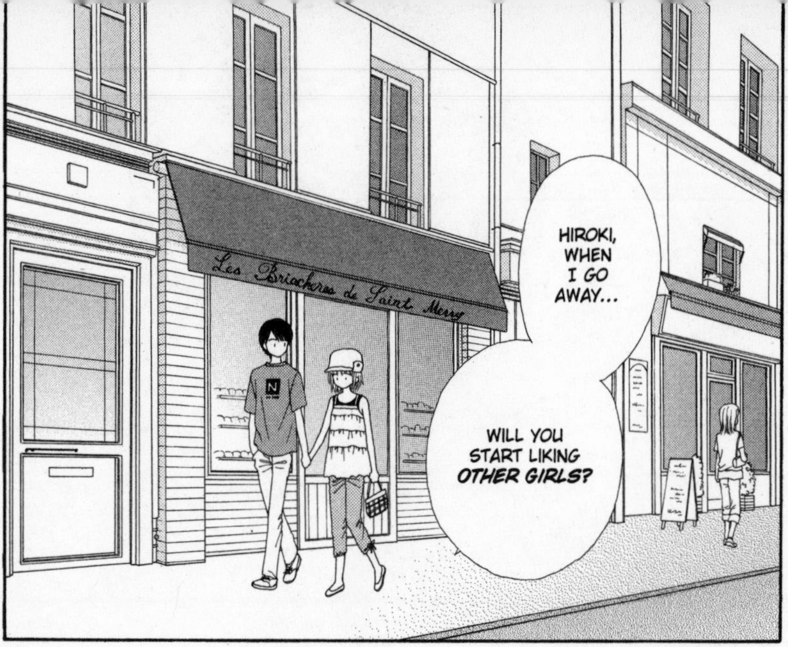
HIROKI, WHEN I GO AWAY...
WILL YOU START LIKING OTHER GIRLS?
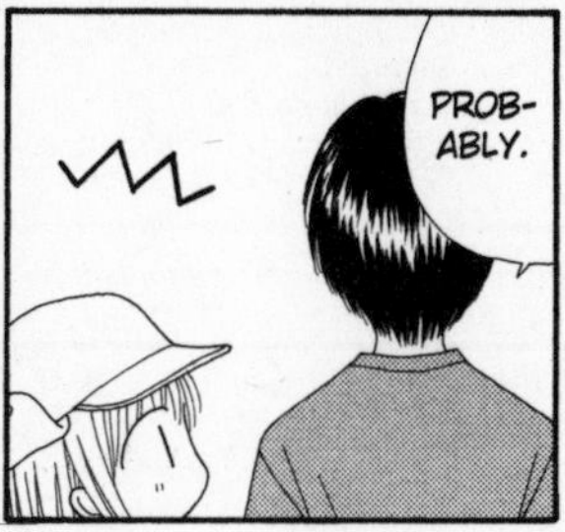
PROB-ABLY.
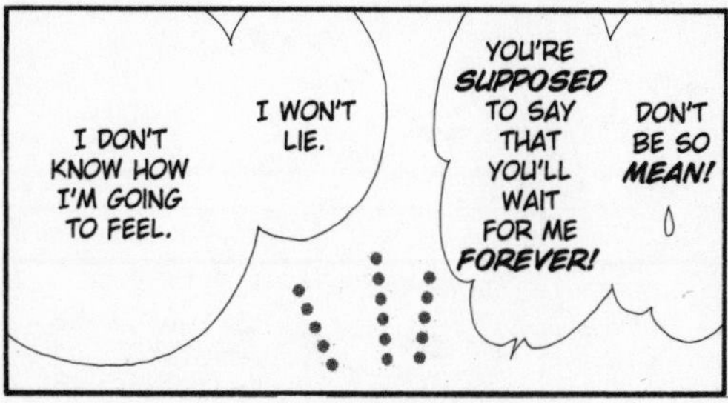
DON'T BE SO MEAN!
YOU'RE SUPPOSED TO SAY THAT YOU'LL WAIT FOR ME FOREVER!
I WON'T LIE.
I DON'T KNOW HOW I'M GOING TO FEEL.
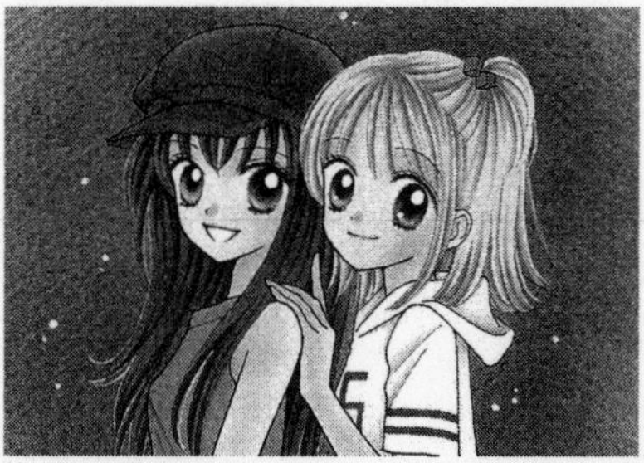

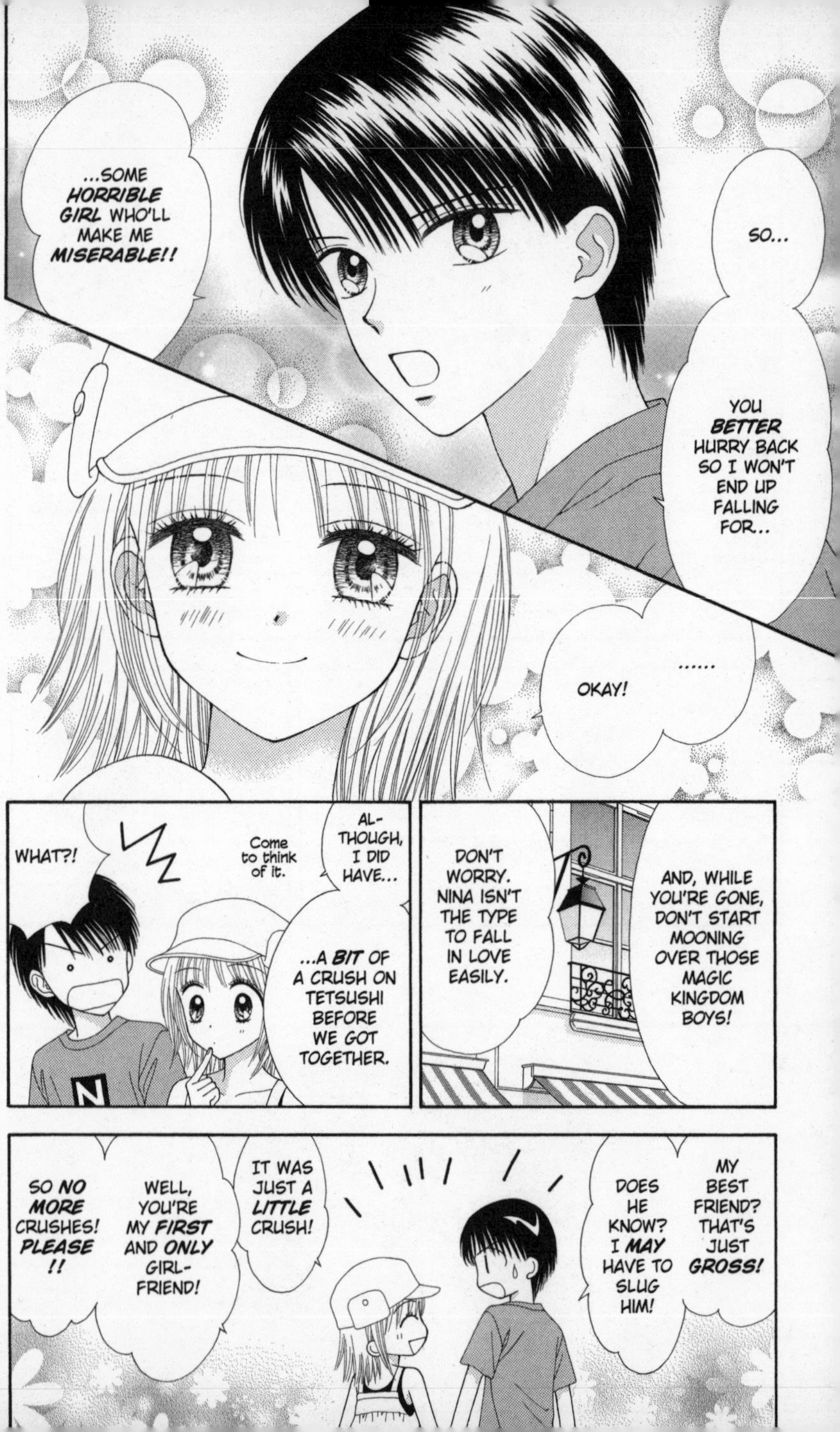
SO...
YOU BETTER HURRY BACK SO I WON'T END UP FALLING FOR...
...SOME HORRIBLE GIRL WHO'LL MAKE ME MISERABLE!!
......
OKAY!
AND, WHILE YOU'RE GONE, DON'T START MOONING OVER THOSE MAGIC KINGDOM BOYS!
DON'T WORRY. NINA ISN'T THE TYPE TO FALL IN LOVE EASILY.
AL-THOUGH, I DID HAVE...
Come to think of it.
...A BIT OF A CRUSH ON TETSUSHI BEFORE WE GOT TOGETHER.
WHAT?!
MY BEST FRIEND? THAT'S JUST GROSS!
DOES HE KNOW? I MAY HAVE TO SLUG HIM!
IT WAS JUST A LITTLE CRUSH!
WELL, YOU'RE MY FIRST AND ONLY GIRL-FRIEND!
SO NO MORE CRUSHES! PLEASE!!

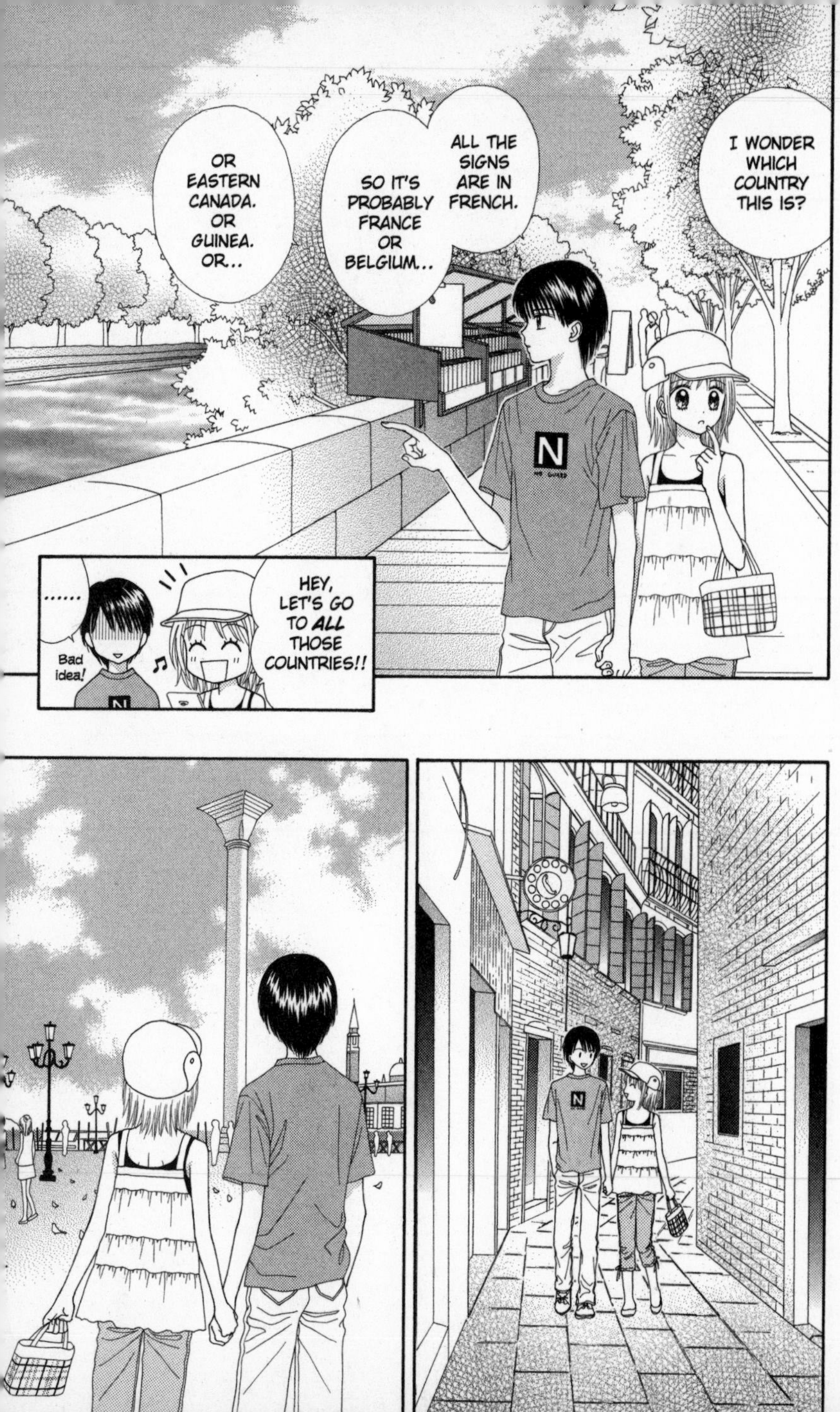
I WONDER WHICH COUNTRY THIS IS?
ALL THE SIGNS ARE IN FRENCH.
SO IT'S PROBABLY FRANCE OR BELGIUM...
OR EASTERN CANADA. OR GUINEA. OR...
HEY, LET'S GO TO ALL THOSE COUNTRIES!!
......
Bad idea!

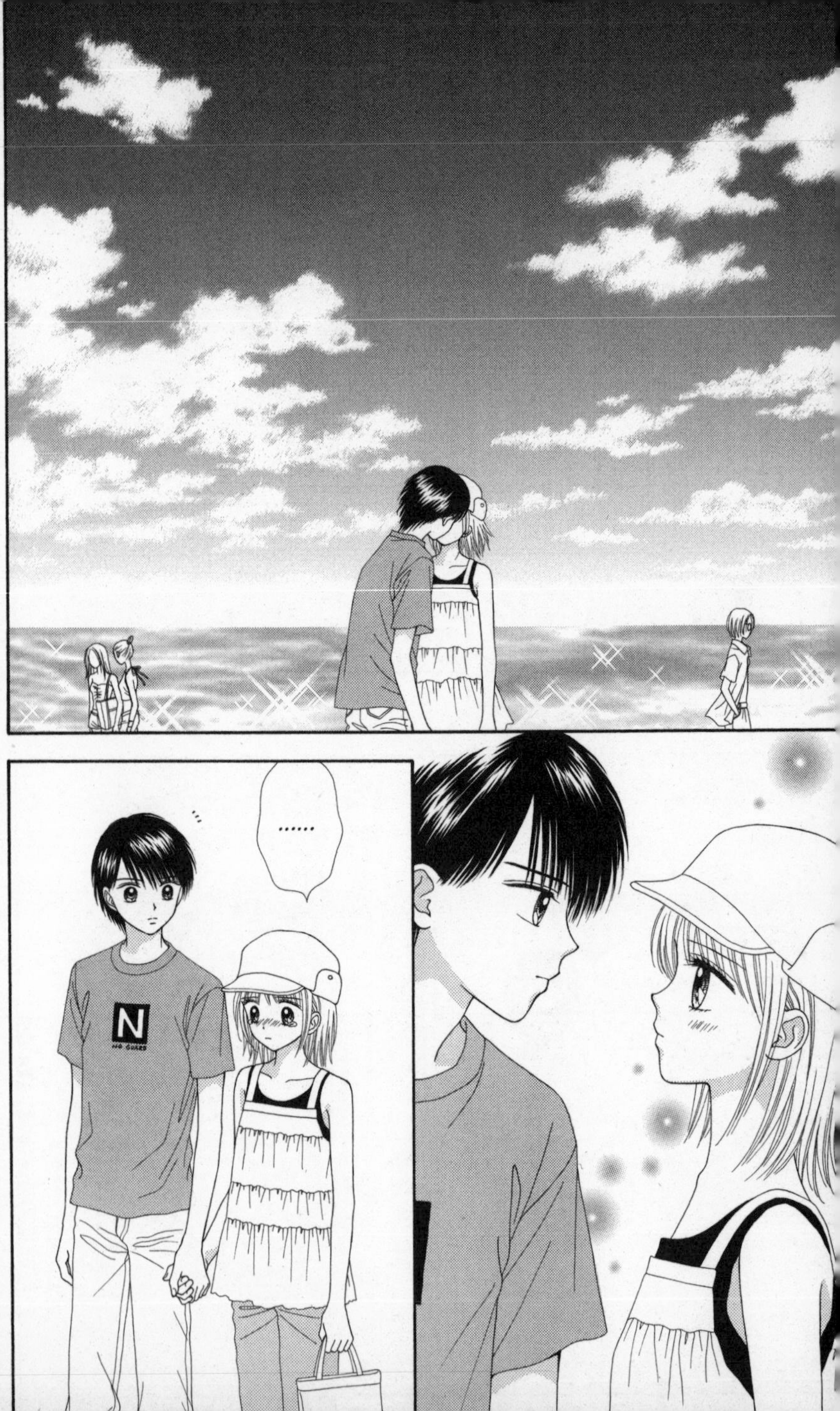
......

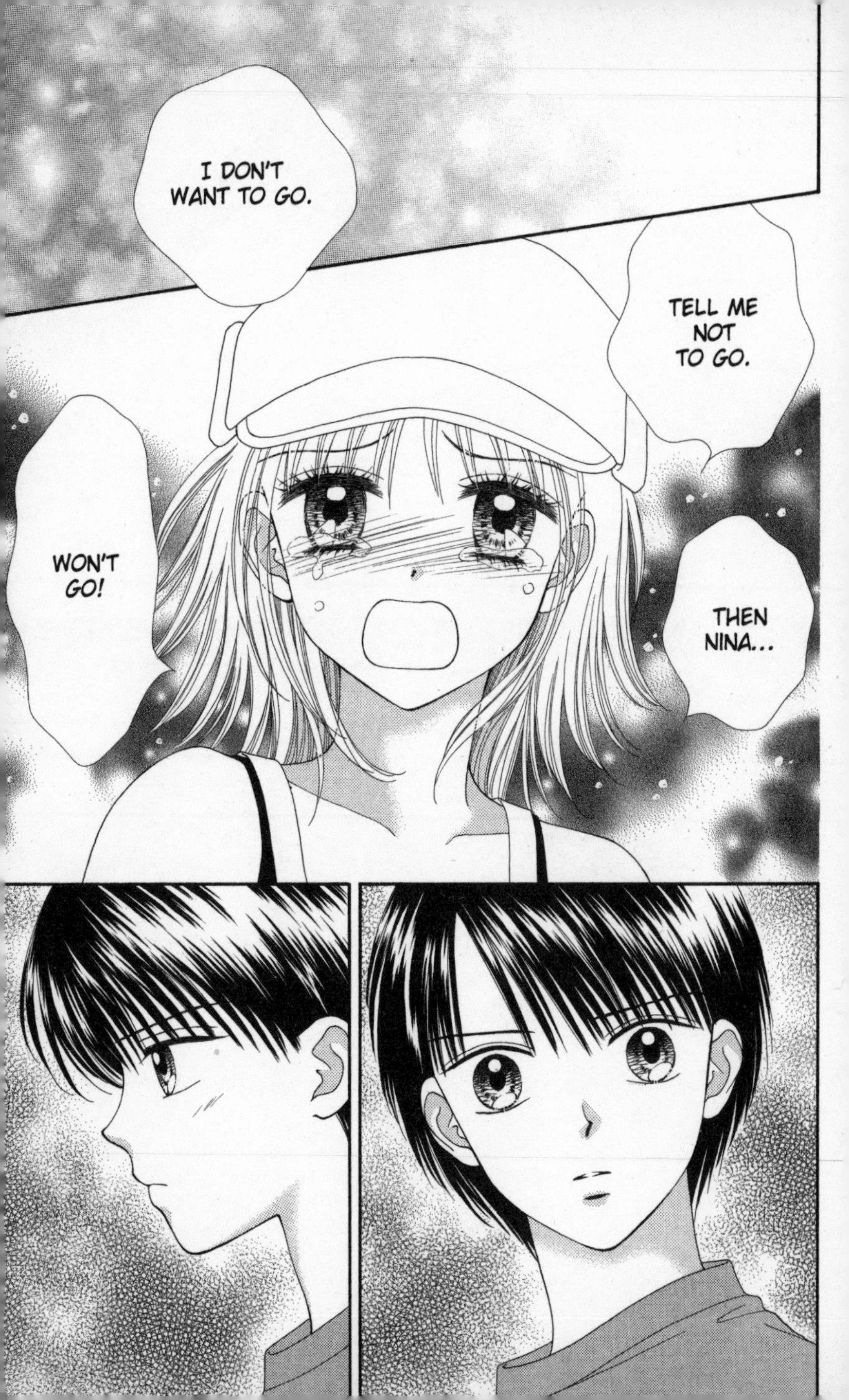
I DON'T WANT TO GO.
TELL ME NOT TO GO.
THEN NINA...
WON'T GO!

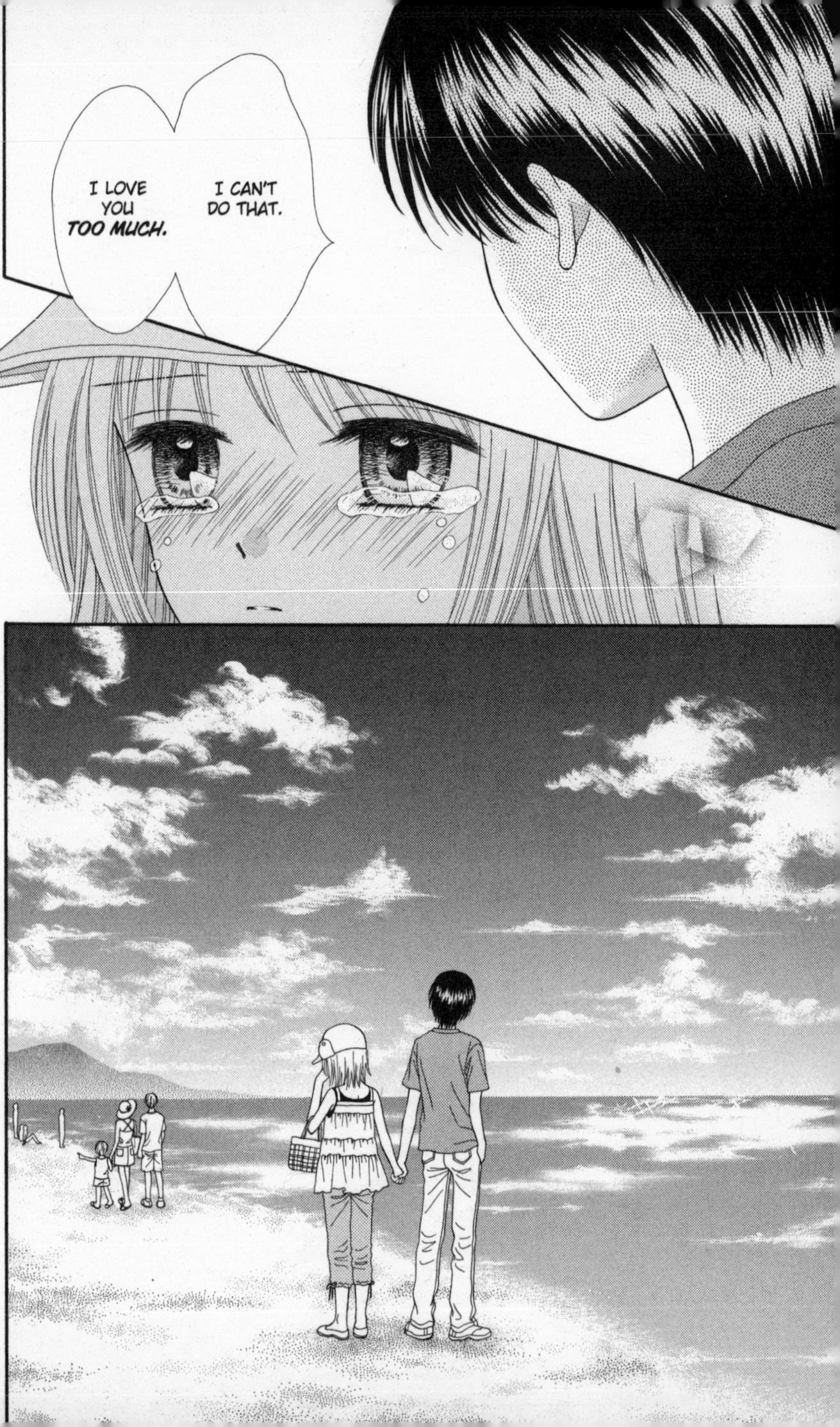
I CAN'T DO THAT.
I LOVE YOU TOO MUCH.

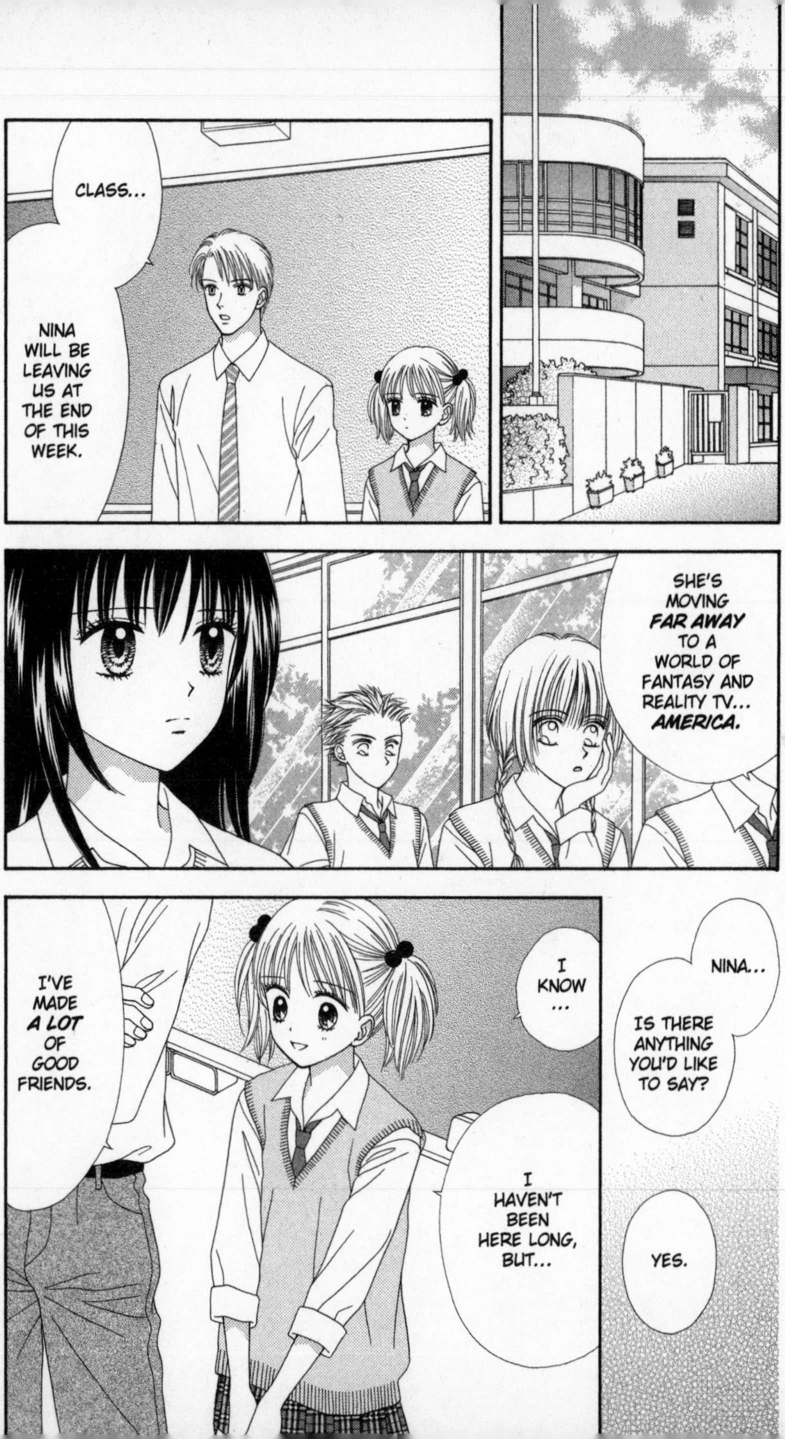
CLASS...
NINA WILL BE LEAVING US AT THE END OF THIS WEEK.
SHE'S MOVING ***FAR AWAY*** TO A WORLD OF FANTASY AND REALITY TV... ***AMERICA.***
NINA...
IS THERE ANYTHING YOU'D LIKE TO SAY?
YES.
I KNOW...
I HAVEN'T BEEN HERE LONG, BUT...
I'VE MADE ***A LOT*** OF GOOD FRIENDS.

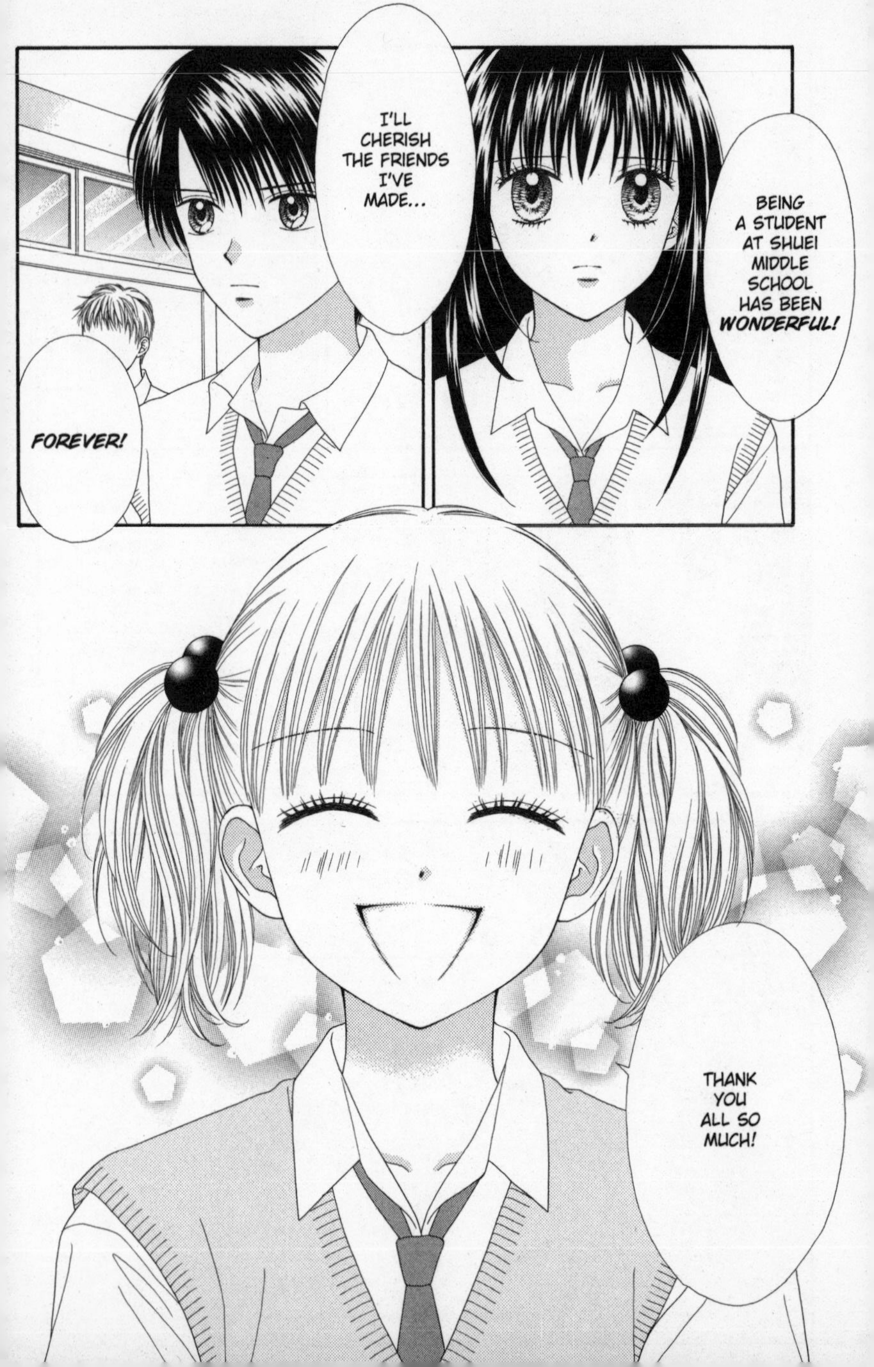
BEING A STUDENT AT SHUEI MIDDLE SCHOOL HAS BEEN WONDERFUL!
I'LL CHERISH THE FRIENDS I'VE MADE...
FOREVER!
THANK YOU ALL SO MUCH!

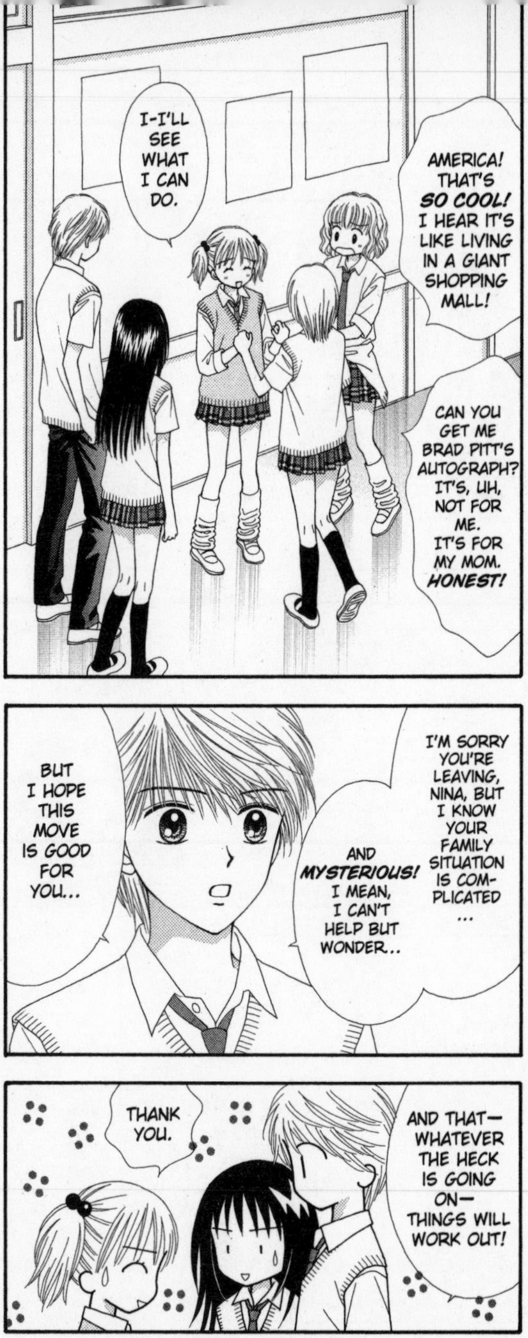
AMERICA! THAT'S **SO COOL!** I HEAR IT'S LIKE LIVING IN A GIANT SHOPPING MALL!
CAN YOU GET ME BRAD PITT'S AUTOGRAPH? IT'S, UH, NOT FOR ME. IT'S FOR MY MOM. **HONEST!**
I-I'LL SEE WHAT I CAN DO.
I'M SORRY YOU'RE LEAVING, NINA, BUT I KNOW YOUR FAMILY SITUATION IS COMPLICATED...
AND **MYSTERIOUS!** I MEAN, I CAN'T HELP BUT WONDER...
BUT I HOPE THIS MOVE IS GOOD FOR YOU...
AND THAT—WHATEVER THE HECK IS GOING ON—THINGS WILL WORK OUT!
THANK YOU.
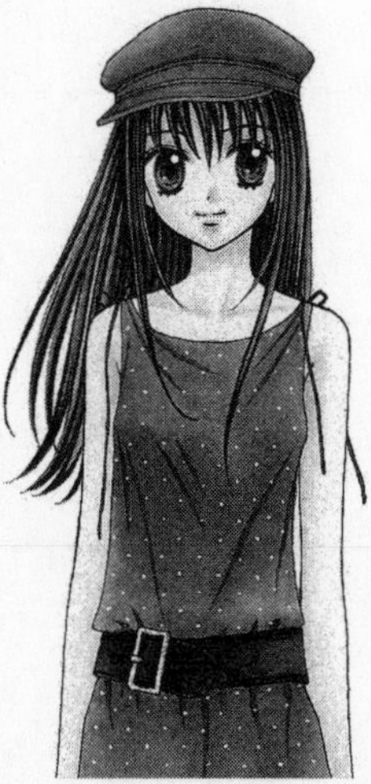

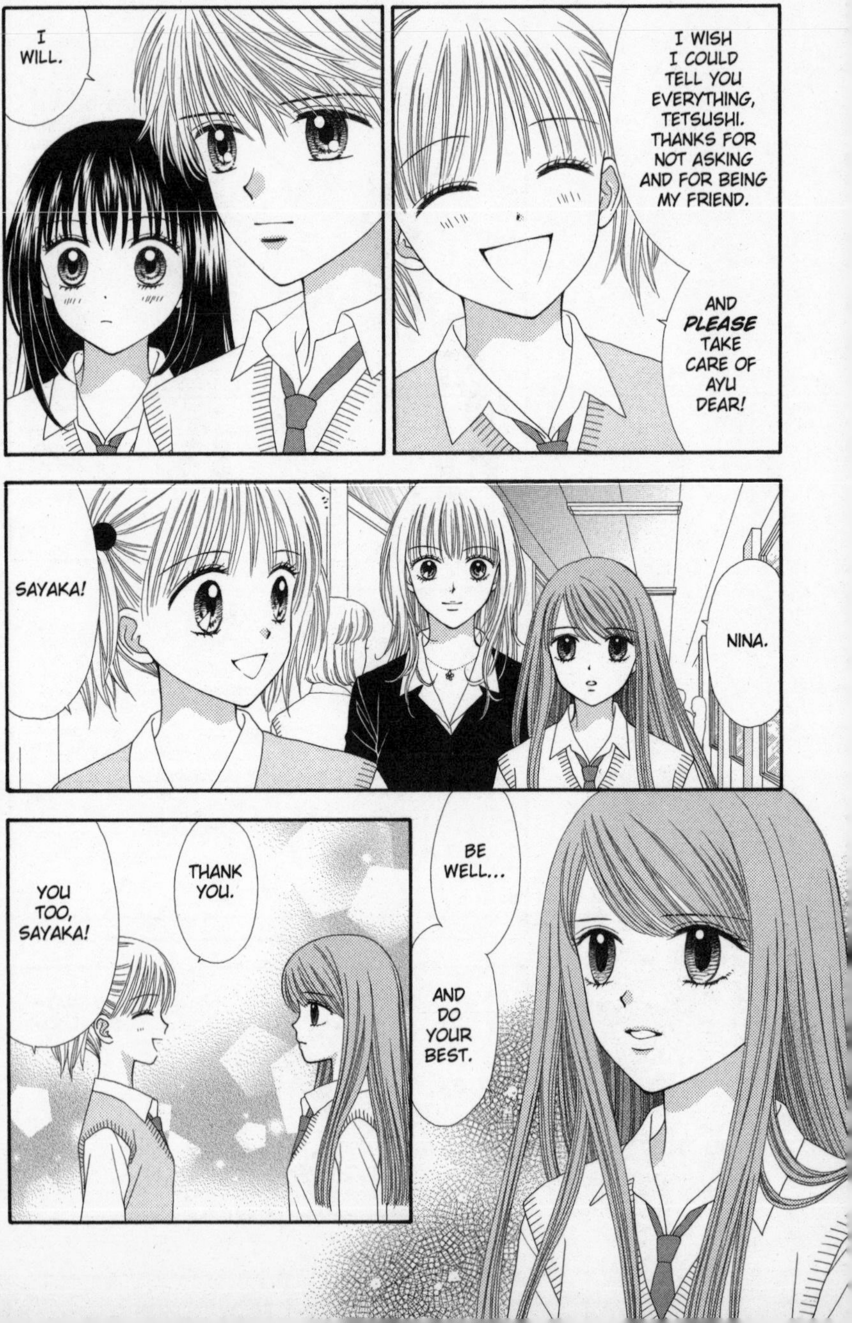
I WISH I COULD TELL YOU EVERYTHING, TETSUSHI. THANKS FOR NOT ASKING AND FOR BEING MY FRIEND.
AND *PLEASE* TAKE CARE OF AYU DEAR!
I WILL.
NINA.
SAYAKA!
BE WELL...
AND DO YOUR BEST.
THANK YOU.
YOU TOO, SAYAKA!

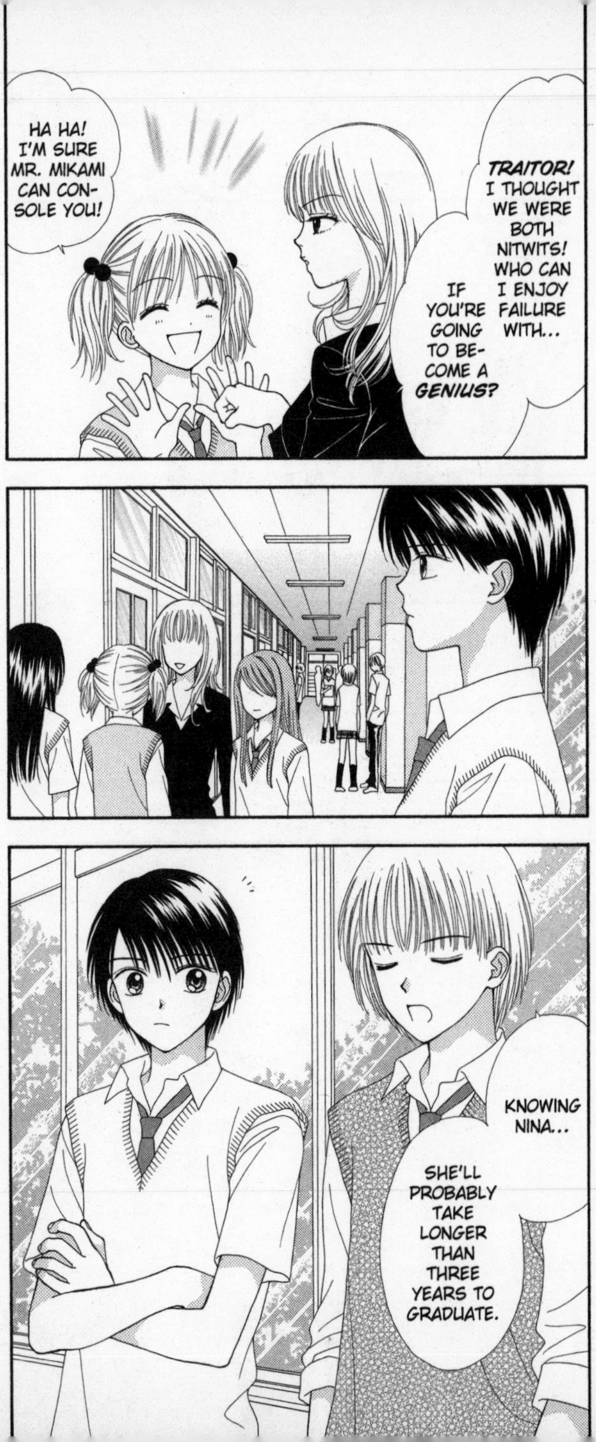
TRAITOR! I THOUGHT WE WERE BOTH NITWITS! WHO CAN I ENJOY FAILURE WITH...
IF YOU'RE GOING TO BECOME A GENIUS?
HA HA! I'M SURE MR. MIKAMI CAN CONSOLE YOU!
KNOWING NINA...
SHE'LL PROBABLY TAKE LONGER THAN THREE YEARS TO GRADUATE.

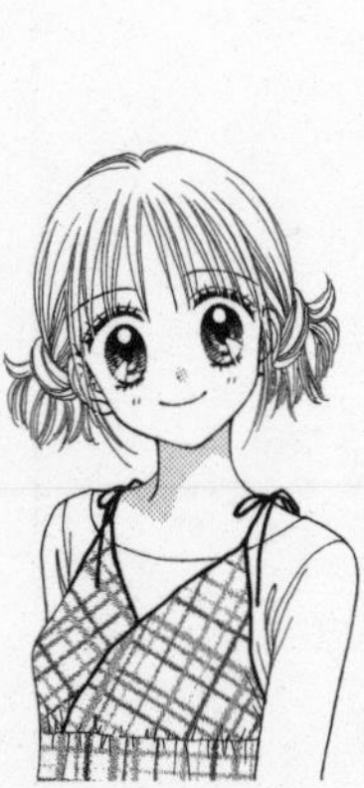

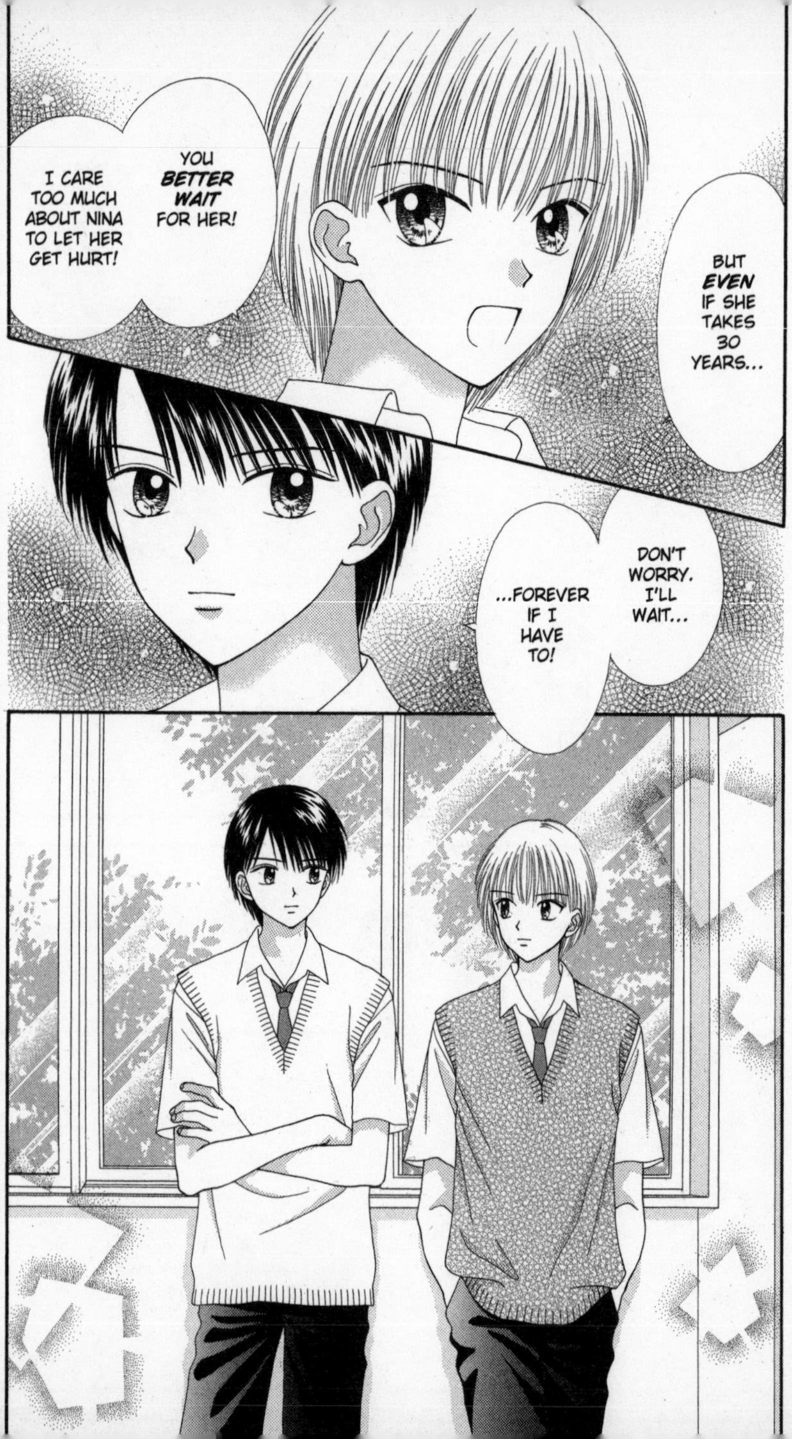
I CARE TOO MUCH ABOUT NINA TO LET HER GET HURT!
YOU BETTER WAIT FOR HER!
BUT EVEN IF SHE TAKES 30 YEARS...
DON'T WORRY. I'LL WAIT...
...FOREVER IF I HAVE TO!

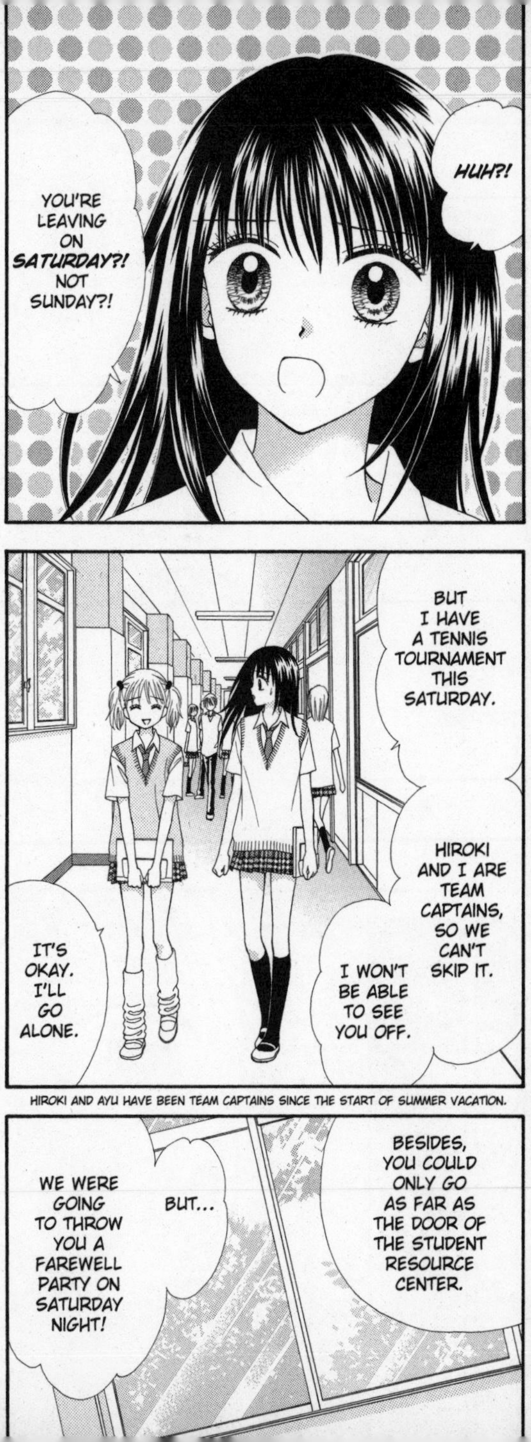
HUH?!
YOU'RE LEAVING ON SATURDAY?! NOT SUNDAY?!
BUT I HAVE A TENNIS TOURNAMENT THIS SATURDAY.
HIROKI AND I ARE TEAM CAPTAINS, SO WE CAN'T SKIP IT.
I WON'T BE ABLE TO SEE YOU OFF.
IT'S OKAY. I'LL GO ALONE.
HIROKI AND AYU HAVE BEEN TEAM CAPTAINS SINCE THE START OF SUMMER VACATION.
BESIDES, YOU COULD ONLY GO AS FAR AS THE DOOR OF THE STUDENT RESOURCE CENTER.
BUT...
WE WERE GOING TO THROW YOU A FAREWELL PARTY ON SATURDAY NIGHT!

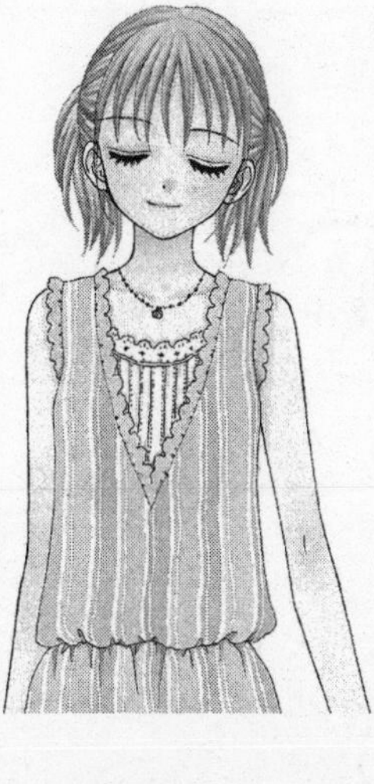

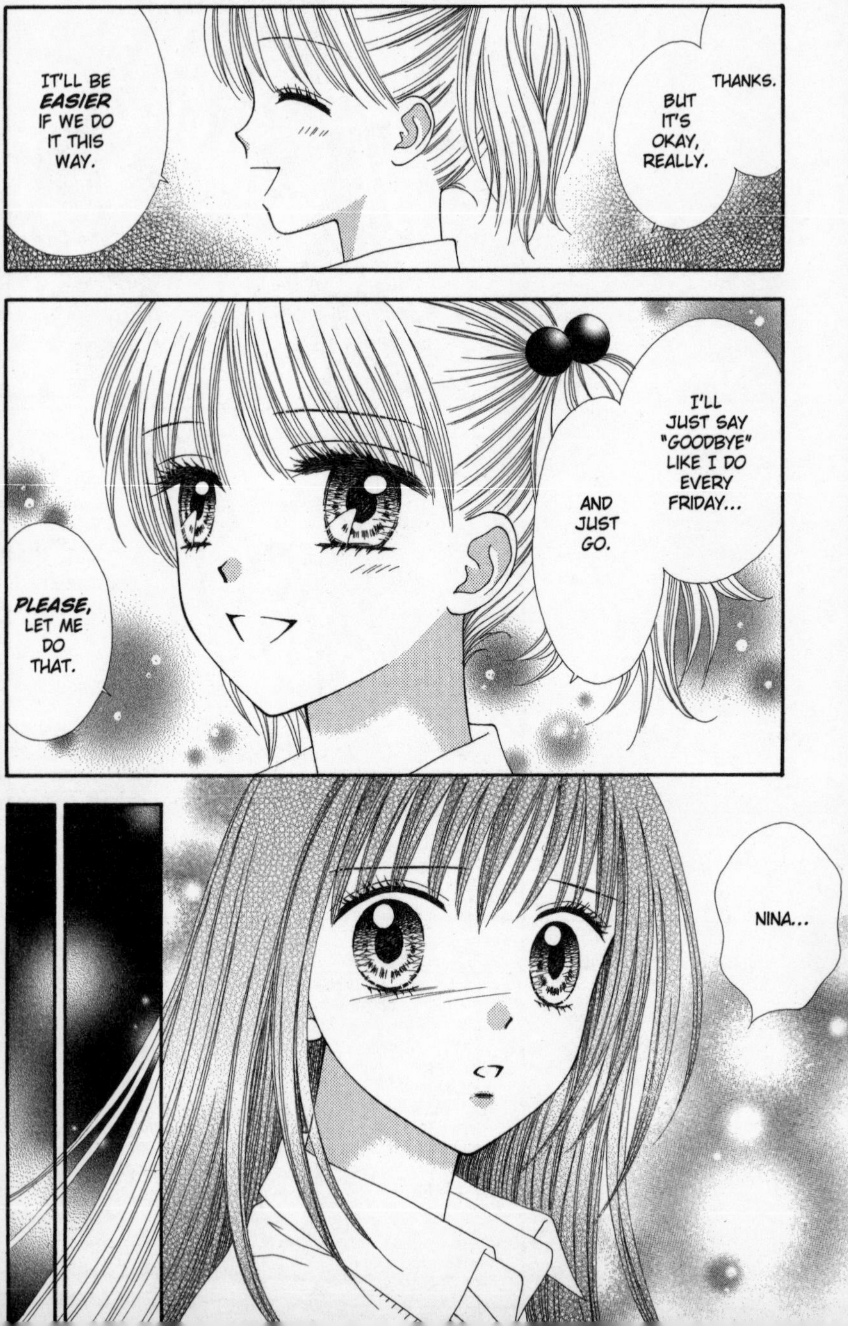
THANKS. BUT IT'S OKAY, REALLY.
IT'LL BE *EASIER* IF WE DO IT THIS WAY.
I'LL JUST SAY "GOODBYE" LIKE I DO EVERY FRIDAY... AND JUST GO.
PLEASE, LET ME DO THAT.
NINA...

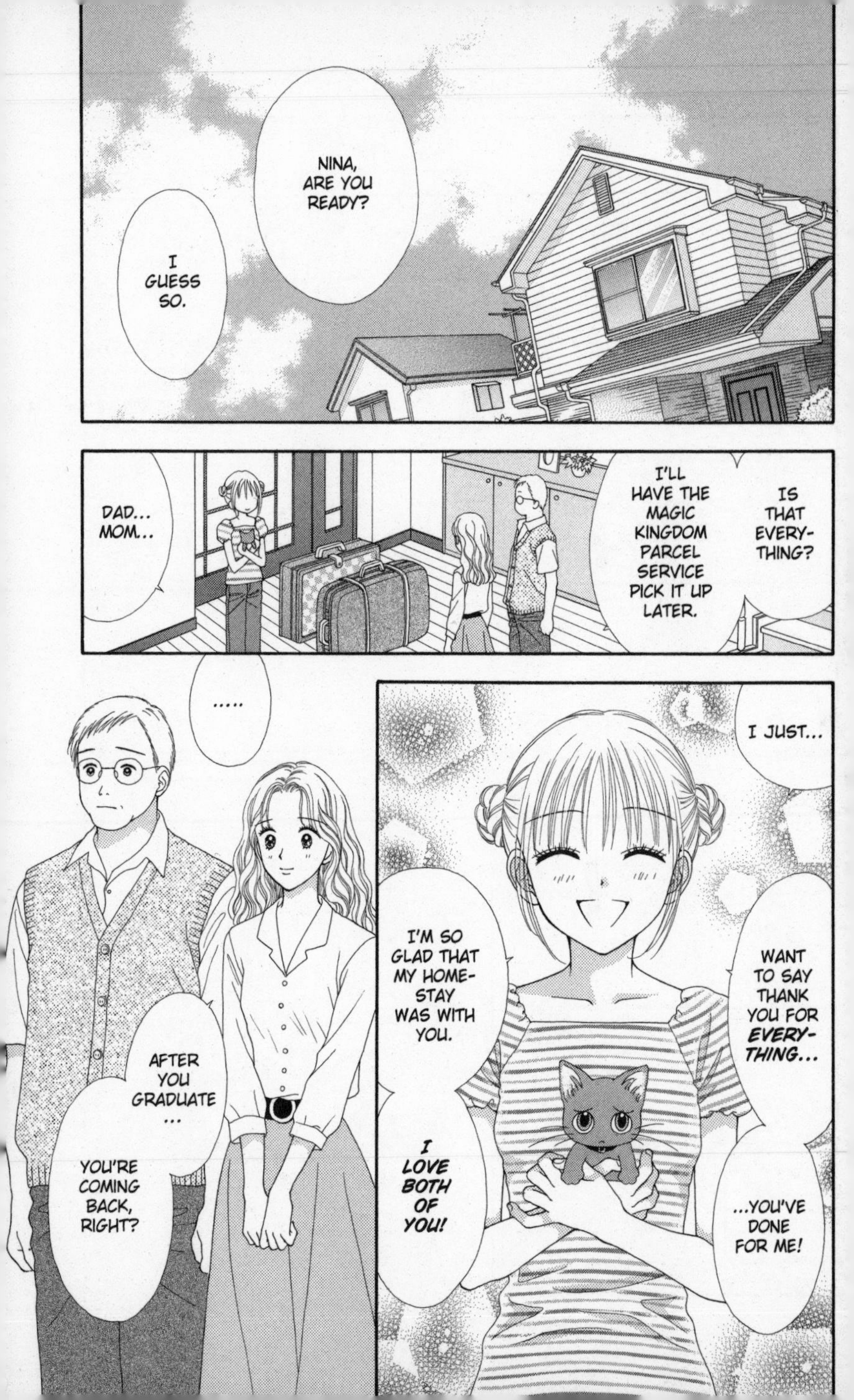
NINA, ARE YOU READY?
I GUESS SO.
IS THAT EVERY-THING?
I'LL HAVE THE MAGIC KINGDOM PARCEL SERVICE PICK IT UP LATER.
DAD... MOM...
I JUST...
WANT TO SAY THANK YOU FOR *EVERY-THING...*
...YOU'VE DONE FOR ME!
I'M SO GLAD THAT MY HOME-STAY WAS WITH YOU.
I LOVE BOTH OF YOU!
.....
AFTER YOU GRADUATE...
YOU'RE COMING BACK, RIGHT?

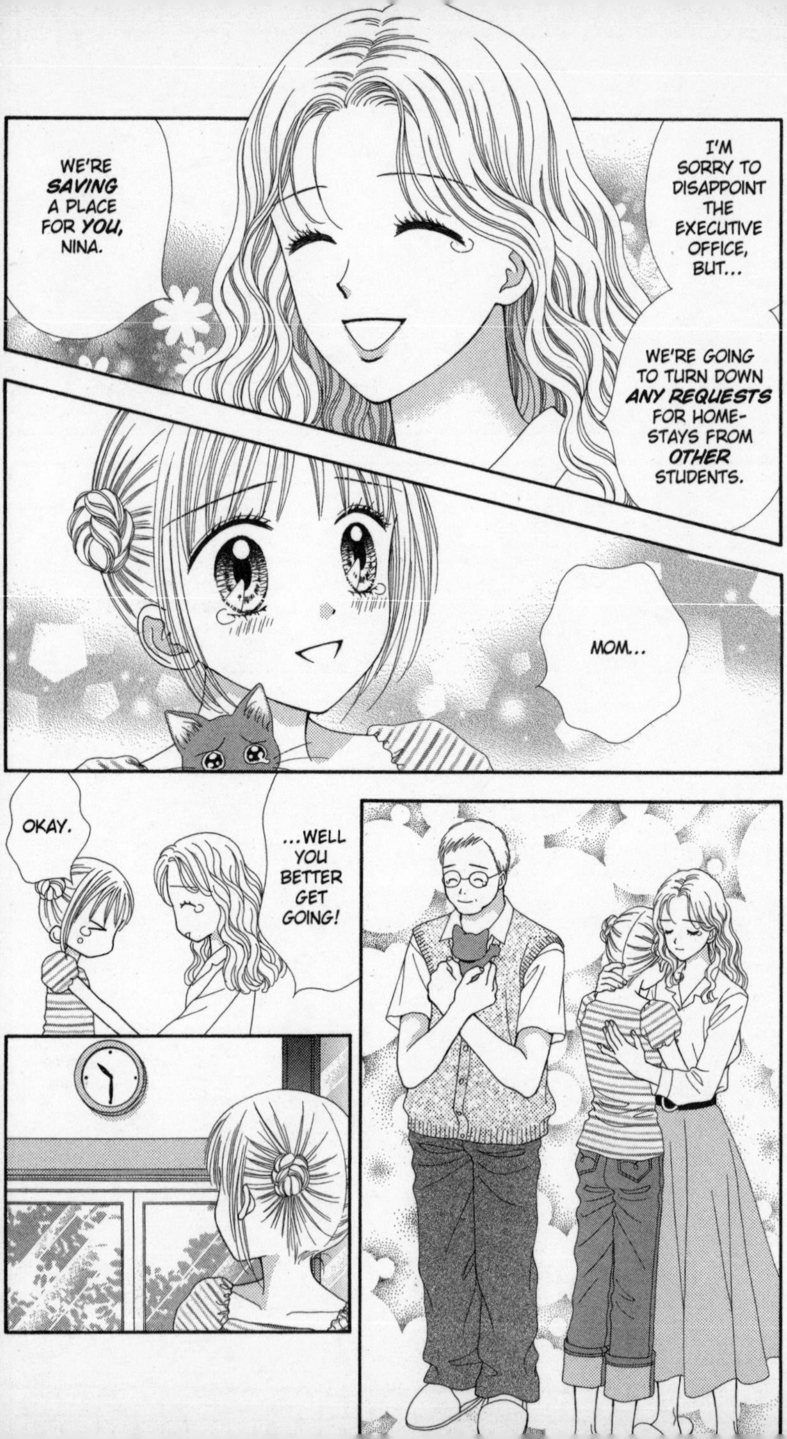
I'M SORRY TO DISAPPOINT THE EXECUTIVE OFFICE, BUT...
WE'RE GOING TO TURN DOWN ANY REQUESTS FOR HOME-STAYS FROM OTHER STUDENTS.
WE'RE SAVING A PLACE FOR YOU, NINA.
MOM...
...WELL YOU BETTER GET GOING!
OKAY.

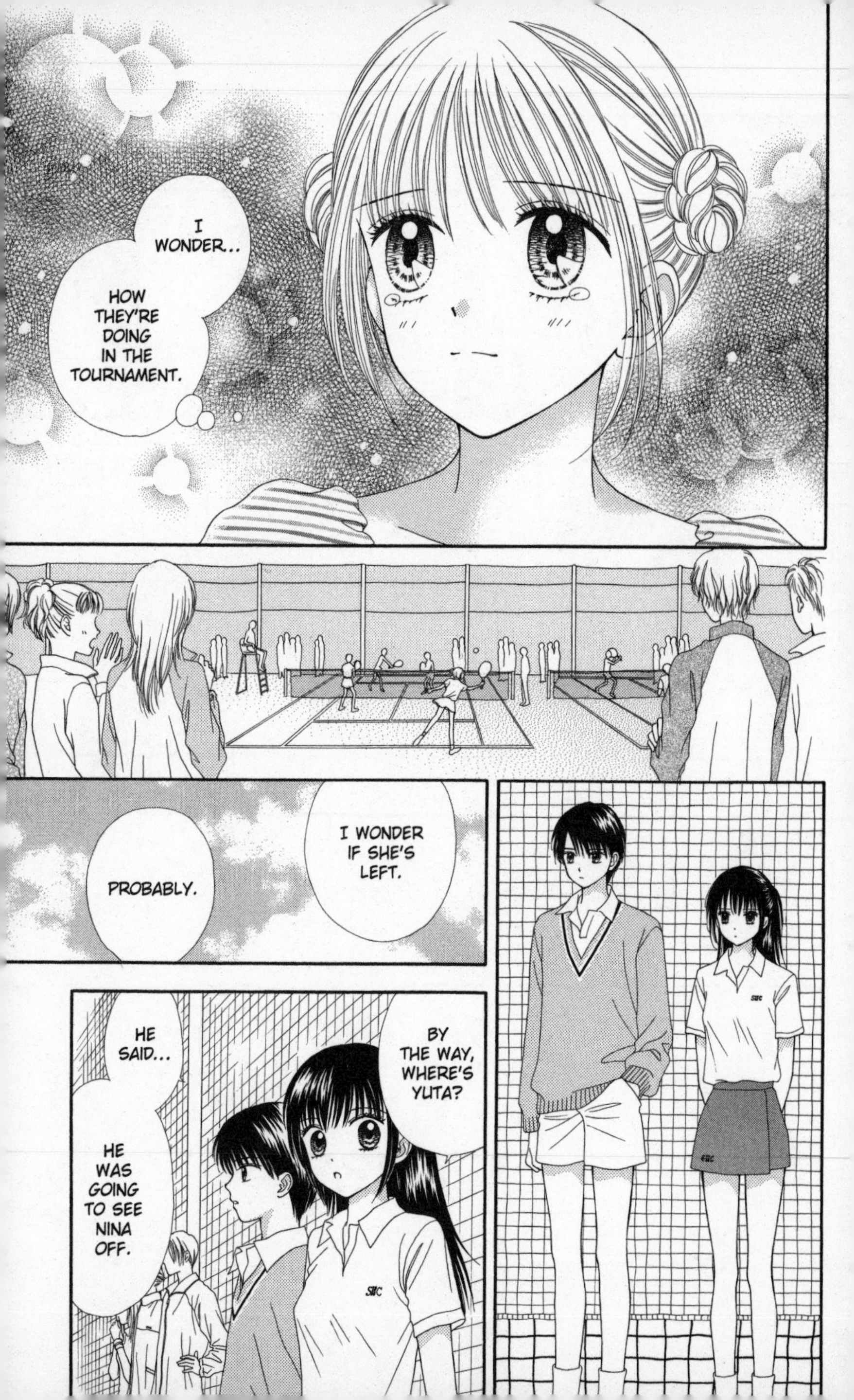
I WONDER...
HOW THEY'RE DOING IN THE TOURNAMENT.
I WONDER IF SHE'S LEFT.
PROBABLY.
BY THE WAY, WHERE'S YUTA?
HE SAID...
HE WAS GOING TO SEE NINA OFF.

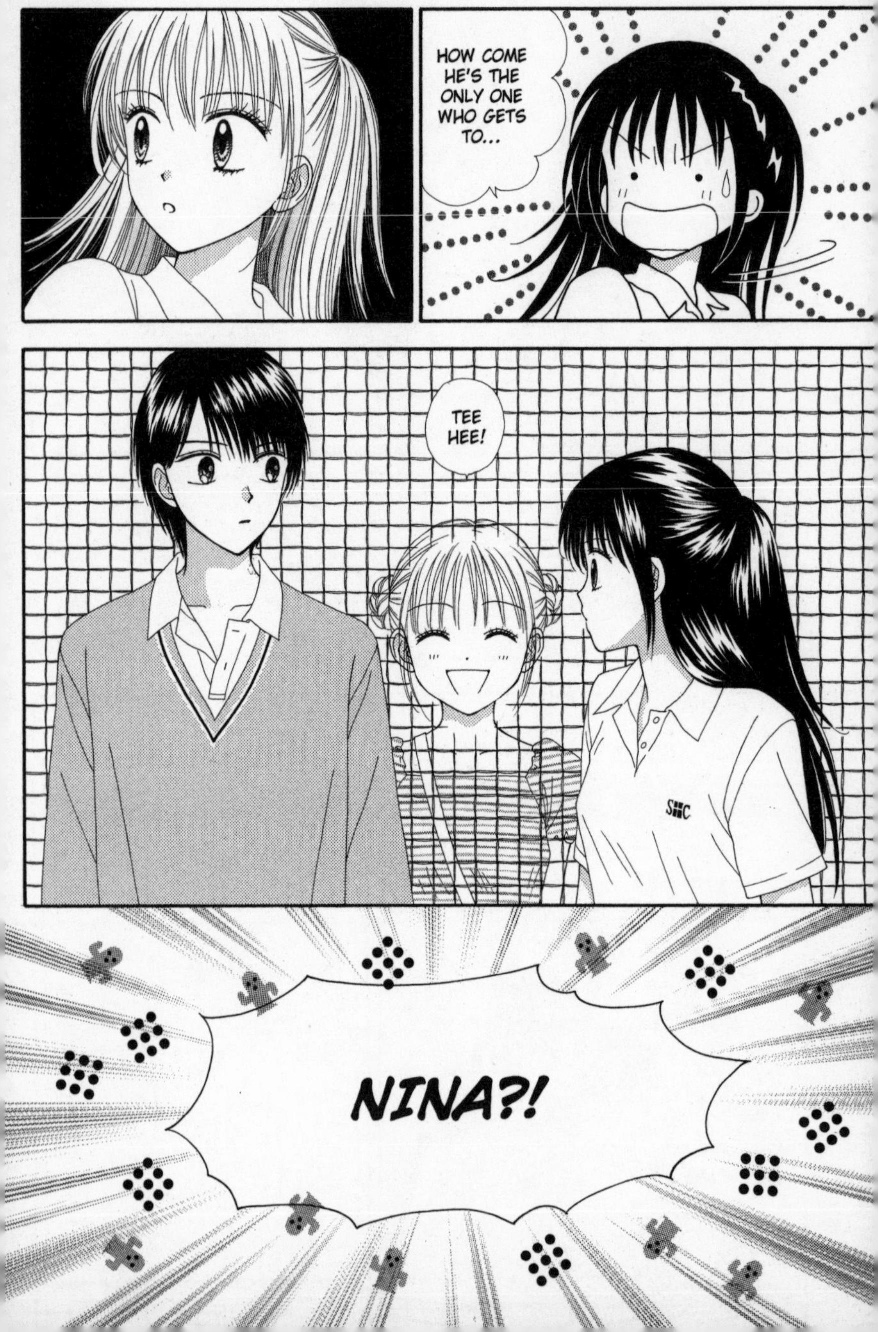
HOW COME HE'S THE ONLY ONE WHO GETS TO...
TEE HEE!
NINA?!

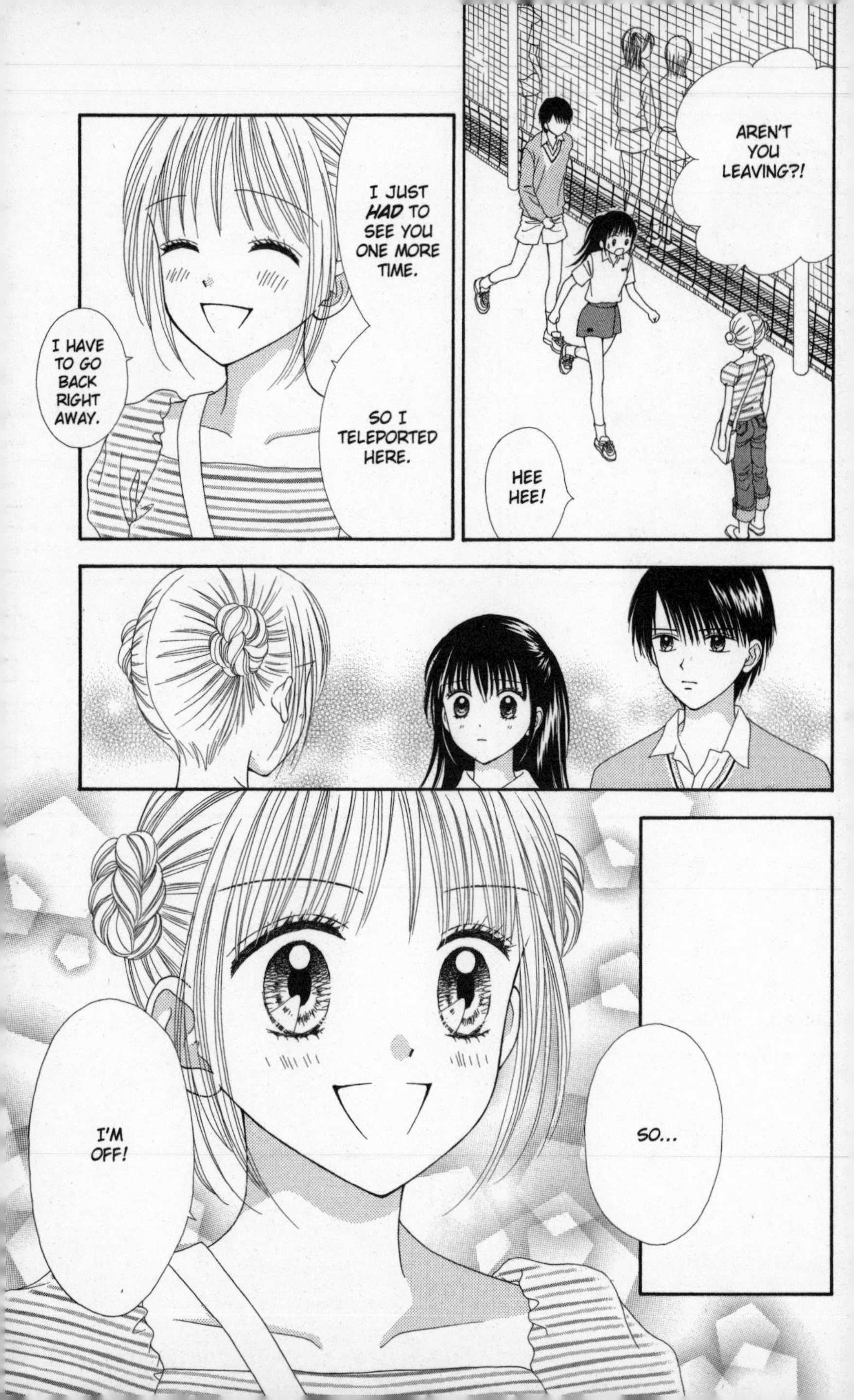
AREN'T YOU LEAVING?!
HEE HEE!
I JUST *HAD* TO SEE YOU ONE MORE TIME.
SO I TELEPORTED HERE.
I HAVE TO GO BACK RIGHT AWAY.
SO...
I'M OFF!

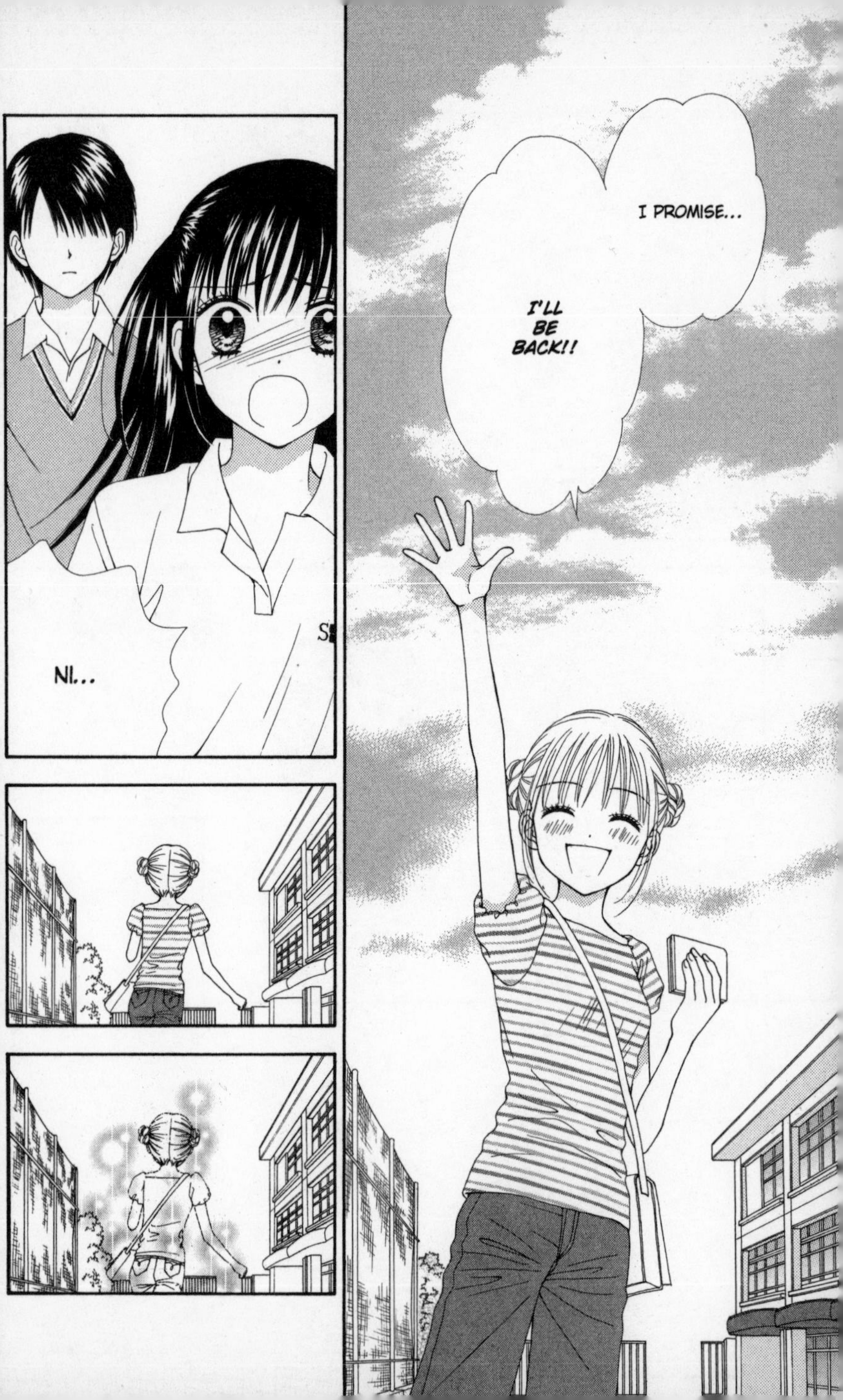
I PROMISE...
I'LL BE BACK!!
NI...

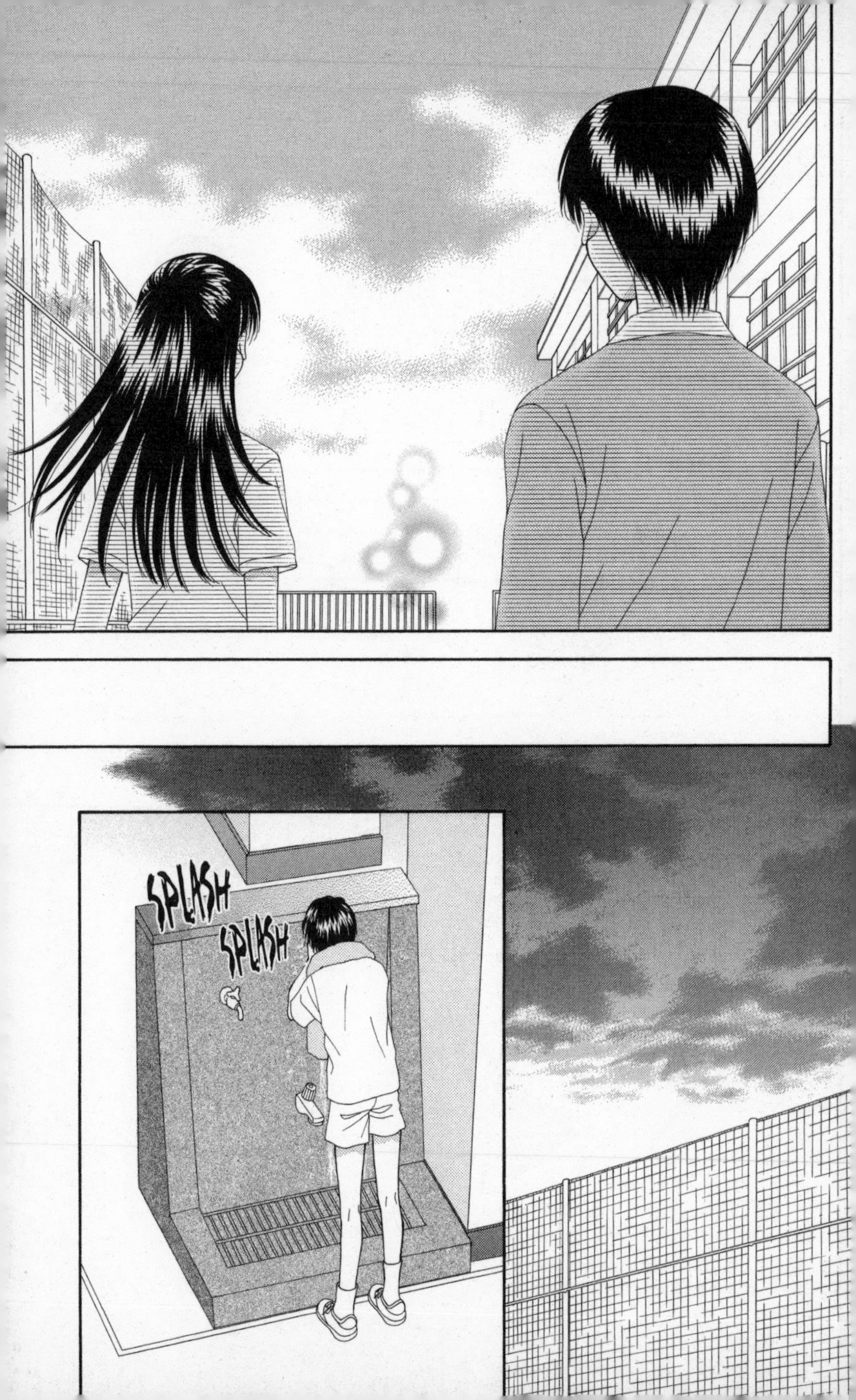
SPLASH
SPLASH

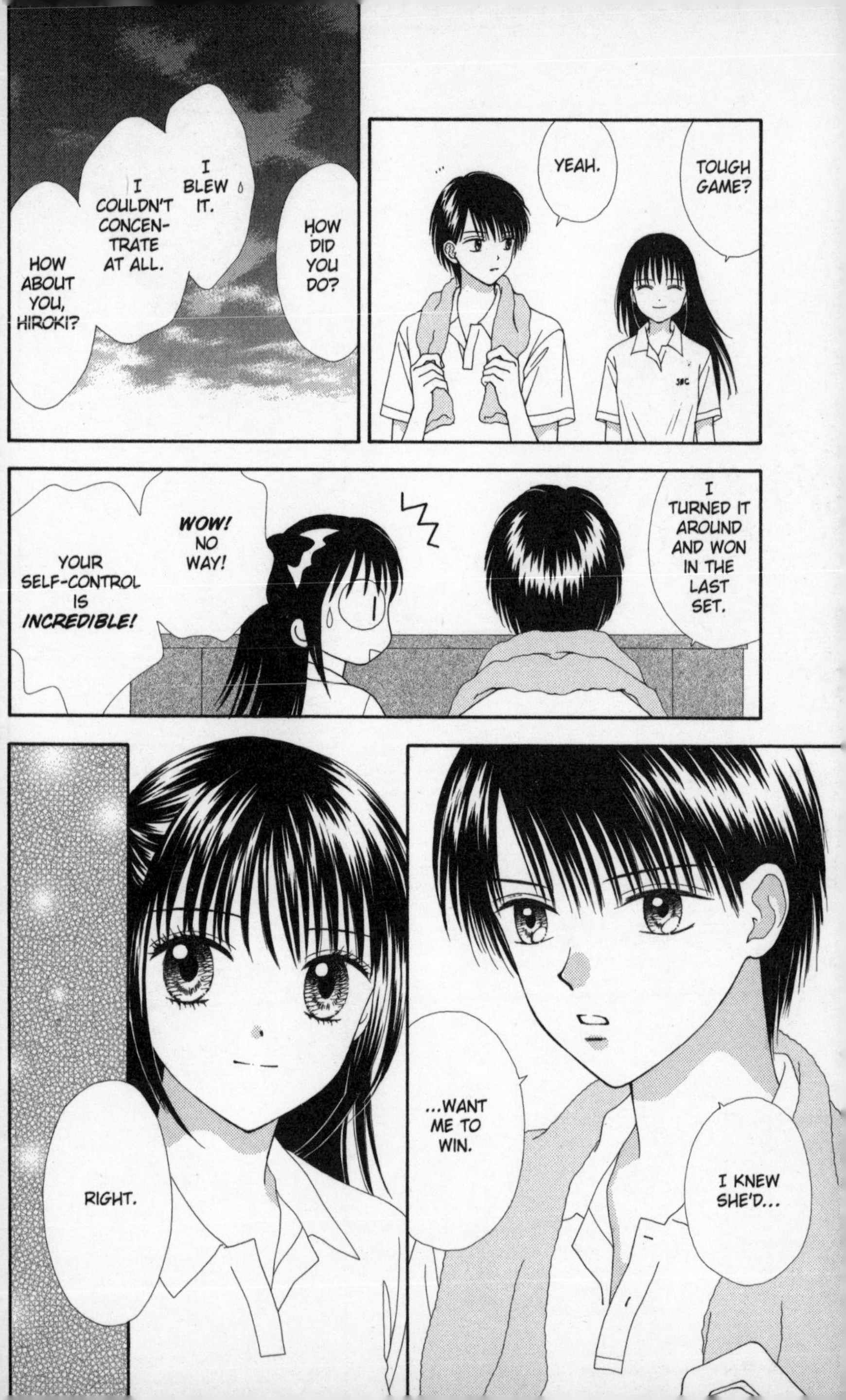
TOUGH GAME?
YEAH.
...
HOW DID YOU DO?
I BLEW IT.
I COULDN'T CONCENTRATE AT ALL.
HOW ABOUT YOU, HIROKI?
I TURNED IT AROUND AND WON IN THE LAST SET.
WOW! NO WAY!
YOUR SELF-CONTROL IS *INCREDIBLE!*
I KNEW SHE'D...
...WANT ME TO WIN.
RIGHT.

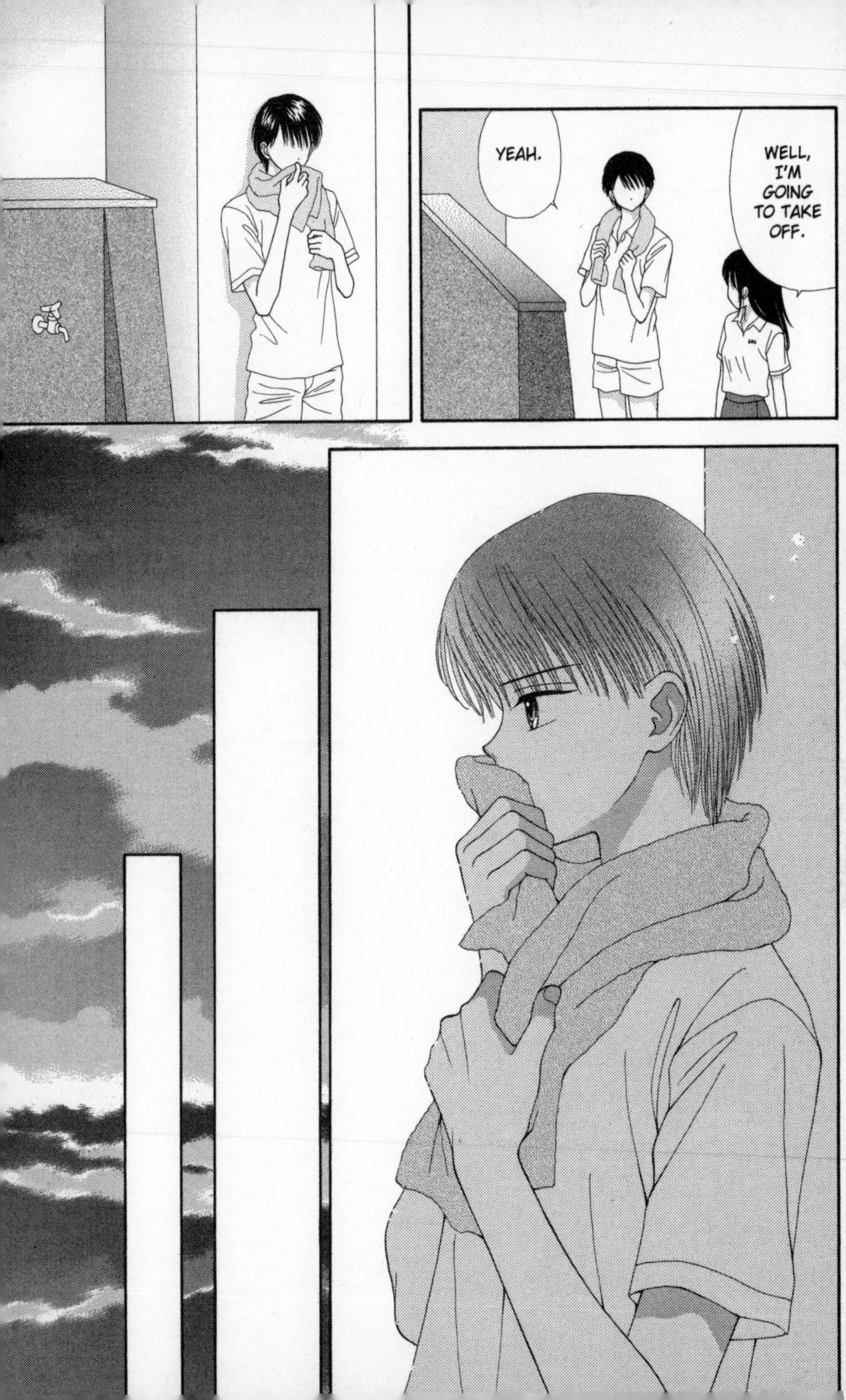
WELL, I'M GOING TO TAKE OFF.
YEAH.

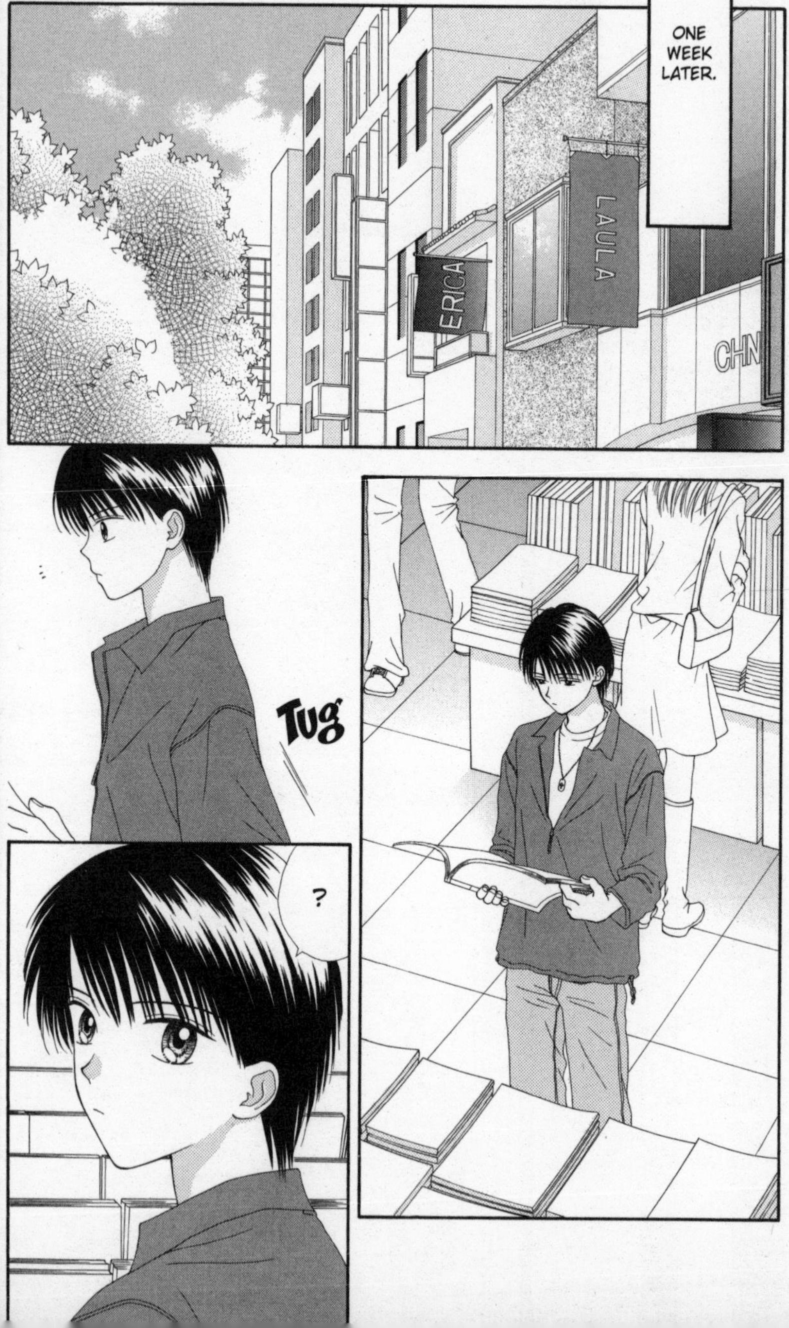
ONE WEEK LATER.
ERICA
LAULA
CHN
...
Tug
?

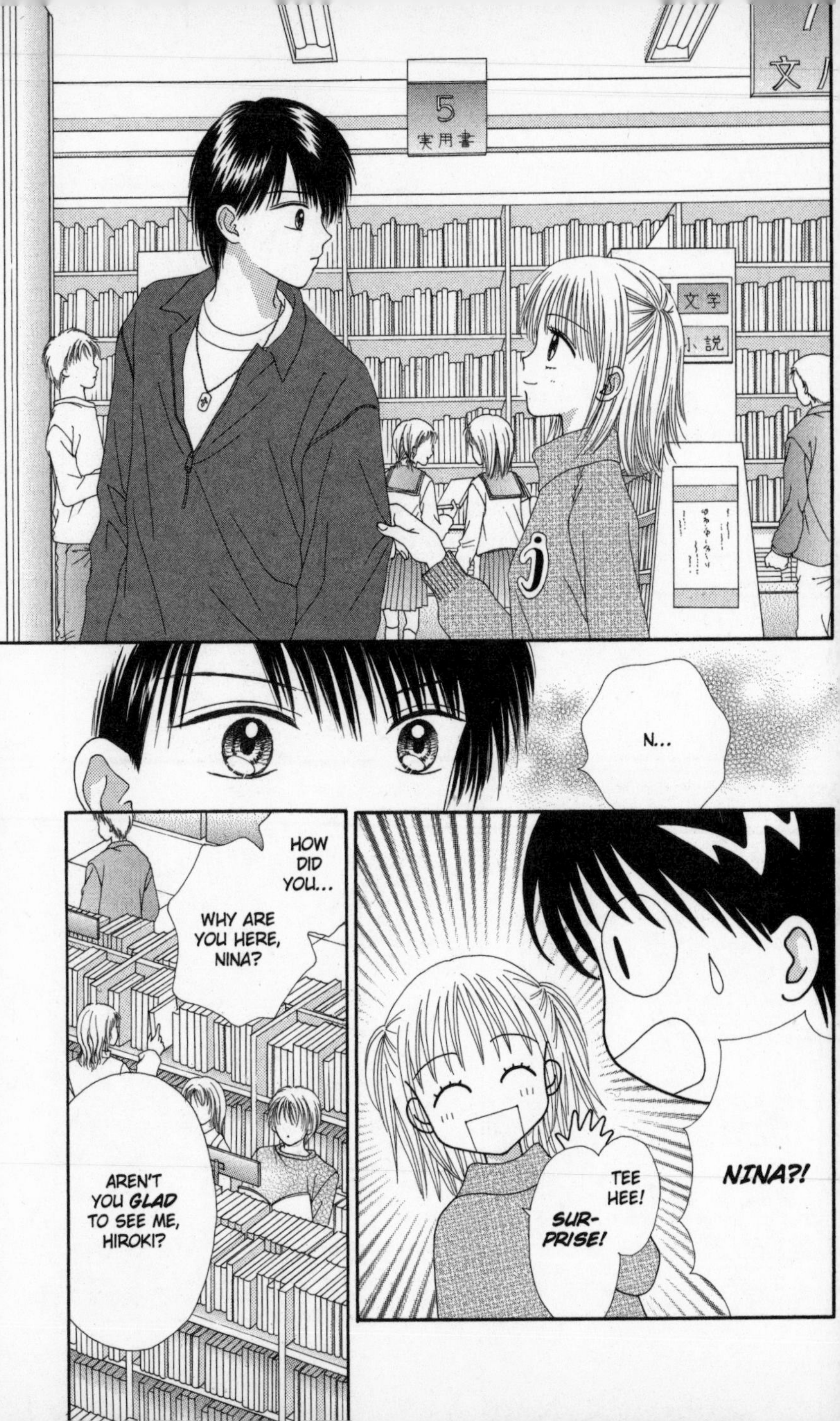
5
実用書
文学
小説
N...
NINA?!
TEE HEE!
SURPRISE!
HOW DID YOU...
WHY ARE YOU HERE, NINA?
AREN'T YOU GLAD TO SEE ME, HIROKI?

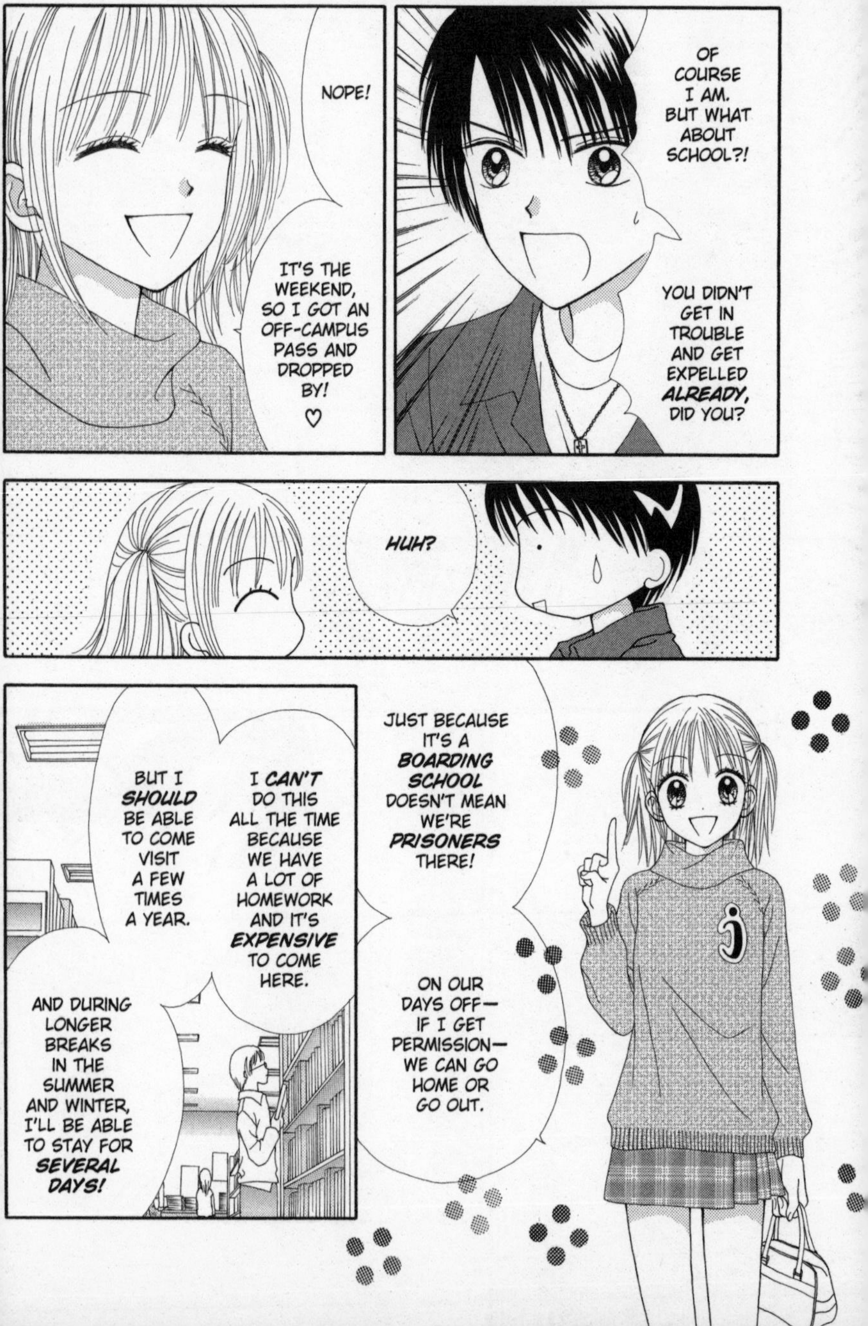
OF COURSE I AM. BUT WHAT ABOUT SCHOOL?!
YOU DIDN'T GET IN TROUBLE AND GET EXPELLED *ALREADY*, DID YOU?
NOPE!
IT'S THE WEEKEND, SO I GOT AN OFF-CAMPUS PASS AND DROPPED BY! ♡
HUH?
JUST BECAUSE IT'S A *BOARDING SCHOOL* DOESN'T MEAN WE'RE *PRISONERS* THERE!
ON OUR DAYS OFF— IF I GET PERMISSION— WE CAN GO HOME OR GO OUT.
I *CAN'T* DO THIS ALL THE TIME BECAUSE WE HAVE A LOT OF HOMEWORK AND IT'S *EXPENSIVE* TO COME HERE.
BUT I *SHOULD* BE ABLE TO COME VISIT A FEW TIMES A YEAR.
AND DURING LONGER BREAKS IN THE SUMMER AND WINTER, I'LL BE ABLE TO STAY FOR *SEVERAL DAYS!*

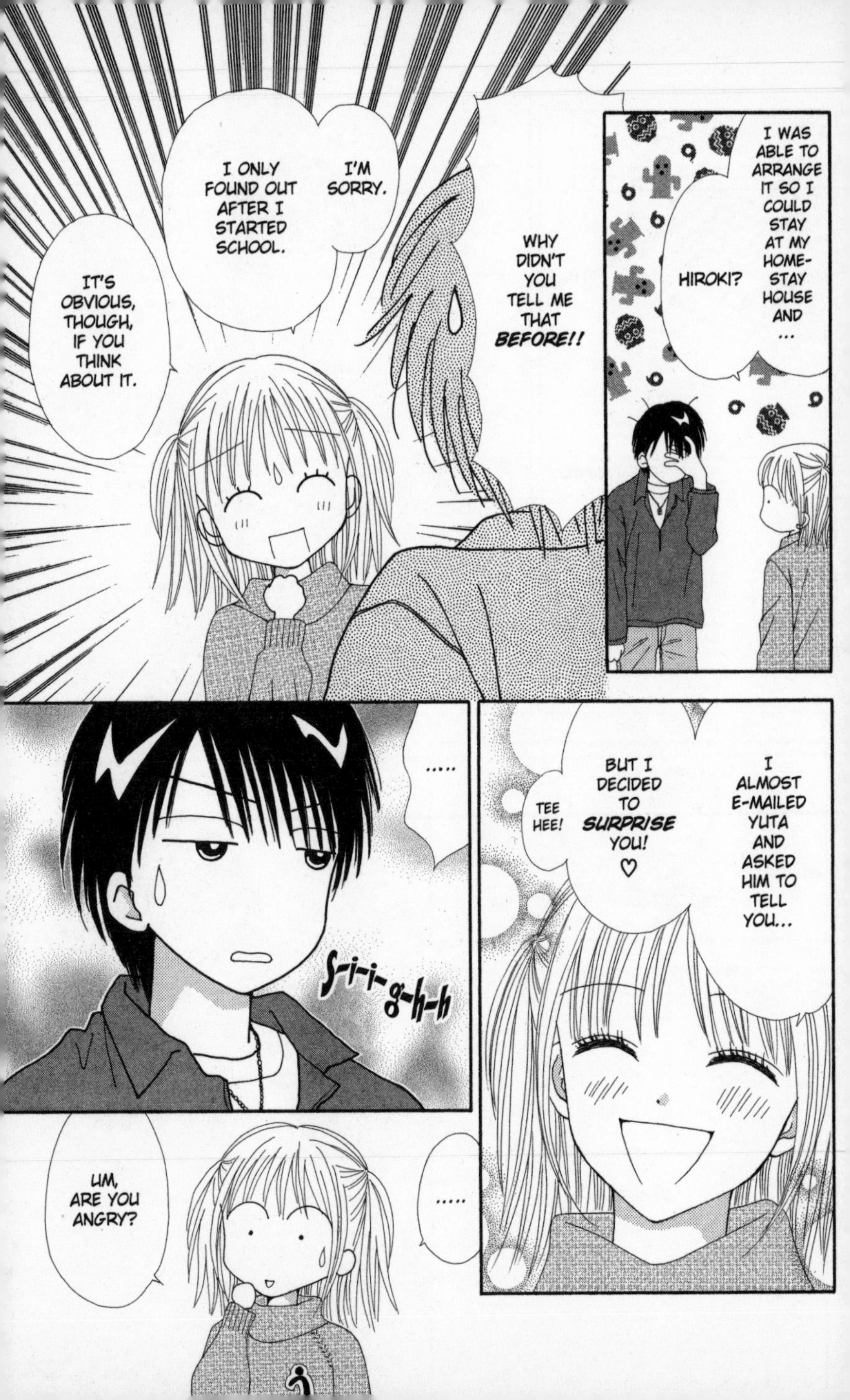
I WAS ABLE TO ARRANGE IT SO I COULD STAY AT MY HOME-STAY HOUSE AND ...
HIROKI?
WHY DIDN'T YOU TELL ME THAT BEFORE!!
I'M SORRY.
I ONLY FOUND OUT AFTER I STARTED SCHOOL.
IT'S OBVIOUS, THOUGH, IF YOU THINK ABOUT IT.
I ALMOST E-MAILED YUTA AND ASKED HIM TO TELL YOU...
BUT I DECIDED TO SURPRISE YOU! ♡
TEE HEE!
.....
S-I-I-G-H-H
.....
UM, ARE YOU ANGRY?

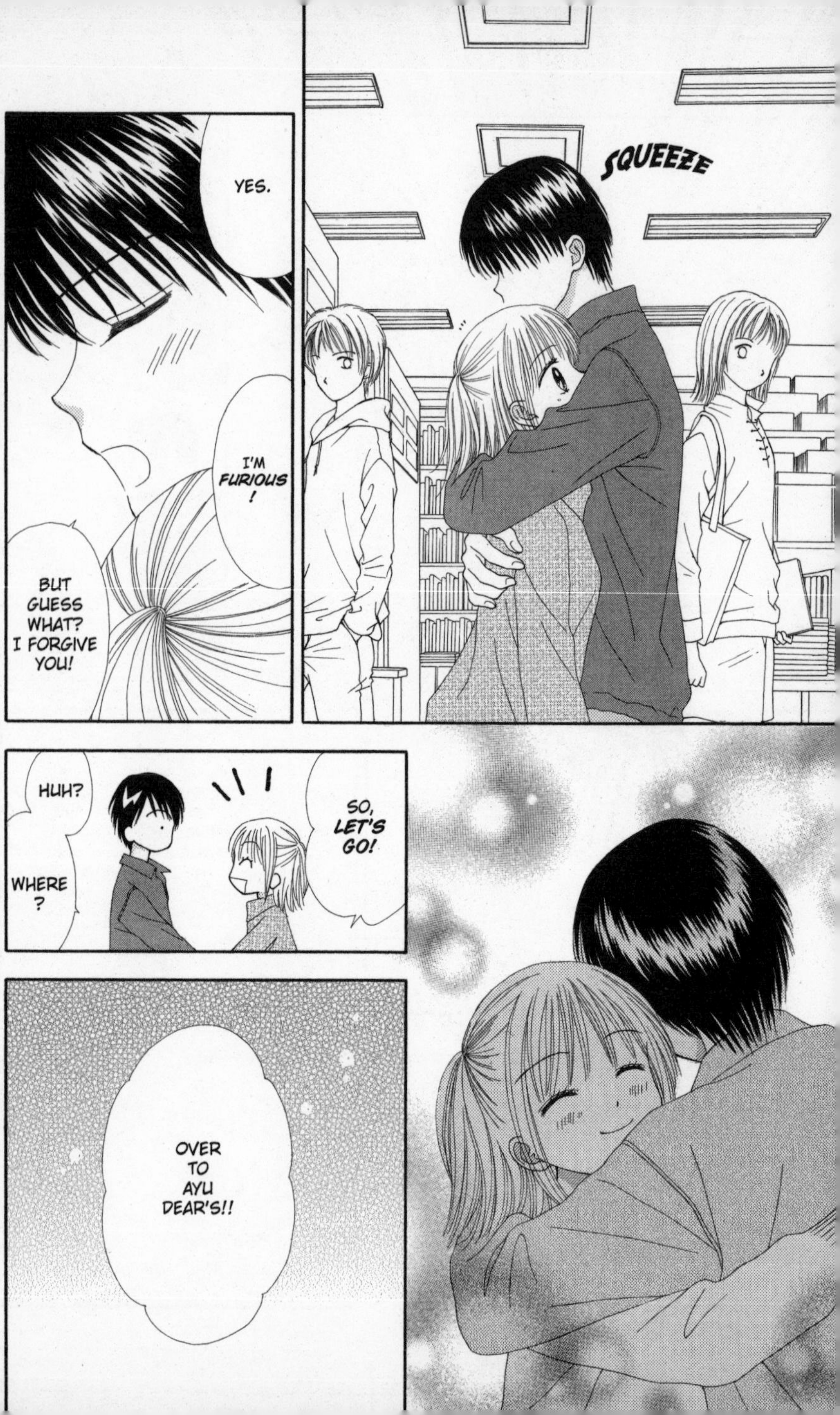
SQUEEZE
YES.
I'M FURIOUS!
BUT GUESS WHAT? I FORGIVE YOU!
SO, LET'S GO!
HUH?
WHERE?
OVER TO AYU DEAR'S!!

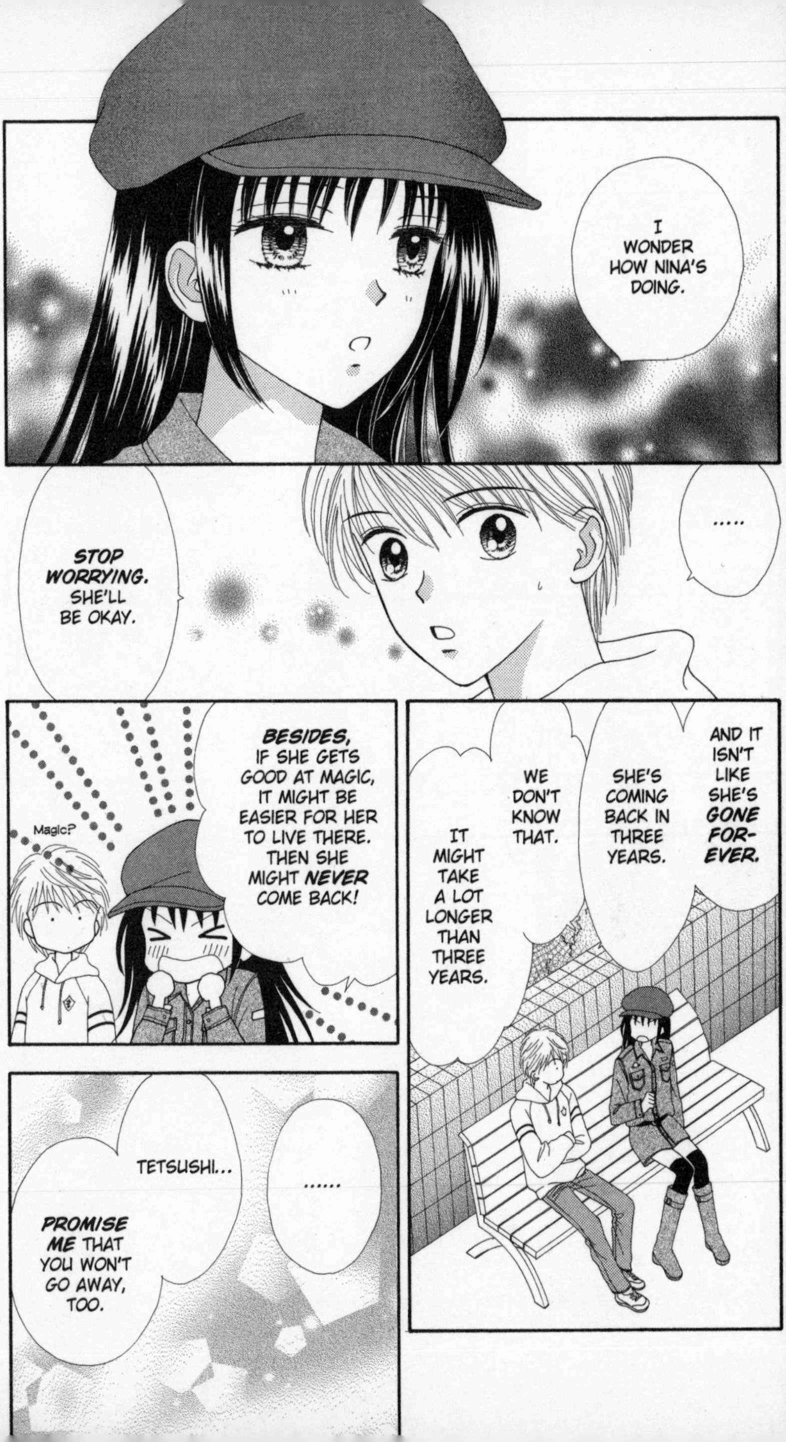
I WONDER HOW NINA'S DOING.
.....
STOP WORRYING. SHE'LL BE OKAY.
AND IT ISN'T LIKE SHE'S GONE FOREVER.
SHE'S COMING BACK IN THREE YEARS.
WE DON'T KNOW THAT.
IT MIGHT TAKE A LOT LONGER THAN THREE YEARS.
BESIDES, IF SHE GETS GOOD AT MAGIC, IT MIGHT BE EASIER FOR HER TO LIVE THERE. THEN SHE MIGHT NEVER COME BACK!
Magic?
......
TETSUSHI...
PROMISE ME THAT YOU WON'T GO AWAY, TOO.

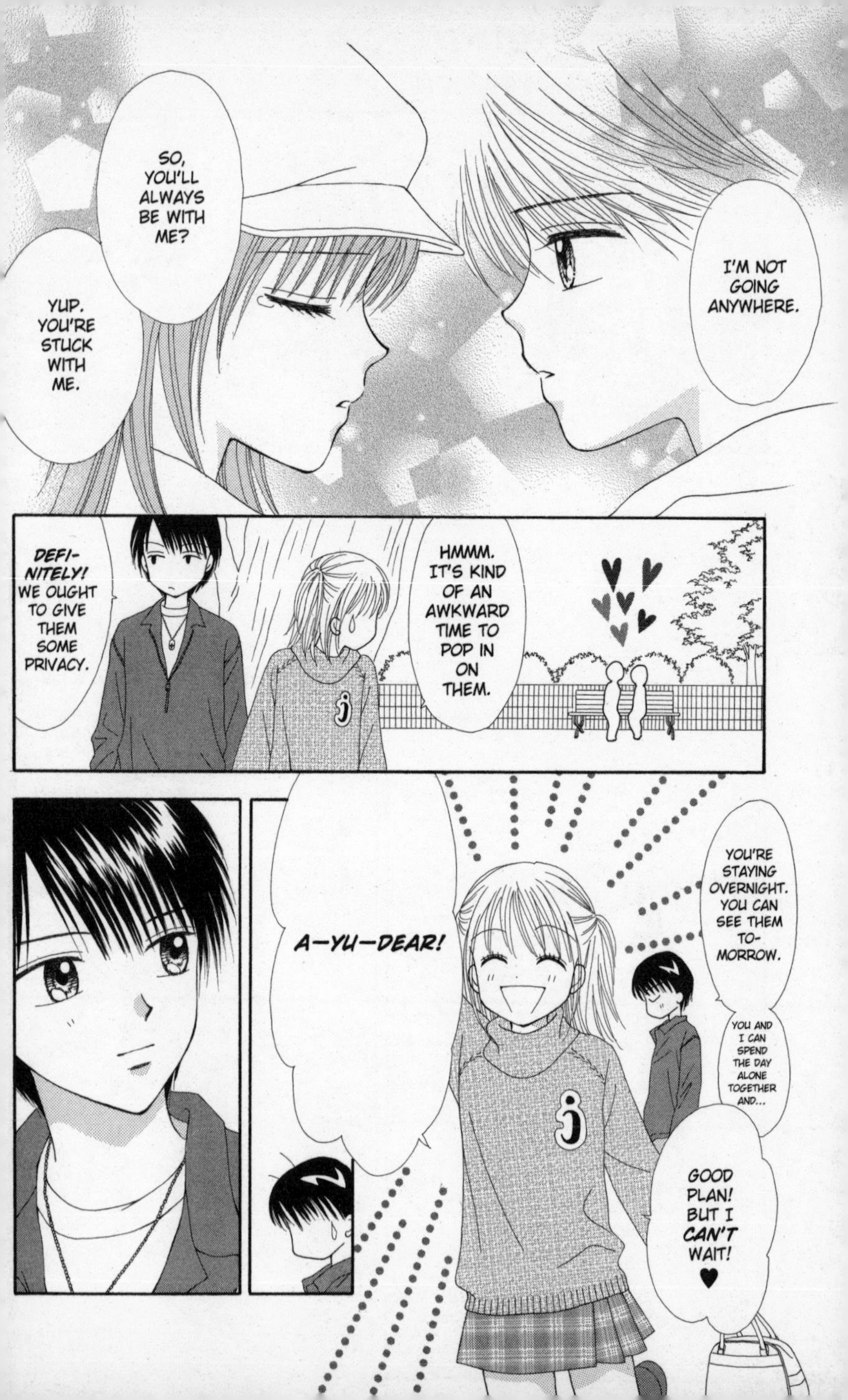
I'M NOT GOING ANYWHERE.
SO, YOU'LL ALWAYS BE WITH ME?
YUP. YOU'RE STUCK WITH ME.
HMMM. IT'S KIND OF AN AWKWARD TIME TO POP IN ON THEM.
DEFI-NITELY! WE OUGHT TO GIVE THEM SOME PRIVACY.
YOU'RE STAYING OVERNIGHT. YOU CAN SEE THEM TO-MORROW.
YOU AND I CAN SPEND THE DAY ALONE TOGETHER AND...
GOOD PLAN! BUT I CAN'T WAIT! ♥
A-YU-DEAR!

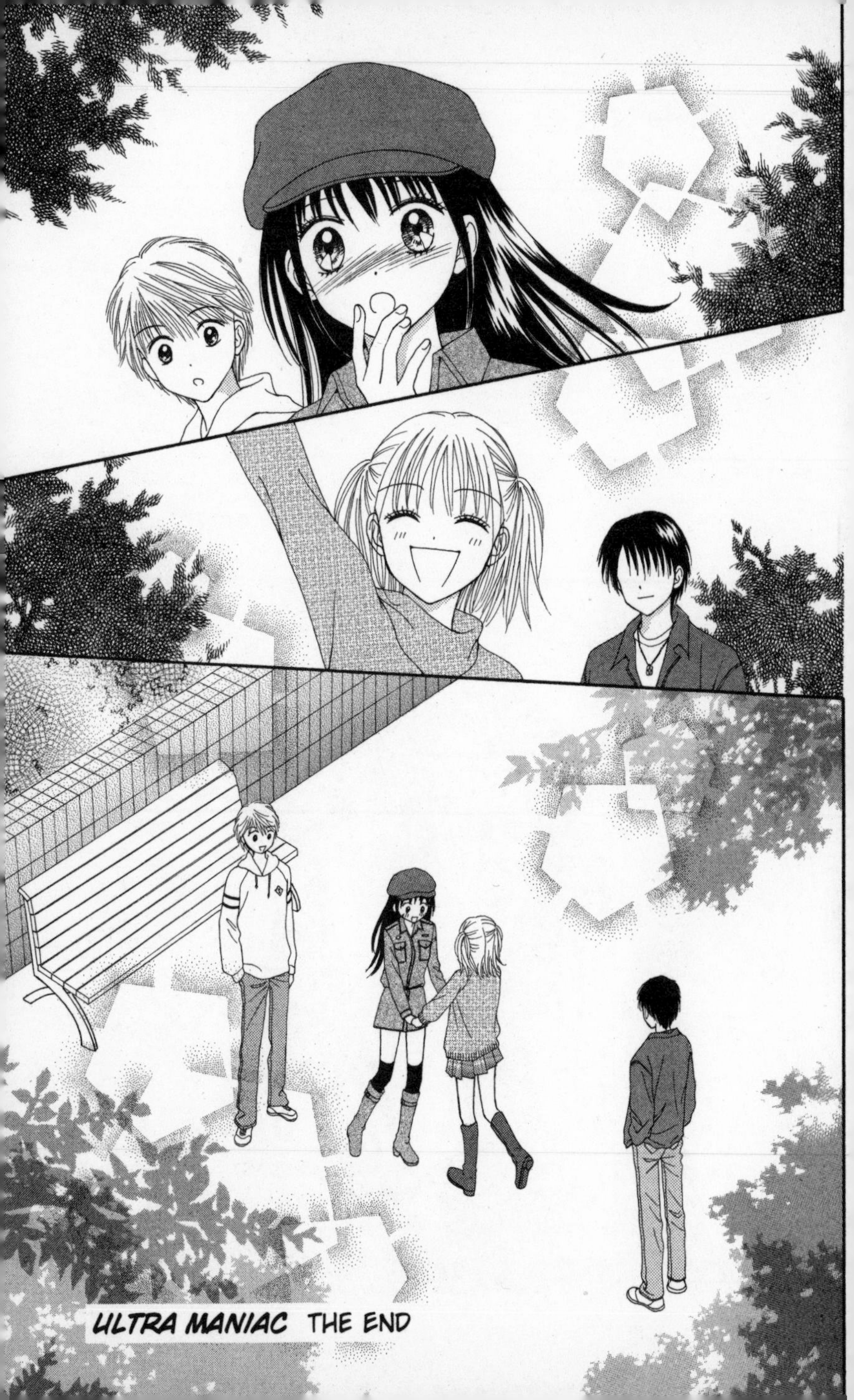
ULTRA MANIAC THE END

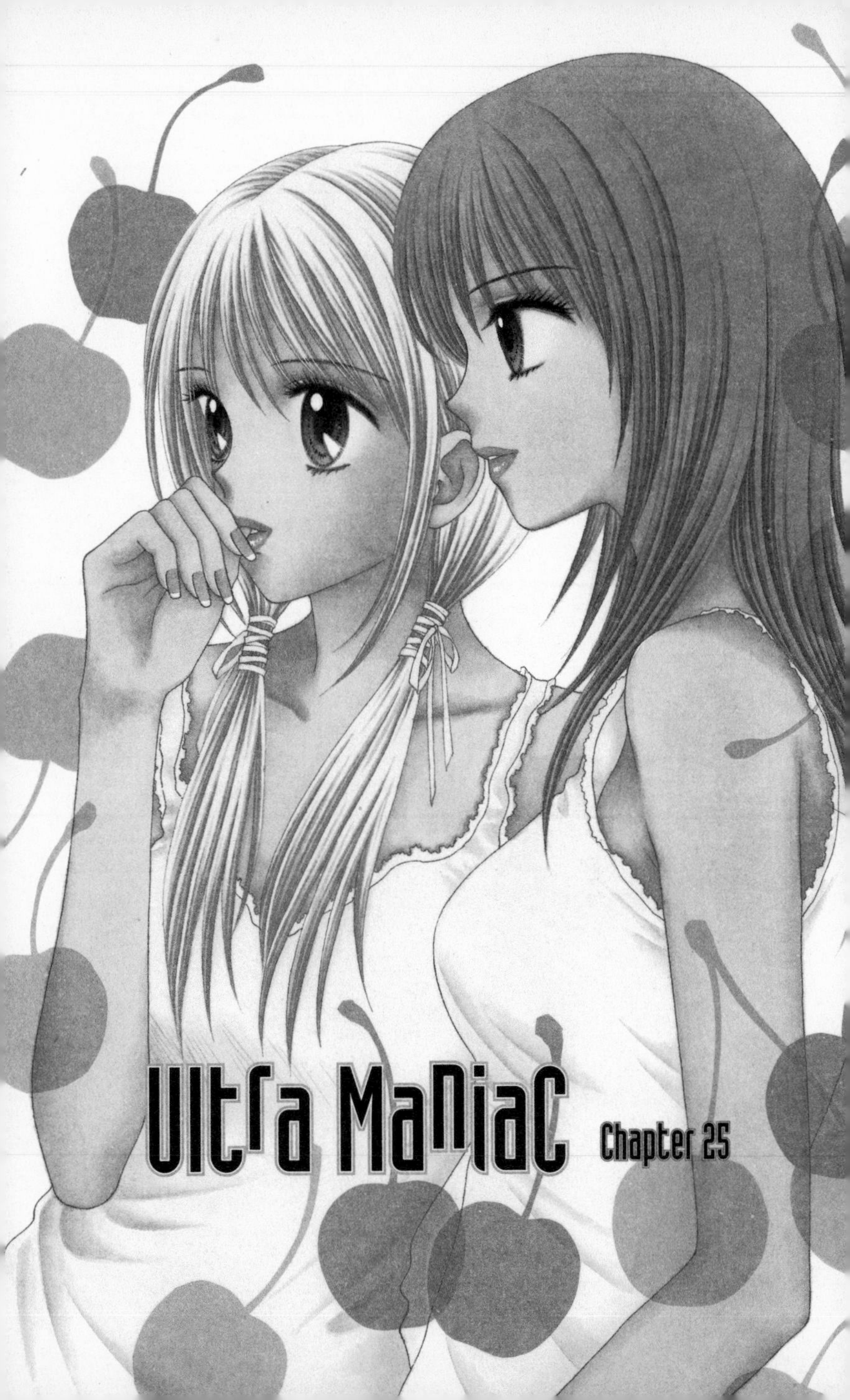
Ultra Maniac
Chapter 25

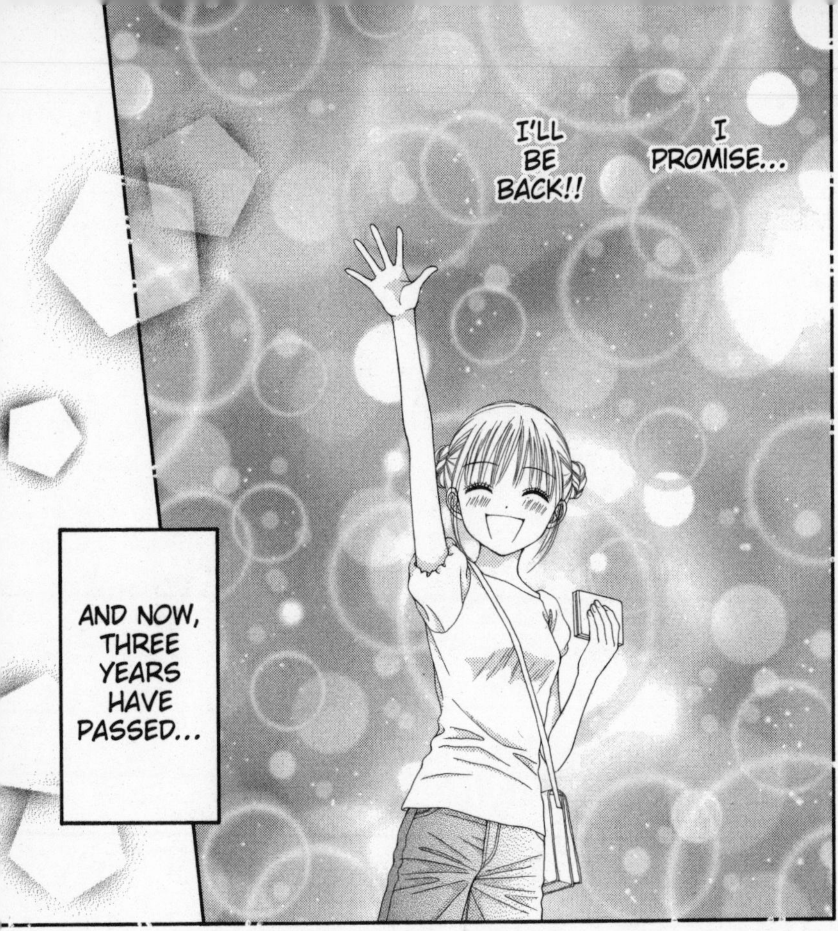
I PROMISE...
I'LL BE BACK!!
AND NOW, THREE YEARS HAVE PASSED...
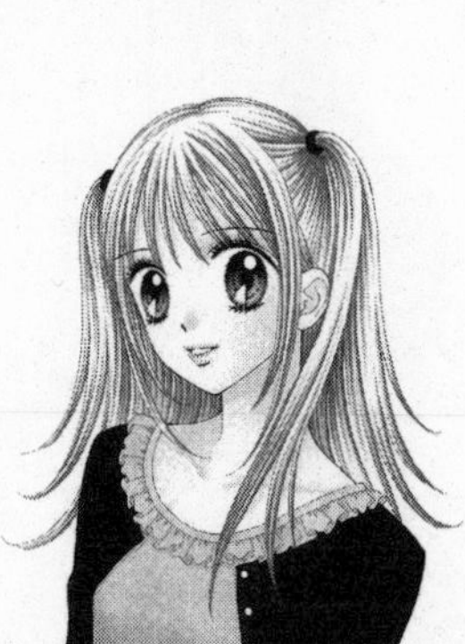

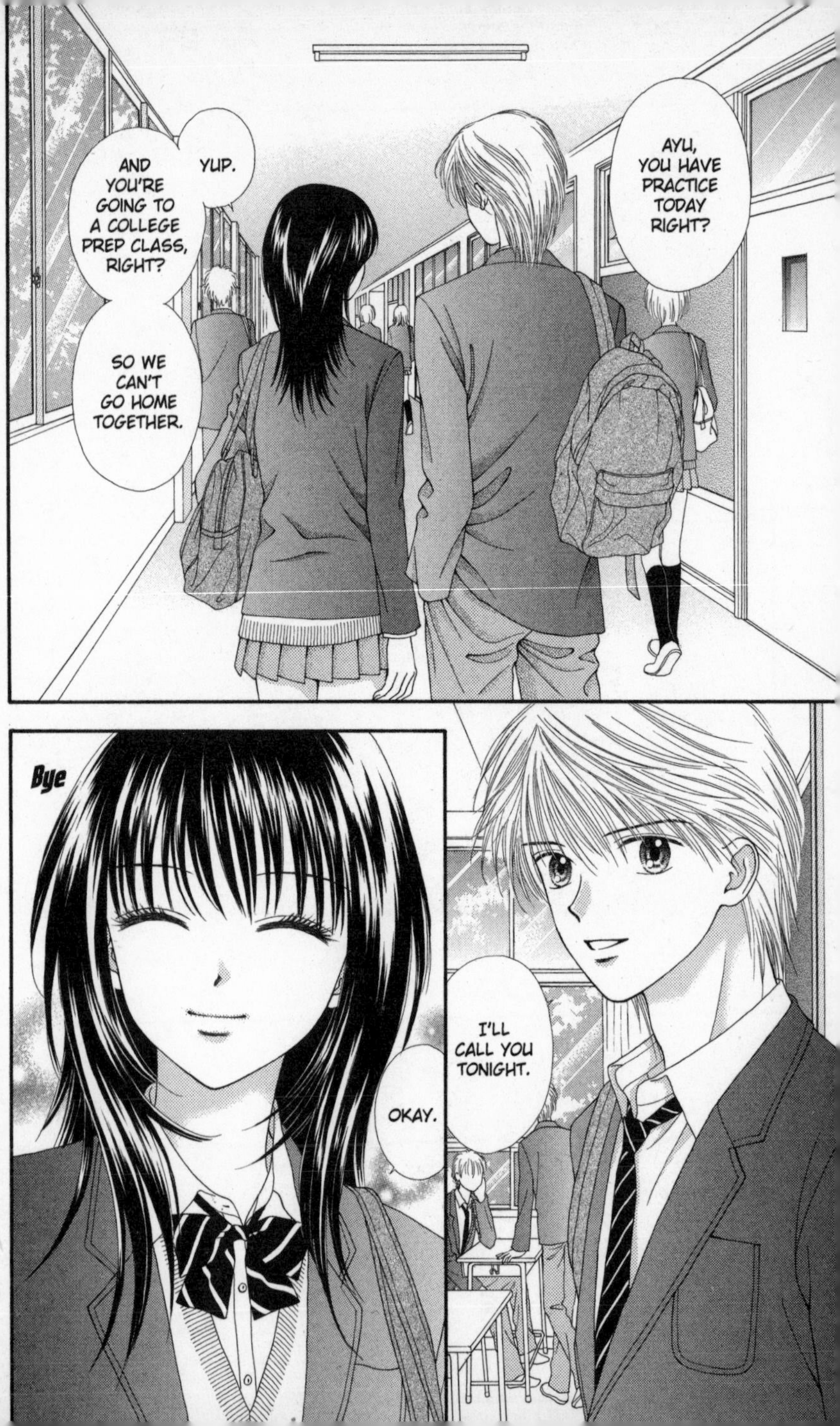
AYU, YOU HAVE PRACTICE TODAY RIGHT?
YUP.
AND YOU'RE GOING TO A COLLEGE PREP CLASS, RIGHT?
SO WE CAN'T GO HOME TOGETHER.
I'LL CALL YOU TONIGHT.
OKAY.
Bye

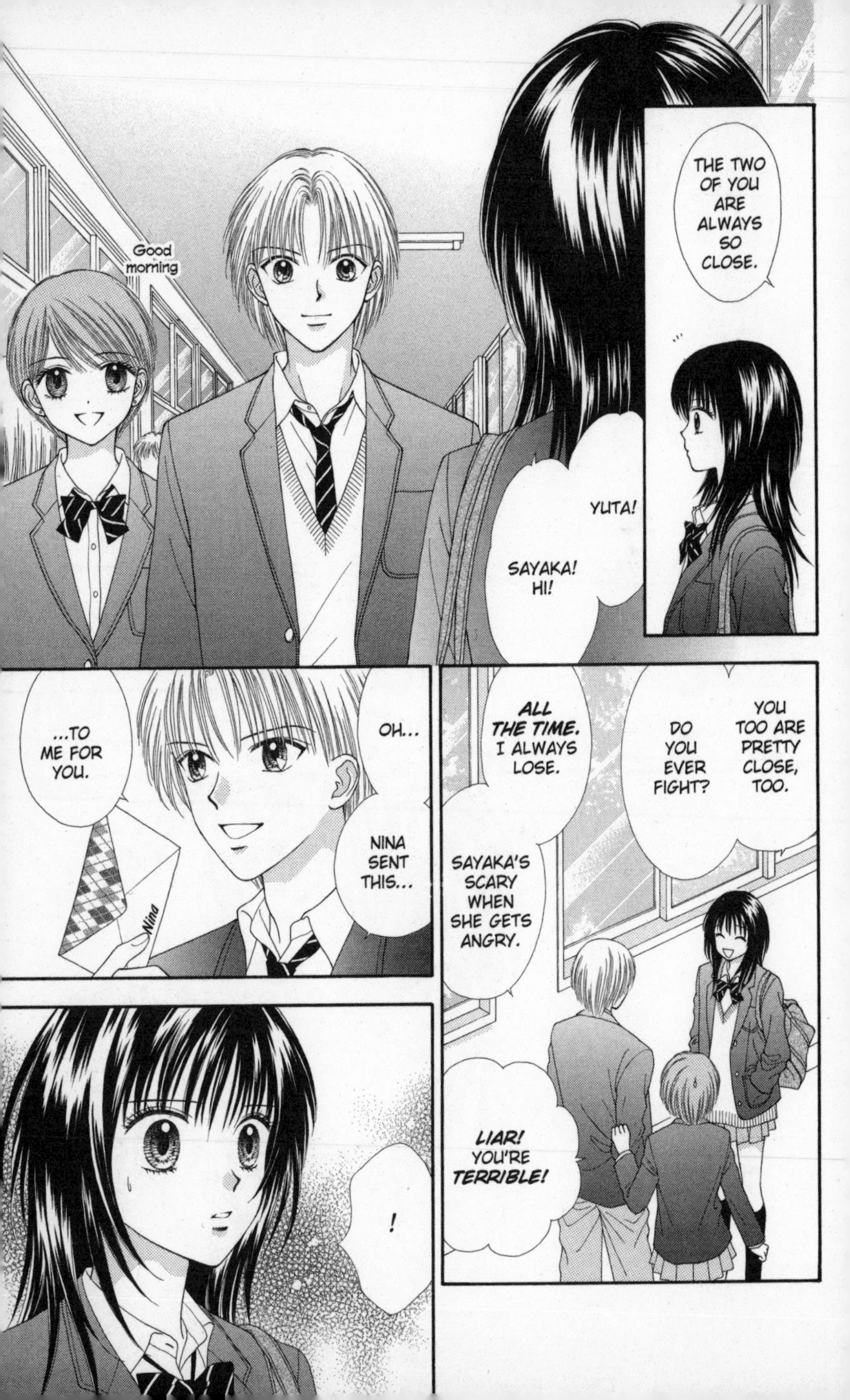
YUTA!
SAYAKA! HI!
Good morning
THE TWO OF YOU ARE ALWAYS SO CLOSE.
...
YOU TOO ARE PRETTY CLOSE, TOO.
DO YOU EVER FIGHT?
ALL THE TIME. I ALWAYS LOSE.
SAYAKA'S SCARY WHEN SHE GETS ANGRY.
LIAR! YOU'RE *TERRIBLE!*
OH...
NINA SENT THIS...
...TO ME FOR YOU.
Nina
!

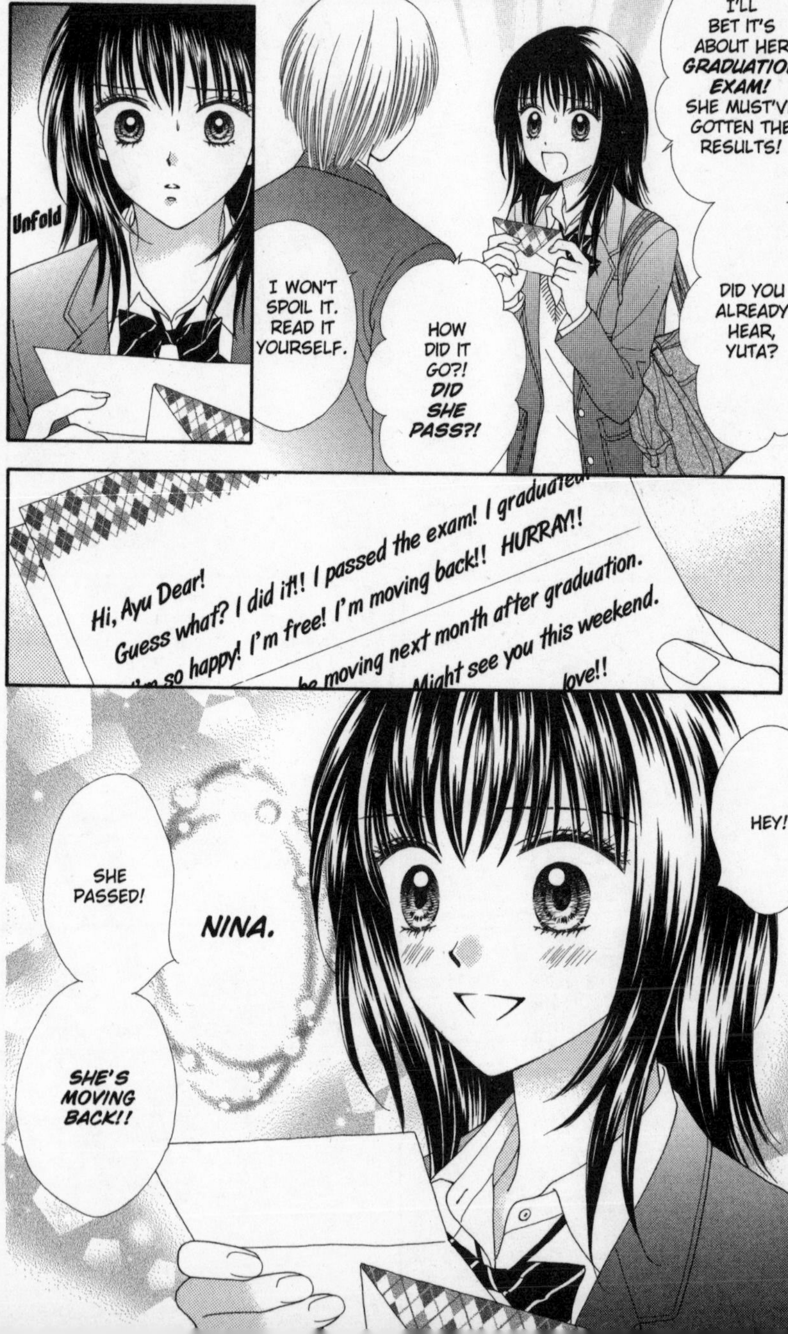
I'LL BET IT'S ABOUT HER GRADUATION EXAM! SHE MUST'VE GOTTEN THE RESULTS!
DID YOU ALREADY HEAR, YUTA?
HOW DID IT GO?! DID SHE PASS?!
I WON'T SPOIL IT. READ IT YOURSELF.
Unfold
Hi, Ayu Dear!
Guess what? I did it!! I passed the exam! I graduate
so happy! I'm free! I'm moving back!! HURRAY!!
moving next month after graduation.
Might see you this weekend.
love!!
HEY!
SHE PASSED!
NINA.
SHE'S MOVING BACK!!

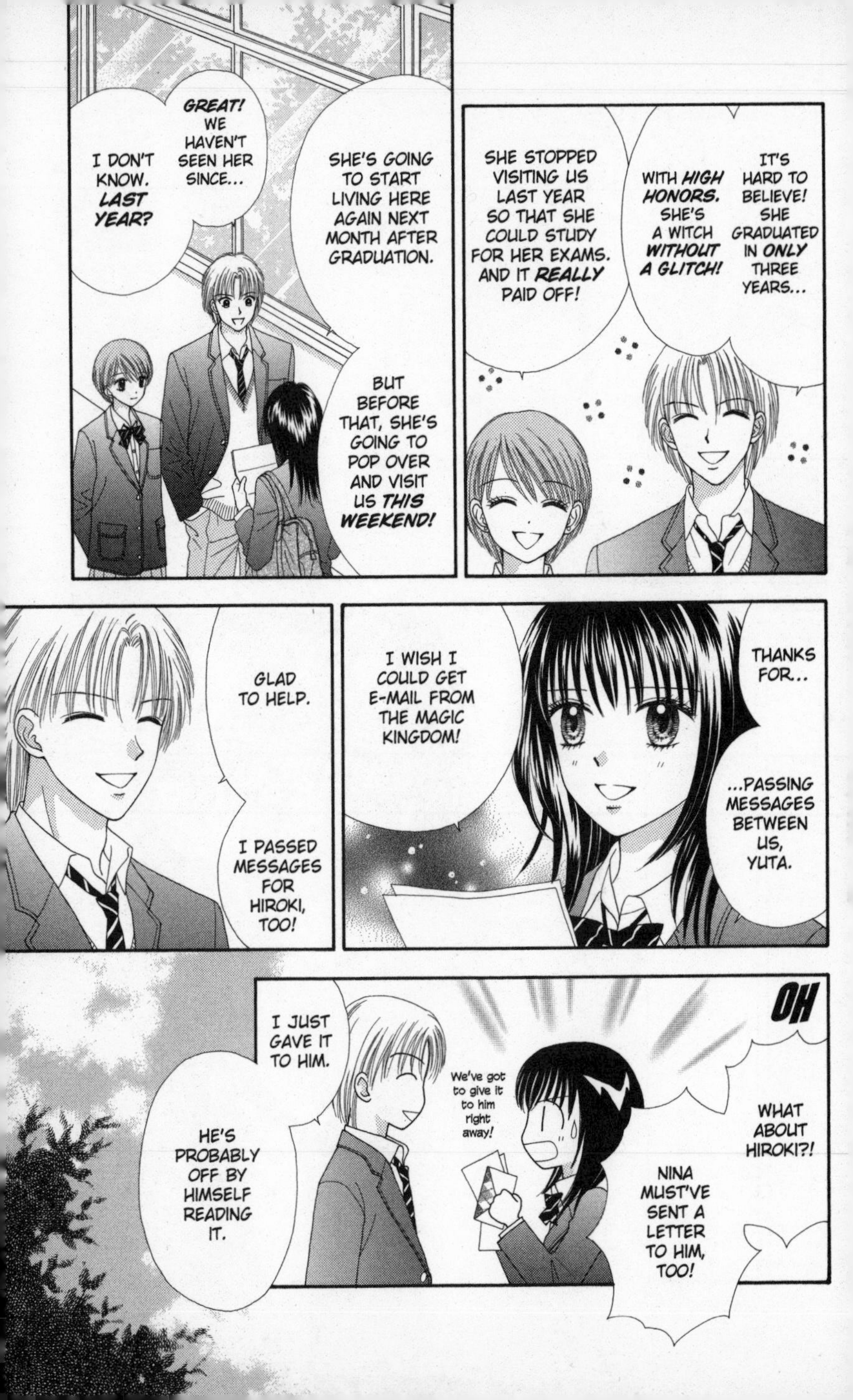
IT'S HARD TO BELIEVE! SHE GRADUATED IN ONLY THREE YEARS...
WITH HIGH HONORS. SHE'S A WITCH WITHOUT A GLITCH!
SHE STOPPED VISITING US LAST YEAR SO THAT SHE COULD STUDY FOR HER EXAMS. AND IT REALLY PAID OFF!
SHE'S GOING TO START LIVING HERE AGAIN NEXT MONTH AFTER GRADUATION.
BUT BEFORE THAT, SHE'S GOING TO POP OVER AND VISIT US THIS WEEKEND!
GREAT! WE HAVEN'T SEEN HER SINCE...
I DON'T KNOW. LAST YEAR?
THANKS FOR...
...PASSING MESSAGES BETWEEN US, YUTA.
I WISH I COULD GET E-MAIL FROM THE MAGIC KINGDOM!
GLAD TO HELP.
I PASSED MESSAGES FOR HIROKI, TOO!
OH
WHAT ABOUT HIROKI?!
NINA MUST'VE SENT A LETTER TO HIM, TOO!
We've got to give it to him right away!
I JUST GAVE IT TO HIM.
HE'S PROBABLY OFF BY HIMSELF READING IT.

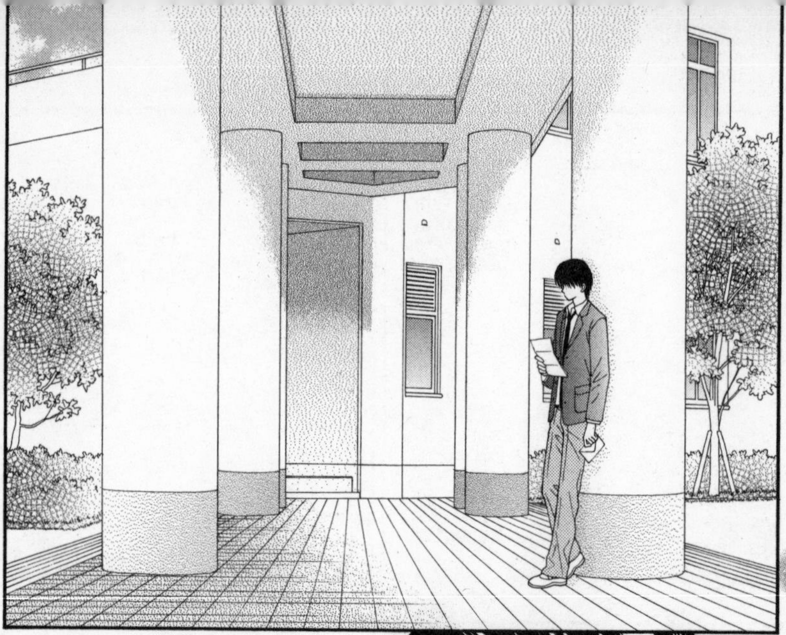
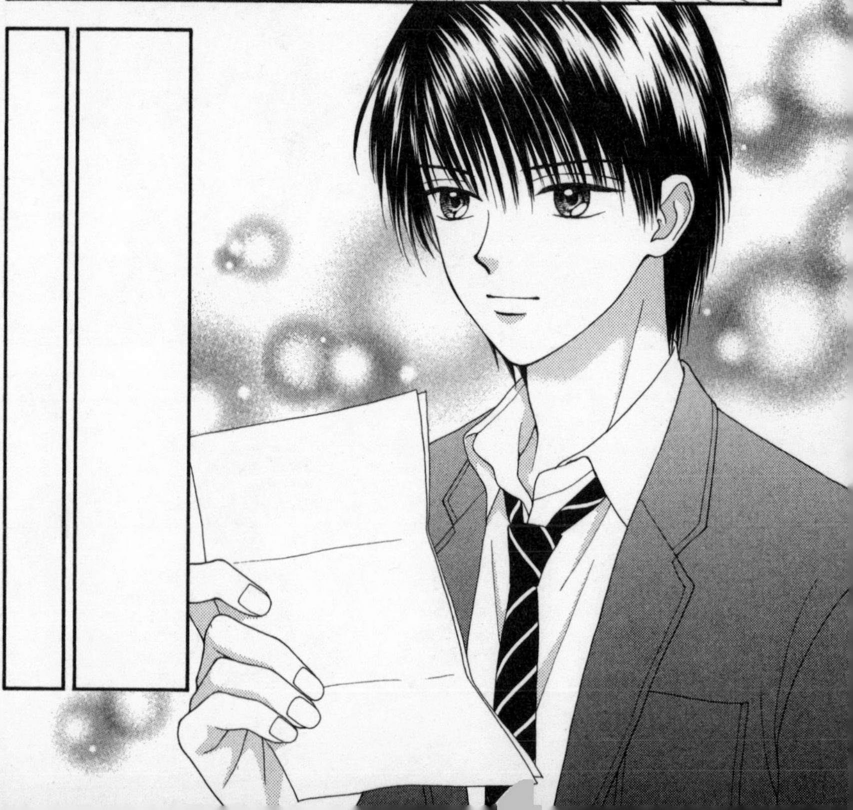

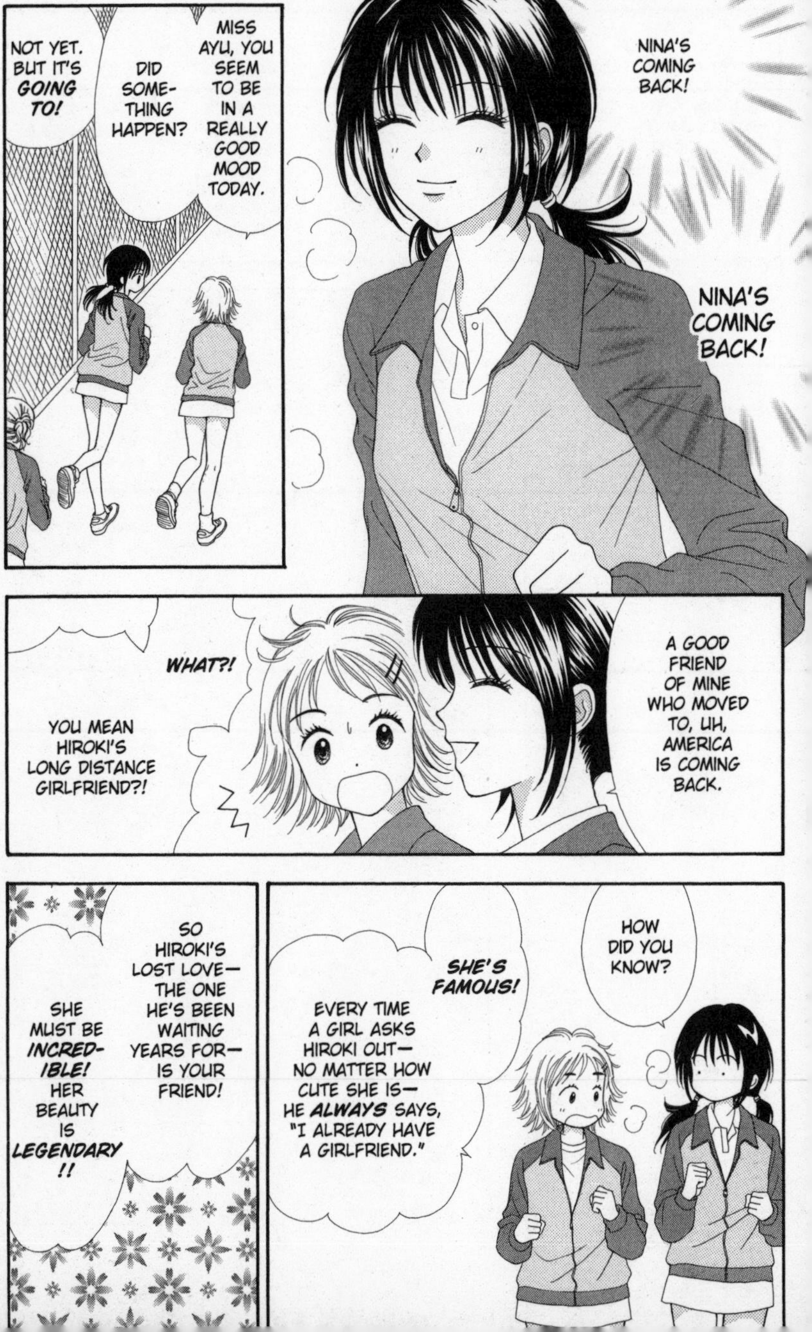
NINA'S COMING BACK!
NINA'S COMING BACK!
MISS AYU, YOU SEEM TO BE IN A REALLY GOOD MOOD TODAY.
DID SOMETHING HAPPEN?
NOT YET. BUT IT'S GOING TO!
A GOOD FRIEND OF MINE WHO MOVED TO, UH, AMERICA IS COMING BACK.
WHAT?!
YOU MEAN HIROKI'S LONG DISTANCE GIRLFRIEND?!
HOW DID YOU KNOW?
SHE'S FAMOUS!
EVERY TIME A GIRL ASKS HIROKI OUT— NO MATTER HOW CUTE SHE IS— HE ALWAYS SAYS, "I ALREADY HAVE A GIRLFRIEND."
SO HIROKI'S LOST LOVE— THE ONE HE'S BEEN WAITING YEARS FOR— IS YOUR FRIEND!
SHE MUST BE INCREDIBLE! HER BEAUTY IS LEGENDARY!!

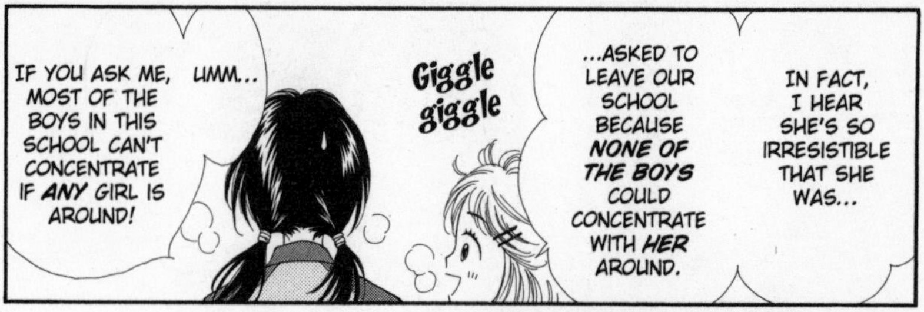
IN FACT, I HEAR SHE'S SO IRRESISTIBLE THAT SHE WAS...
...ASKED TO LEAVE OUR SCHOOL BECAUSE NONE OF THE BOYS COULD CONCENTRATE WITH HER AROUND.
Giggle giggle
UMM...
IF YOU ASK ME, MOST OF THE BOYS IN THIS SCHOOL CAN'T CONCENTRATE IF ANY GIRL IS AROUND!
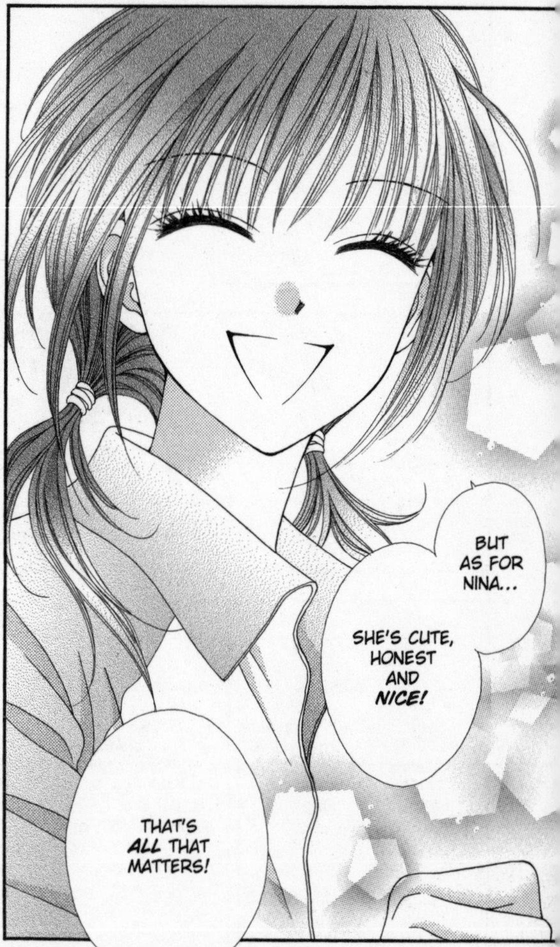
BUT AS FOR NINA...
SHE'S CUTE, HONEST AND NICE!
THAT'S ALL THAT MATTERS!
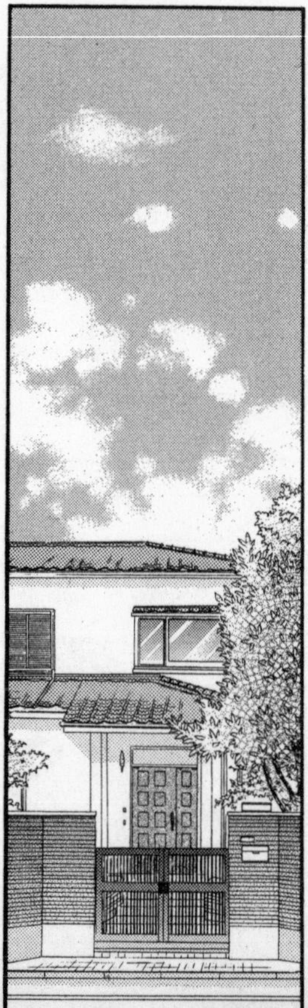

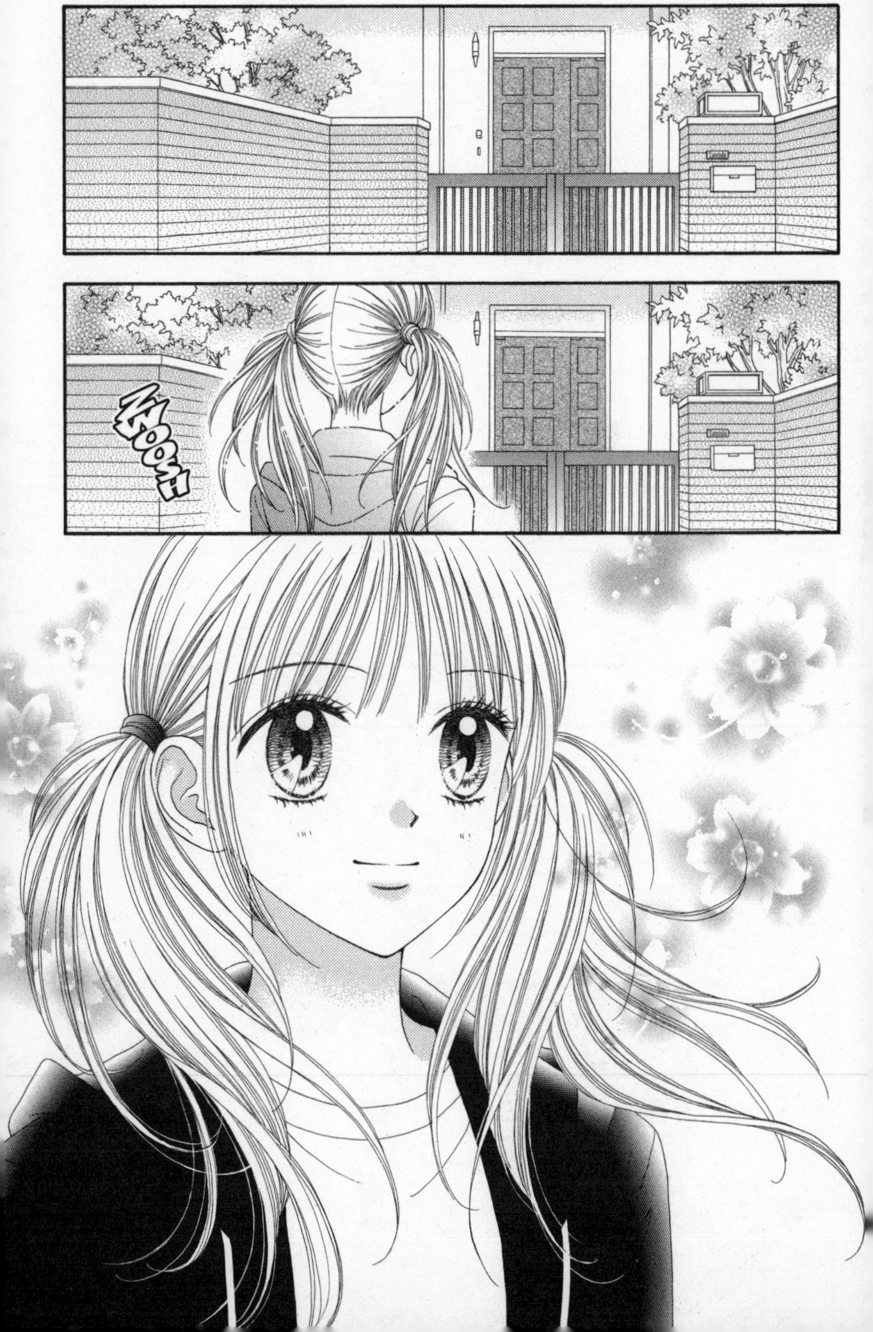
WOOSH!

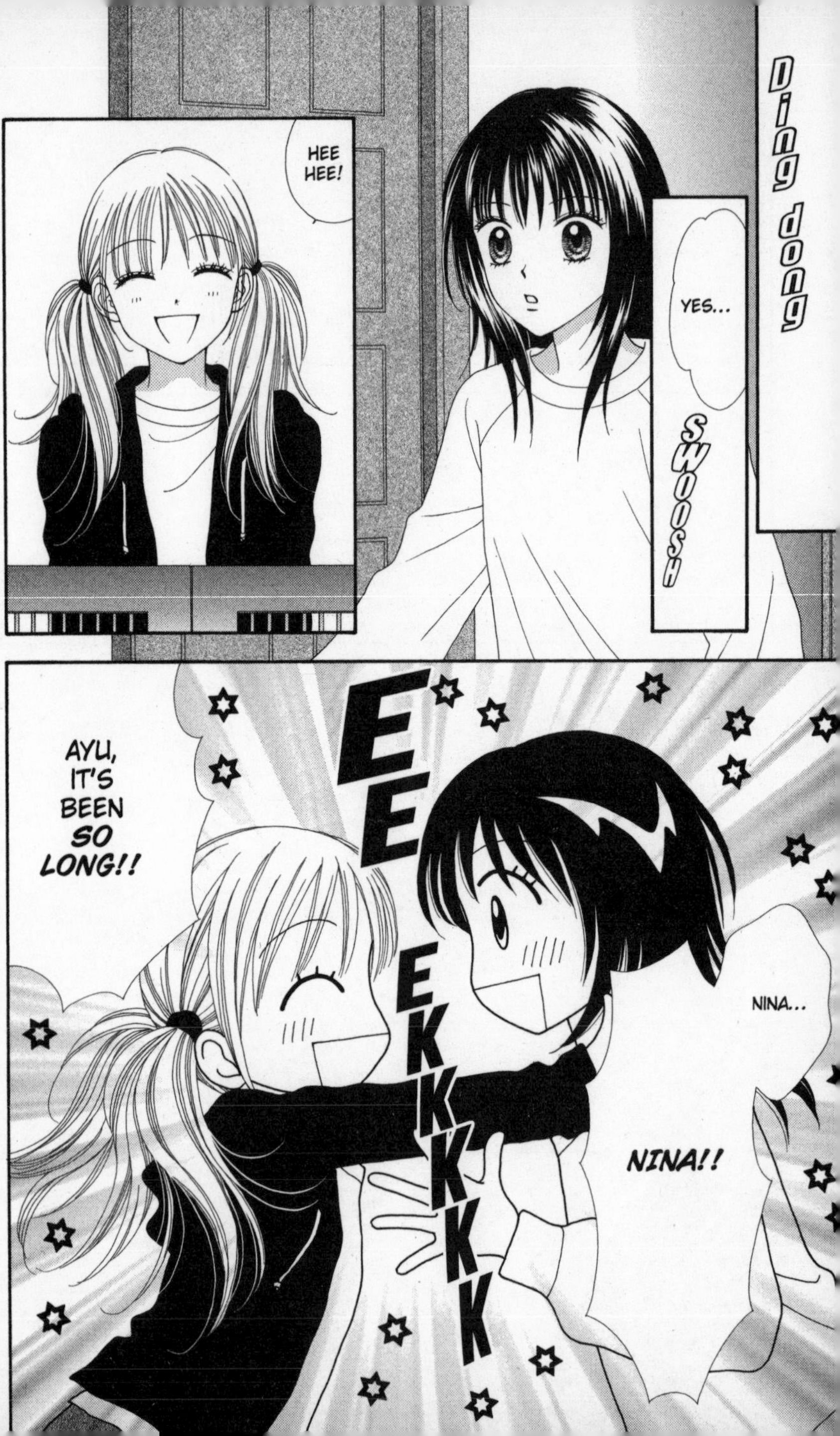
Ding dong
YES...
SWOOSH
HEE HEE!
EEEKKKKKKK
NINA!!
NINA...
AYU, IT'S BEEN SO LONG!!

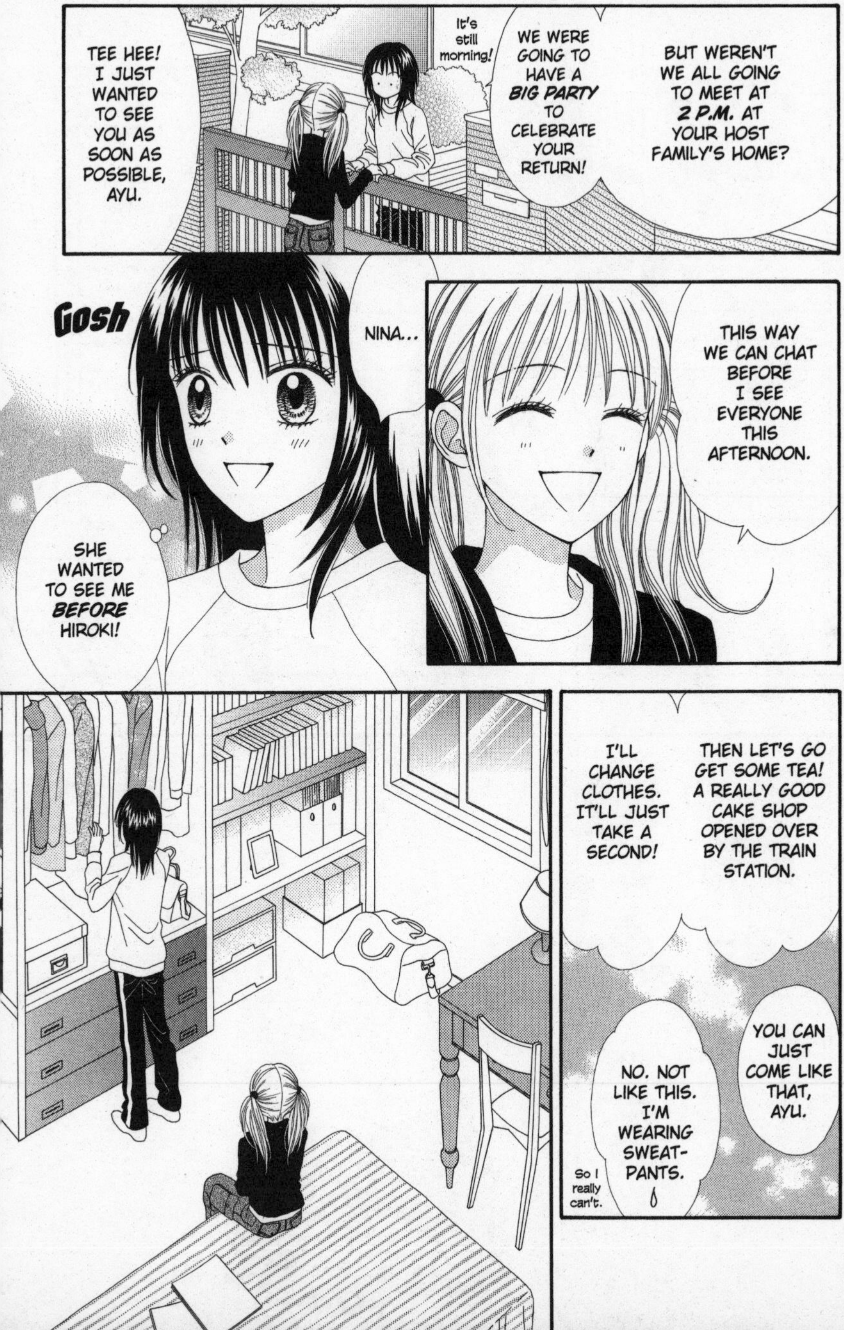
BUT WEREN'T WE ALL GOING TO MEET AT 2 P.M. AT YOUR HOST FAMILY'S HOME?
WE WERE GOING TO HAVE A BIG PARTY TO CELEBRATE YOUR RETURN!
It's still morning!
TEE HEE! I JUST WANTED TO SEE YOU AS SOON AS POSSIBLE, AYU.
THIS WAY WE CAN CHAT BEFORE I SEE EVERYONE THIS AFTERNOON.
NINA...
Gosh
SHE WANTED TO SEE ME BEFORE HIROKI!
THEN LET'S GO GET SOME TEA! A REALLY GOOD CAKE SHOP OPENED OVER BY THE TRAIN STATION.
I'LL CHANGE CLOTHES. IT'LL JUST TAKE A SECOND!
YOU CAN JUST COME LIKE THAT, AYU.
NO. NOT LIKE THIS. I'M WEARING SWEAT-PANTS.
So I really can't.

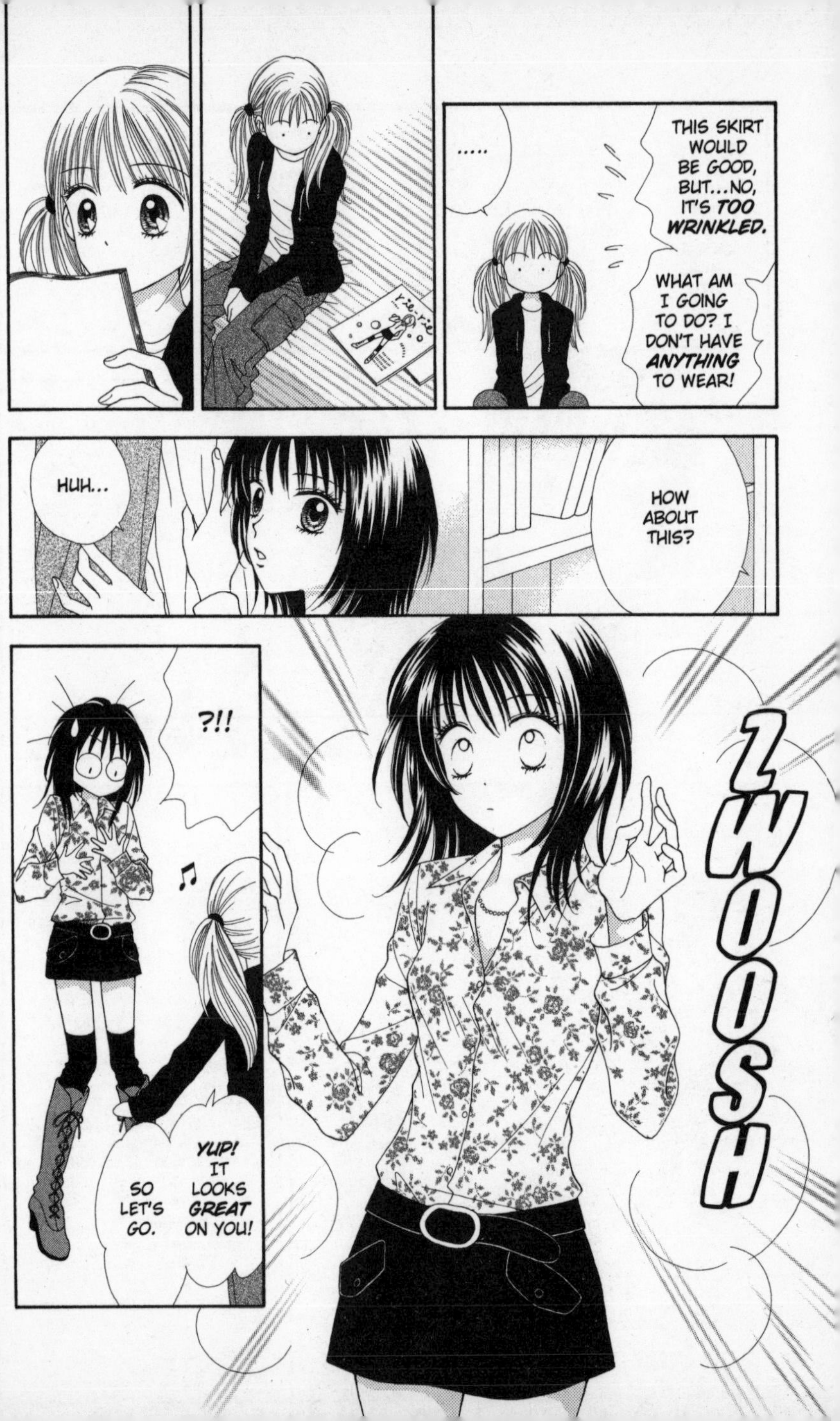
THIS SKIRT WOULD BE GOOD, BUT...NO, IT'S TOO WRINKLED.
WHAT AM I GOING TO DO? I DON'T HAVE ANYTHING TO WEAR!
.....
HOW ABOUT THIS?
HUH...
ZWOOSH
?!!
YUP! IT LOOKS GREAT ON YOU!
SO LET'S GO.

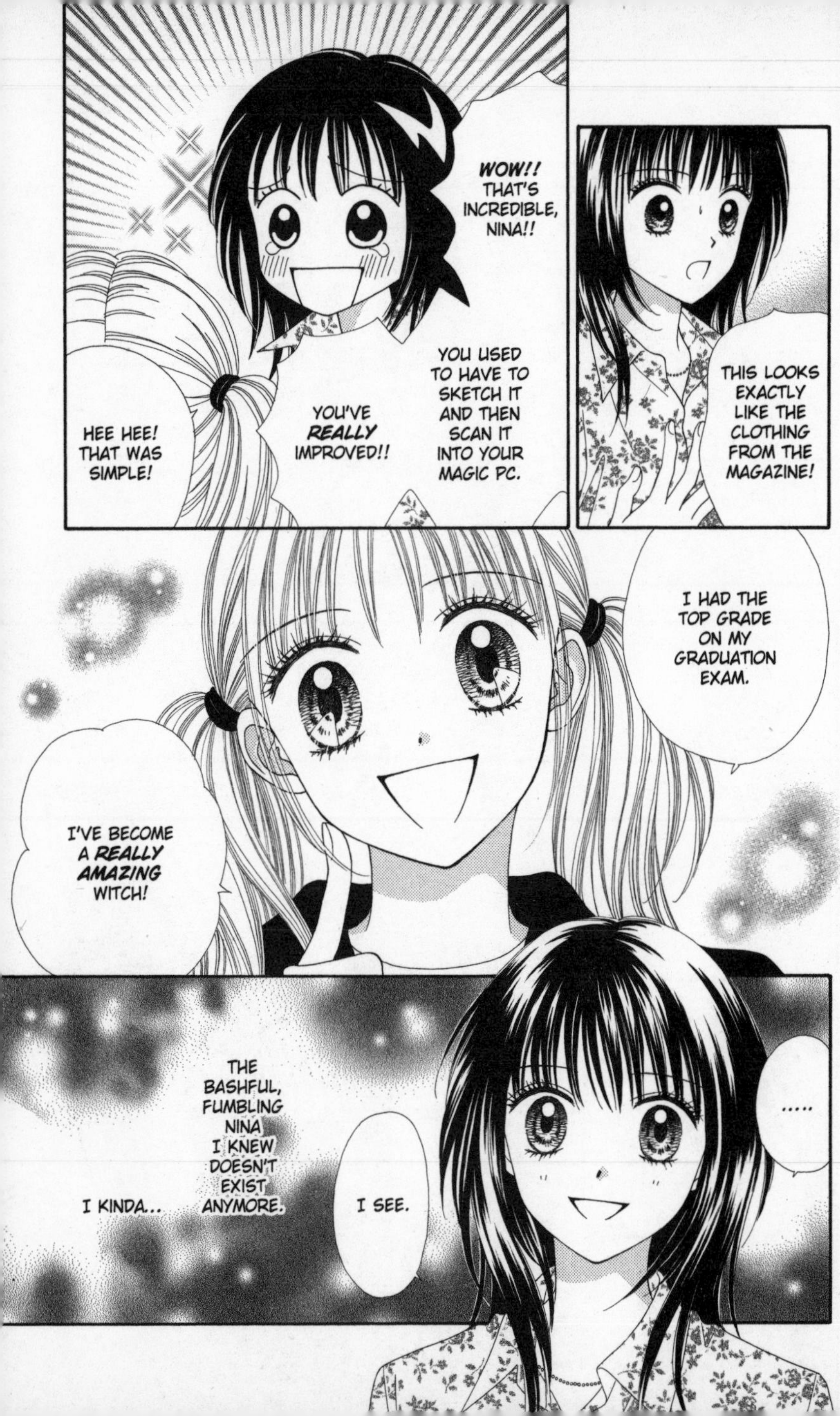
THIS LOOKS EXACTLY LIKE THE CLOTHING FROM THE MAGAZINE!
WOW!! THAT'S INCREDIBLE, NINA!!
YOU USED TO HAVE TO SKETCH IT AND THEN SCAN IT INTO YOUR MAGIC PC.
YOU'VE REALLY IMPROVED!!
HEE HEE! THAT WAS SIMPLE!
I HAD THE TOP GRADE ON MY GRADUATION EXAM.
I'VE BECOME A REALLY AMAZING WITCH!
.....
I SEE.
THE BASHFUL, FUMBLING NINA I KNEW DOESN'T EXIST ANYMORE.
I KINDA...

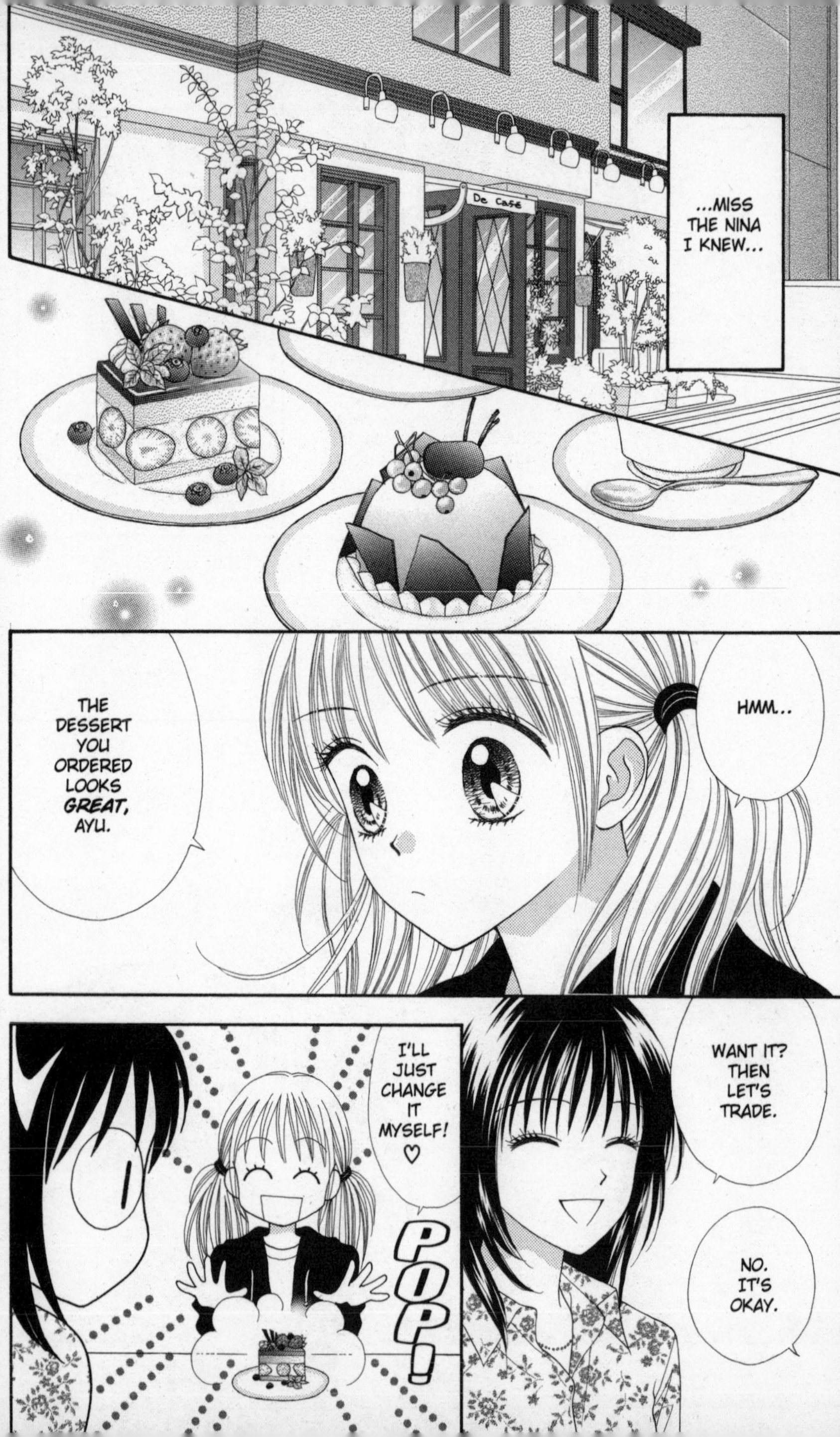
...MISS THE NINA I KNEW...
De Café
HMM...
THE DESSERT YOU ORDERED LOOKS GREAT, AYU.
WANT IT? THEN LET'S TRADE.
NO. IT'S OKAY.
I'LL JUST CHANGE IT MYSELF! ♡
POP!

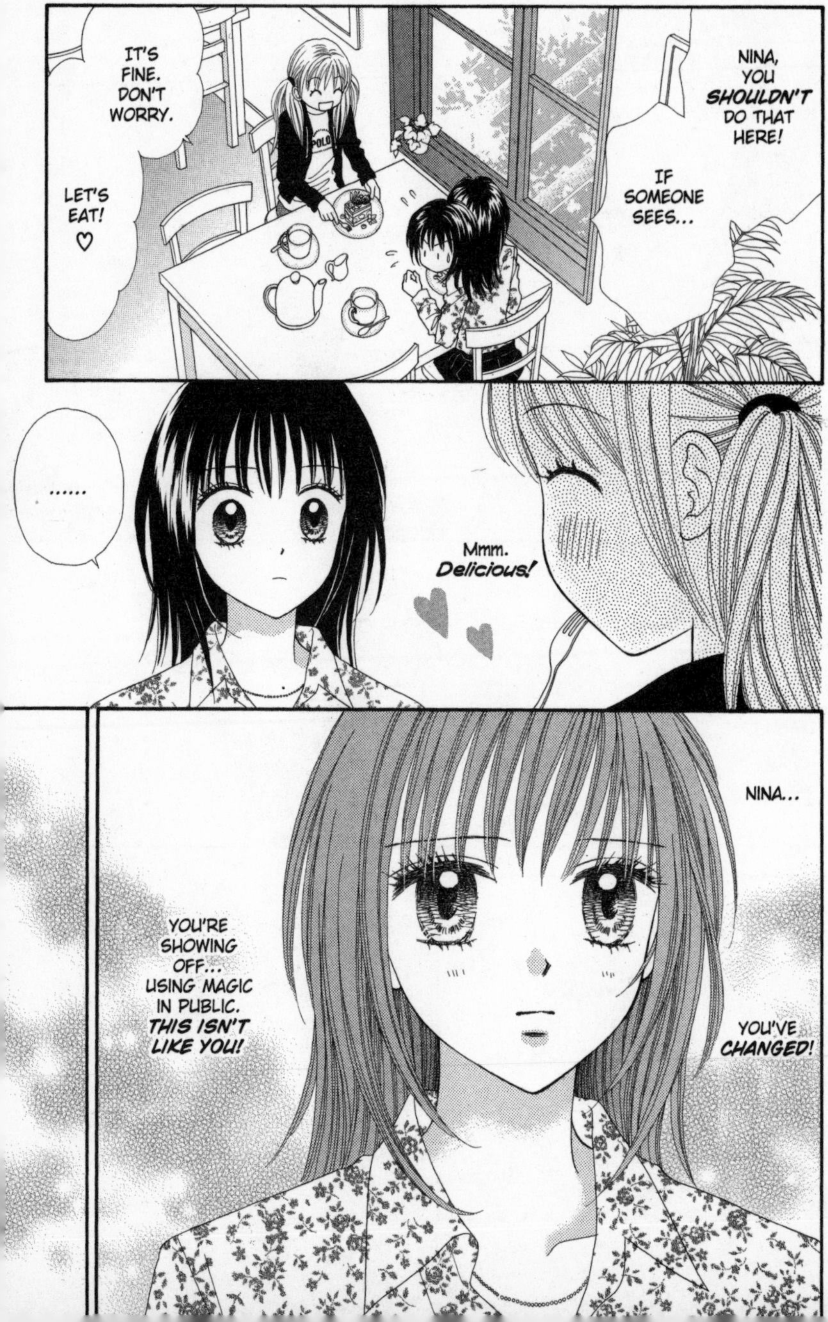
NINA, YOU SHOULDN'T DO THAT HERE!
IF SOMEONE SEES...
IT'S FINE. DON'T WORRY.
LET'S EAT! ♡
POLO
Mmm. Delicious!
......
NINA...
YOU'RE SHOWING OFF... USING MAGIC IN PUBLIC. THIS ISN'T LIKE YOU!
YOU'VE CHANGED!

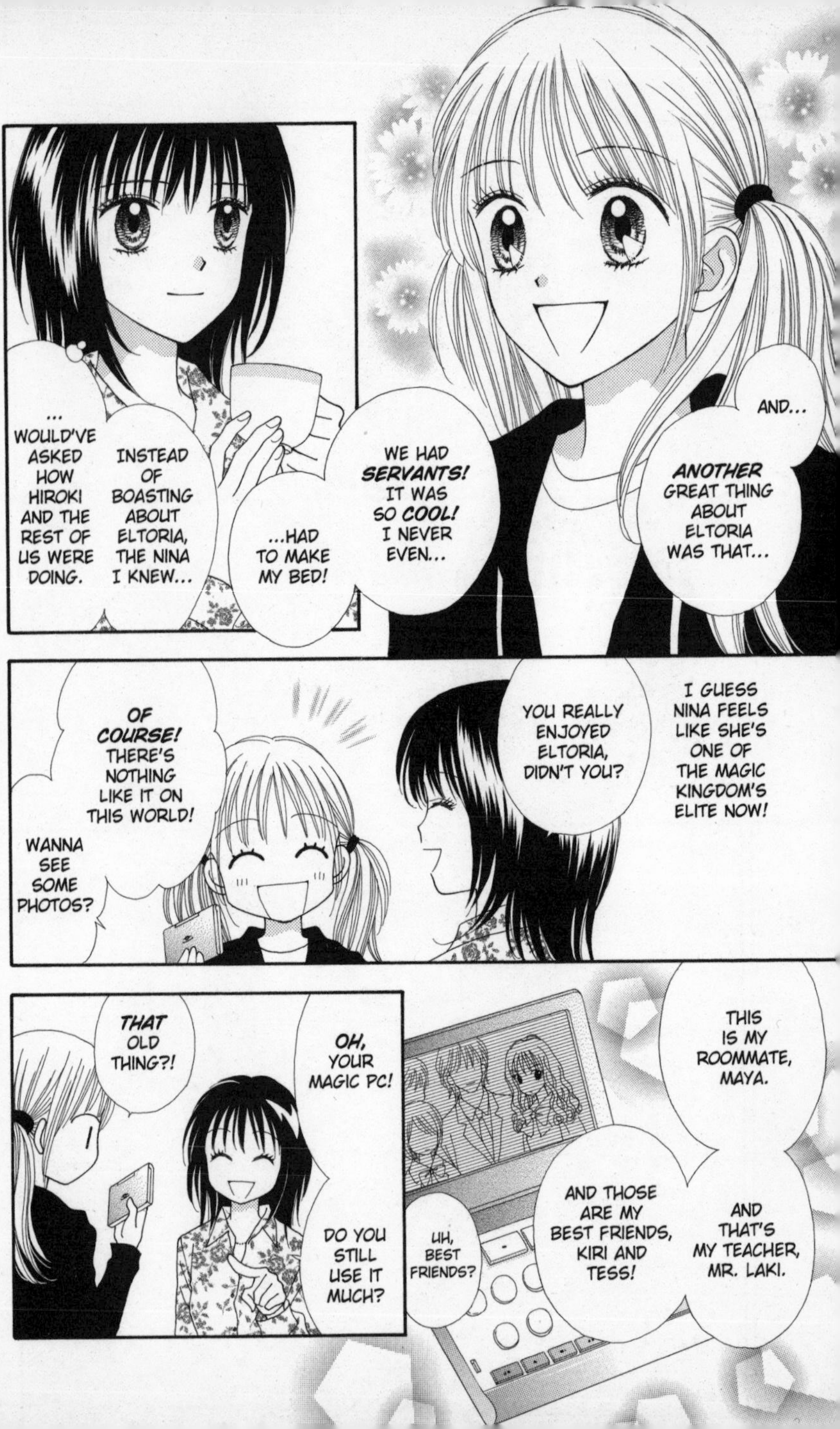
AND...
ANOTHER GREAT THING ABOUT ELTORIA WAS THAT...
WE HAD SERVANTS! IT WAS SO COOL! I NEVER EVEN...
...HAD TO MAKE MY BED!
INSTEAD OF BOASTING ABOUT ELTORIA, THE NINA I KNEW...
...WOULD'VE ASKED HOW HIROKI AND THE REST OF US WERE DOING.
I GUESS NINA FEELS LIKE SHE'S ONE OF THE MAGIC KINGDOM'S ELITE NOW!
YOU REALLY ENJOYED ELTORIA, DIDN'T YOU?
OF COURSE! THERE'S NOTHING LIKE IT ON THIS WORLD!
WANNA SEE SOME PHOTOS?
THIS IS MY ROOMMATE, MAYA.
AND THAT'S MY TEACHER, MR. LAKI.
AND THOSE ARE MY BEST FRIENDS, KIRI AND TESS!
UH, BEST FRIENDS?
OH, YOUR MAGIC PC!
DO YOU STILL USE IT MUCH?
THAT OLD THING?!

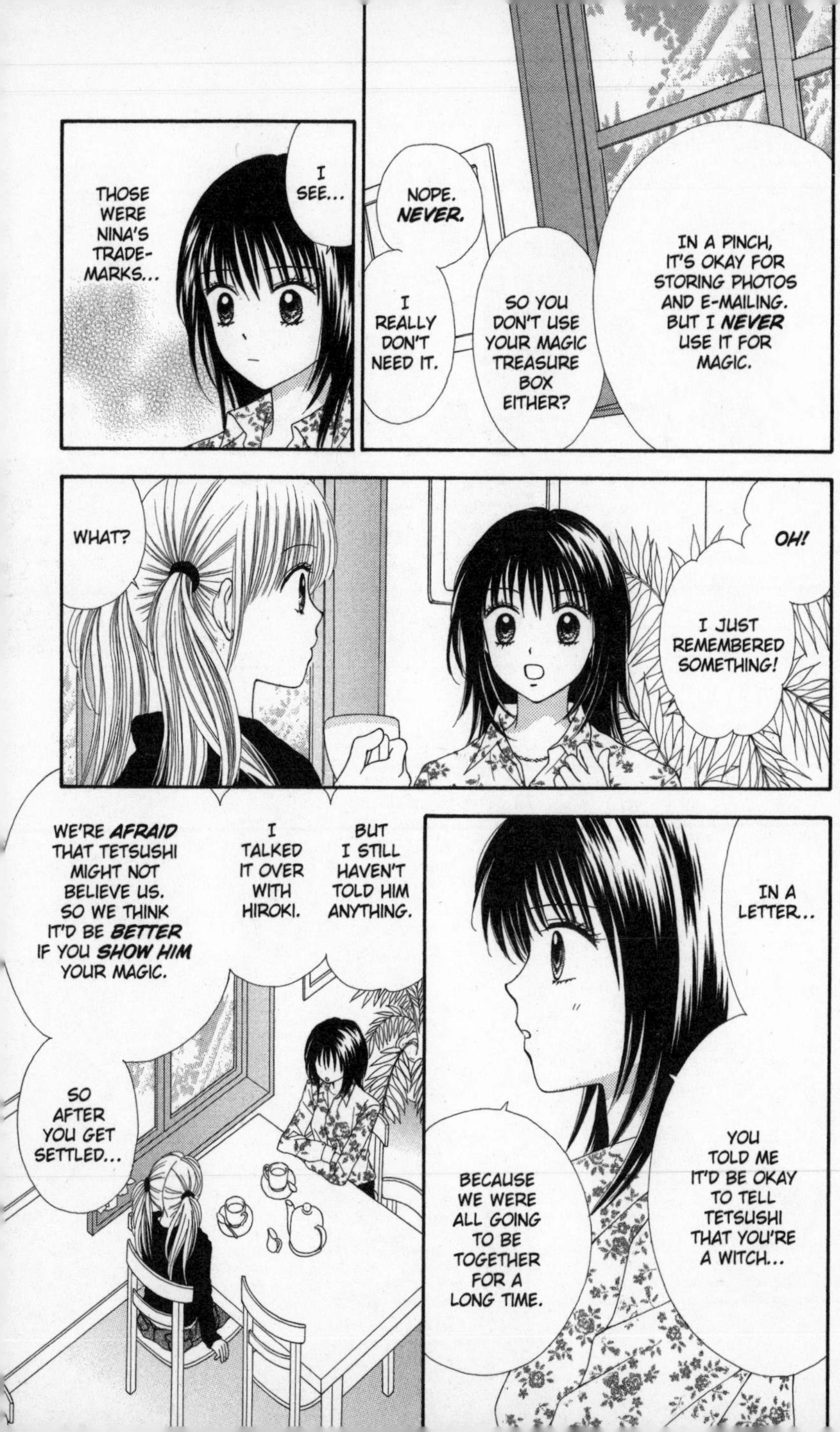
IN A PINCH, IT'S OKAY FOR STORING PHOTOS AND E-MAILING. BUT I ***NEVER*** USE IT FOR MAGIC.
SO YOU DON'T USE YOUR MAGIC TREASURE BOX EITHER?
NOPE. ***NEVER.***
I REALLY DON'T NEED IT.
I SEE...
THOSE WERE NINA'S TRADE-MARKS...
OH!
I JUST REMEMBERED SOMETHING!
WHAT?
IN A LETTER..
YOU TOLD ME IT'D BE OKAY TO TELL TETSUSHI THAT YOU'RE A WITCH...
BECAUSE WE WERE ALL GOING TO BE TOGETHER FOR A LONG TIME.
BUT I STILL HAVEN'T TOLD HIM ANYTHING.
I TALKED IT OVER WITH HIROKI.
WE'RE ***AFRAID*** THAT TETSUSHI MIGHT NOT BELIEVE US. SO WE THINK IT'D BE ***BETTER*** IF YOU ***SHOW HIM*** YOUR MAGIC.
SO AFTER YOU GET SETTLED...

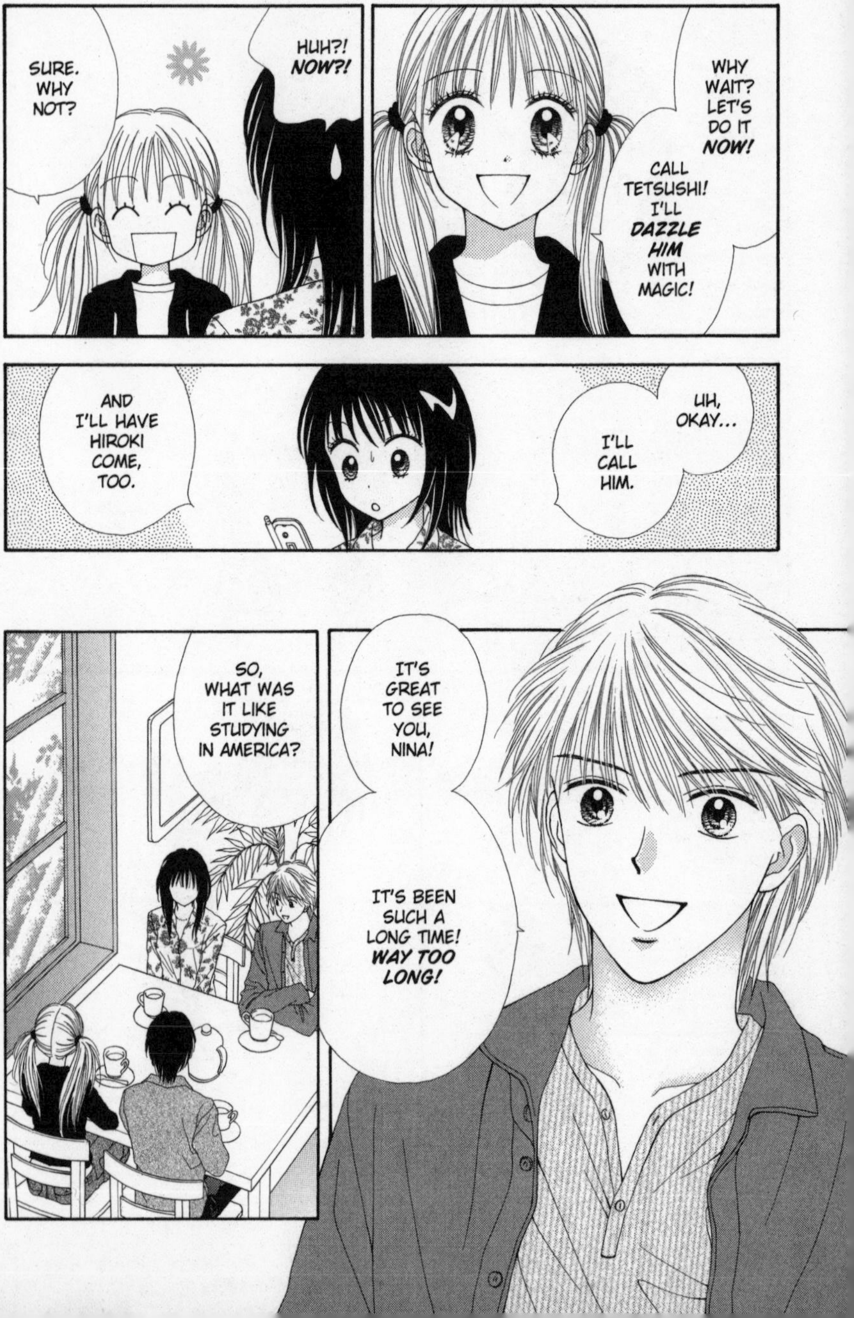
WHY WAIT? LET'S DO IT **NOW!**
CALL TETSUSHI! I'LL ***DAZZLE HIM*** WITH MAGIC!
HUH?! ***NOW?!***
SURE. WHY NOT?
UH, OKAY...
I'LL CALL HIM.
AND I'LL HAVE HIROKI COME, TOO.
IT'S GREAT TO SEE YOU, NINA!
IT'S BEEN SUCH A LONG TIME! ***WAY TOO LONG!***
SO, WHAT WAS IT LIKE STUDYING IN AMERICA?

FREE TALK 8

The Bonus Chapter is a story that takes place three years after Nina leaves. It was a lot of fun to draw my characters older. I mostly just made the girls emotionally more mature. But boys typically grow a lot in three years. So I really changed the appearances of Tetsushi, Hiroki and Yuta.

While I was drawing this chapter I was trying really hard to make distinctive changes. But looking at the characters now, it seems they REALLY changed! Maybe too much? (Ha ha.) A lot of my readers were probably surprised by the changes.

The last scene is a little different from the way it was when it was originally published in the magazine. I added a little to it. Those of you who still have the magazine, can see the differences.

Please send your questions and impressions to the following address:

Ultra Maniac
c/o Shojo Beat
VIZ Media
P.O. Box 77010
San Francisco, CA 94107

I hope you enjoyed *Ultra Maniac*. Take care.
Wataru Yoshizumi

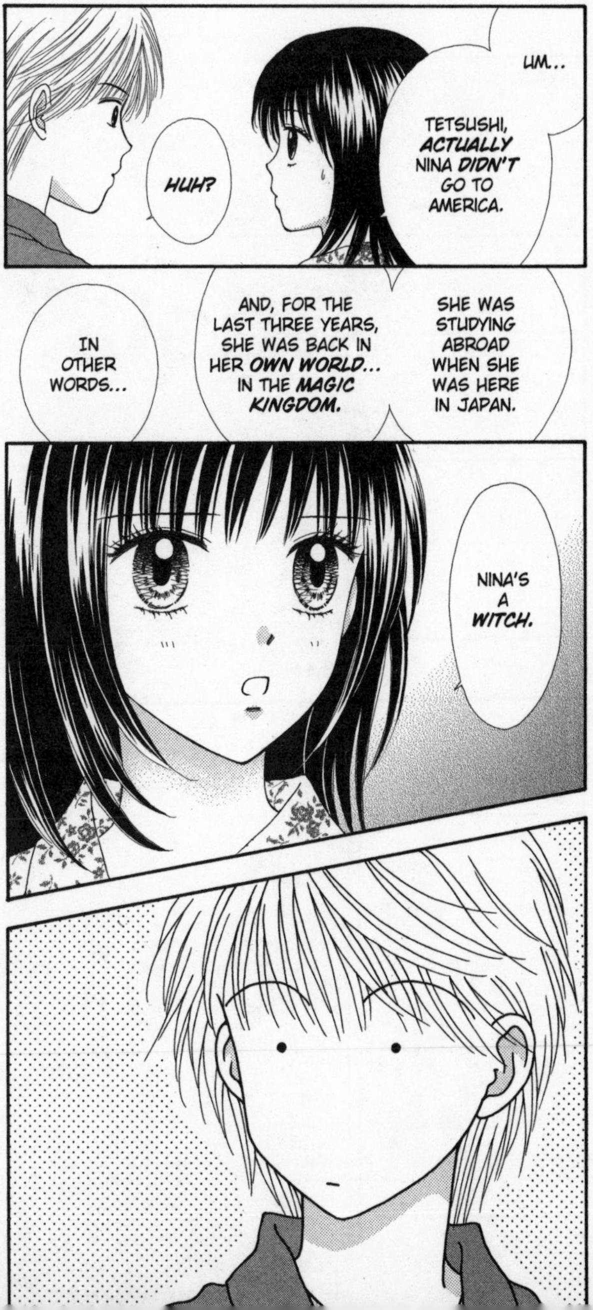
UM...
TETSUSHI, ***ACTUALLY*** NINA ***DIDN'T*** GO TO AMERICA.
HUH?
SHE WAS STUDYING ABROAD WHEN SHE WAS HERE IN JAPAN.
AND, FOR THE LAST THREE YEARS, SHE WAS BACK IN HER ***OWN WORLD...*** IN THE ***MAGIC KINGDOM.***
IN OTHER WORDS...
NINA'S A ***WITCH.***

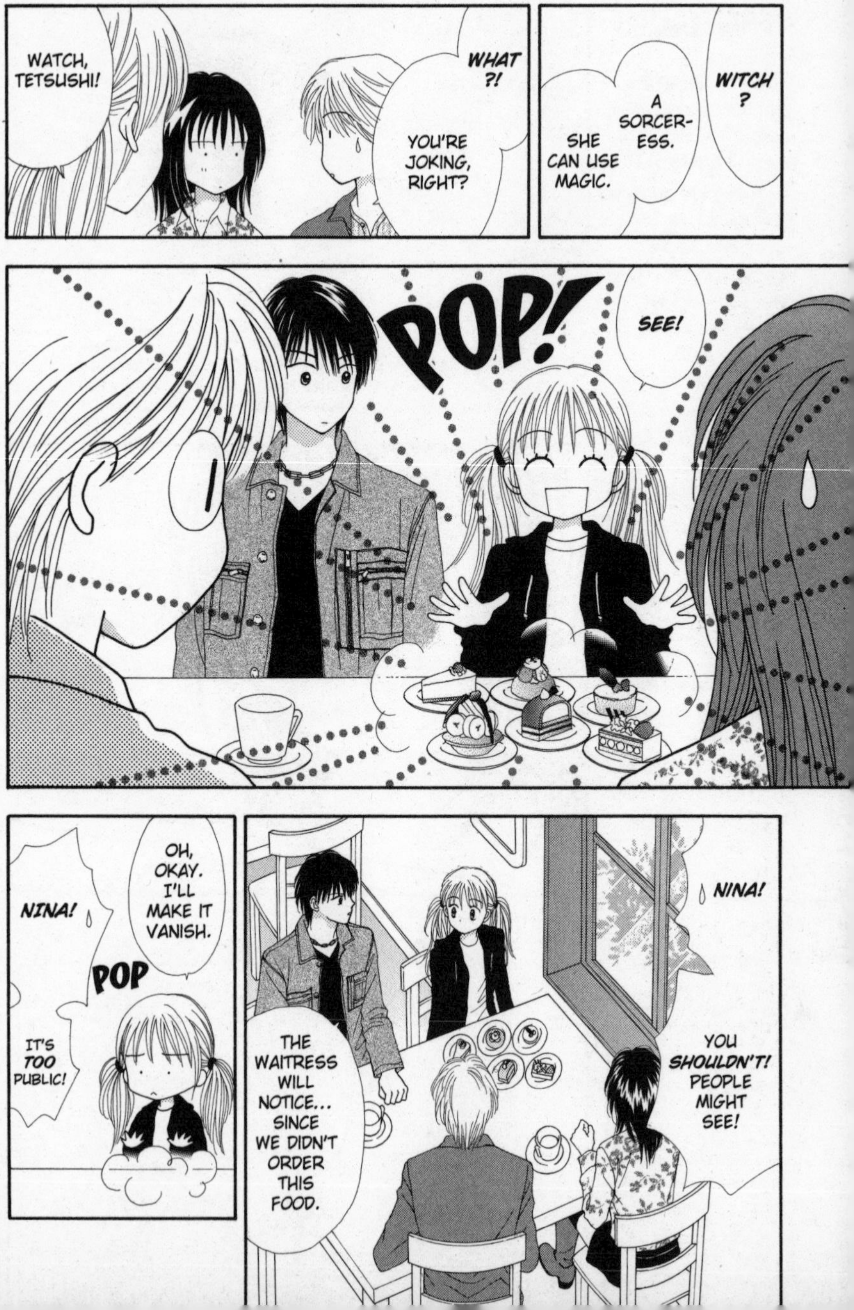
WITCH?
A SORCERESS. SHE CAN USE MAGIC.
WHAT?! YOU'RE JOKING, RIGHT?
WATCH, TETSUSHI!
POP!
SEE!
NINA!
YOU *SHOULDN'T!* PEOPLE MIGHT SEE!
THE WAITRESS WILL NOTICE... SINCE WE DIDN'T ORDER THIS FOOD.
OH, OKAY. I'LL MAKE IT VANISH.
NINA!
POP
IT'S *TOO* PUBLIC!

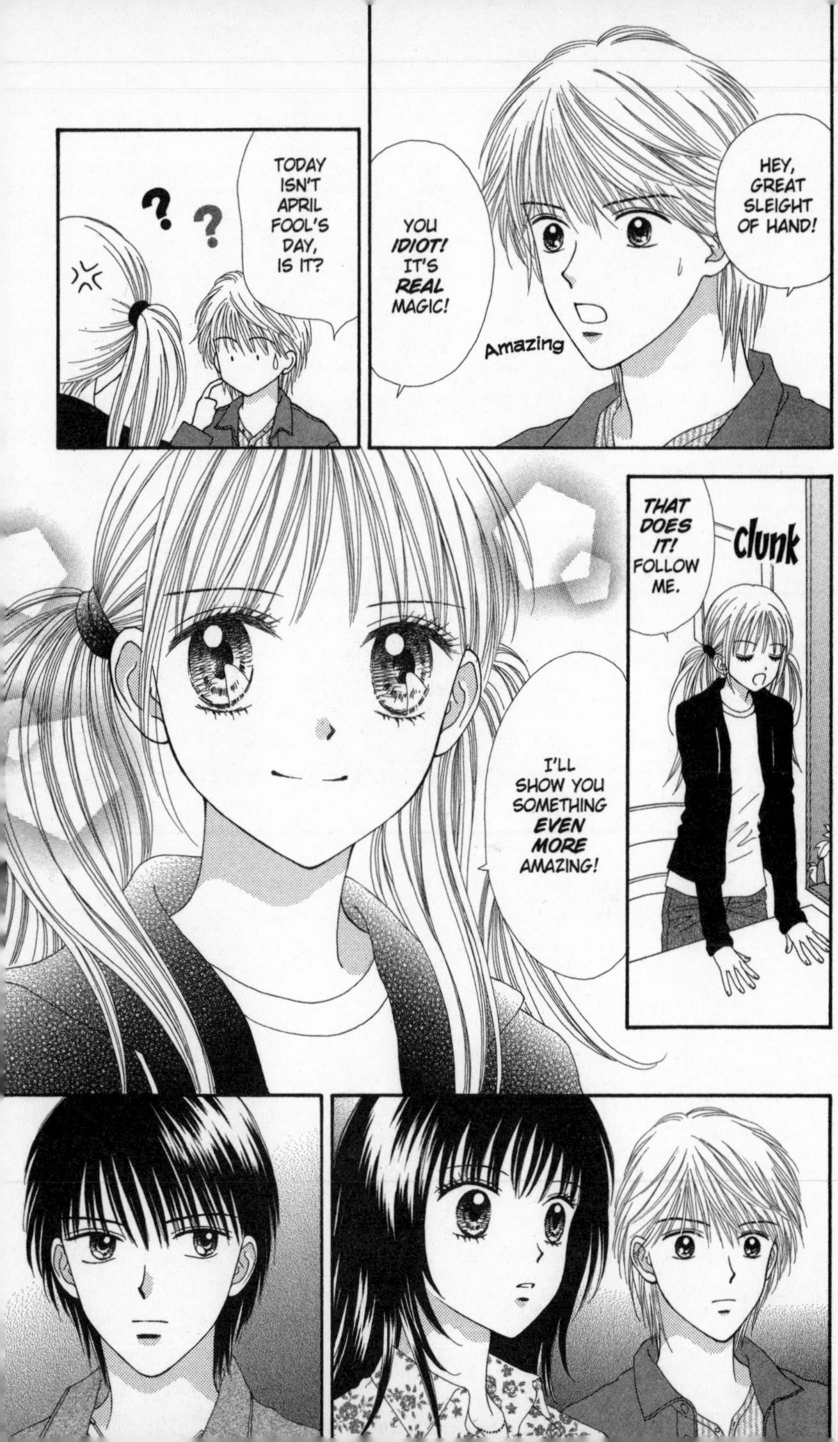
HEY, GREAT SLEIGHT OF HAND!
YOU IDIOT! IT'S REAL MAGIC!
Amazing
TODAY ISN'T APRIL FOOL'S DAY, IS IT?
THAT DOES IT! FOLLOW ME.
Clunk
I'LL SHOW YOU SOMETHING EVEN MORE AMAZING!

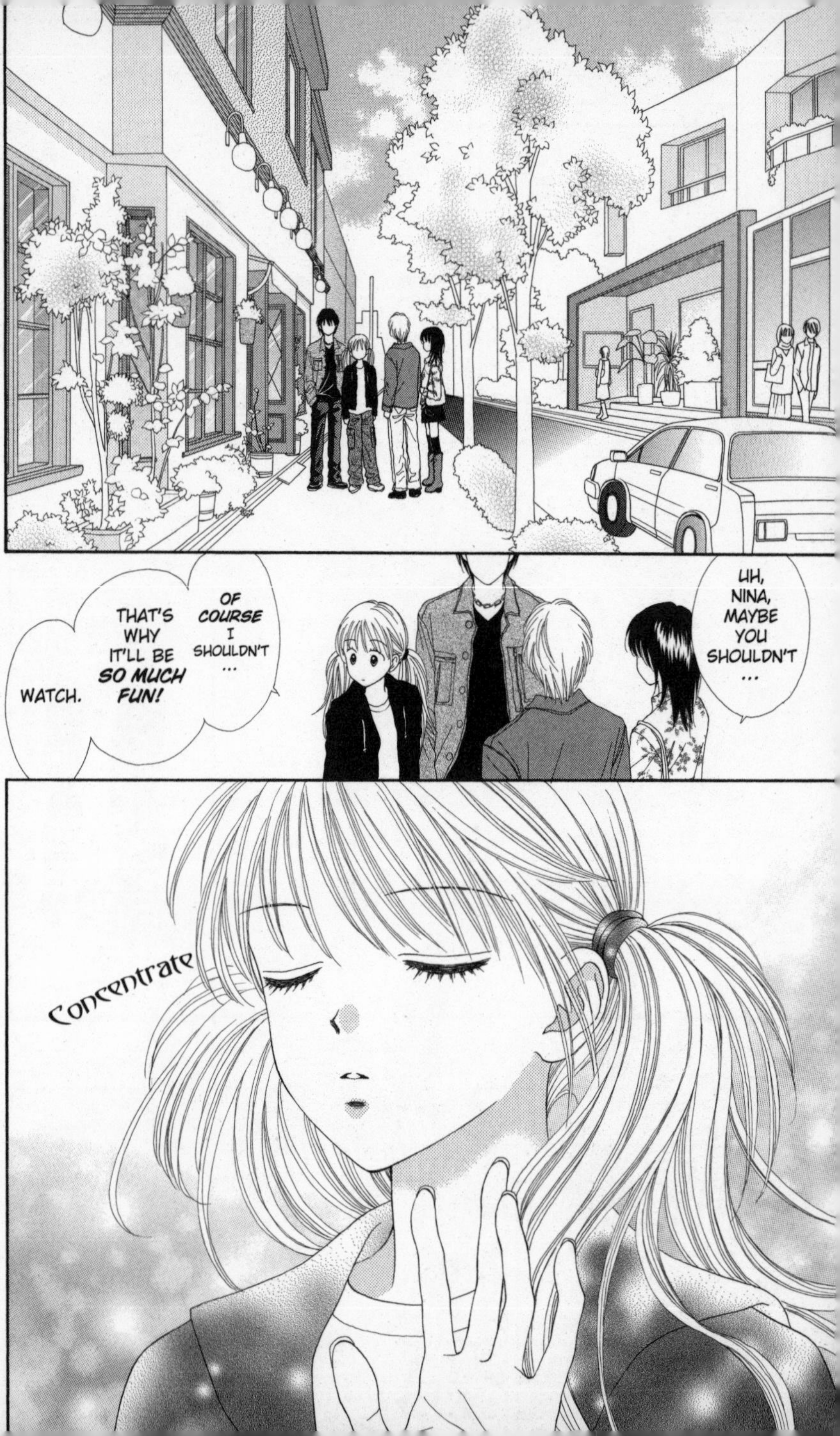
UH, NINA, MAYBE YOU SHOULDN'T ...
OF COURSE I SHOULDN'T ...
THAT'S WHY IT'LL BE **SO MUCH FUN!**
WATCH.
Concentrate

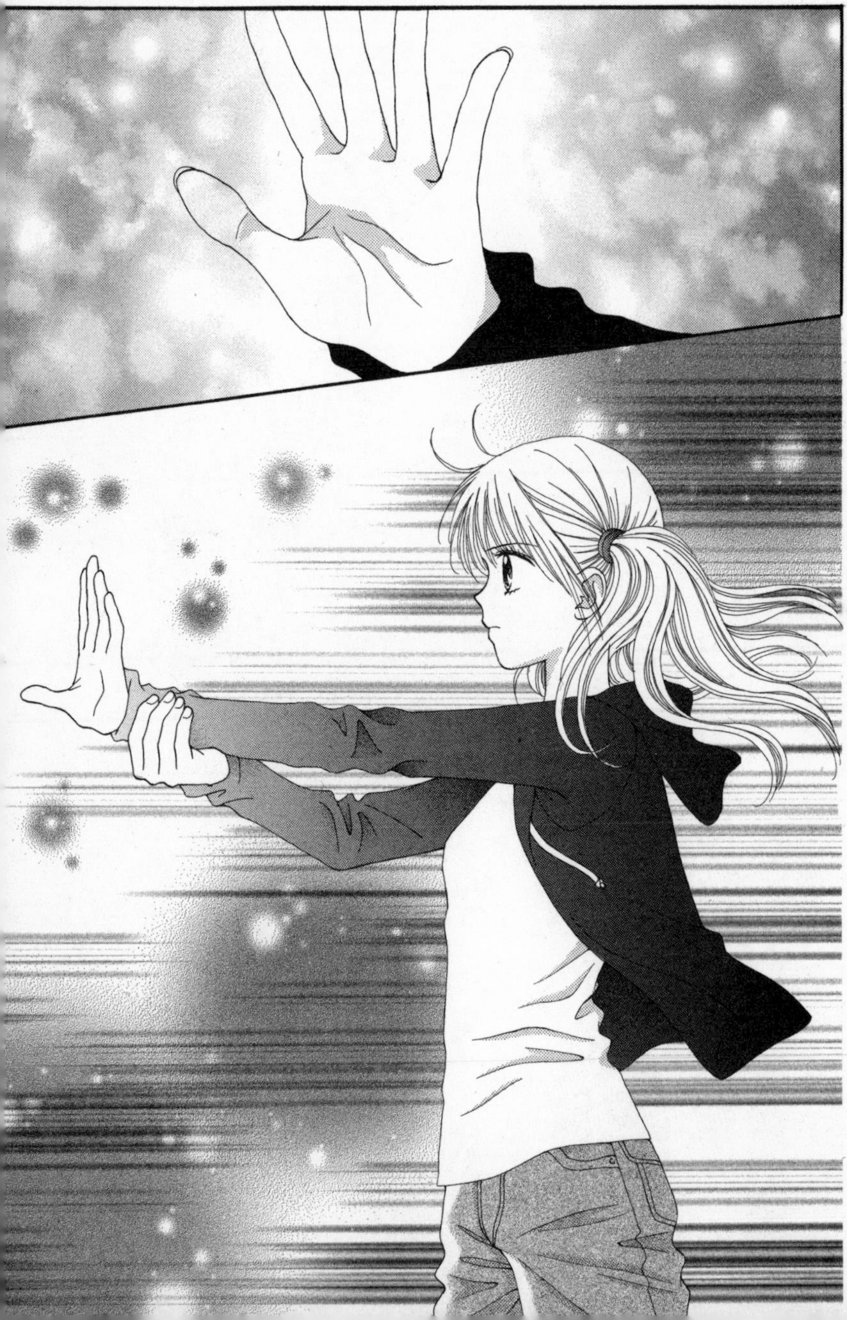

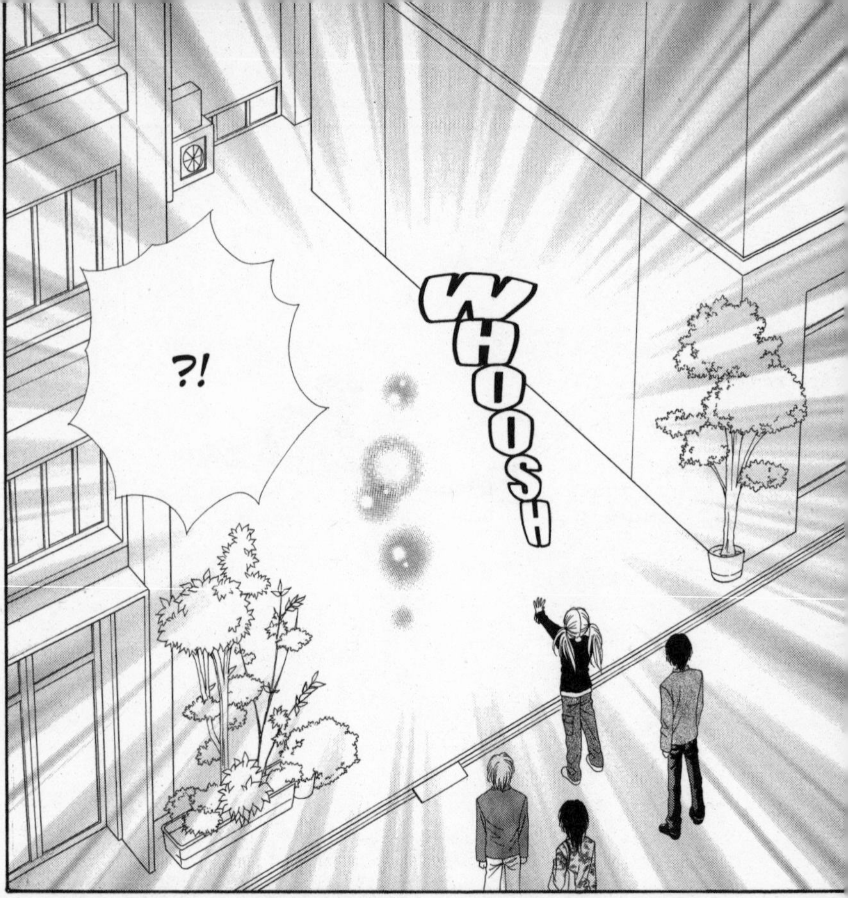
?!
WHOOSH
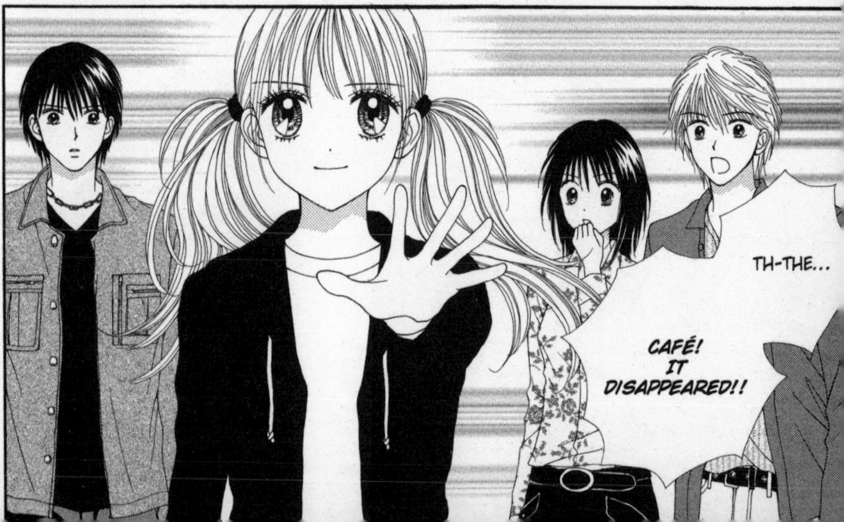
TH-THE...
CAFÉ! IT DISAPPEARED!!

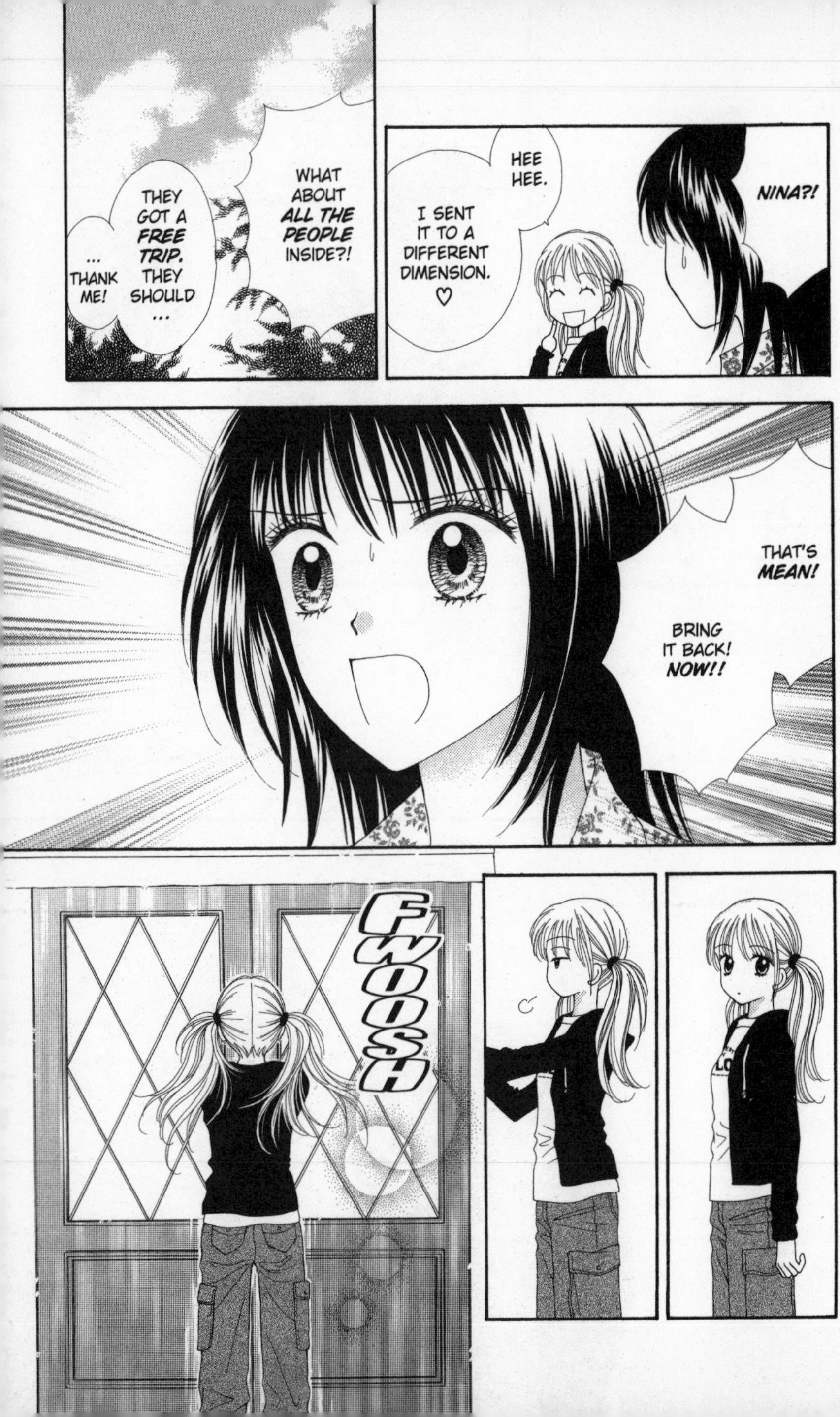
NINA?!
HEE HEE.
I SENT IT TO A DIFFERENT DIMENSION. ♡
WHAT ABOUT ALL THE PEOPLE INSIDE?!
THEY GOT A FREE TRIP. THEY SHOULD ...
... THANK ME!
THAT'S MEAN!
BRING IT BACK! NOW!!
FWOOSH

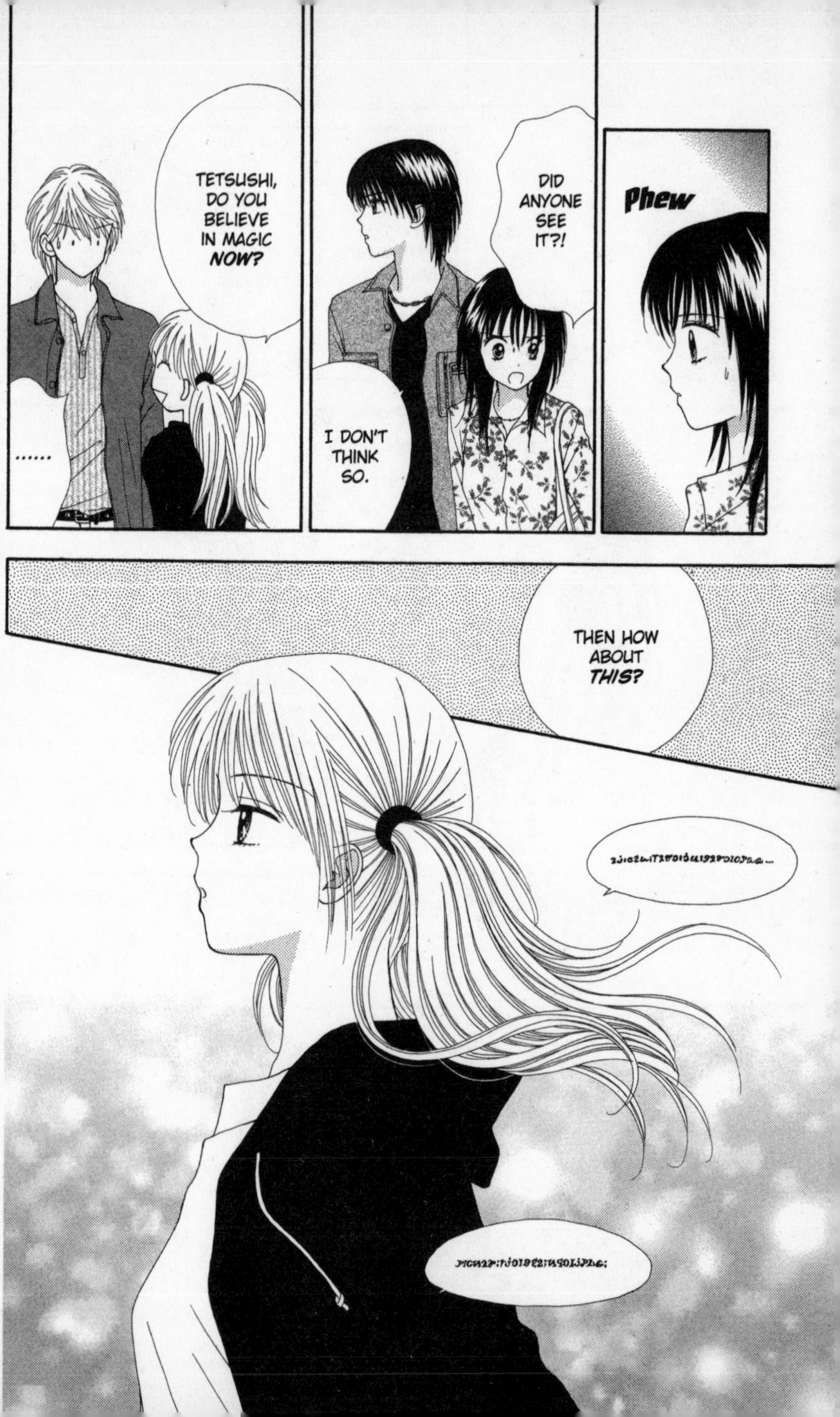
Phew
DID ANYONE SEE IT?!
I DON'T THINK SO.
TETSUSHI, DO YOU BELIEVE IN MAGIC *NOW?*
......
THEN HOW ABOUT *THIS?*

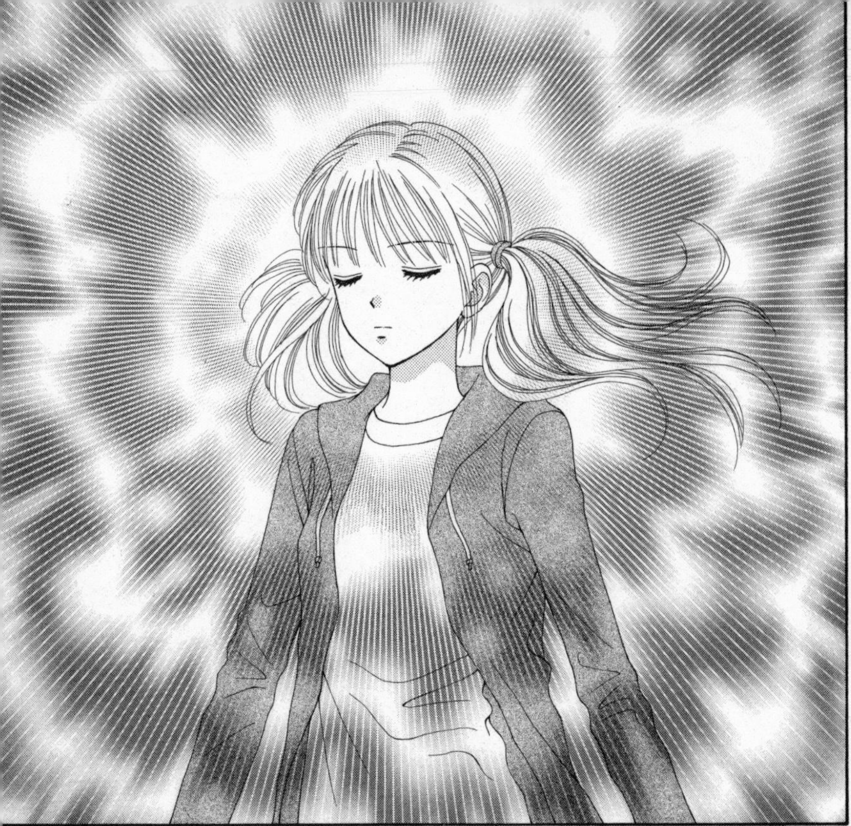
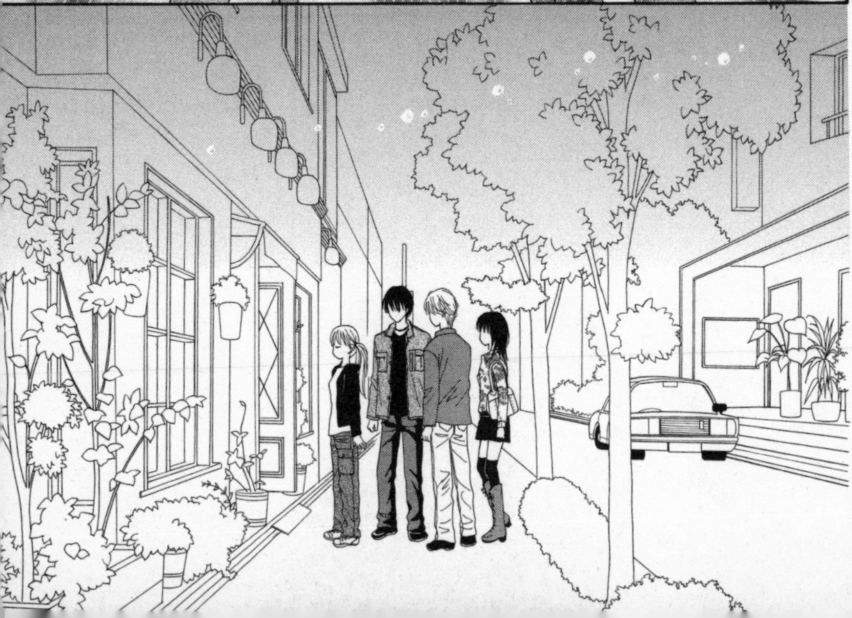

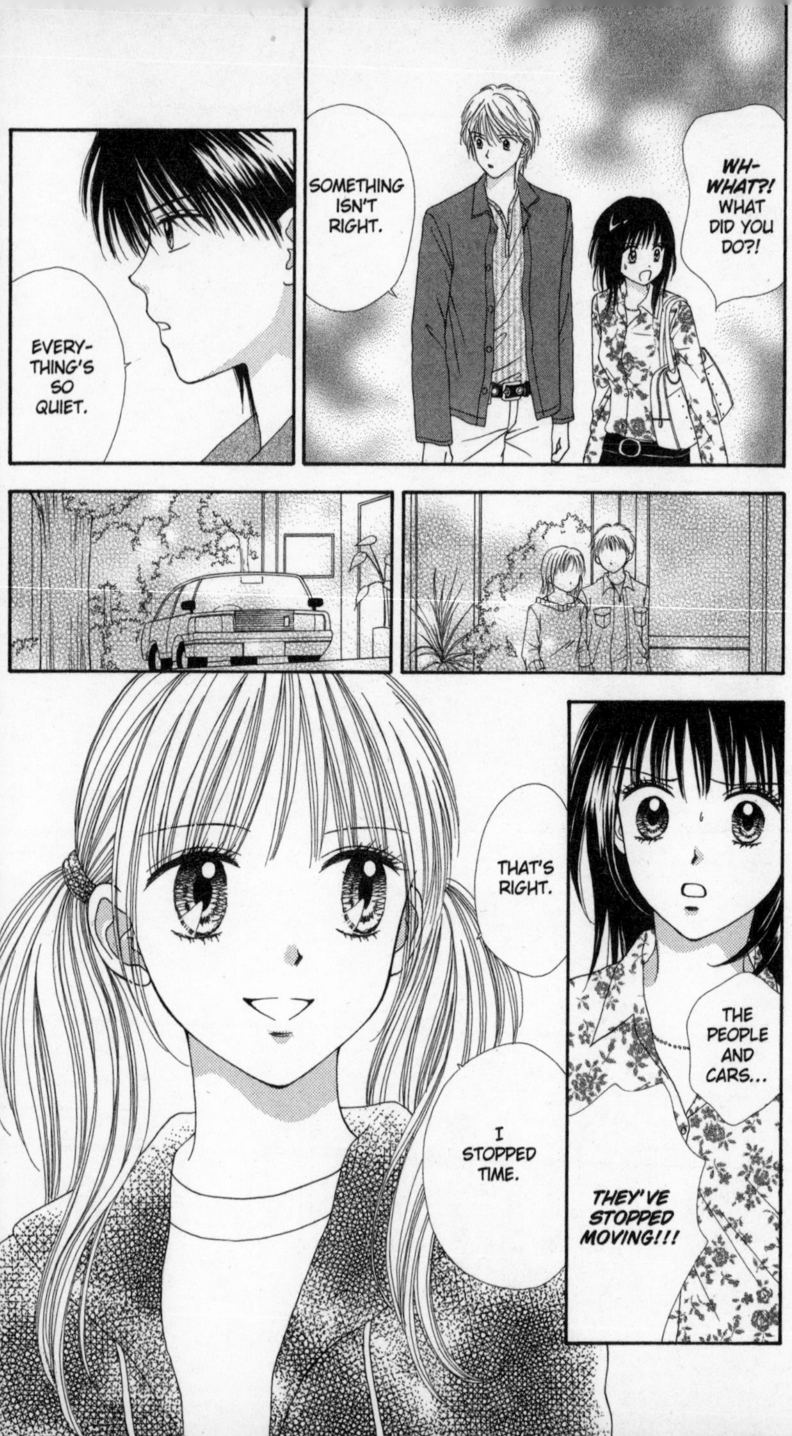
WH-WHAT?! WHAT DID YOU DO?!
SOMETHING ISN'T RIGHT.
EVERY-THING'S SO QUIET.
THE PEOPLE AND CARS...
THEY'VE STOPPED MOVING!!!
THAT'S RIGHT.
I STOPPED TIME.

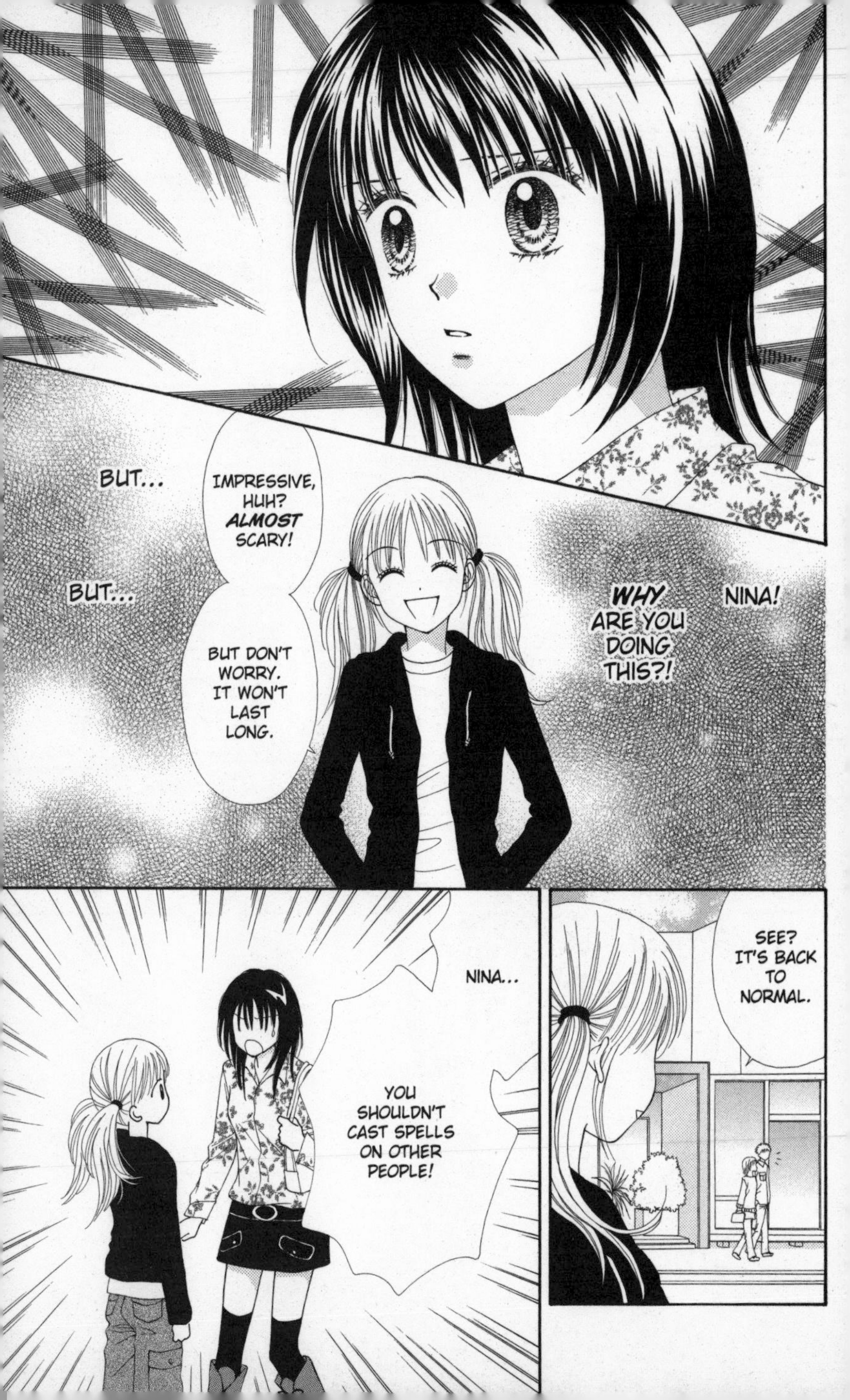
NINA!
WHY ARE YOU DOING THIS?!
IMPRESSIVE, HUH? ALMOST SCARY!
BUT...
BUT DON'T WORRY. IT WON'T LAST LONG.
BUT...
SEE? IT'S BACK TO NORMAL.
NINA...
YOU SHOULDN'T CAST SPELLS ON OTHER PEOPLE!

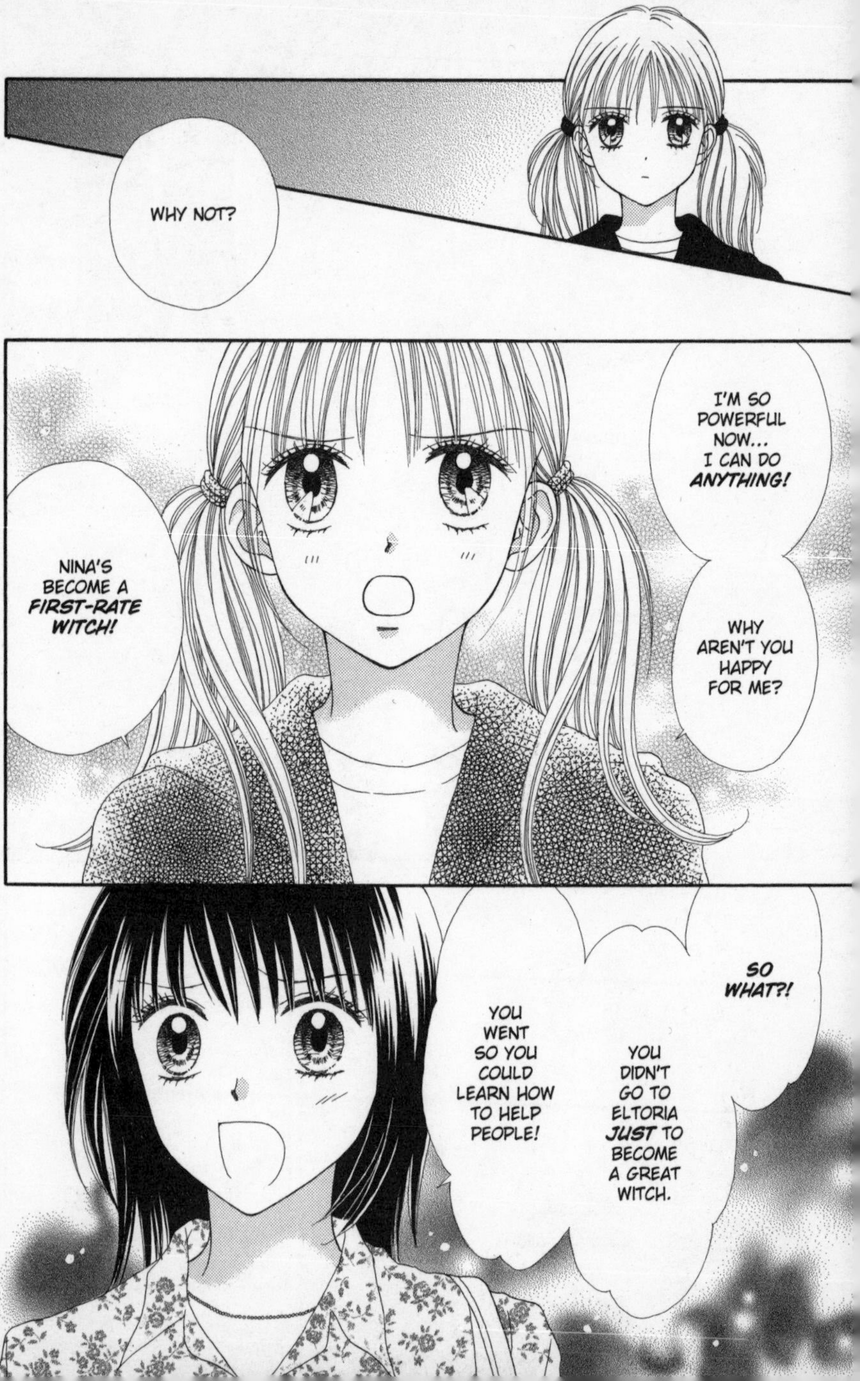
WHY NOT?
I'M SO POWERFUL NOW... I CAN DO *ANYTHING!*
NINA'S BECOME A *FIRST-RATE WITCH!*
WHY AREN'T YOU HAPPY FOR ME?
SO *WHAT?!*
YOU DIDN'T GO TO ELTORIA *JUST* TO BECOME A GREAT WITCH.
YOU WENT SO YOU COULD LEARN HOW TO HELP PEOPLE!

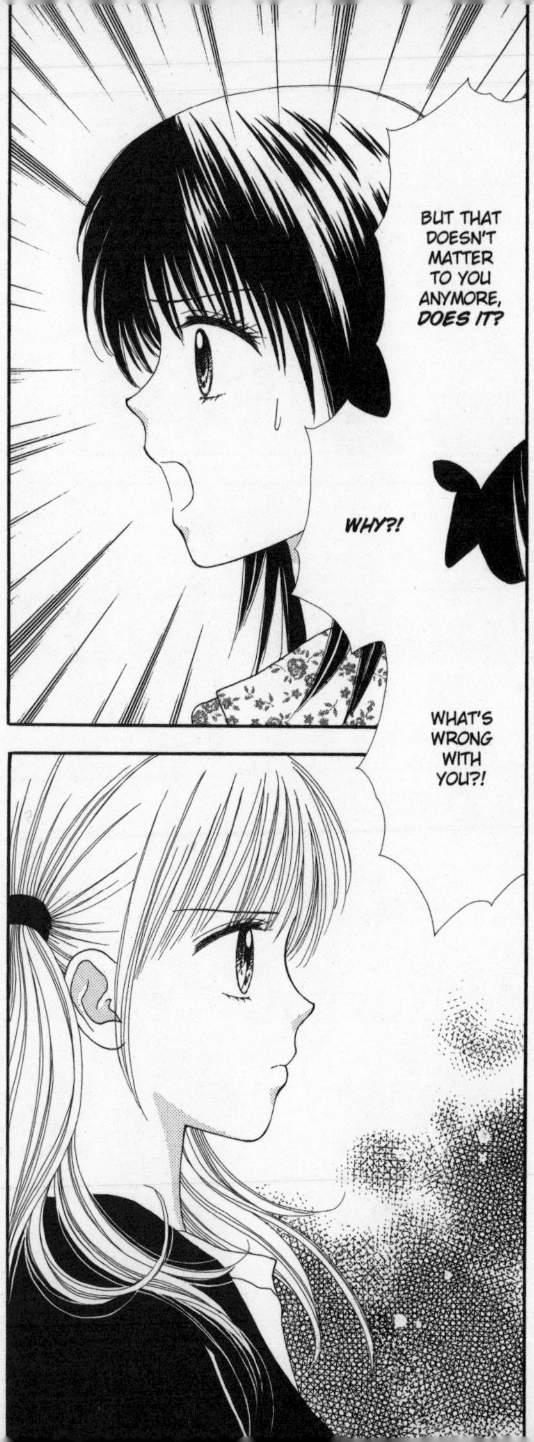
BUT THAT DOESN'T MATTER TO YOU ANYMORE, DOES IT?
WHY?!
WHAT'S WRONG WITH YOU?!

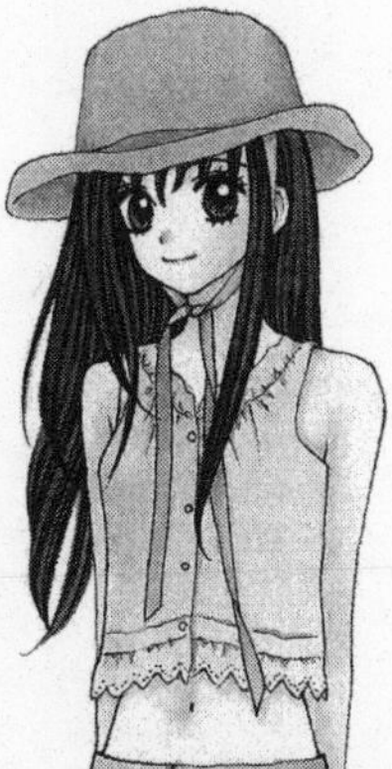

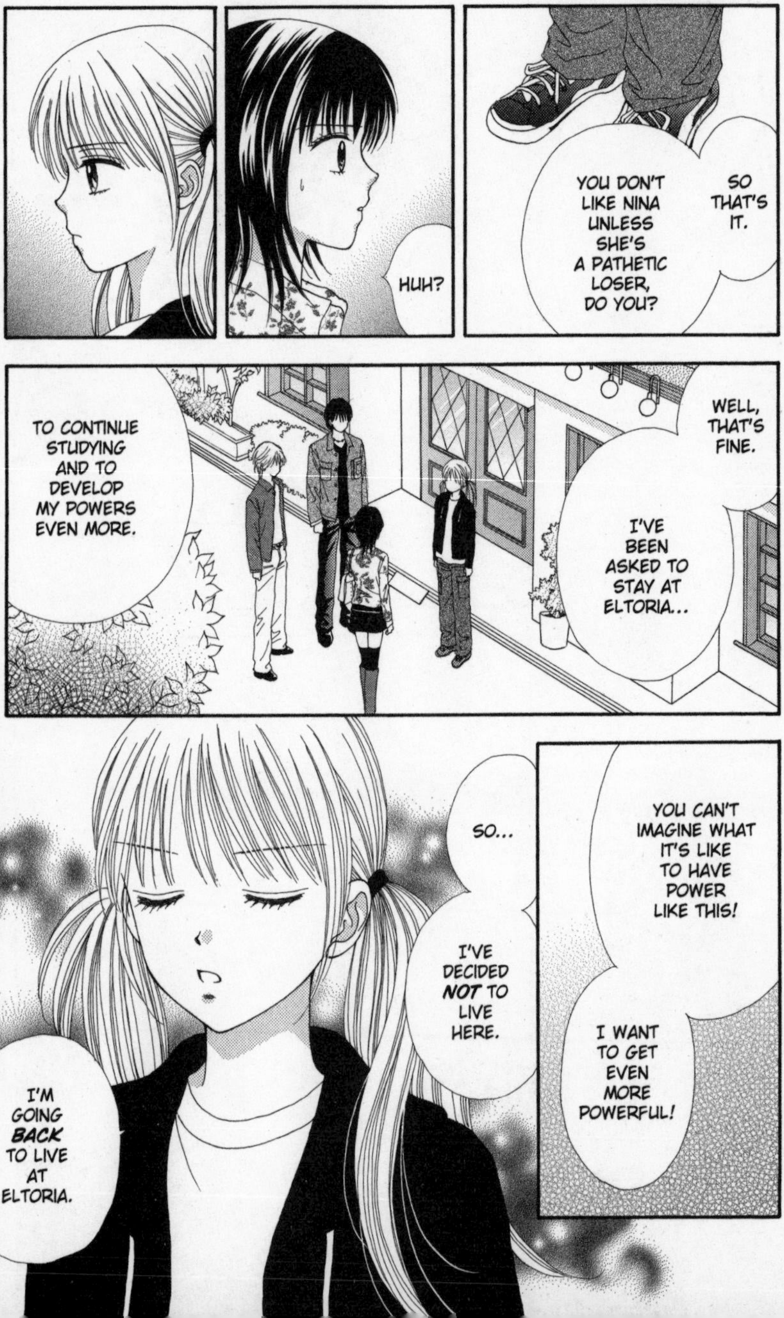
SO THAT'S IT.
YOU DON'T LIKE NINA UNLESS SHE'S A PATHETIC LOSER, DO YOU?
HUH?
WELL, THAT'S FINE.
I'VE BEEN ASKED TO STAY AT ELTORIA...
TO CONTINUE STUDYING AND TO DEVELOP MY POWERS EVEN MORE.
YOU CAN'T IMAGINE WHAT IT'S LIKE TO HAVE POWER LIKE THIS!
I WANT TO GET EVEN MORE POWERFUL!
SO...
I'VE DECIDED *NOT* TO LIVE HERE.
I'M GOING *BACK* TO LIVE AT ELTORIA.

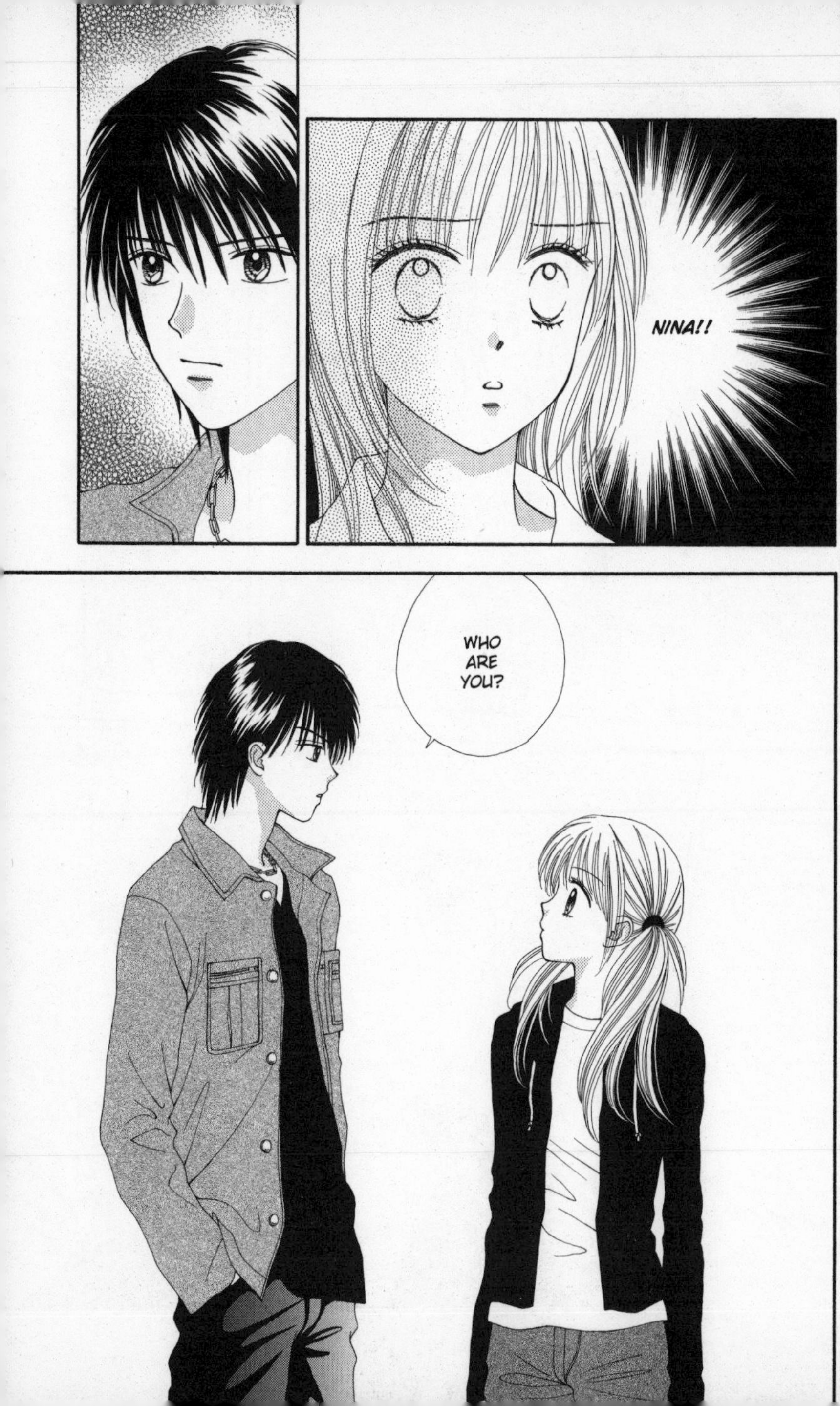
NINA!!
WHO ARE YOU?

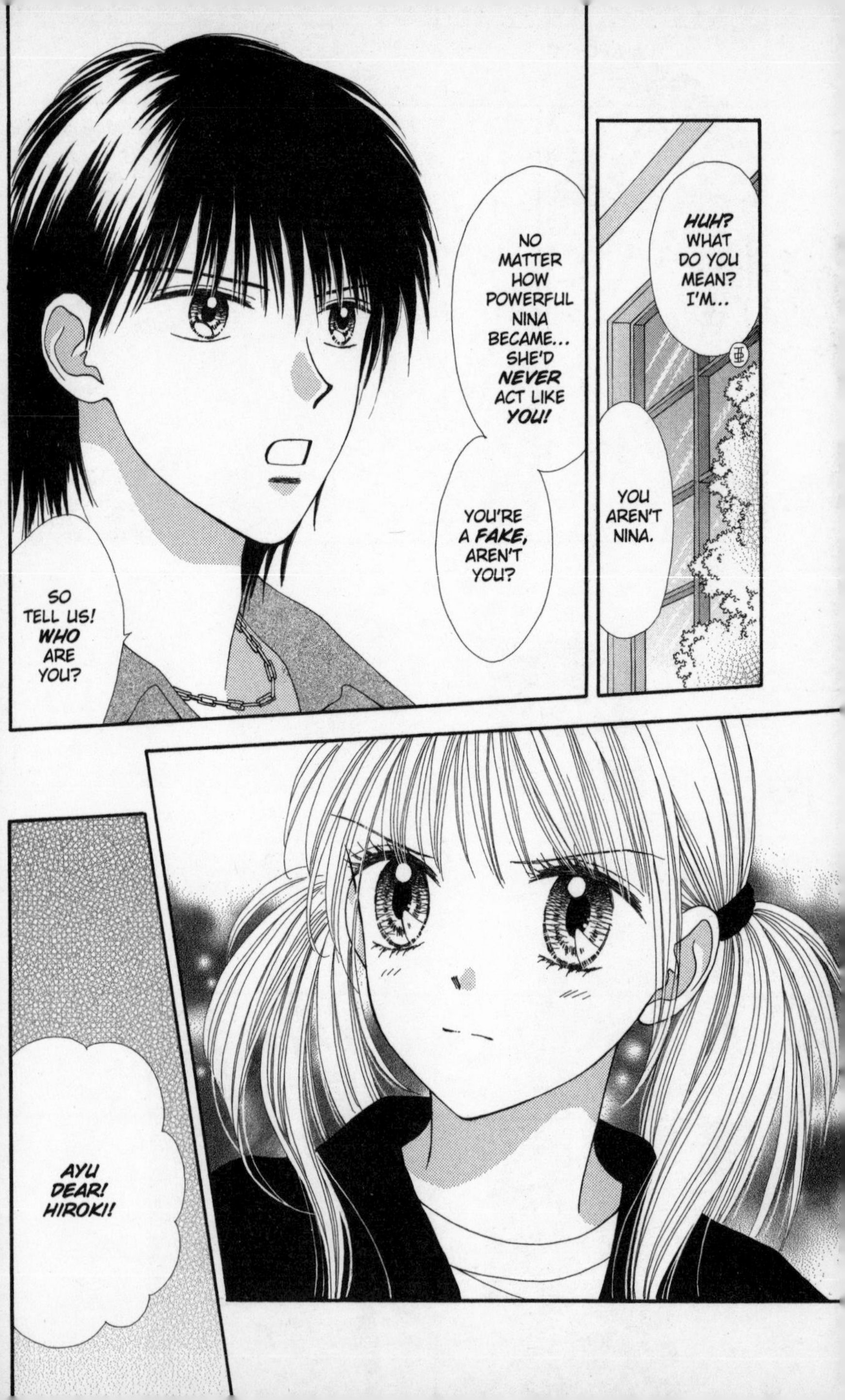
HUH? WHAT DO YOU MEAN? I'M...
YOU AREN'T NINA.
NO MATTER HOW POWERFUL NINA BECAME... SHE'D NEVER ACT LIKE YOU!
YOU'RE A FAKE, AREN'T YOU?
SO TELL US! WHO ARE YOU?
AYU DEAR! HIROKI!

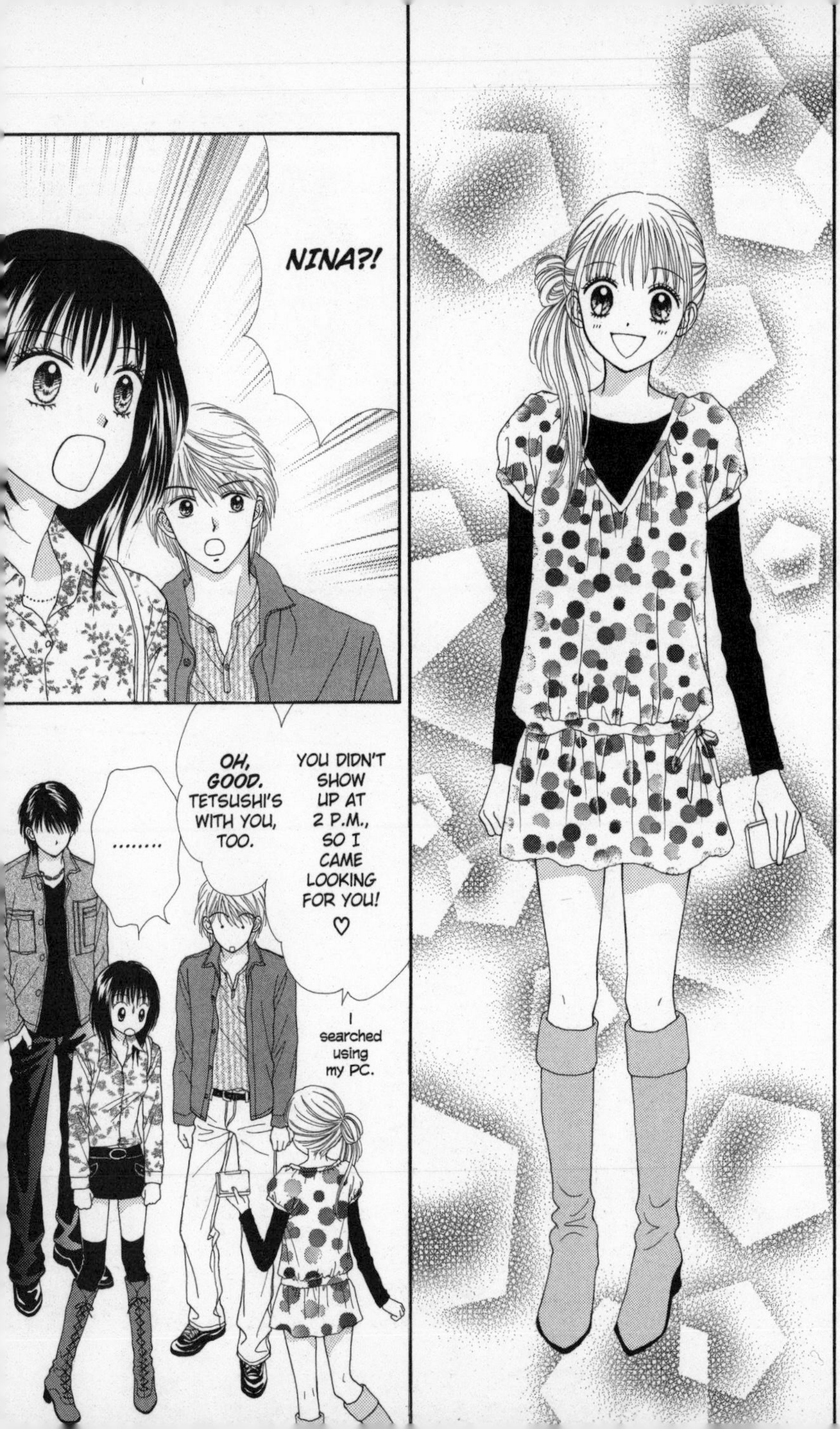
NINA?!
YOU DIDN'T SHOW UP AT 2 P.M., SO I CAME LOOKING FOR YOU! ♡
I searched using my PC.
OH, GOOD. TETSUSHI'S WITH YOU, TOO.
....

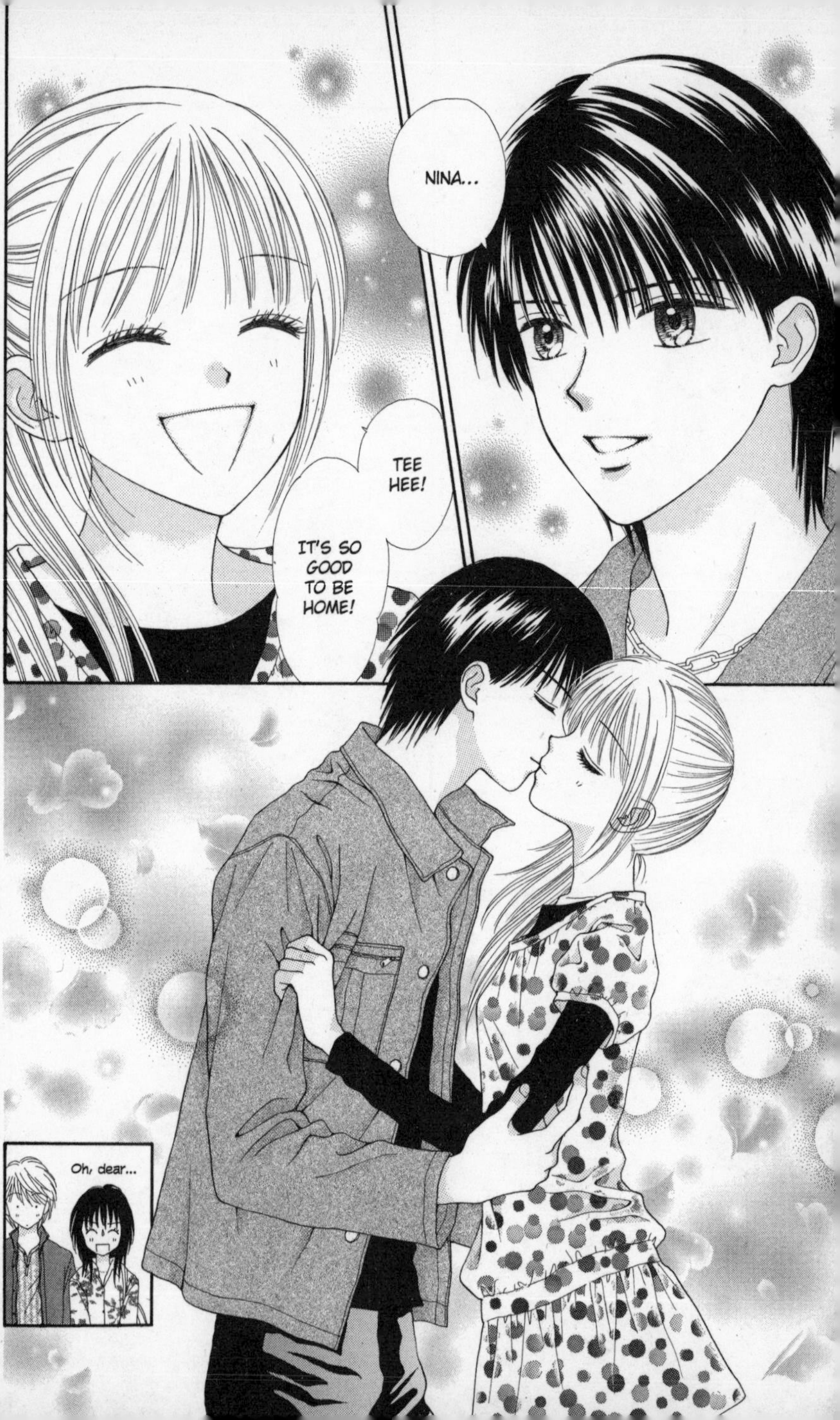
NINA...
TEE HEE!
IT'S SO GOOD TO BE HOME!
Oh, dear...

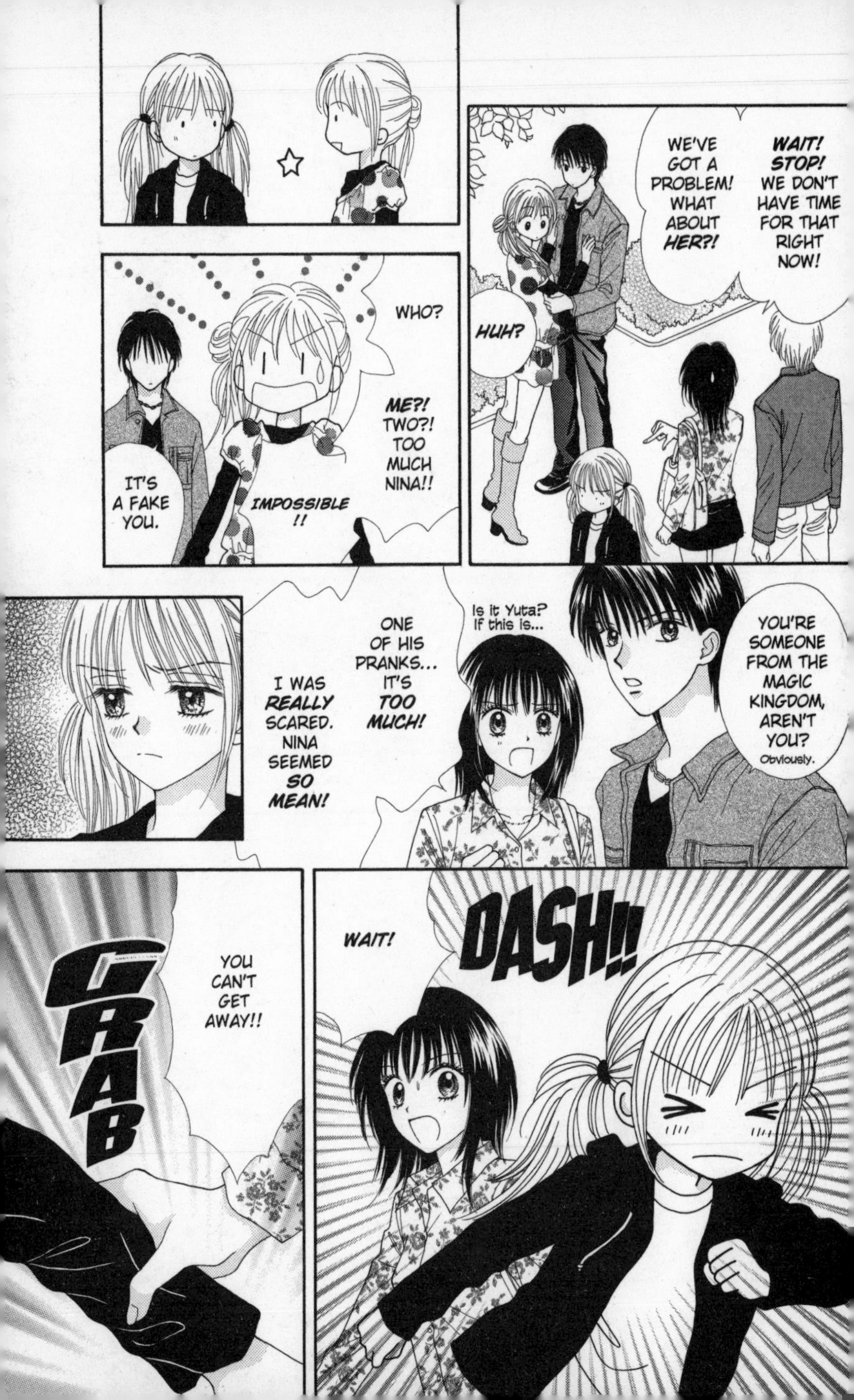
WAIT! STOP! WE DON'T HAVE TIME FOR THAT RIGHT NOW!
WE'VE GOT A PROBLEM! WHAT ABOUT HER?!
HUH?
WHO?
ME?! TWO?! TOO MUCH NINA!!
IMPOSSIBLE !!
IT'S A FAKE YOU.
YOU'RE SOMEONE FROM THE MAGIC KINGDOM, AREN'T YOU?
Obviously.
Is it Yuta? If this is...
ONE OF HIS PRANKS... IT'S TOO MUCH!
I WAS REALLY SCARED. NINA SEEMED SO MEAN!
DASH!!
WAIT!
GRAB
YOU CAN'T GET AWAY!!

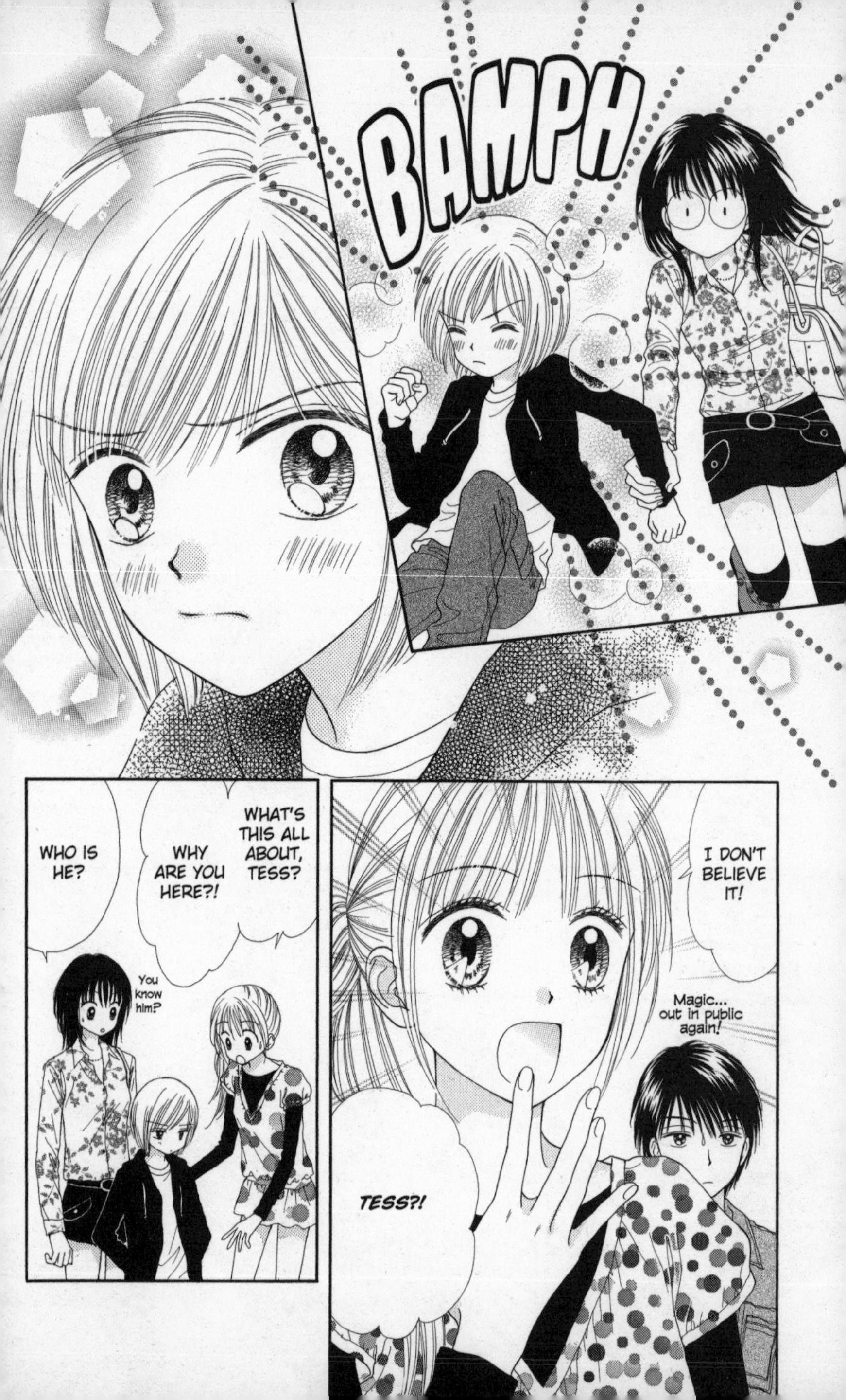
BAMPH
I DON'T BELIEVE IT!
Magic... out in public again!
TESS?!
WHAT'S THIS ALL ABOUT, TESS?
WHY ARE YOU HERE?!
WHO IS HE?
You know him?

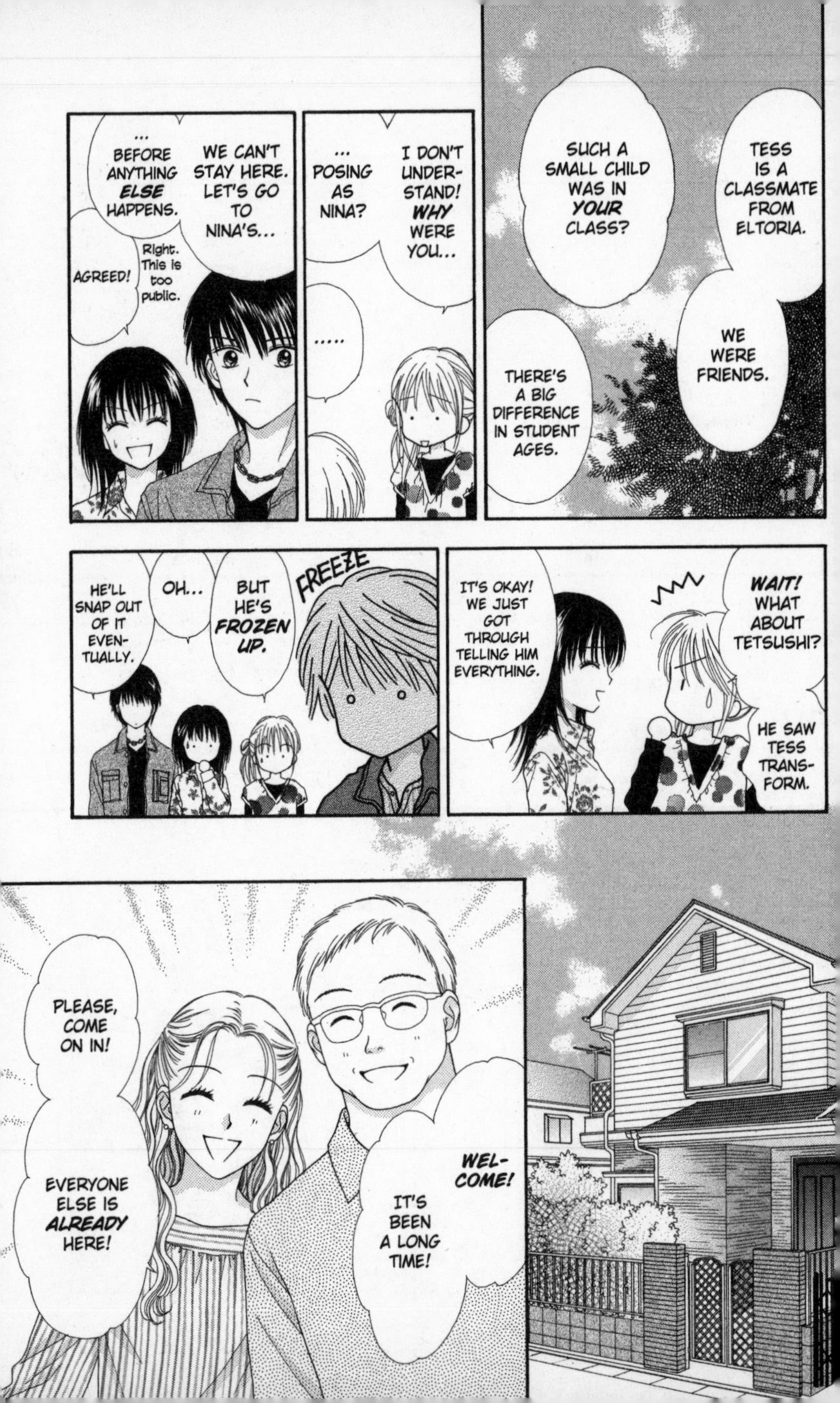
TESS IS A CLASSMATE FROM ELTORIA.
SUCH A SMALL CHILD WAS IN *YOUR* CLASS?
WE WERE FRIENDS.
THERE'S A BIG DIFFERENCE IN STUDENT AGES.
I DON'T UNDERSTAND! *WHY* WERE YOU...
... POSING AS NINA?
.....
WE CAN'T STAY HERE. LET'S GO TO NINA'S...
... BEFORE ANYTHING *ELSE* HAPPENS.
Right. This is too public.
AGREED!
WAIT! WHAT ABOUT TETSUSHI?
HE SAW TESS TRANSFORM.
IT'S OKAY! WE JUST GOT THROUGH TELLING HIM EVERYTHING.
FREEZE
BUT HE'S *FROZEN UP.*
OH...
HE'LL SNAP OUT OF IT EVEN-TUALLY.
WEL-COME!
IT'S BEEN A LONG TIME!
PLEASE, COME ON IN!
EVERYONE ELSE IS *ALREADY* HERE!

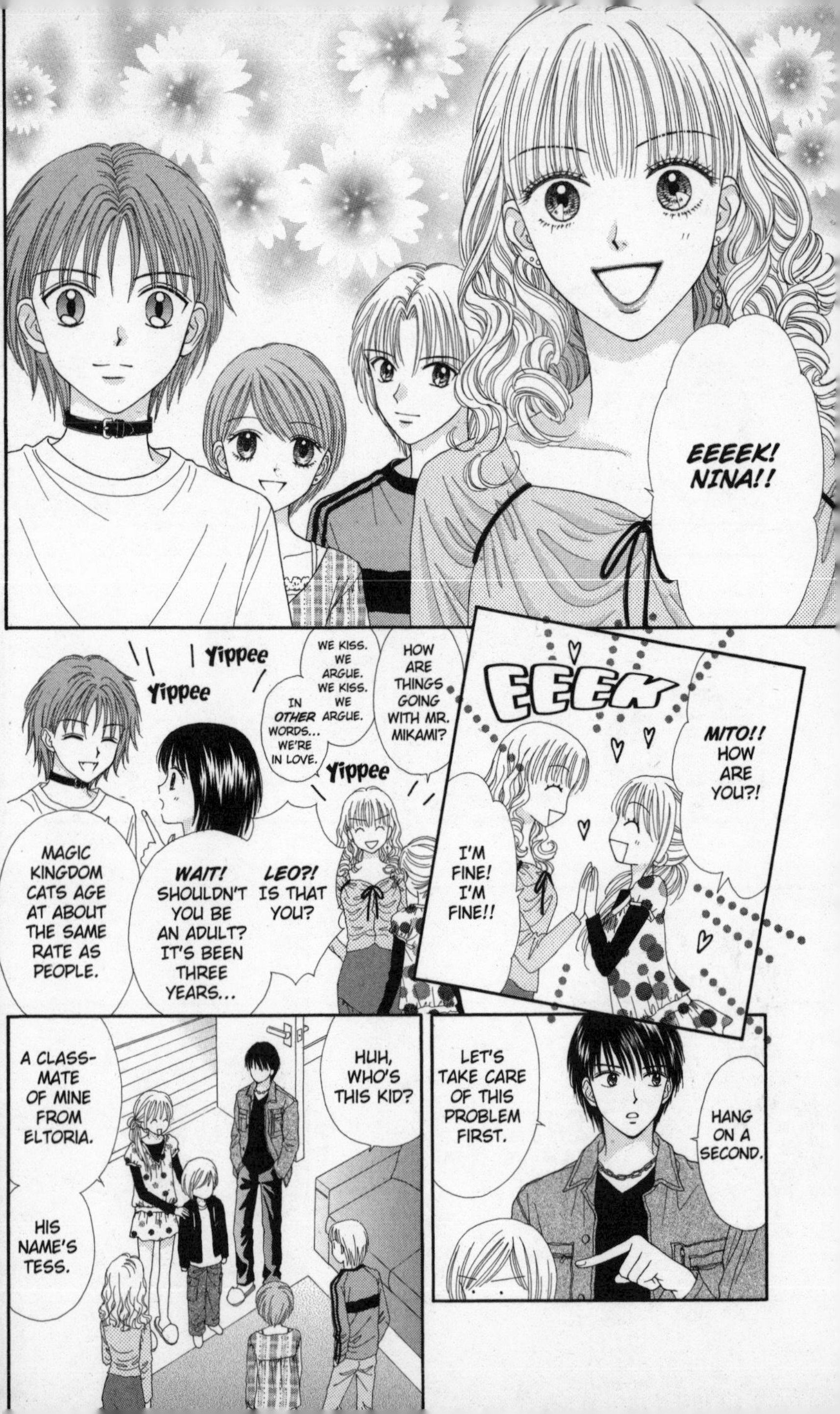
EEEEK! NINA!!
EEEK
MITO!! HOW ARE YOU?!
I'M FINE! I'M FINE!!
HOW ARE THINGS GOING WITH MR. MIKAMI?
WE KISS. WE ARGUE. WE KISS. WE ARGUE. IN OTHER WORDS... WE'RE IN LOVE.
Yippee
Yippee
Yippee
LEO?! IS THAT YOU?
WAIT! SHOULDN'T YOU BE AN ADULT? IT'S BEEN THREE YEARS...
MAGIC KINGDOM CATS AGE AT ABOUT THE SAME RATE AS PEOPLE.
HANG ON A SECOND.
LET'S TAKE CARE OF THIS PROBLEM FIRST.
HUH, WHO'S THIS KID?
A CLASSMATE OF MINE FROM ELTORIA.
HIS NAME'S TESS.

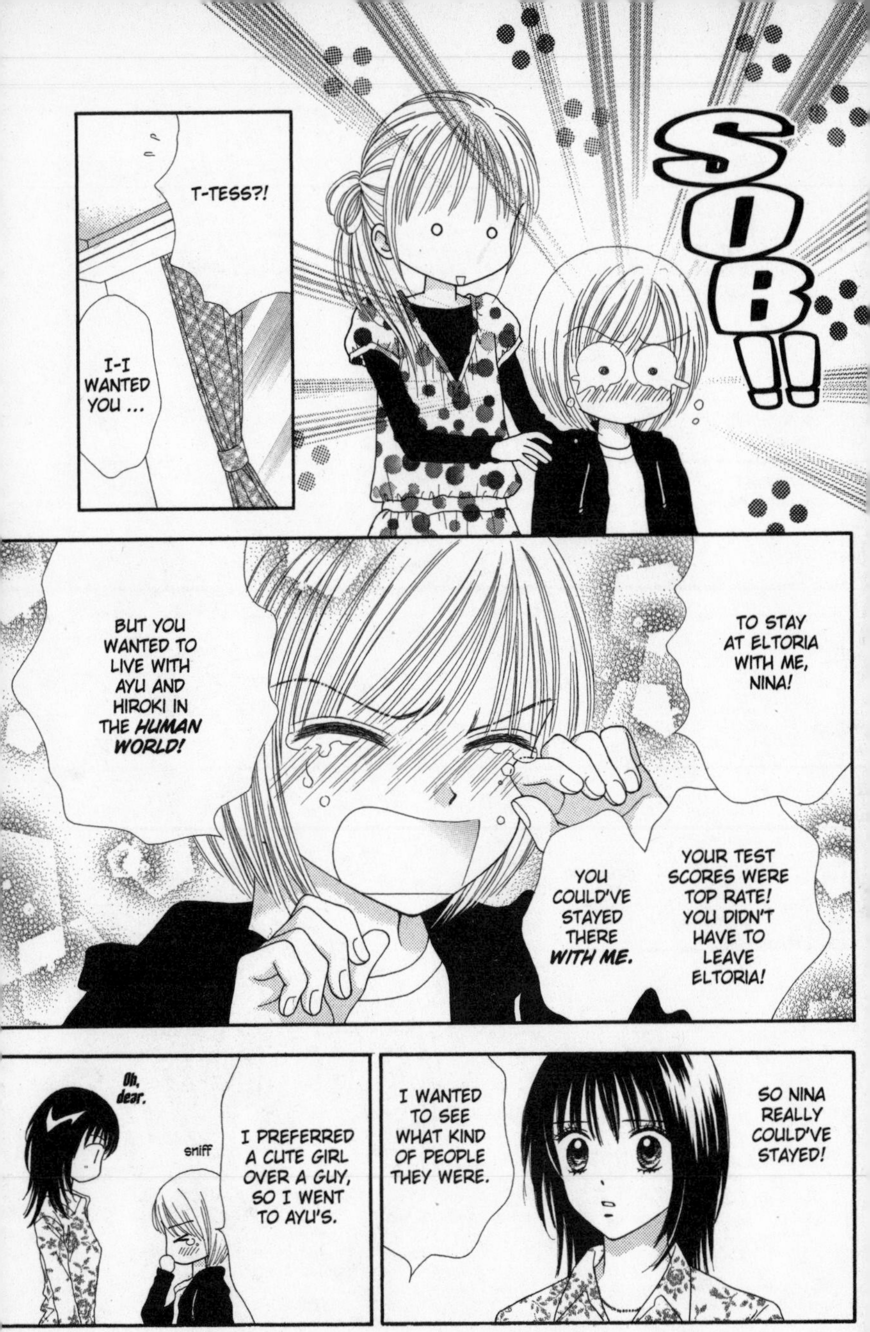
SOB!!
T-TESS?!
I-I WANTED YOU ...
TO STAY AT ELTORIA WITH ME, NINA!
BUT YOU WANTED TO LIVE WITH AYU AND HIROKI IN THE *HUMAN WORLD!*
YOUR TEST SCORES WERE TOP RATE! YOU DIDN'T HAVE TO LEAVE ELTORIA!
YOU COULD'VE STAYED THERE *WITH ME.*
SO NINA REALLY COULD'VE STAYED!
I WANTED TO SEE WHAT KIND OF PEOPLE THEY WERE.
I PREFERRED A CUTE GIRL OVER A GUY, SO I WENT TO AYU'S.
sniff
Oh, dear.

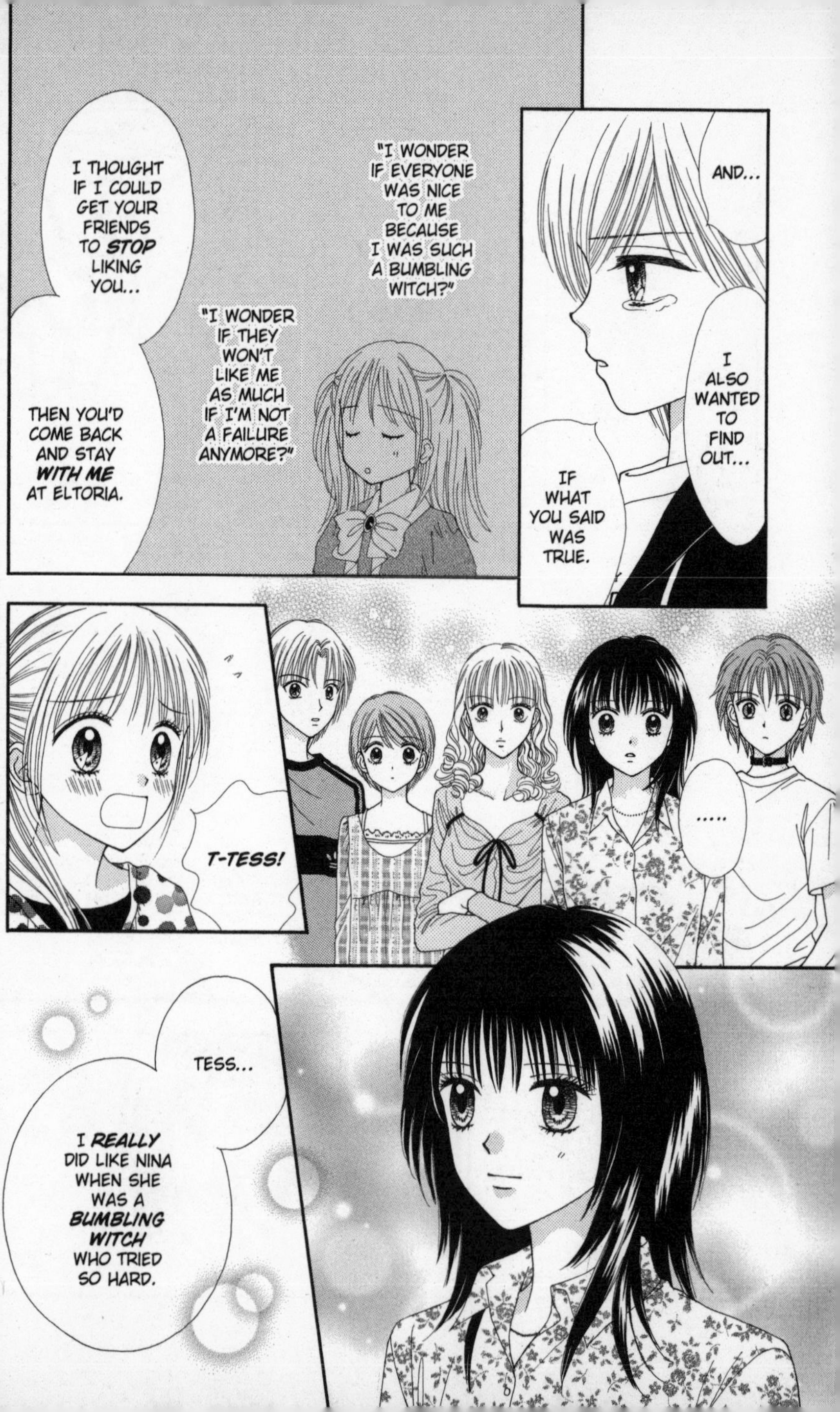
AND...
I ALSO WANTED TO FIND OUT...
IF WHAT YOU SAID WAS TRUE.
"I WONDER IF EVERYONE WAS NICE TO ME BECAUSE I WAS SUCH A BUMBLING WITCH?"
"I WONDER IF THEY WON'T LIKE ME AS MUCH IF I'M NOT A FAILURE ANYMORE?"
I THOUGHT IF I COULD GET YOUR FRIENDS TO **STOP** LIKING YOU...
THEN YOU'D COME BACK AND STAY **WITH ME** AT ELTORIA.
.....
T-TESS!
TESS...
I **REALLY** DID LIKE NINA WHEN SHE WAS A **BUMBLING WITCH** WHO TRIED SO HARD.

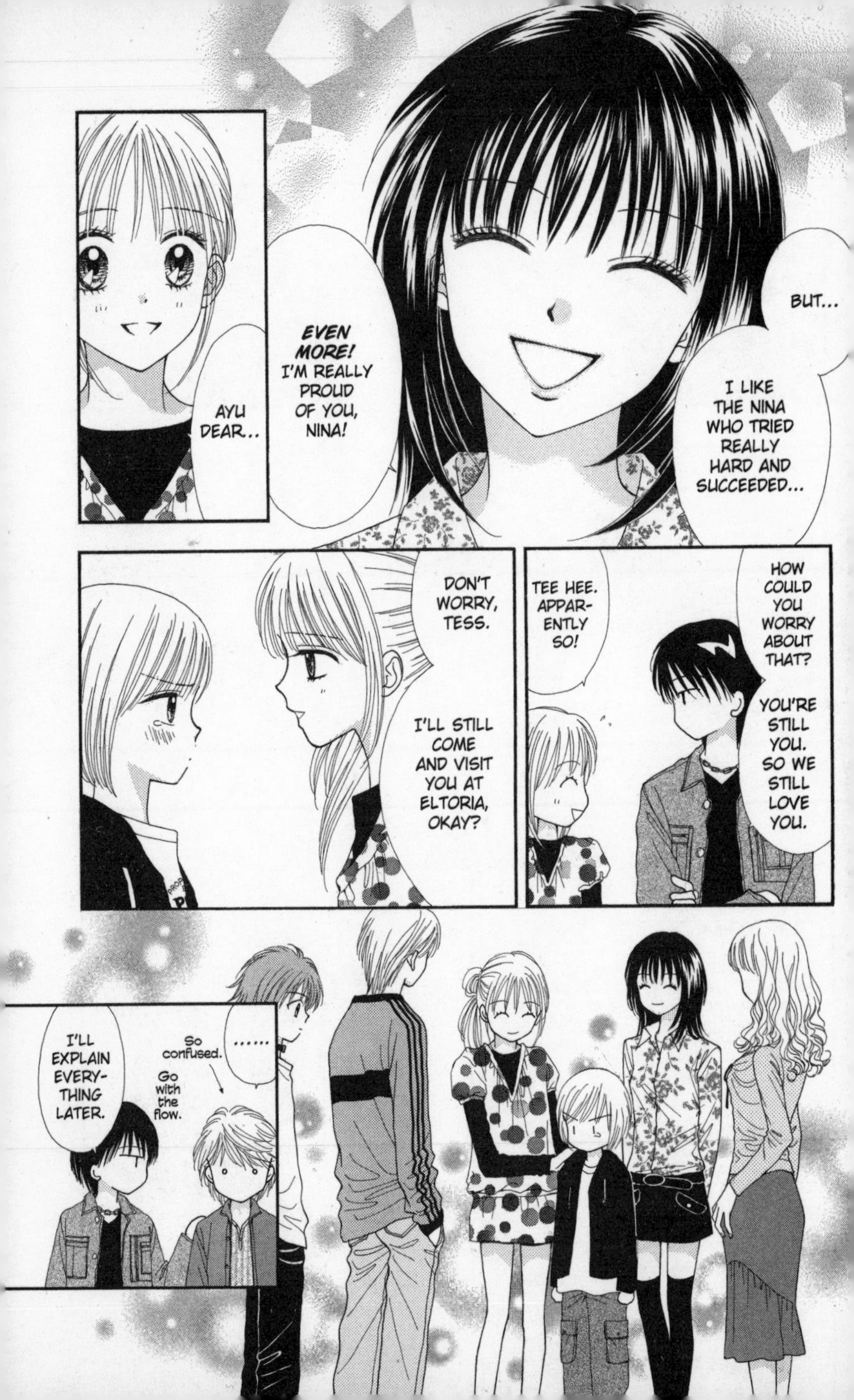
BUT...
I LIKE THE NINA WHO TRIED REALLY HARD AND SUCCEEDED...
EVEN MORE! I'M REALLY PROUD OF YOU, NINA!
AYU DEAR...
HOW COULD YOU WORRY ABOUT THAT? YOU'RE STILL YOU. SO WE STILL LOVE YOU.
TEE HEE. APPARENTLY SO!
DON'T WORRY, TESS.
I'LL STILL COME AND VISIT YOU AT ELTORIA, OKAY?
......
So confused.
Go with the flow.
I'LL EXPLAIN EVERYTHING LATER.

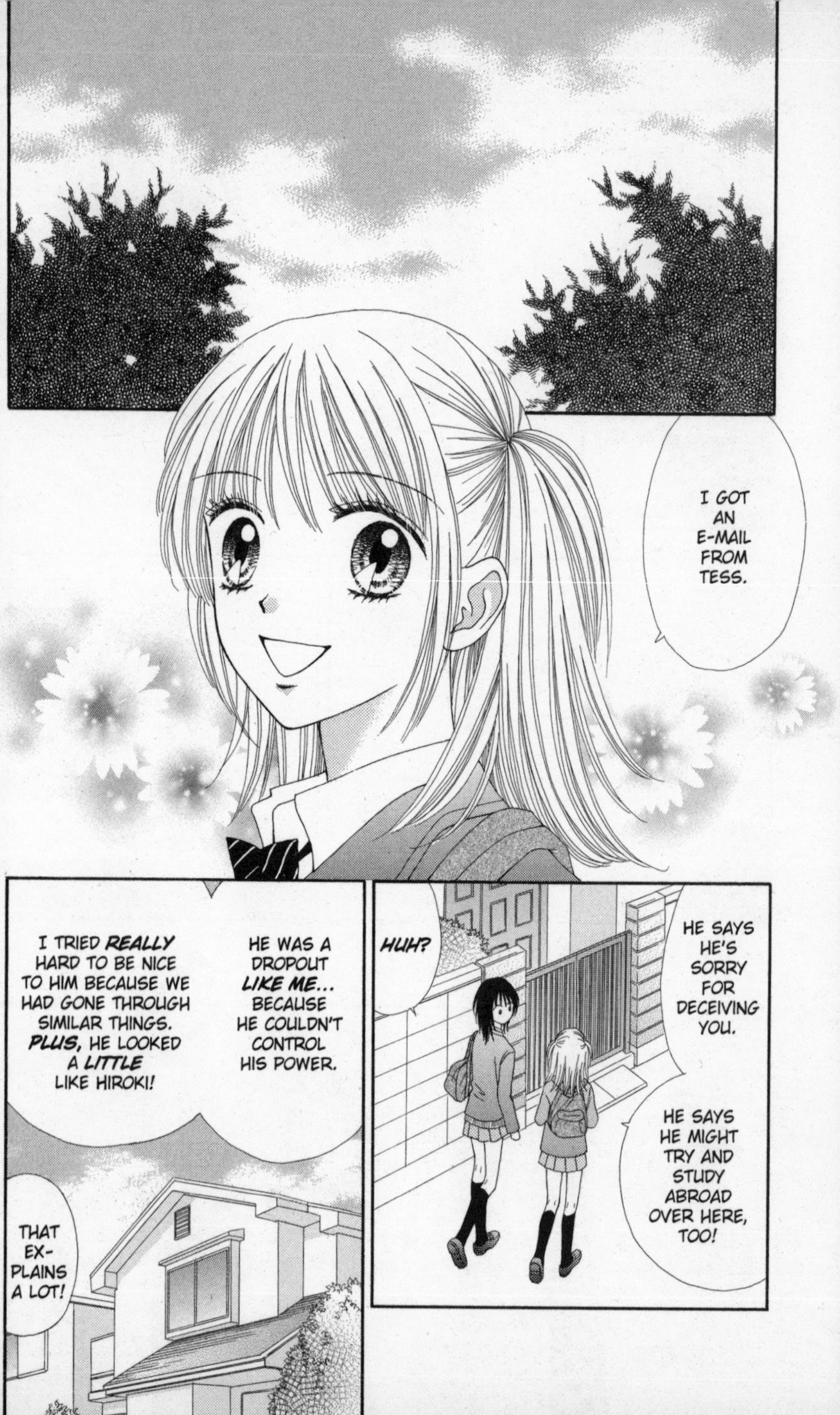
I GOT AN E-MAIL FROM TESS.
HE SAYS HE'S SORRY FOR DECEIVING YOU.
HUH?
HE SAYS HE MIGHT TRY AND STUDY ABROAD OVER HERE, TOO!
HE WAS A DROPOUT *LIKE ME*... BECAUSE HE COULDN'T CONTROL HIS POWER.
I TRIED *REALLY* HARD TO BE NICE TO HIM BECAUSE WE HAD GONE THROUGH SIMILAR THINGS. *PLUS,* HE LOOKED A *LITTLE* LIKE HIROKI!
THAT EX-PLAINS A LOT!

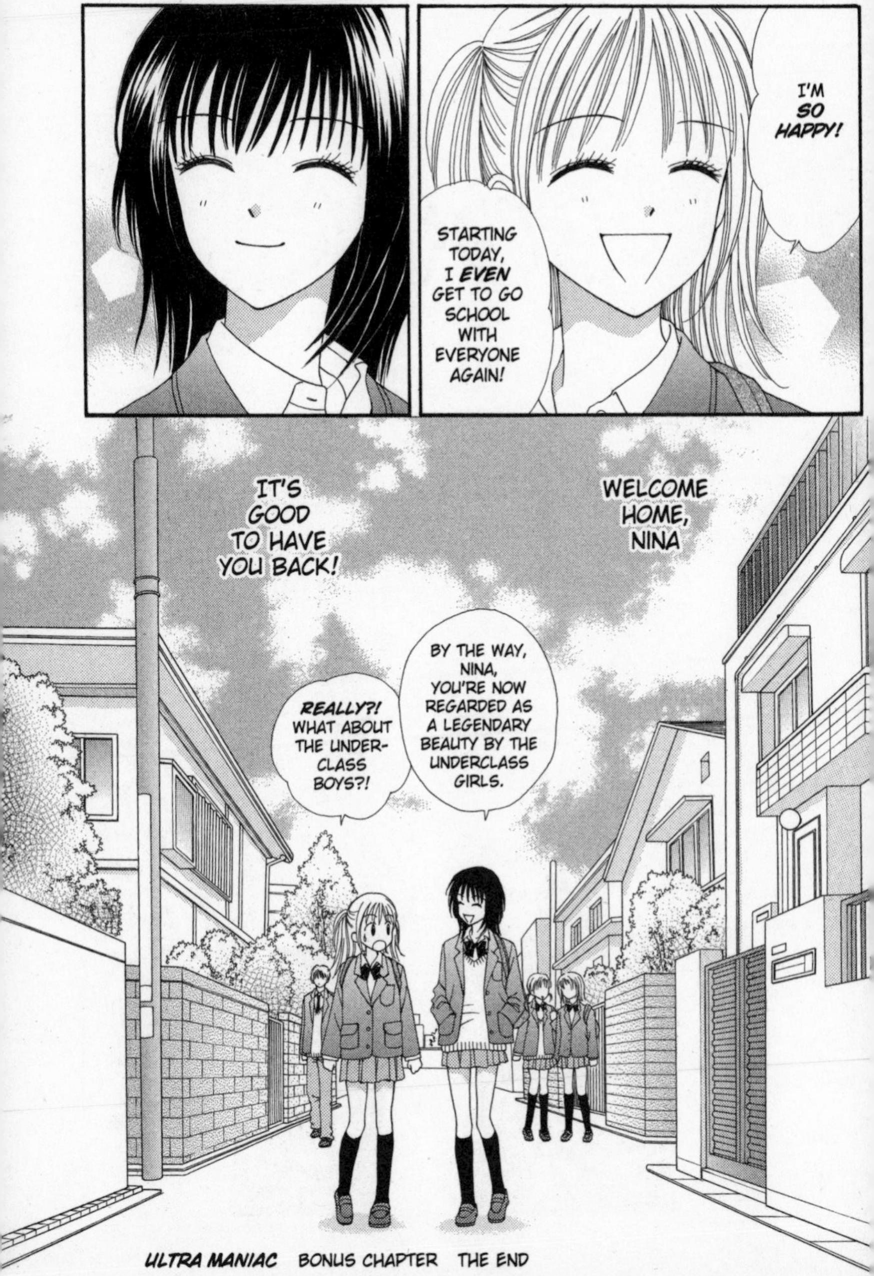
I'M *SO HAPPY!*
STARTING TODAY, I *EVEN* GET TO GO SCHOOL WITH EVERYONE AGAIN!
WELCOME HOME, NINA
IT'S GOOD TO HAVE YOU BACK!
BY THE WAY, NINA, YOU'RE NOW REGARDED AS A LEGENDARY BEAUTY BY THE UNDERCLASS GIRLS.
REALLY?! WHAT ABOUT THE UNDER-CLASS BOYS?!

ULTRA MANIAC BONUS CHAPTER THE END

BONUS

TESS' TRANSFORMATION SCENE FROM THE MAGAZINE PUBLICATION.

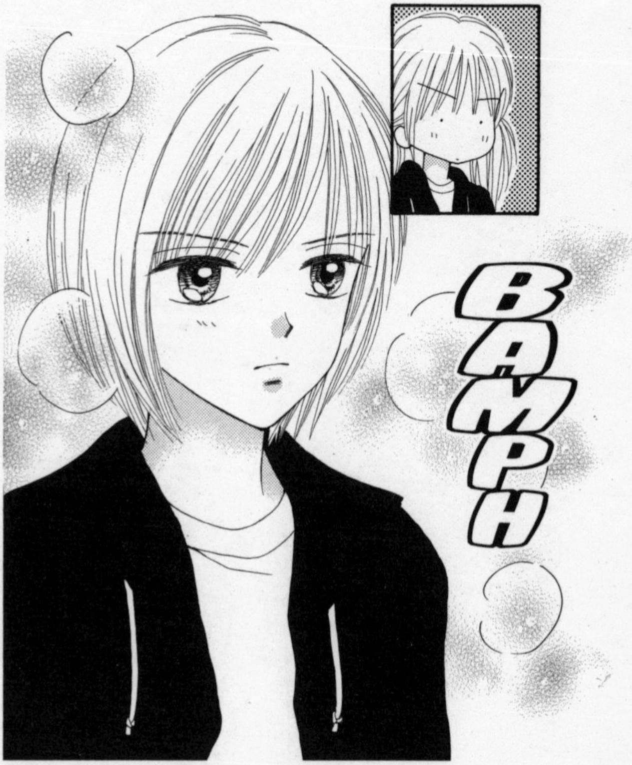
BAMPH

Wataru Yoshizumi

Comments

"*Ultra Maniac* was my first attempt at a fantasy," says Wataru Yoshizumi. "After I started, I realized that I had even less interest in magic than I thought I did (laughs). So sometimes I was at a loss as to what I should do. But I really liked all the characters. Plus I got to meet a lot of great people involved with the anime. So I don't regret writing this story at all. Thank you very much for reading it!"

Bio

Wataru Yoshizumi hails from Tokyo and made her manga debut in 1984 with *Radical Romance* in *Ribon Original* magazine. The artist has since produced a string of fan-favorite titles, including *Quartet Game*, *Handsome na Kanojo* (Handsome Girl), *Marmalade Boy*, and *Random Walk*. *Ultra Maniac*, a magical screwball comedy, is only the second time her work has been available in the U.S. Many of her titles, however, are available throughout Asia and Europe. Yoshizumi loves to travel and is keen on making original accessories out of beads.

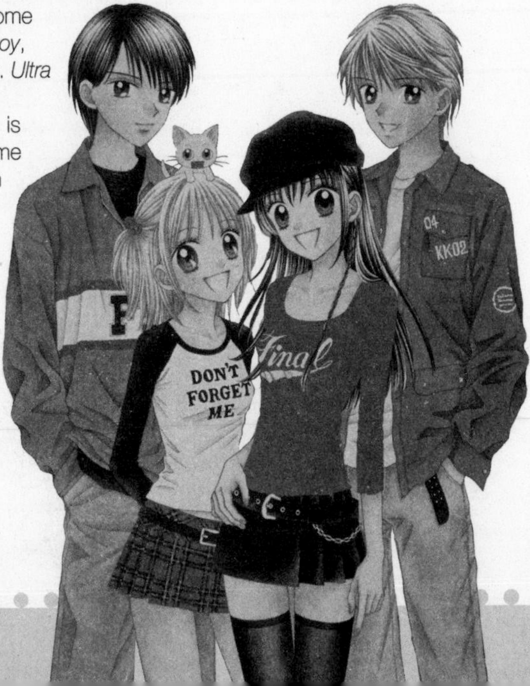
DON'T FORGET ME
Final
04
KK02

ULTRA MANIAC VOL. 5

The Shojo Beat Manga Edition

STORY AND ART BY
WATARU YOSHIZUMI

English Adaptation/John Lustig
Translation/Koji Goto
Touch-up Art & Lettering/Elizabeth Watasin
Cover & Graphic Design/Izumi Evers
Editor/Eric Searleman

Editor in Chief, Books/Alvin Lu
Editor in Chief, Magazines/Marc Weidenbaum
VP of Publishing Licensing/Rika Inouye
VP of Sales/Gonzalo Ferreyra
Sr. VP of Marketing/Liza Coppola
Publisher/Hyoe Narita

Printed in Canada

Published by VIZ Media, LLC
P.O. Box 77010
San Francisco, CA 94107

Shojo Beat Manga Edition
10 9 8 7 6 5 4 3
First printing, March 2006
Third printing, November 2007

store.viz.com